FILM

Allen Kirschner
and Linda Kirschner

FILM

READINGS IN THE MASS MEDIA

The Odyssey Press · New York

A division of
The Bobbs-Merrill Company, Inc.

Printed in the United States
Library of Congress Catalog Card Number: 70–158977

Second printing

ACKNOWLEDGMENTS

Academy of Motion Picture Arts and Sciences. For "The Modern Photoplay," by Irving Thalberg, From *Introduction to the Photoplay.* Reprinted by permission.

The Baltimore *Sun.* For "The Movies," by H. L. Mencken. Reprinted by permission.

Berkley Publishing Corporation. For "Movies, the Desperate Art" by Pauline Kael. Copyright 1956. Reprinted by permission of Berkley Publishing Corporation.

Crown Publishers, Inc. For "The Writer and the Film," by Dudley Nichols, from *Great Film Plays,* edited by John Gassner and Dudley Nichols. Copyright © 1959 by Crown Publishers, Inc. Reprinted by permission.

Peter Davies Ltd. For "Direction," by Alfred Hitchcock. From *Footnotes to the Film,* edited by Charles Davy. Reprinted by permission of the publishers.

Doubleday & Company, Inc. For "Mike Nichols Talks About *The Graduate."* From "Mike Nichols Talks about His Films," by Joseph Gelmis. From the book *The Film Director as Superstar,* by Joseph Gelmis. Copyright © 1970 by Joseph Gelmis. Reprinted by permission of Doubleday & Company, Inc.

Film Culture. For "Reflections on the Film Actor," by Michelangelo Antonioni. *Film Culture,* Summer 1961, nos. 22–23. Reprinted by permission of the publisher.

Grosset & Dunlap, Inc. For "Comedy's Greatest Era," by James Agee. Reprinted from *Agee on Film:* Vol. I, by James Agee. Copyright © 1958 by The James Agee Trust. Published by Grosset & Dunlap, Inc. Reprinted by permission.

Grove Press, Inc. For "What Is 'Film Making,'" by Ingmar Bergman. From *Cahiers du Cinema,* XI, no. 61 (July 1956). Reprinted by permission of Grove Press, Inc.

Harper and Row, Publishers, Inc. For "The Film Generation," from *A World on Film,* by Stanley Kauffmann. Copyright © 1966 by Stanley Kauffmann. Reprinted by permission of Harper and Row, Publishers.

Ken Kelman. For "The Reality of New Cinema," by Ken Kelman. Copyright © 1967 by Ken Kelman. From *The New American Cinema,* edited by Gregory Battcock (New York: E. P. Dutton, 1967). Reprinted by permission of the author.

Alfred A. Knopf, Inc. For "What Makes a Good Screen Story?" from *It Takes More than Talent,* by Mervyn LeRoy. Copyright 1953 by Alfred A. Knopf, Inc. Reprinted by permission.

Look Magazine. For "Movies: Morals, Violence, and Sex—Anything Goes," by Judith Crist. From the January 9, 1968 issue of *Look Magazine.* Copyright 1967 by Cowles Communications, Inc. By permission of the editors.

McGraw-Hill Book Company. For "The Reel World," from *Understanding Media: The Extensions of Man,* by Marshall McLuhan. Copyright © 1964 by Marshall McLuhan. Used with permission of McGraw-Hill Book Company.

Jonas Mekas. For "Where Are We—The Underground?" Reprinted by permission of the author.

Motion Picture Association of America, Inc. For "Rating Code." Reprinted by permission.

Newsweek. For "Summa Cum Laude," by Joseph Morgenstern. From *Newsweek,* 71:63 Jan. 1, 1968. Copyright Newsweek, Inc., 1968. Reprinted by permission.

The New York Times. For "Film: Tales Out of School," by Bosley Crowther. © 1967 by The New York Times Company. Reprinted by permission.

——. For "The Movies Are Better Than the Theater," by Walter Kerr. © 1968 by The New York Times Company. Reprinted by permission.

———. For "The Movies Are Now High Art," by Richard Schickel. © 1969 by The New York Times Company. Reprinted by permission.

——. For "On Reviewing, I: Turnstiles," by Renata Adler. © 1968 by The New York Times Company. Reprinted by permission.

Raymond Rohauer. For selection from *King of Comedy* by Mack Sennett (New York: Doubleday & Company, 1954). Copyright © 1954 Raymond Rohauer. Reprinted by permission.

Saturday Review. For "Engaging the Eye-Minded," by Arthur Knight. Copyright 1968 Saturday Review, Inc. Reprinted by permission.

———. For "Film as Environment," by Anthony Schillaci. Copyright 1968 Saturday Review, Inc. Reprinted by permission.

———. For "The Graduate Makes Out," by Hollis Alpert. Copyright 1968 Saturday Review, Inc. Reprinted by permission.

———. For "Should American Films Be Subsidized," by William Fadiman. Copyright 1967 Saturday Review, Inc. Reprinted by permission.

Richard Schickel. For "The Future of Film," from *Film 67 68,* by Members of the National Society of Film Critics, Richard Schickel, editor. © 1968 National Society of Film Critics. Reprinted by permission.

Parker Tyler. For "Is Film Criticism Only Propaganda," by Parker Tyler. Copyright © 1967 Parker Tyler. From *The New American Cinema,* edited by Gregory Battcock (New York: E. P. Dutton, 1967). Reprinted by permission of the author.

The University of California Press. For "Film and Reality," from *Film as Art,* by Rudolf Arnheim. Reprinted by permission of the Regents of The University of California.

———. For "The Graduate," by Stephen Farber and Estelle Changas. © 1968 by The Regents of the University of California. Reprinted from *Film Quarterly,* Vol. XXI, No. 3, pp. 37–41, by permission of The Regents.

———. For "The Movie Industry and the Film Culture," by Ernest Callenbach. © 1968 by The Regents of the University of California. Reprinted from *Film Quarterly,* Vol. XXII, No. 1, pp. 1–10, by permission of The Regents.

University of Southern California. For "The Modern Photoplay," by Irving Thalberg. From *Introduction to the Photoplay.* Reprinted by permission.

The University of Wisconsin Press. For Richard S. Randall, "Freedom of Speech in a Mass Medium," *Censorship of the Movies* (Madison: The University of Wisconsin Press; © 1970 by the Regents of the University of Wisconsin), 227–233. Reprinted by permission.

Thomas Wolfe. For "Loverboy of the Bourgeoisie," by Thomas Wolfe. Copyright © 1963, New York Herald-Tribune, Inc. Reprinted with permission of W. C. C. Publishing Company, Inc.

For M. Jerry Weiss,
a great teacher, who never forgets that
students are more important than schools.

CONTENTS

Introduction, 3

1 FORM AND TECHNIQU[E]

Marshall McLuhan: MOVIES: THE REEL WORLD, 11
James Agee: COMEDY'S GREATEST ERA, 21
Mack Sennett: from KING OF COMEDY, 39
David Wark Griffith: THE MOVIES 100 YEARS FROM NOW, 49
Irving Thalberg: THE MODERN PHOTOPLAY, 55
H. L. Mencken: THE MOVIES, 59
Rudolf Arnheim: FILM AND REALITY, 63
Alfred Hitchcock: DIRECTION, 79
Michelangelo Antonioni: REFLECTIONS ON THE FILM ACTOR, 87
Ingmar Bergman: WHAT IS "FILM MAKING"? 91
Ken Kelman: THE REALITY OF NEW CINEMA, 103
Jonas Mekas: WHERE ARE WE—THE UNDERGROUND? 107

2 AUDIENCE AND EFFECT

Mervyn LeRoy: WHAT MAKES A GOOD SCREEN STORY? 113
Dudley Nichols: THE WRITER AND THE FILM, 117
Richard Schickel: THE MOVIES ARE NOW HIGH ART, 129
Walter Kerr: THE MOVIES ARE BETTER THAN THE THEATER, 141
Stanley Kauffmann: THE FILM GENERATION, 151
Arthur Knight: ENGAGING THE EYE-MINDED, 165
Judith Crist: MOVIES: MORALS, VIOLENCE, SEX—ANYTHING GOES, 173
Anthony Schillaci: FILM AS ENVIRONMENT, 183
Tom Wolfe: LOVERBOY OF THE BOURGEOISIE, 195
Richard S. Randall: FREEDOM OF SPEECH IN A MASS MEDIUM, 201
Motion Picture Association of America: RATING CODE, 209

3 CRITICS AND CRITICISM

Pauline Kael: MOVIES, THE DESPERATE ART, 213

William Fadiman: SHOULD AMERICAN FILMS BE SUBSIDIZED? 233

Ernest Callenbach: THE MOVIE INDUSTRY AND THE FILM CULTURE, 243

Renata Adler: ON REVIEWING, I: TURNSTILES, 257

Parker Tyler: IS FILM CRITICISM ONLY PROPAGANDA? 261

THE GRADUATE: FOUR REVIEWS, 271

- *Hollis Alpert:* THE GRADUATE MAKES OUT, 271
- *Bosley Crowther:* TALES OUT OF SCHOOL, 277
- *Joseph Morgenstern:* SUMMA CUM LAUDE, 279
- *Stephen Farber and Estelle Changas:* THE GRADUATE, 280

Joseph Gelmis: MIKE NICHOLS TALKS ABOUT *THE GRADUATE,* 287

Members of the National Society of Film Critics: THE FUTURE OF FILM, 293

- *Hollis Alpert,* 293
- *Brendan Gill,* 297
- *Philip T. Hartung,* 298
- *Stanley Kauffmann,* 299
- *Arthur Knight,* 301
- *Joseph Morgenstern,* 304
- *Andrew Sarris,* 306
- *Richard Schickel,* 307
- *Wilfrid Sheed,* 310
- *John Simon,* 311

Selected Bibliography, 313

FILM

INTRODUCTION

PAUL NEWMAN IS HUD shouts the neighborhood theater marquee! And all across America millions flock to *Hud,* not to see a representation of a man but to see Hud himself. "Paul Newman IS Hud," a living, breathing man, not just a piece of celluloid with light shining through it.

We believe in our films—through them we live lives far different in time, place, or circumstance from our prosaic existences. And we believe in our film heroes—they are our alter egos, exciting, romantic extensions of ourselves. We dream and we imitate. We become.

We are what we pretend to be, the novelist Kurt Vonnegut, Jr., has suggested. And films, despite our belief in their reality, are pretend. As such, they offer both a great opportunity and a great danger. To view a world larger than our own may enoble us. Such a world may lend insight into our own lives. Like Dustin Hoffman in *The Graduate,* we too may be able to maintain our own identity in a hostile world. But films can also diminish us. Seeing a world we never made nor can ever hope to make may lessen our view of ourselves and in so doing thwart our own growth. We can't be James Bond in *Goldfinger,* and in attempting to imitate him we may only fail to develop our own potentials. Films, we must remember, are a reproduction, not reality, even though we have been assured for over a century now that "the camera does not lie."

Well, maybe it doesn't lie; perhaps it just fibs a bit, exaggerates, glamorizes, and romanticizes. But, above all, the camera does influence. The audience watching Clark Gable remove his shirt in *It Happened One Night* observes that he wears no undershirt. Within a year the men's underwear industry reflects a fifty percent decline in its business. Peter Fonda races across America on his motorcycle in *Easy*

Rider, and the motorcycle craze reaches new heights. Many of our ideas of courage, love, loyalty, integrity, virtue, stem from the screen. Our views of ourselves are conditioned and changed by what we see and hear in a darkened theater.

"ONE MINUTE, PLEASE" (1896–1912)

It began on an April evening in 1896. Thomas A. Edison's latest marvel, the Vitascope, was being shown publicly for the first time. A novelty, little more than a scientific toy, it shared the bill with seven acts at Koster and Bials' Music Hall in New York City. The audience's response was immediate and overwhelming. America's love affair with the films began.

What fun we have today looking back on those old movies filled with baggy-pants comedians endlessly bumping into each other or falling off ladders, good guys forever chasing bad guys, heroines pulled from the tracks in the very nick of time—each scene performed in a silent pantomime never more than twelve minutes in length. How ancient they all seem, how primitive, how insignificant. Who could have predicted then that Edison's crude moving pictures would develop into an artistic medium of tremendous force? Who could have predicted the enormous impact of films on our society and on our national character?

Yet, in retrospect, it all seems so fated and so logical. The movies and the moment were mated. In the 1890's hordes of European immigrants were descending on New York in search of the Promised Land. Instead they found themselves confined to ghettos, mired in poverty on the Lower East Side. Small wonder then that they turned to the old silent movies. There, for five cents the Promised Land opened to them. From the drabness of their tenements and their sweatshops, they could be transported to Niagara Falls or the Grand Canyon. They could "see" their adopted land. Their unfamiliarity with the English language was no barrier. Their awkward sense of isolation, of "greenness," diminished as they watched the flickering images on the screen. As the movies gave them comfort and strength, so they, in turn, gave support to the movies. For the next decade the immigrant and working classes provided the foundation for a new industry.

"One Minute, Please" flashed the words on the screen. And those who couldn't read English soon learned the significance of the three familiar words. One minute to repair the break in the film or to breathe life back into a stalled projecter. But it would take more than one minute for the films to mature and to change forever the character of a nation.

"YOU ARE *LIVING* THE STORY" (1912–1927)

Those first movies were a novelty, a toy. They were short films offering a few minutes of escape and entertainment, little more. The travelogues, the pantomime comedians, the obvious little melodramas with their obligatory "chases" continued to attract the working classes, but the audience base was not expanding. Had the movies so continued, they would most likely be found today only in penny arcades and amusement parks.

That the films did mature and broaden their base of support is to a great extent the accomplishment of one man, David Wark Griffith. Griffith recognized the film's potential: if the movies could make people laugh, they could also make them feel and think. They did not have to be one-reel mindless experiences, twelve minutes to be seen and forgotten. They could tell a story and in so doing affect and influence audiences.

In the years from 1912 to 1915, Griffith advanced movies from their infancy to their adolescence. Utilizing the raw elements of film that had been developed to that time, he refined and mastered them to serve his concept of what film should be. Working with imaginative stories, Griffith discarded the tradition that the movies consist of one or at most two reels. Drawing upon writers such as Shakespeare, Tolstoy, Maupassant, and Poe, he introduced to the working classes, who patronized the movies of the day, an entire new concept of what film could be. The *New York Times* reported that audiences "received it with applause and are asking for more." Not only had Griffith tapped an unsuspected mine, but his films also drew to the theaters the middle class and the intelligentsia, which had heretofore ignored movies.

With *The Birth of a Nation* in 1915, Griffith produced a three-hour film, a film so monumental in design and impact that it dwarfed all that had preceded it. So great was its effect that riots accompanied its showing in the United States. Depicting the Civil War and its aftermath, *The Birth of a Nation* inspired an awakening of the dormant Ku Klux Klan and demonstrated conclusively the power and impact of the film medium. It was, as President Woodrow Wilson said, "like writing history with lightning." What once had been little more than a moment's diversion had become an awesome social force.

Now the movies presented stories, and the stories influenced and changed the nation's fashions, behavior, and attitudes. Patronized by all social classes, they became a major source of ideas about life and the world. Films flowed from Hollywood. Griffith epics gave way to the titillating and tantalizing productions of men like Cecil B. De Mille and Irving Thalberg. Titles such as *Male and Female, The Golden Bed, Saturday Night,* and *Forbidden Fruit* lured audiences with promises of romantic and exotic adventure. Stars like Lillian Gish and Mary Pickford projected slim, delicate images, and American girls who previously tended toward plumpness suddenly slimmed down. Theda Bara contributed "vamp" to the language and the word has remained. The breezy cheerfulness of Douglas Fairbanks was admired and imitated. And, of course, there was Valentino who had American women yearning and American men despairing.

"Before you know it you are *living* the story," proclaimed the old ads for the silent films. Americans did indeed live the stories and were changed by them. The Twenties, Hollywood's golden age of silent films, was an unprecedented period of moral and social changes in the American national character.

"YOU AIN'T HEARD NOTHING YET" (1927–1950)

So, the silent films swept the nation. Cities and hamlets felt their influence. The country was creating its own royalty. Names such as Gloria Swanson, Rudolph Valentino, Clara Bow, Ramon Novarro glittered through the Roaring Twenties, a decade led, paradoxically, by drab, faceless men like Harding, Coolidge, and Hoover. But the glitter and the glory of the silent films and the silent stars, like the decade itself, showed signs of fading.

That the movies have prospered for so long has been a tribute to their ability to change when their development depended on change. The film in its infancy, in those early years of the century, changed and grew by creating stories and stars. So in its adolescence the silent films, challenged by a society's new-found amusements, mobility, and freedom to which the movies themselves had contributed greatly, began to lose ground. And so they changed. They talked.

Warner Brothers, a struggling, silent film studio began it in 1927 when they released *The Jazz Singer* with Al Jolson. And Jolson talked! From the heretofore silent screen came the prophetic words to the audience: "You ain't heard nothing yet, folks." *Variety,* the newspaper of show business, best summed it up by saying that the impact of sound "didn't do any more to the industry than turn it upside down, shake the entire bag of tricks from its pocket and advance Warner Brothers from the last place to first in the league."

The talking movie was as much a revelation as the first inchoate film itself. Once again the sensation began. In 1927, the last year of the silent film domination, the industry collected $60 million dollars in admissions. By 1929, the first year of sound domination, admissions revenue had jumped to $110 million dollars. Through the years of the Great Depression and World War II, the American public was spending more money each year for admissions, a remarkable record in view of the nation's economic difficulties and preoccupations.

By 1930, the silent film was as forgotten as a Civil War daguerreotype. The movies talked, and because talk was what audiences wanted, the movies talked and talked and talked. Where once the picture was all, now words were all. The script writer and the sound editor reigned; the director and the photographer no longer ruled. The movies had changed. Observing this change, the old master D. W. Griffith expressed the feelings of many: "The moving picture is beautiful, the moving of wind on beautiful trees is more beautiful than a painting. Too much today depends on the voice. We have taken beauty and exchanged it for stilted voices."

But stilted or not, the voices were here to stay. Now that the images on the screen talked as well as moved, they became an even greater influence. For example, simple speech patterns, idioms, vocabulary drifted toward standardization. The once rich regional dialects of a nation blended into Hollywood American. As the movies' influence expanded, our own sense of identity and consciousness contracted. More and more frequently the world on the screen became our world. From a depression and a war, we sought escape, entertainment, and a vicarious life. We talked of going to the "show" knowing that there we were somehow safe. Although we may have been safe, we were also subtly and subconsciously changed. We were seeing models and behavior that would forever shape our sensibility. Clark Gable was our king, John Wayne, our hero, Scarlett O'Hara, our dream, Captain Bligh, our villain. Although we lived their lives, sometimes learned from them, often imitated them, never shall we know what part of ourselves remained undeveloped because of them.

"THE MOVIES ARE BETTER THAN EVER" (SINCE 1950)

Until 1950 the movies had been able to withstand challenges from other forms of entertainment as well as from a fickle public constantly in search of something new. But the years following World War II were to test the movie industry's very survival.

Television, heretofore little more than a scientific toy, as the movies themselves had once been, now reached into virtually every home in the nation. All that movies could provide for its audience, television could provide easier and cheaper.

The film industry, on the defensive now, loudly proclaimed, "The Movies Are Better Than Ever." Perhaps they weren't better than ever, but certainly they were changing. Color, which had been used sparingly before, flooded the screen. Television didn't have color—not yet anyway. Perhaps television could show a little picture, but the movie theaters could show a big picture and a bigger and a bigger picture. Cinerama, 3-D movies, VistaVision, CinemaScope, the industry was willing to try anything to regain a public suddenly entrenched firmly in front of its television set. Still, as the movie screens grew larger, movie audiences grew steadily smaller. By 1956 movie attendance had dropped to less than 35 million people a week. A decade earlier the industry had boasted of 90 million per week. Gone was a public whose habit it was to attend movies weekly regardless of the attraction.

Yet strangely enough in almost destroying the movie industry, television liberated it. No longer did films have to serve a mass audience for television had preempted that audience. To survive now the movies had to direct their attention to varied audiences with specific tastes. Television unwittingly helped. Its shows got worse and worse; the novelty palled. This is not to imply that millions deserted their little box. They didn't. But new audiences matured, audiences which were not satisfied with the stultifying product brought daily into their living room.

As the sixties came and went, the very landscape of American society changed dramatically and unalterably. A new frankness, a new freedom swept the country and with it a new wave of film producers and film productions. From France, Italy, Sweden, Japan, and from the United States itself, a new kind of film made its presence felt. Directors such as Fellini, Bergman, Antonioni, Nichols, Cassavetes made films that were strong personal statements as well as universal comments on the human condition. "Experimental Cinema" and "Underground Films" gained strength on the college campus and in the city alike. A television-bred generation discovered the glory of the movies' past, and cults grew around stars such as W. C. Fields, Charlie Chaplin, and the incomparable "Bogey." Film societies sprung up across the country. Universities instituted the study of films as a part of their curriculum. Films became a legitimate art. Edison's crude moving pictures of the 1890's had come a long way. The infant had grown up.

1

FORM AND TECHNIQUE

Marshall McLuhan
MOVIES: THE REEL WORLD

Marshall McLuhan, Director of the Center for Culture and Technology at the University of Toronto, has been one of the most vital intellectual forces of our time. His explanations of what is happening to man in this age of technology have had profound influences on the mass media as well as on society as a whole. "Movies: The Reel World" is a chapter from McLuhan's germinal book Understanding Media.

IN ENGLAND the movie theater was originally called "The Bioscope," because of its visual presentation of the actual movements of the forms of life (from Greek *bios,* way of life). The movie, by which we roll up the real world on a spool in order to unroll it as a magic carpet of fantasy, is a spectacular wedding of the old mechanical technology and the new electric world. In the chapter on The Wheel, the story was told of how the movie had a kind of symbolic origin in an attempt to photograph the flying hooves of galloping horses, for to set a series of cameras to study animal movement is to merge the mechanical and the organic in a special way. In the medieval world, curiously, the idea of change in organic beings was that of the substitution of one static form for another, in sequence. They imagined the life of a flower as a kind of cinematic strip of phases or essences. The movie is the total realization of the medieval idea of change, in the form of an entertaining illusion. Physiologists had very much to do with the development of film, as they did with the telephone. On film the mechanical appears as organic, and the growth of a flower can be portrayed as easily and as freely as the movement of a horse.

If the movie merges the mechanical and organic in a world of undulating forms, it also links with the technology of print. The reader in projecting words, as it were, has to follow the black and white sequences of stills that is typography, providing his own sound track. He tries to follow the contours of the author's mind, at varying speeds and with various illusions of understanding. It would be difficult to exaggerate the bond between print and movie in terms of their power to generate fantasy in the viewer or reader. Cervantes devoted his *Don Quixote* entirely to this aspect of the printed word and its power to create what James Joyce throughout *Finnegans Wake* designates as "the ABCED-minded," which can be taken as "ab-said" or "ab-sent," or just alphabetically controlled.

The business of the writer or the film-maker is to transfer the reader or viewer from one world, his *own,* to another, the world created by typography and film. That is so obvious, and happens so completely, that those undergoing the experience accept it subliminally and without critical awareness. Cervantes lived in a world in which print was as new as movies are in the West, and it seemed obvious to him that print, like the images now on the screen, had usurped the real world. The reader or spectator had become a dreamer under their spell, as René Clair said of film in 1926.

Movies as a nonverbal form of experience are like photography, a form of statement without syntax. In fact, however, like the print and the photo, movies assume a high level of literacy in their users and prove baffling to the nonliterate. Our literate acceptance of the mere movement of the camera eye as it follows or drops a figure from view is not acceptable to an African film audience. If somebody disappears off the side of the film, the African wants to know what happened to him. A literate audience, however, accustomed to following printed imagery line by line without questioning the logic of lineality, will accept film sequence without protest.

It was René Clair who pointed out that if two or three people were together on a stage, the dramatist must ceaselessly motivate or explain their being there at all. But the film audience, like the book reader, accepts mere sequence as rational. Whatever the camera turns to, the audience accepts. We are transported to another world. As René Clair observed, the screen opens its white door into a harem of beautiful visions and adolescent dreams, compared to which the loveliest real body seems defective. Yeats saw the movie as a world of Platonic ideals with the film projector playing "a spume upon a ghostly paradigm of things." This was the world that haunted Don Quixote, who found it through the folio door of the newly printed romances.

The close relation, then, between the reel world of film and the private fantasy experience of the printed word is indispensable to our Western acceptance of the film form. Even the film industry regards all of its greatest achievements as derived from novels, nor is this unreasonable. Film, both in its reel form and in its scenario or script form, is completely involved with book culture. All one need do is to imagine for a moment a film based on newspaper form in order to see how close film is to book. Theoretically, there is no reason why the camera should not be used to photograph complex groups of items and events in dateline configurations, just as they are presented on the page of a newspaper. Actually, poetry tends to do this configuring or "bunching" more than prose. Symbolist poetry has much in common with the mosaic of the newspaper page, yet very few people can detach themselves from uniform and connected space sufficiently to grasp symbolist poems. Natives, on the other hand, who have very little contact with phonetic literary and lineal print, have to learn to "see" photographs or film just as much as we have to learn our letters. In fact, after having tried for years to teach Africans their letters by film, John Wilson of London University's African Institute found it easier to teach them their letters as a means to film literacy. For even when natives have learned to "see" pictures, they cannot accept our ideas of time and space "illusions." On seeing Charlie Chaplin's *The Tramp,* the African audience concluded that Europeans were magicians who could restore life. They saw a character who survived a mighty blow on the head without any indication of being hurt. When the camera shifts, they think they see trees moving, and buildings growing or shrinking, because they cannot make the literate assumption that space is continuous and uniform. Nonliterate people simply don't get perspective or distancing effects of light and shade that we assume are innate human equipment. Literate people think of cause and effect as sequential, as if one thing pushed another along by physical force. Nonliterate people register very little interest in this kind of "efficient" cause and effect, but are fascinated by hidden forms that produce magical results. Inner, rather than outer, causes interest the nonliterate and nonvisual cultures. And that is why the literate West sees the rest of the world as caught in the seamless web of superstition.

Like the oral Russian, the African will not accept sight and sound together. The talkies were the doom of Russian film-making because, like any backward or oral culture, Russians have an irresistible need for participation that is defeated by the addition of sound to the visual image. Both Pudovkin and Eisenstein denounced the sound film but considered that if sound were used symbolically and contrapuntally, rather than realistically, there would result less harm to the visual image. The African insistence on group participation and on chanting and shouting during films is wholly frustrated by sound track. Our own talkies were a further completion of the visual package as a mere consumer commodity. For with silent film we automatically provide sound for ourselves by way of "closure" or completion. And when it is filled in for us there is very much less participation in the work of the image.

Again, it has been found that nonliterates do not know how to fix their eyes, as Westerners do, a few feet in front of the movie screen, or some distance in front of a photo. The result is that they move their eyes over photo or screen as they might their hands. It is this same habit of using the eyes as hands that makes European men so "sexy" to American women. Only an extremely literate and abstract society learns to fix the eyes, as we must learn to do in reading the printed page. For those who thus fix their eyes, perspective results. There is great subtlety and synesthesia in native art, but no perspective. The old belief that everybody really saw in perspective, but only that Renaissance painters had learned how to paint it, is erroneous. Our own first TV generation is rapidly losing this habit of visual perspective as a sensory modality, and along with this change comes an interest in words not as visually uniform and continuous, but as unique worlds in depth. Hence the craze for puns and word-play, even in sedate ads.

In terms of other media such as the printed page, film has the power to store and to convey a great deal of information. In an instant it presents a scene of landscape with figures that would require several pages of prose to describe. In the next instant it repeats, and can go on repeating, this detailed information. The writer, on the other hand, has no means of holding a mass of detail before his reader in a large bloc or *gestalt.* As the photograph urged the painter in the direction of abstract, sculptural art, so the film has confirmed the writer in verbal economy and depth symbolism where the film cannot rival him.

Another facet of the sheer quantity of data possible in a movie shot is exemplified in historical films like *Henry V* or *Richard III.* Here extensive research went into the making of the sets and costumes that any six-year-old can now enjoy as readily as any adult. T. S. Eliot reported how, in the making of the film of his *Murder in the Cathedral,* it was not only necessary to have costumes of the period, but—so great is the precision and tyranny of the camera eye—these costumes had to be woven by the same techniques as those used in the twelfth century. Hollywood, amidst much illusion, had also to provide authentic scholarly replicas of many past scenes. The stage and TV can make do with very rough approximations, because they offer an image of low definition that evades detailed scrutiny.

At first, however, it was the detailed realism of writers like Dickens that inspired movie pioneers like D. W. Griffith, who carried a copy of a Dickens novel on location. The realistic novel, that arose with the newspaper form of communal cross-section and human-interest coverage in the eighteenth century, was a complete anticipation of film form. Even the poets took up the same panoramic style, with human interest vignettes and close-ups as variant. Gray's *Elegy,* Burns' *The Cotter's Saturday Night,* Wordsworth's *Michael,* and Byron's *Childe Harold* are all like shooting scripts for some contemporary documentary film.

"The kettle began it. . . ." Such is the opening of Dickens' *Cricket and the Hearth.* If the modern novel came out of Gogol's *The Overcoat,* the modern movie, says Eisenstein, boiled up out of that kettle. It should be plain that the American and even British approach to film is much lacking in that free interplay among the senses and the media that seems so natural to Eisenstein or René Clair. For the Russian, especially, it is easy to approach any situation structurally, which is to say, sculpturally. To Eisenstein, the overwhelming fact of film was that it is an "act of juxtaposition." But to a culture in an extreme reach of typographic conditioning, the juxtaposition must be one of uniform and connected characters and qualities. There must be no leaps from the unique space of the tea kettle to the unique space of the kitten or the boot. If such objects appear, they must be leveled off by some continuous narrative, or be "contained" in some uniform pictorial space. All that Salvador Dali had to do to create a furor was to allow the chest of drawers or the grand piano to exist in its own space against some Sahara or Alpine backdrop. Merely by releasing objects from the uniform continuous space of typography we got modern art and poetry. We can measure the psychic pressure of typography by the uproar generated by that release. For most people, their own ego image seems to have been typographically conditioned, so that the electric age with its return to inclusive experience threatens their idea of self. These are the fragmented ones, for whom specialist toil renders the mere prospect of leisure or jobless security a nightmare. Electric simultaneity ends specialist learning and activity, and demands interrelation in depth, even of the personality.

The case of Charlie Chaplin films helps to illumine this problem. His *Modern Times* was taken to be a satire on the fragmented character of modern tasks. As clown, Chaplin presents the acrobatic feat in a mime of elaborate incompetence, for any specialist task leaves out most of our faculties. The clown reminds us of our fragmented state by tackling acrobatic or special jobs in the spirit of the whole or integral man. This is the formula for helpless incompetence. On the street, in social situations, on the assembly line, the worker continues his compulsive twitchings with an imaginary wrench. But the mime of this Chaplin film and others is precisely that of the robot, the mechanical doll whose deep pathos it is to approximate so closely to the condition of human life. Chaplin, in all his work, did a puppetlike ballet of the Cyrano de Bergerac kind. In order to capture this puppetlike pathos, Chaplin (a devotee of ballet and personal friend of Pavlova) adopted from the first the foot postures of classical ballet. Thus he could have the aura of *Spectre de la Rose* shimmering around his clown getup. From the British music hall, his first training ground, with a sure touch of genius he took images like that of Mr. Charles Pooter, the haunting figure of a nobody. This shoddy-genteel image he invested with an envelope of fairy romance by means of adherence to the classic ballet postures. The new film form was perfectly adapted to this composite image, since film is itself a jerky mechanical ballet of flicks that yields a sheer dream world of romantic illusions. But the film form is not just a puppetlike dance of arrested still shots, for it manages to approximate and even to surpass real life by means of illusion. That is why Chaplin, in his silent pictures at least, was never tempted to abandon the Cyrano role of the puppet who could never really be a lover. In this stereotype Chaplin discovered the heart of the film illusion, and he manipulated that heart with easy mastery, as the key to the pathos of a mechanized civilization. A mechanized world is always in the process of getting ready to live, and to this end it brings to bear the most appalling pomp of skill and method and resourcefulness.

The film pushed this mechanism to the utmost mechanical verge and beyond, into a surrealism of dreams that money can buy. Nothing is more congenial to the film form than this pathos of superabundance and power that is the dower of a puppet for whom they can never be real. This is the key to *The Great Gatsby* that reaches its moment of truth when Daisy breaks down in contemplating Gatsby's superb collection of shirts. Daisy and Gatsby live in a tinsel world that is both corrupted by power, yet innocently pastoral in its dreaming.

The movie is not only a supreme expression of mechanism, but paradoxically it offers as product the most magical of consumer commodities, namely dreams. It is, therefore, not accidental that the movie has excelled as a medium that offers poor people roles of riches and power beyond the dreams of avarice. In the chapter on The Photograph, it was pointed out how the press photo in particular had discouraged the really rich from the paths of conspicuous consumption. The life of display that the photo had taken from the rich, the movie gave to the poor with lavish hand:

> Oh, lucky, lucky me,
> I shall live in luxury,
> For I've got a pocketful of dreams.

The Hollywood tycoons were not wrong in acting on the assumption that movies gave the American immigrant a means of self-fulfillment without any delay. This strategy, however deplorable in the light of the "absolute ideal good," was perfectly in accord with film form. It meant that in the 1920s the American way of life was exported to the entire world in cans. The world eagerly lined up to buy canned dreams. The film not only accompanied the first great consumer age, but was also incentive, advertisement and, in itself, a major commodity. Now in terms of media study it is clear that the power of film to store information in accessible form is unrivaled. Audio tape and video tape were to excel film eventually as information storehouses. But film remains a major information resource, a rival of the book whose technology it did so much to continue and also to surpass. At the present time, film is still in its manuscript phase, as it were; shortly it will, under TV pressure, go into its portable, accessible, printed-book phase. Soon everyone will be able to have a small, inexpensive film projector that plays an 8-mm sound cartridge as if on a TV screen. This type of development is part of our present technological implosion. The present dissociation of projector and screen is a vestige of our older mechanical world of explosion and separation of functions that is now ending with the electrical implosion.

Typographic man took readily to film just because, like books, it offers an inward world of fantasy and dreams. The film viewer sits in psychological solitude like the silent book reader. This was not the case with the manuscript reader, nor is it true of the watcher of television. It is not pleasant to turn on TV just for oneself in a hotel room, nor even at home. The TV mosaic image demands social completion and dialogue. So with the manuscript before typography, since manuscript culture is oral and demands dialogue and debate, as the entire culture of the ancient and medieval worlds demonstrates. One of the major pressures of TV has been to encourage the "teaching machine." In fact, these devices are adaptations of the book in the direction of dialogue. These teaching machines are really private tutors, and their being misnamed on the principle that produced the names "wireless" and "horseless carriage" is another instance in that long list that illustrates how every innovation must pass through a primary phase in which the new effect is secured by the old method, amplified or modified by some new feature.

Film is not really a single medium like song or written word, but a collective art form with different individuals directing color, lighting, sound, acting, speaking. The press, radio and TV, and the comics are also art forms dependent upon entire teams and hierarchies of skill in corporate action. Prior to the movies, the most obvious example of such corporate artistic action had occurred early in the industrialized world, with the large new symphony orchestras of the nineteenth century. Paradoxically, as industry went its ever more specialized fragmented course, it demanded more and more teamwork in sales and supplies. The symphony orchestra became a major expression of the ensuing power of such coordinated effort, though for the players themselves this effect was lost, both in the symphony and in industry.

When the magazine editors recently introduced film scenario procedures to the constructing of idea articles, the idea article supplanted the short story. The film is the rival of the book in that sense. (TV in turn is the rival of the magazine because of its mosaic power.) Ideas presented as a sequence of shots or pictorialized situations, almost in the manner of a teaching machine, actually drove the short story out of the magazine field.

Hollywood has fought TV mainly by becoming a subsidiary of TV. Most of the film industry is now engaged in supplying TV programs. But one new strategy has been tried, namely the big-budget picture. The fact is that Technicolor is the closest the movie can get to the effect of the TV image. Technicolor greatly lowers photographic intensity and creates, in part, the visual conditions for participant viewing. Had Hollywood understood the reasons for *Marty's* success, TV might have given us a revolution in film. *Marty* was a TV show that got onto the screen in the form of low definition or low-intensity visual realism. It was not a success story, and it had no stars, because the low-intensity TV image is quite incompatible with the high-intensity star image. *Marty,* which in fact looked like an early silent movie or an old Russian picture, offered the film industry all the clues it needed for meeting the TV challenge.

This kind of casual, cool realism has given the new British films easy ascendancy. *Room at the Top* features the new cool realism. Not only is it not a success story, it is as much an announcement of the end of the Cinderella package as Marilyn Monroe was the end of the star system. *Room at the Top* is the story of how the higher a monkey climbs, the more you see of his backside. The moral is that success is not only wicked but also the formula for misery. It is very hard for a hot medium like film to accept the cool message of TV. But the Peter Sellers movies *I'm All Right, Jack* and *Only Two Can Play* are perfectly in tune with the new temper created by the cool TV image. Such is also the meaning of the ambiguous success of *Lolita.* As a novel, its acceptance announced the antiheroic approach to romance. The film industry had long beaten out a royal road to romance in keeping with the crescendo of the success story. *Lolita* announced that the royal road was only a cowtrack, after all, and as for success, it shouldn't happen to a dog.

In the ancient world and in medieval times, the most popular of all stories were those dealing with *The Falls of Princes.* With the coming of the very hot print medium, the preference changed to a rising rhythm and to tales of success and sudden elevation in the world. It seemed possible to achieve anything by the new typographic method of minute, uniform segmentation of problems. It was by this method, eventually, that film was made. Film was, as a form, the final fulfillment of the great potential of typographic fragmentation. But the electric implosion has now reversed the entire process of expansion by fragmentation. Electricity has brought back the cool, mosaic world of implosion, equilibrium, and stasis. In our electric age, the one-way expansion of the berserk individual on his way to the top now appears as a gruesome image of trampled lives and disrupted harmonies. Such is the subliminal message of the TV mosaic with its total field of simultaneous impulses. Film strip and sequence cannot but bow to this superior power. Our own youngsters have taken the TV message to heart in their beatnik rejection of consumer mores and of the private success story.

Since the best way to get to the core of a form is to study its effect in some unfamiliar setting, let us note what President Sukarno of Indonesia announced in 1956 to a large group of Hollywood executives. He said that he regarded them as political radicals and revolutionaries who had greatly hastened political change in the East. What the Orient saw in a Hollywood movie was a world in which all the *ordinary people* had cars and electric stoves and refrigerators. So the Oriental now regards himself as an ordinary person who has been deprived of the ordinary man's birthright.

That is another way of getting a view of the film medium as monster ad for consumer goods. In America this major aspect of film is merely subliminal. Far from regarding our pictures as incentives to mayhem and revolution, we take them as solace and compensation, or as a form of deferred payment by daydreaming. But the Oriental is right, and we are wrong about this. In fact, the movie is a mighty limb of the industrial giant. That it is being amputated by the TV image reflects a still greater revolution going on at the center of American life. It is natural that the ancient East should feel the political pull and industrial challenge of our movie industry. The movie, as much as the alphabet and the printed word, is an aggressive and imperial form that explodes outward into other cultures. Its explosive force was significantly greater in silent pictures than in talkies, for the electromagnetic sound track already forecast the substitution of electric implosion for mechanical explosion. The silent pictures were immediately acceptable across language barriers as the talkies were not. Radio teamed up with film to give us the talkie and to carry us further on our present reverse course of implosion or re-integration after the mechanical age of explosion and expansion. The extreme form of this implosion or contraction is the image of the astronaut locked into his wee bit of wraparound space. Far from enlarging our world, he is announcing its contraction to village size. The rocket and the space capsule are ending the rule of the wheel and the machine, as much as did the wire services, radio, and TV.

We may now consider a further instance of the film's influence in a most conclusive aspect. In modern literature there is probably no more celebrated technique than that of the stream of consciousness or interior monologue. Whether in Proust, Joyce, or Eliot, this form of sequence permits the reader an extraordinary identification with personalities of the utmost range and diversity. The stream of consciousness is really managed by the transfer of film technique to the printed page, where, in a deep sense it really originated; for as we have seen, the Gutenberg technology of movable types is quite indispensable to any industrial or film process. As much as the infinitesimal calculus that *pretends* to deal with motion and change by minute fragmentation, the film *does* so by making motion and change into a series of static shots. Print does likewise while pretending to deal with the whole mind in action. Yet film and the stream of consciousness alike seemed to provide a deeply desired release from the mechanical world of increasing standardization and uniformity. Nobody ever felt oppressed by the monotony or uniformity of the Chaplin ballet or by the monotonous, uniform musings of his literary twin, Leopold Bloom.

In 1911 Henri Bergson in *Creative Evolution* created a sensation by associating the thought process with the form of the movie. Just at the extreme point of mechanization represented by the factory, the film, and the press, men seemed by the stream of consciousness, or interior film to obtain release into a world of spontaneity, of dreams, and of unique personal experience. Dickens perhaps began it all with his Mr. Jingle in *Pickwick Papers.* Certainly in *David Copperfield* he made a great technical discovery, since for the first time the world unfolds realistically through the use of the eyes of a growing child as camera. Here was the stream of consciousness, perhaps, in its original form before it was adopted by Proust and Joyce and Eliot. It indicates how the enrichment of human experience can occur unexpectedly with the crossing and interplay of the life of media forms.

The film imports of all nations, especially those from the United States, are very popular in Thailand, thanks in part to a deft Thai technique for getting round the foreign-language obstacle. In Bangkok, in place of subtitles, they use what is called "Adam-and-Eving." This takes the form of live Thai dialogue read through a loudspeaker by Thai actors concealed from the audience. Split-second timing and great endurance enable these actors to demand more than the best-paid movie stars of Thailand.

Everyone has at some time wished he were equipped with his own sound system during a movie performance, in order to make appropriate comments. In Thailand, one might achieve great heights of interpretive interpolation during the inane exchanges of great stars.

James Agee
COMEDY'S GREATEST ERA

James Agee, poet, novelist, screenwriter, and film critic for Time *and* The Nation, *produced in the 1940's weekly film criticism, which W. H. Auden called "the most remarkable regular event in American journalism today." Week after week, Agee's film column gave stature to a medium struggling to overcome its reputation as solely a form of mindless mass entertainment. In, perhaps, his most famous piece of film criticism, Agee examines the "masters," those renowned silent film comedians who constituted "Comedy's Greatest Era."*

IN THE language of screen comedians four of the main grades of laugh are the titter, the yowl, the belly laugh and the boffo. The titter is just a titter. The yowl is a runaway titter. Anyone who has even had the pleasure knows all about a belly laugh. The boffo is the laugh that kills. An ideally good gag, perfectly constructed and played, would bring the victim up this ladder of laughs by cruelly controlled degrees to the top rung, and would then proceed to wobble, shake, wave and brandish the ladder until he groaned for mercy. Then, after the shortest possible time out for recuperation, he would feel the first wicked tickling of the comedian's whip once more and start up a new ladder.

The reader can get a fair enough idea of the current state of screen comedy by asking himself how long it has been since he has had that treatment. The best of comedies these days hand out plenty of titters and once in a while it is possible to achieve a yowl without overstraining. Even those who have never seen anything better must occasionally have the feeling, as they watch the current run or, rather, trickle of screen comedy, that they are having to make a little cause for laughter go an awfully long way. And anyone who has watched screen comedy over the past ten or fifteen years is bound to realize that it has quietly but steadily deteriorated. As for those happy atavists who remember silent comedy in its heyday and the belly laughs and boffos that went with it, they have something close to an absolute standard by which to measure the deterioration.

When a modern comedian gets hit on the head, for example, the most he is apt to do is look sleepy. When a silent comedian got hit on the head he seldom let it go so flatly. He realized a broad license, and a ruthless discipline within that license. It was his business to be as funny as possible physically, without the help or hindrance of words. So he gave us a figure of speech, or rather of vision, for loss of consciousness. In other words he gave us a poem, a kind of poem, moreover, that everybody understands. The least he might do was to straighten up stiff as a plank and fall over backward with such skill that his whole length seemed to slap the floor at the same instant. Or he might make a cadenza of it—look vague, smile like an angel, roll up his eyes, lace his fingers, thrust his hands palms downward as far as they would go, hunch his shoulders, rise on tiptoe, prance ecstatically in narrowing circles until, with tallow knees, he sank down the vortex of his dizziness to the floor and there signified nirvana by kicking his heels twice, like a swimming frog.

Startled by a cop, this same comedian might grab his hatbrim with both hands and yank it down over his ears, jump high in the air, come to earth in a split violent enough to telescope his spine, spring thence into a coattail-flattening sprint and dwindle at rocket speed to the size of a gnat along the grand, forlorn perspective of some lazy back boulevard.

Those are fine clichés from the language of silent comedy in its infancy. The man who could handle them properly combined several of the more difficult accomplishments of the acrobat, the dancer, the clown and the mime. Some very gifted comedians, unforgettably Ben Turpin, had an immense vocabulary of these clichés and were in part so lovable because they were deep conservative classicists and never tried to break away from them. The still more gifted men, of course, simplified and invented, finding out new and much deeper uses for the idiom. They learned to show emotion through it, and comic psychology, more eloquently than most language has even managed to, and they discovered beauties of comic motion which are hopelessly beyond reach of words.

It is hard to find a theater these days where a comedy is playing; in the days of the silents it was equally hard to find a theater which was not showing one. The laughs today are pitifully few, far between, shallow, quiet and short. They almost never build, as they used to, into something combining the jabbering frequency of a machine gun with the delirious momentum of a roller coaster. Saddest of all, there are few comedians now below middle age and there are none who seem to learn much from picture to picture, or to try anything new.

To put it unkindly, the only thing wrong with screen comedy today is that it takes place on a screen which talks. Because it talks, the only comedians who ever mastered the screen cannot work, for they cannot combine their comic style with talk. Because there is a screen, talking comedians are trapped into a continual exhibition of their inadequacy as screen comedians on a surface as big as the side of a barn.

At the moment, as for many years past, the chances to see silent comedy are rare. There is a smattering of it on television—too often treated as something quaintly archaic, to be laughed at, not with. Some two hundred comedies—long and short—can be rented for home projection. And a lucky minority has access to the comedies in the collection of New York's Museum of Modern Art, which is still incomplete but which is probably the best in the world. In the near future, however, something of this lost art will return to regular theaters. A thick straw in the wind is the big business now being done by a series of revivals of W. C. Fields's memorable movies, a kind of comedy more akin to the old silent variety than anything which is being made today. Mack Sennett now is preparing a sort of potpourri variety show called *Down Memory Lane* made up out of his old movies, featuring people like Fields and Bing Crosby when they were movie beginners, but including also interludes from silents. Harold Lloyd has re-released *Movie Crazy,* a talkie, and plans to revive four of his best silent comedies, *Grandma's Boy, Safety Last, Speedy* and *The Freshman.* Buster Keaton hopes to remake at feature length, with a minimum of dialogue, two of the funniest short comedies ever made, one about a porous homemade boat and one about a prefabricated house.

Awaiting these happy events, we will discuss here what has gone wrong with screen comedy and what, if anything, can be done about it. But mainly we will try to suggest what it was like in its glory in the years from 1912 to 1930, as practiced by the employees of Mack Sennett, the father of American screen comedy, and by the four most eminent masters: Charlie Chaplin, Harold Lloyd, the late Harry Langdon and Buster Keaton.

Mack Sennett made two kinds of comedy: parody laced with slapstick, and plain slapstick. The parodies were the unceremonious burial of a century of hamming, including the new hamming in serious movies, and nobody who has missed Ben Turpin in *A Small Town Idol,* or kidding Erich von Stroheim in *Three Foolish Weeks* or as *The Shriek of Araby,* can imagine how rough parody can get and still remain subtle and roaringly funny. The plain slapstick, at its best, was even better: a profusion of hearty young women in disconcerting bathing suits, frisking around with a gaggle of insanely incompetent policemen and of equally certifiable male civilians sporting museum-piece mustaches. All these people zipped and caromed about the pristine world of the screen as jazzily as a convention of water bugs. Words can hardly suggest how energetically they collided and bounced apart, meeting in full gallop around the corner of a house; how hard and how often they fell on their backsides; or with what fantastically adroit clumsiness they got themselves fouled up in folding ladders, garden hoses, tethered animals and each other's headlong cross-purposes. The gestures were ferociously emphatic; not a line or motion of the body was wasted or inarticulate. The reader may remember how splendidly upright wandlike old Ben Turpin could stand for a Renunciation Scene, with his lampshade mustache twittering and his sparrowy chest stuck out and his head flung back like Paderewski assaulting a climax and the long babyish back hair trying to look lionlike, while his Adam's apple, an orange in a Christmas stocking, pumped with noble emotion. Or huge Mack Swain, who looked like a hairy mushroom, rolling his eyes in a manner patented by French romantics and gasping in some dubious ecstasy. Or Louise Fazenda, the perennial farmer's daughter and the perfect low-comedy housemaid, primping her spit curl; and how her hair tightened a good-looking face into the incarnation of rampant gullibility. Or snouty James Finlayson, gleefully foreclosing a mortgage, with his look of eternally tasting a spoiled pickle. Or Chester Conklin, a myopic and inebriated little walrus stumbling around in outsize pants. Or Fatty Arbuckle, with his cold eye and his loose, serene smile, his silky manipulation of his bulk and his satanic marksmanship with pies (he was ambidextrous and could simultaneously blind two people in opposite directions).

The intimate tastes and secret hopes of these poor ineligible dunces were ruthlessly exposed whenever a hot stove, an electric fan or a bulldog took a dislike to their outer garments: agonizingly elaborate drawers, worked up on some lonely evening out of some Godforsaken lace curtain; or men's underpants with big round black spots on them. The Sennett sets—delirious wallpaper, megalomaniacally scrolled iron beds, Grand Rapids *in extremis*—outdid even the underwear. It was their business, after all, to kid the squalid braggadocio which infested the domestic interiors of the period, and that was almost beyond parody. These comedies told their stories to the unaided eye, and by every means possible they screamed to it. That is one reason for the India ink silhouettes of the cops, and for convicts and prison bars and their shadows in hard sunlight, and for barefooted husbands, in tigerish pajamas, reacting like dervishes to stepped-on tacks.

The early silent comedians never strove for or consciously thought of anything which could be called artistic "form," but they achieved it. For Sennett's rival, Hal Roach, Leo McCarey once devoted almost the whole of a Laurel and Hardy two-reeler to pie throwing. The first pies were thrown thoughtfully, almost philosophically. Then innocent bystanders began to get caught into the vortex. At full pitch it was Armageddon. But everything was calculated so nicely that until late in the picture, when havoc took over, every pie made its special kind of point and piled on its special kind of laugh.

Sennett's comedies were just a shade faster and fizzier than life. According to legend (and according to Sennett) he discovered the tempo proper to screen comedy when a green camerman, trying to save money, cranked too slow.[1] Realizing the tremendous drumlike power of mere motion to exhilarate, he gave inanimate objects a mischievous life of their own, broke every law of nature the tricked camera would serve him for and made the screen dance like a witches' Sabbath. The thing one is surest of all to remember is how toward the end of nearly every Sennett comedy, a chase (usually called the "rally") built up such a majestic trajectory of pure anarchic motion that bathing girls, cops, comics, dogs, cats, babies, automobiles, locomotives, innocent bystanders, sometimes what seemed like a whole city, an entire civilization, were hauled along head over heels in the wake of that energy like dry leaves following an express train.

"Nice" people, who shunned all movies in the early days, condemned the Sennett comedies as vulgar and naïve. But millions of less pretentious people loved their sincerity and sweetness, their wild-animal innocence and glorious vitality. They could not put these feelings into words, but they flocked to the silents. The reader who gets back deep enough into that world will probably even remember the theater: the barefaced honky-tonk and the waltzes by Waldteufel, slammed out on a mechanical piano; and searing redolence of peanuts and demirep perfumery, tobacco and feet and sweat; the laughter of unrespectable people having a hell of a fine time, laughter as violent and steady and deafening as standing under a waterfall.

Sennett wheedled his first financing out of a couple of ex-bookies to whom he was already in debt. He took his comics out of music halls, burlesque, vaudeville, circuses and limbo, and through them he tapped in on that great pipeline of horsing and miming which runs back unbroken through the fairs of the Middle Ages at least to ancient Greece. He added all that he himself had learned about the large and spurious gesture, the late decadence of the Grand Manner, as a stage-struck boy in East Berlin, Connecticut, and as a frustrated opera singer and actor. The only thing he claims to have invented is the pie in the face,

1 Silent comedy was shot at twelve to sixteen frames per second and was speeded up by being shown at sixteen frames per second, the usual rate of theater projectors at that time. Theater projectors today run at twenty-four, which makes modern film taken at the same speed seem smooth and natural. But it makes silent movies fast and jerky.

and he insists, "Anyone who tells you he has discovered something new is a fool or a liar or both."

The silent-comedy studio was about the best training school the movies have ever known, and the Sennett studio was about as free and easy and as fecund of talent as they came. All the major comedians we will mention worked there, at least briefly. So did some of the major stars of the '20s and since—notably Gloria Swanson, Phyllis Haver, Wallace Beery, Marie Dressler and Carole Lombard. Directors Frank Capra, Leo McCarey and George Stevens also got their start in silent comedy; much that remains most flexible, spontaneous and visually alive in sound movies can be traced, through them and others, to this silent apprenticeship. Everybody did pretty much as he pleased on the Sennett lot, and everybody's ideas were welcome. Sennett posted no rules, and the only thing he strictly forbade was liquor. A Sennett story conference was a most informal affair. During the early years, at least, only the most important scenario might be jotted on the back of an envelope. Mainly Sennett's men thrashed out a few primary ideas and carried them in their heads, sure that better stuff would turn up while they were shooting, in the heat of physical action. This put quite a load on the prop man; he had to have the most improbable apparatus on hand—bombs, trick telephones, what not—to implement whatever idea might suddenly turn up. All kinds of things did—and were recklessly used. Once a low-comedy auto got out of control and killed the cameraman, but he was not visible in the shot, which was thrilling and undamaged; the audience never knew the difference.

Sennett used to hire a "wild man" to sit in on his gag conferences, whose whole job was to think up "wildies." Usually he was an all but brainless, speechless man, scarcely able to communicate his idea; but he had a totally uninhibited imagination. He might say nothing for an hour; then he'd mutter, "You take . . . " and all the relatively rational others would shut up and wait. "You take this cloud . . ." he would get out, sketching vague shapes in the air. Often he could get no further; but thanks to some kind of thought transference, saner men would take this cloud and make something of it. The wild man seems in fact to have functioned as the group's subconscious mind, the source of all creative energy. His ideas were so weird and amorphous that Sennett can no longer remember a one of them, or even how it turned out after rational processing. But a fair equivalent might be one of the best comic sequences in a Laurel and Hardy picture. It is simple enough —simple and real, in fact, as a nightmare. Laurel and Hardy are trying to move a piano across a narrow suspension bridge. The bridge is slung over a sickening chasm, between a couple of Alps. Midway they meet a gorilla.

Had he done nothing else, Sennett would be remembered for giving a start to three of the four comedians who now began to apply their sharp individual talents to this newborn language. The one whom he did not train (he was on the lot briefly but Sennett barely remembers seeing him around) wore glasses, smiled a great deal and looked like the sort of eager young man who might have quit divinity school to hustle brushes. That was Harold Lloyd. The others were grotesque and poetic in their screen characters in degrees which appear to be impossible when the magic of silence is broken. One, who never smiled, carried a face as still and sad as a daguerreotype through some of the most preposterously ingenious and visually satisfying physical comedy ever invented. That was Buster Keaton. One looked like an elderly baby and, at times, a baby dope fiend; he could do more with less than any other comedian. That was Harry Langdon. One looked like Charlie Chaplin, and he was the first man to give the silent language a soul.

When Charlie Chaplin started to work for Sennett he had chiefly to reckon with Ford Sterling, the reigning comedian. Their first picture together amounted to a duel before the assembled professionals. Sterling, by no means untalented, was a big man with a florid Teutonic style which, under this special pressure, he turned on full blast. Chaplin defeated him within a few minutes with a wink of the mustache, a hitch of the trousers, a quirk of the little finger.

With *Tillie's Punctured Romance,* in 1914, he became a major star. Soon after, he left Sennett when Sennett refused to start a landslide among the other comedians by meeting the raise Chaplin demanded. Sennett is understandably wry about it in retrospect, but he still says, "I was right at the time." Of Chaplin he says simply, "Oh well, he's just the greatest artist that ever lived." None of Chaplin's former rivals rates him much lower than that; they speak of him no more jealously than they might of God. We will try here only to suggest the essence of his supremacy. Of all comedians he worked most deeply and most shrewdly within a realization of what a human being is, and is up against. The Tramp is as centrally representative of humanity, as many-sided and as mysterious, as Hamlet, and it seems unlikely that any dancer or actor can ever have excelled him in eloquence, variety or poignancy of motion. As for pure motion, even if he had never gone on to make his magnificent feature-length comedies, Chaplin would have made his period in movies a great one singlehanded even if he had made nothing except *The Cure,* or *One A.M.* In the latter, barring one immobile taxi driver, Chaplin plays alone, as a drunk trying to get upstairs and into bed. It is a sort of inspired elaboration on a soft-shoe dance, involving an angry stuffed wildcat, small rugs on slippery floors, a Lazy Susan table, exquisite footwork on a flight of stairs, a contretemps with a huge, ferocious pendulum and the funniest and most perverse Murphy bed in movie history—and, always made physically lucid, the delicately weird mental processes of a man ethereally sozzled.

Before Chaplin came to pictures people were content with a couple of gags per comedy; he got some kind of laugh every second. The minute he began to work he set standards—and continually forced them higher. Anyone who saw Chaplin eating a boiled shoe like brook trout in *The Gold Rush,* or embarrassed by a swallowed whistle in *City Lights,* has seen perfection. Most of the time, however, Chaplin got his laughter less from the gags, or from milking them in any ordinary sense, than through his genius for what may be called *inflection* —the perfect, changeful shading of his physical and emotional attitudes toward the gag. Funny as his bout with the Murphy bed is, the glances of awe, expostulation and helpless, almost whimpering desire for vengeance which he darts at this infernal machine are even better.

A painful and frequent error among tyros is breaking the comic line with a too-big laugh, then a letdown; or with a laugh which is out of key or irrelevant. The masters could ornament the main line beautifully; they never addled it. In *A Night Out* Chaplin, passed out, is hauled along the sidewalk by the scruff of his coat by staggering Ben Turpin. His toes trail; he is as supine as a sled. Turpin himself is so drunk he can hardly drag him. Chaplin comes quietly to, realizes how well he is being served by his struggling pal, and with a royally delicate gesture plucks and savors a flower.

The finest pantomime, the deepest emotion, the richest and most poignant poetry were in Chaplin's work. He could probably pantomime Bryce's *The American Commonwealth* without ever blurring a syllable and make it paralyzingly funny into the bargain. At the end of *City Lights* the blind girl who has regained her sight, thanks to the Tramp, sees him for the first time. She has imagined and anticipated him as princely, to say the least; and it has never seriously occurred to him that he is inadequate. She recognizes who he must be by his shy, confident, shining joy as he comes silently toward her. And he recognizes himself, for the first time, through the terrible changes in her face. The camera just exchanges a few quiet close-ups of the emotions which shift and intensify in each face. It is enough to shrivel the heart to see, and it is the greatest piece of acting and the highest moment in movies.

Harold Lloyd worked only a little while with Sennett. During most of his career he acted for another major comedy producer, Hal Roach. He tried at first to offset Chaplin's influence and establish his own individuality by playing Chaplin's exact opposite, a character named Lonesome Luke who wore clothes much too small for him and whose gestures were likewise as un-Chaplinesque as possible. But he soon realized that an opposite in itself was a kind of slavishness. He discovered his own comic identity when he saw a movie about a fighting parson: a hero who wore glasses. He began to think about those glasses day and night. He decided on horn rims because they were youthful, ultravisible on the screen and on the verge of becoming fashionable (he was to make them so). Around these large lensless horn rims he began to develop a new character, nothing grotesque or eccentric, but a fresh, believable young man who could fit into a wide variety of stories.

Lloyd depended more on story and situation than any of the other major comedians (he kept the best stable of gagmen in Hollywood, at one time hiring six); but unlike most "story" comedians he was also a very funny man from inside. He had, as he has written, "an unusually large comic vocabulary." More particularly he had an expertly expressive body and even more expressive teeth, and out of his thesaurus of smiles he could at a moment's notice blend prissiness, breeziness and asininity, and still remain tremendously likable. His movies were more extroverted and closer to ordinary life than any others of the best comedies: the vicissitudes of a New York taxi driver; the unaccepted college boy who, by desperate courage and inspired ineptitude, wins the Big Game. He was especially good at putting a very timid, spoiled or brassy young fellow through devastating embarrassments. He went through one of his most uproarious Gethsemanes as a shy country youth courting the nicest girl in town in *Grandma's Boy.* He arrived dressed "strictly up to date for the Spring of 1862," as a subtitle observed, and found that the ancient colored butler wore a similar flowered waistcoat and moldering cutaway. He got one wandering, nervous forefinger dreadfully stuck in a fancy little vase. The girl began cheerfully to try to identify that queer smell which dilated from him; Grandpa's best suit was rife with mothballs. A tenacious litter of kittens feasted off the goose grease on his home-shined shoes.

Lloyd was even better at the comedy of thrills. In *Safety Last,* as a rank amateur, he is forced to substitute for a human fly and to climb a medium-sized skyscraper. Dozens of awful things happen to him. He gets fouled up in a tennis net. Popcorn falls on him from a window above, and the local pigeons treat him like a cross between a lunch wagon and St. Francis of Assisi. A mouse runs up his britches leg, and the crowd below salutes his desperate dance on the window ledge with wild applause of the daredevil. A good deal of this full-length picture hangs thus by its eyelashes along the face of a building. Each new floor is like a new stanza in a poem; and the higher and more horrifying it gets, the funnier it gets.

In this movie Lloyd demonstrates beautifully his ability to do more than merely milk a gag, but to top it. (In an old, simple example of topping, an incredible number of tall men get, one by one, out of a small closed auto. After as many have clambered out as the joke will bear, one more steps out: a midget. That tops the gag. Then the auto collapses. That tops the topper.) In *Safety Last* Lloyd is driven out to the dirty end of a flagpole by a furious dog; the pole breaks and he falls, just managing to grab the minute hand of a huge clock. His weight promptly pulls the hand down from IX to VI. That would be more than enough for any ordinary comedian, but there is further logic in the situation. Now, hideously, the whole clockface pulls loose and slants from its trembling springs above the street. Getting out of difficulty with the clock, he makes still further use of the instrument by getting one foot caught in one of these obstinate springs.

A proper delaying of the ultrapredictable can of course be just as funny as a properly timed explosion of the unexpected. As Lloyd approaches the end of his horrible hegira up the side of the building in *Safety Last,* it becomes clear to the audience, but not to him, that if he raises his head another couple of inches he is going to get murderously conked by one of the four arms of a revolving wind gauge. He delays the evil moment almost interminably, with one distraction and another, and every delay is a suspense-tightening laugh; he also gets his foot nicely entangled in a rope, so that when he does get hit, the payoff of one gag sends him careening head downward through the abyss into another. Lloyd was outstanding even among the master craftsmen at setting up a gag clearly, culminating and getting out of it deftly, and linking it smoothly to the next. Harsh experience also taught him a deep and fundamental rule: Never try to get "above" the audience.

Lloyd tried it in *The Freshman.* He was to wear an unfinished, basted-together tuxedo to a college party, which would gradually, fall apart as he danced. Lloyd decided to skip the pants, a low-comedy cliché, and lose just the coat. His gag men warned him. A preview proved how right they were. Lloyd had to reshoot the whole expensive sequence, build it around defective pants and climax it with the inevitable. It was one of the funniest things he ever did.

When Lloyd was still a very young man he lost about half his right hand (and nearly lost his sight) when a comedy bomb exploded prematurely. But in spite of his artificially built-out hand he continued to do his own dirty work, like all of the best comedians. The side of the building he climbed in *Safety Last* did not overhang the street, as it appears to. But the nearest landing place was a roof three floors below him, as he approached the top, and he did everything, of course, the hard way, i.e., the comic way, keeping his bottom stuck well out, his shoulders hunched, his hands and feet skidding over perdition.

If great comedy must involve something beyond laughter, Lloyd was not a great comedian. If plain laughter is any criterion—and it is a healthy counterbalance to the other—few people have equaled him, and nobody has ever beaten him.

Chaplin and Keaton and Lloyd were all more like each other, in one important way, than Harry Langdon was like any of them. Whatever else the others might be doing, they all used more or less elaborate physical comedy; Langdon showed how little of that one might use and still be a great silent-screen comedian. In his screen character he symbolized something as deeply and centrally human, though by no means as rangily so, as the Tramp. There was, of course, an immense difference in inventiveness and range of virtuosity. It seemed as if Chaplin could do literally anything, on any instrument in the orchestra. Langdon had one queerly toned, unique little reed. But out of it he could get incredible melodies.

Like Chaplin, Langdon wore a coat which buttoned on his wishbone and swung out wide below, but the effect was very different: he seemed like an outsized baby who had begun to outgrow his clothes. The crown of his hat was rounded and the brim was turned up all around, like a little boy's hat, and he looked as if he wore diapers under his pants. His walk was that of a child which has just got sure on its feet, and his body and hands fitted that age. His face was kept pale to show off, with the simplicity of a nursery school drawing, the bright, ignorant, gentle eyes and the little twirling mouth. He had big moon cheeks, with dimples, and a Napoleonic forelock of mousy hair; the round, docile head seemed large in ratio to the cream-puff body. Twitchings of his face were signals of tiny discomforts too slowly registered by a tinier brain; quick, squirty little smiles showed his almost prehuman pleasures, his incurably premature trustfulness. He was a virtuoso of hesitations and of delicately indecisive motions, and he was particularly fine in a high wind, rounding a corner with a kind of skittering toddle, both hands nursing his hatbrim.

He was as remarkable a master as Chaplin of subtle emotional and mental process and operated much more at leisure. He once got a good three hundred feet of continuously bigger laughs out of rubbing his chest, in a crowded vehicle, with Limburger cheese, under the misapprehension that it was a cold salve. In another long scene, watching a brazen show girl change her clothes, he sat motionless, back to the camera, and registered the whole lexicon of lost innocence, shock, disapproval and disgust, with the back of his neck. His scenes with women were nearly always something special. Once a lady spy did everything in her power (under the Hays Office) to seduce him. Harry was polite, willing, even flirtatious in his little way. The only trouble was that he couldn't imagine what in the world she was leering and pawing at him for, and that he was terribly ticklish. The Mata Hari wound up foaming at the mouth.

There was also a sinister flicker of depravity about the Langdon character, all the more disturbing because babies are premoral. He had an instinct for bringing his actual adulthood and figurative babyishness into frictions as crawly as a fingernail on a slate blackboard, and he wandered into areas of strangeness which were beyond the other comedians. In a nightmare in one movie he was forced to fight a large, muscular young man; the girl Harry loved was the prize. The young man was a good boxer; Harry could scarcely lift his gloves. The contest took place in a fiercely lighted prize ring, in a prodigious pitch-dark arena. The only spectator was the girl, and she was rooting against Harry. As the fight went on, her eyes glittered ever more brightly with blood lust and, with glittering teeth, she tore her big straw hat to shreds.

Langdon came to Sennett from a vaudeville act in which he had fought a losing battle with a recalcitrant automobile. The minute Frank Capra saw him he begged Sennett to let him work with him. Langdon was almost as childlike as the character he played. He had only a vague idea of his story or even of each scene as he played it; each time he went before the camera Capra would brief him on the general situation and then, as this finest of intuitive improvisers once tried to explain his work, "I'd go into my routine." The whole tragedy of the coming of dialogue as far as these comedians were concerned —and one reason for the increasing rigidity of comedy ever since— can be epitomized in the mere thought of Harry Langdon confronted with a script.

Langdon's magic was in his innocence, and Capra took beautiful care not to meddle with it. The key to the proper use of Langdon, Capra always knew, was "the principle of the brick." "If there was a rule for writing Langdon material," he explains, "it was this: His only ally was God. Langdon might be saved by the brick falling on the cop, but it was *verboten* that he in any way motivate the brick's fall." Langdon became quickly and fantastically popular with three pictures, *Tramp, Tramp, Tramp, The Strong Man* and *Long Pants;* from then on he went downhill even faster. "The trouble was," Capra says, "that high-brow critics came around to explain his art to him. Also he developed an interest in dames. It was a pretty high life for such a little fellow." Langdon made two more pictures with high-brow writers, one of which (*Three's a Crowd*) had some wonderful passages in it, including the prize-ring nightmare; then First National canceled his contract. He was reduced to mediocre roles and two-reelers which were more rehashes of his old gags; this time around they no longer seemed funny. "He never did really understand what hit him," says Capra. "He died broke [in 1944]. And he died of a broken heart. He was the most tragic figure I ever came across in show business."

Buster Keaton started work at the age of three and a half with his parents in one of the roughest acts in vaudeville ("The Three Keatons"); Harry Houdini gave the child the name Buster in admiration for a fall he took down a flight of stairs. In his first movies Keaton teamed with Fatty Arbuckle under Sennett. He went on to become one of Metro's biggest stars and earners; a Keaton feature cost about $200,000 to make and reliably grossed $2 million. Very early in his movie career friends asked him why he never smiled on the screen. He didn't realize he didn't. He had got the deadpan habit in variety; on the screen he had merely been so hard at work it had never occurred to him there was anything to smile about. Now he tried it just once and never again. He was by his whole style and nature so much the most deeply "silent" of the silent comedians that even a smile was as deafeningly out of key as a yell. In a way his pictures are like a transcendent juggling act in which it seems that the whole universe is in exquisite flying motion and the one point of repose is the juggler's effortless, uninterested face.

Keaton's face ranked almost with Lincoln's as an early American archetype; it was haunting, handsome, almost beautiful, yet it was irreducibly funny; he improved matters by topping it off with a deadly horizontal hat, as flat and thin as a phonograph record. One can never forget Keaton wearing it, standing erect at the prow as his little boat is being launched. The boat goes grandly down the skids and, just as grandly, straight on to the bottom. Keaton never budges. The last you see of him, the water lifts the hat off the stoic head and it floats away.

No other comedian could do as much with the deadpan. He used this great, sad, motionless face to suggest various related things: a one-track mind near the track's end of pure insanity; mulish imperturbability under the wildest of circumstances; how dead a human being can get and still be alive; an awe-inspiring sort of patience and power to endure, proper to granite but uncanny in flesh and blood. Everything that he was and did bore out this rigid face and played laughs against it. When he moved his eyes, it was like seeing them move in a statue. His short-legged body was all sudden, machinelike angles, governed by a daft aplomb. When he swept a semaphorelike arm to point, you could almost hear the electrical impulse in the signal block. When he ran from a cop his transitions from accelerating walk to easy jog trot to brisk canter to headlong gallop to flogged-piston sprint—always floating, above this frenzy, the untroubled, untouchable face—were as distinct and as soberly in order as an automatic gearshift.

Keaton was a wonderfully resourceful inventor of mechanistic gags (he still spends much of his time fooling with Erector sets); as he ran afoul of locomotives, steamships, prefabricated and overelectrified houses, he put himself through some of the hardest and cleverest punishment ever designed for laughs. In *Sherlock Jr.*, boiling along on the handlebars of a motorcycle quite unaware that he has lost his driver, Keaton whips through city traffic, breaks up a tug-of-war, gets a shovelful of dirt in the face from each of a long line of Rockettetimed ditchdiggers, approaches at high speed a log which is hinged open by dynamite precisely soon enough to let him through and, hitting an obstruction, leaves the handlebars like an arrow leaving a bow, whams through the window of a shack in which the heroine is about to be violated, and hits the heavy feet first, knocking him through the opposite wall. The whole sequence is as clean in motion as the trajectory of a bullet.

Much of the charm and edge of Keaton's comedy, however, lay in the subtle leverages of expression he could work against his nominal deadpan. Trapped in the side wheel of a ferryboat, saving himself from drowning only by walking, then desperately running, inside the accelerating wheel like a squirrel in a cage, his only real concern was, obviously, to keep his hat on. Confronted by Love, he was not as deadpan as he was cracked up to be, either; there was an odd, abrupt motion of his head which suggested a horse nipping after a sugar lump.

Keaton worked strictly for laughs, but his work came from so far inside a curious and original spirit that he achieved a great deal besides, especially in his feature-length comedies. (For plain hard laughter his nineteen short comedies—the negatives of which have been lost—were even better.) He was the only major comedian who kept sentiment almost entirely out of his work, and he brought pure physical comedy to its greatest heights. Beneath his lack of emotion he was also uninsistently sardonic; deep below that, giving a disturbing tension and grandeur to the foolishness, for those who sensed it, there was in his comedy a freezing whisper not of pathos but of melancholia. With the humor, the craftsmanship and the action there was often, besides, a fine, still and sometimes dreamlike beauty. Much of his Civil War picture *The General* is within hailing distance of Mathew Brady. And there is a ghostly, unforgettable moment in *The Navigator* when, on a deserted, softly rolling ship, all the pale doors along a deck swing open as one behind Keaton and, as one, slam shut, in a hair-raising illusion of noise.

Perhaps because "dry" comedy is so much more rare and odd than "dry" wit, there are people who never much cared for Keaton. Those who do cannot care mildly.

As soon as the screen began to talk, silent comedy was pretty well finished. The hardy and prolific Mack Sennett made the transfer; he was the first man to put Bing Crosby and W. C. Fields on the screen. But he was essentially a silent-picture man, and by the time the Academy awarded him a special Oscar for his "lasting contribution to the comedy technique of the screen" (in 1938), he was no longer active. As for the comedians we have spoken of in particular, they were as badly off as fine dancers suddenly required to appear in plays.

Harold Lloyd, whose work was most nearly realistic, naturally coped least unhappily with the added realism of speech; he made several talking comedies. But good as the best were, they were not so good as his silent work, and by the late '30s he quit acting. A few years ago he returned to play the lead (and play it beautifully) in Preston Sturges' *The Sin of Harold Diddlebock,* but this exceptional picture—which opened, brilliantly, with the closing reel of Lloyd's *The Freshman*—has not yet been generally released.

Like Chaplin, Lloyd was careful of his money; he is still rich and active. Last June, in the presence of President Truman, he became Imperial Potentate of the A.A.O.N.M.S. (Shriners). Harry Langdon, as we have said, was a broken man when sound came in.

Up to the middle '30s Buster Keaton made several feature-length pictures (with such players as Jimmy Durante, Wallace Beery and Robert Montgomery); he also made a couple of dozen talking shorts. Now and again he managed to get loose into motion, without having to talk, and for a moment or so the screen would start singing again. But his dark, dead voice, though it was in keeping with the visual character, tore his intensely silent style to bits and destroyed the illusion within which he worked. He gallantly and correctly refuses to regard himself as "retired." Besides occasional bits, spots and minor roles in Hollywood pictures, he has worked on summer stages, made talking comedies in France and Mexico and clowned in a French circus. This summer he has played the straw hats in *Three Men on a Horse.* He is planning a television program. He also has a working agreement with Metro. One of his jobs there is to construct comedy sequences for Red Skelton.

The only man who really survived the flood was Chaplin, the only one who was rich, proud and popular enough to afford to stay silent. He brought out two of his greatest nontalking comedies, *City Lights* and *Modern Times,* in the middle of an avalanche of talk, spoke gibberish and, in the closing moments, plain English in *The Great Dictator,* and at last made an all-talking picture, *Monsieur Verdoux,* creating for that purpose an entirely new character who might properly talk a blue streak. *Verdoux* is the greatest of talking comedies though so cold and savage that it had to find its public in grimly experienced Europe.

Good comedy, and some that was better than good, outlived silence, but there has been less and less of it. The talkies brought one great comedian, the late, majestically lethargic W. C. Fields, who could not possibly have worked as well in silence; he was the toughest and the most warmly human of all screen comedians, and *It's a Gift* and *The Bank Dick,* fiendishly funny and incisive white-collar comedies, rank high among the best comedies (and best movies) ever made. Laurel and Hardy, the only comedians who managed to preserve much of the large, low style of silence and who began to explore the comedy of sound, have made nothing since 1945. Walt Disney, at his best an inspired comic inventor and teller of fairy stories, lost his stride during the war and has since regained it only at moments. Preston Sturges has made brilliant, satirical comedies, but his pictures are smart, nervous comedy-dramas merely italicized with slapstick. The Marx Brothers were sidesplitters but they made their best comedies years ago. Jimmy Durante is mainly a night-club genius; Abbott and Costello are semiskilled laborers, at best; Bob Hope is a good radio comedian with a pleasing presence, but not much more, on the screen.

There is no hope that screen comedy will get much better than it is without new, gifted young comedians who really belong in movies, and without freedom for their experiments. For everyone who may appear we have one last, invidious comparison to offer as a guidepost.

One of the most popular recent comedies is Bob Hope's *The Paleface.* We take no pleasure in blackening *The Paleface;* we single it out, rather, because it is as good as we've got. Anything that is said of it here could be said, with interest, of other comedies of our time. Most of the laughs in *The Paleface* are verbal. Bob Hope is very adroit with his lines and now and then, when the words don't get in the way, he makes a good beginning as a visual comedian. But only the beginning, never the middle or the end. He is funny, for instance, reacting to a shot of violent whisky. But he does not know how to get still funnier (i.e., how to build and milk) or how to be funniest last (i.e., how to top or cap his gag). The camera has to fade out on the same old face he started with.

One sequence is promisingly set up for visual comedy. In it, Hope and a lethal local boy stalk each other all over a cow town through streets which have been emptied in fear of their duel. The gag here is that through accident and stupidity they keep just failing to find each other. Some of it is quite funny. But the fun slackens between laughs like a weak clothesline, and by all the logic of humor (which is ruthlessly logical) the biggest laugh should come at the moment, and through the way, they finally spot each other. The sequence is so weakly thought out that at that crucial moment the camera can't afford to watch them; it switches to Jane Russell.

Now we turn to a masterpiece. In *The Navigator* Buster Keaton works with practically the same gag as Hope's duel. Adrift on a ship which he believes is otherwise empty, he drops a lighted cigarette. A girl finds it. She calls out and he hears her; each then tries to find the other. First each walks purposefully down the long, vacant starboard deck, the girl, then Keaton, turning the corner just in time not to see each other. Next time around each of them is trotting briskly, very much in earnest; going at the same pace, they miss each other just the same.

Next time around each of them is going like a bat out of hell. Again they miss. Then the camera withdraws to a point of vantage at the stern, leans its chin in its hand and just watches the whole intricate superstructure of the ship as the protagonists stroll, steal and scuttle from level to level, up, down and sidewise, always managing to miss each other by hairbreadths, in an enchantingly neat and elaborate piece of timing. There are no subsidiary gags to get laughs in this sequence and there is little loud laughter; merely a quiet and steadily increasing kind of delight. When Keaton has got all he can out of this fine modification of the movie chase he invents a fine device to bring the two together: the girl, thoroughly winded, sits down for a breather, indoors, on a plank which workmen have left across sawhorses. Keaton pauses on an upper deck, equally winded and puzzled. What follows happens in a couple of seconds at most: Air suction whips his silk topper backward down a ventilator; grabbing frantically for it, he backs against the lip of the ventilator, jackknifes and falls in backward. Instantly the camera cuts back to the girl. A topper falls through the ceiling and lands tidily, right side up, on the plank beside her. Before she can look more than startled, its owner follows, head between his knees, crushes the topper, breaks the plank with the point of his spine and proceeds to the floor. The breaking of the plank smacks Boy and Girl together.

It is only fair to remember that the silent comedians would have as hard a time playing a talking scene as Hope has playing his visual ones, and that writing and directing are as accountable for the failure as Hope himself. But not even the humblest journeymen of the silent years would have let themselves off so easily. Like the masters, they knew, and sweated to obey, the laws of their craft.

Mack Sennett
from KING OF COMEDY

"We lived our art," said Mack Sennett. And if the millions who laughed at the Turpins, the Langdons, and the Chaplins failed to see the art for the pie in the face, what difference? The tremendous appeal of "the little guys coping with a mean universe" was enough. We can look back on the crudeness of the early film with amusement, but we must acknowledge the popularity developed by those long-departed silent stars who did, indeed, live their art.

WHEN I started these recollections, I opened up with some remarks that might be taken as unbecoming and even downright immodest. I claimed that it had been a long, tired time since any citizens had been rolled in the aisles of a motion-picture house or had been doubled up with laughter while watching television comedians. I was implying, of course, that my own comedies truly murdered the people.

Don't get me wrong. It wasn't me, the Old Man, who was so funny; it was the comical people I had around me. I called myself "King of Comedy," a solemn and foolish title if there ever was one, but I was a harassed monarch. I worried most of the time. It was only in the evenings that I laughed.

I sat in a heavy, creaking rocking chair in the rear of my screening room at Keystone and examined our dizzy productions with a hard eye. When there was anything to laugh at I rocked back and forth with the contented rhythm of a broad-beamed Percheron in a bareback riding act. I seldom needed to say much to my writers, gag men, and actors. They watched the rhythm of the rocker. When I was in full gallop, they assumed that everything was as ridiculous as it should be. If I didn't rock and roar as the rushes went on the screen, everybody took it for granted that the work of art under eye was no good. Then we'd shoot scenes over again.

My main contribution to motion-picture comedy seems to have resided in my boiling point. I was equipped with a natural, built-in thermostat. It turned out that when I got up a full head of steam over a film and began to roll and spout, millions of moviegoers were likely to react the same way. I was a reliable one-man audience.

Since I did produce the Keystone Comedies, it turns out that I have been credited with considerably more inventiveness than I actually possessed. For instance, historians of the drama put me down for the creation of what was once a distinguished facet of cineplastic art—pie-throwing. I'd be glad to claim this honor, if I could claim it honestly, since a pie in the face represents a fine, wish-fulfilling, universal idea, especially in the face of authority, as in cop or mother-in-law. Also, these sequences in which we started building from the tossing of one pie, quickly increasing the tempo and the quantity until we had dozens of pastries in flight across the screen simultaneously, were wholesome releases of nervous tension for the people and made them laugh. But honor for the pie is not mine. It belongs to Mabel Normand.

Mabel was always shown on the screen as a comely girl, usually poor and unfashionable, whose fate was to find herself surrounded by ruffians, villains, and amiable boobs such as Ben Turpin, Ford Sterling, or 285-pound "Fatty" Arbuckle. As our story would begin to release doses of our stock commodity, pandemonium, Miss Normand would invariably be caught in the middle.

But one afternoon in Edendale we were having trouble shooting the simplest possible kind of a scene. Ben Turpin had to stick his head through a door. Since Mr. Turpin's eyes were aimed in all directions, we thought the scene would be funny. It wasn't.

"Don't look into the camera," I instructed Ben. "This is the kind of quick scene we throw away, casual-like."

Turpin stared at me, or approximately at me, with the affronted dignity of a Wagnerian soprano ordered to conceal her tonsils.

"Shoot the eyes! Shoot the eyes!" he squalled. "What do millions of people go to movies for?"

If Turpin had ever seen the Mona Lisa he could have explained an ancient mystery. He would have claimed she was about to break out laughing at him.

Ben squinted, peered, and mouthed, but still the scene was not comical. Suddenly it was one of the funniest shots ever flashed on any motion-picture screen.

Mabel, who had nothing to do with this sequence, had been watching. She was sitting quietly, minding her own business for once, when she found a pie in her hand. It was a custard pie.

Miss Normand was not startled. At Keystone you were likely to find anything in your hand from a lion to a raw egg. You were as likely to meet an ape on the sidewalk as Gloria Swanson. If you were unwary you were likely to get a shock treatment in the seat of the trousers, mustard in your make-up, or a balloonful of water on your head. We lived our art.

As it turned out, the projectile in Mabel's hand was neither a joke nor an accident. Two carpenters were having custard for dessert. Mabel sniffed, and was inspired.

She weighed and hefted the pastry in her right palm, considered it benevolently, balanced herself on the balls of her feet, went into a windup like a big-league pitcher, and threw. Motion-picture history, millions of dollars, and a million laughs hung on her aim as the custard wabbled in a true curve and splashed with a dull explosion in Ben Turpin's face.

No one expected this memorable heave, least of all Turpin. The grinding camera, going sixteen frames to the second, was full on him. When the custard smote him, Ben's face was as innocent of anticipation as a plate. His aplomb vanished in a splurch* of goo that drooled and dripped down his shirt front. As the camera held on him his magnificent eyes emerged, batting in stunned outrage in all directions.

Worse luck for scholars, I don't remember the name of the picture in which the first custard was thrown. The date would have been sometime in 1913. But if we failed in later years to understand the long words laid on us by heavy-duty professors who explain our art to us, we knew a good thing when we saw it, seized upon pie-throwing, refined it, perfected its techniques, and presented it to the theater as a new art. It became, in time, a learned routine like the pratt-fall, the double-take, the slow burn, and the frantic leap, all stock equipment of competent comedians. When the Turpin pie scene was shown that night in a screening room we saw at once why it was funny.

It was funny, not only because a pie in the face is an outrage to pumped-up dignity, but because Turpin received the custard without a flick of premonition. Nonanticipation on the part of the recipient of a pastry is the chief ingredient of the recipe. And it takes an actor with a stern artistic conscience to stand still and innocent, never wagging an eyelash, while a strong man takes aim at him with such ammunition.

If you don't run with show people you may find this incredible, but it is a fact that many actors are frustrated because they never had a chance to display their integrity and facial control by taking a pie.

* *Splurch:* A technical and onomatopoetic word coined by Mack Sennett; applies only to the effect of sudden custard in the puss.

Franklin Pangborn, for instance, a gentle comedian and a fine artist, pined for many years to receive a custard. When he finally worked for me, we had to write in a scene for him in which he got splurched. Frank did well, too, but he said being pushed backwards into swimming pools while wearing top hat and cutaway was more in his line.

We became scientists in custard. A man named Greenburg, who ran a small restaurant-bakery near the studio, became a throwing-pie entrepreneur. Our consumption was so enormous that this man got rich. After several experiments he invented a special Throwing Pie, just right in heft and consistency, filled with paste, and inedible. He lost most of his eating customers when he began to sell them throwing custards by mistake.

Del Lord, my ace comedy director, soon became the world-champion pie tosser. And "Fatty" Arbuckle, who in spite of his suet was an agile man—the kind of fat man known as light on his feet—became a superb pie pitcher. Arbuckle was ambidextrous and had double vision like a T-formation quarterback. He could throw two pies at once in different directions, but he was not precise in this feat. The Christy Mathewson of the custard was Del Lord.

"This is a delicate and serious art," says Mr. Lord, "and not one in which amateurs or inexperienced flingers should try to win renown. Pie-throwing, like tennis or golf, which depend upon form, requires a sense of balance and a definite follow-through.

"Actually, you don't throw like a shortstop rifling to first base. You *push* the pie toward the face, leaning into your follow-through. Six or eight feet is the limit for an artistic performance.

"You must never let the actor know when you're going to give him the custard in the choppers. Even the most skillful actor, José Ferrer or John Gielgud, for instance, finds it difficult to conceal anticipation.

"The wisest technique is to con your victim into a sense of security and then slip it to him.

"In my day, when I was the acknowledged world-champeen pie heaver, I developed a prejudice for berries with whipped cream. After the actual whomp in the face, the berries trickle beautifully down the actor's shirt and the whipped cream besplashes his suit. This is muddy, frothy, and photogenic."

Soon after we discovered that a pie is as theatrical a device as Bette Davis's handkerchief or Cyrano's nose, we made a picture called *The Great Pie Mystery.* Pies were thrown every time the heavy would try to do dirt to the girl or the comic. Pies came from everywhere and the audience couldn't see who was throwing them. Our pay-off gag was that the fellow who began telling the story in the first scene was throwing the pies.

We also invented a way to throw pies around telephone poles. We did this by having an expert fly caster out of camera range atop a step-ladder. After a little practice he could let fly with rod and reel and make a pie do a figure eight before it hit a guy in the face.

As I was saying a while back, we demanded at least some kind of motivation in our pictures. Always the improbable, never the impossible. The introduction of pie-throwing was no stumbling block at all to our scenario writers. They simply inserted a restaurant or a bakery into the scene whenever it seemed like a good idea to fling a pie.

In speaking of the impossible, one of our most notable laugh-making scenes was one in which we had Charlie Murray tied to a steam boiler in a basement. The boiler actually expanded before the audience's eyes. Now that would be impossible, but that is how the boiler would *seem* to a man who was tied to it.

This rudimentary notion seems to be beyond the capacity of movie makers today. With my boys it was merely the beginning of a laugh sequence. They went on from the expanding boiler and had the *whole house* expand.

There are four kinds of laughs in the theatre: the titter, the yowl, the belly-laugh, and the boffo, according to Mr. James Agee, poet and motion-picture critic.

I don't want to create the impression that the titter, the yowl, the belly-laugh, and the boffo were purely mechanical affairs, even when the switcheroo was as charming a device as a tastefully flung pie. Neither my rocking-chair responses nor the genius of my thinker-uppers in the gag room was responsible for all the fun. The Keystone studio was a university of nonsense where, if an actor or actress had any personality at all, that personality developed in full blossom without inhibition. Two of the most special performers who ever came my way were Harry Langdon and Ben Turpin, both prime comics, and as different in outlook, philosophy, and abilities as men could be. Like most of our people—it was some years before we employed the already famous—they came to us from the knockabout stage with no money and no fame.

Harry Langdon came from a small-town vaudeville act in which his specialty was helpless frustration with a balky automobile. Frank Capra, who had progressed from gag man to director, wanted Langdon as soon as he set eyes on him. Harry had a kind of dough-faced baby innocence about him, combined with malice, that delighted Capra. Harry Langdon actually was as innocent as an infant. He had his routines, well learned in vaudeville, and he could do them on demand, but he seldom had the mistiest notion of what his screen stories were about. Like Charlie Chaplin, you had to let him take his time and go through his motions. His twitters and hesitations built up a ridiculous but sympathetic little character. It was difficult for us at first to know how to use Langdon, accustomed as we were to firing the gags and the falls at the audience as fast as possible, but as new talent arrived, we found ways to screen it and to cope with it. I thought for a while Langdon was as good as Chaplin. In some of his pathetic scenes he was certainly as good.

Langdon was an oddly gifted fellow. He drew cartoons for *Judge* and *Puck,* was an expert designer, and curiously handy at carpentry.

On screen he resembled Chaplin in one kind of appeal. He was always the small figure of frustrated good will beset and bewildered by a cruel world of hard rules and economics. But Chaplin, who could be as pitiful as a kicked spaniel or as forlorn and brave as he was in that wonderful scene in which he ate his shoes in *The Gold Rush,* was a man. He was adult. His impulses were often venal. He chased girls with pretentious gallantry and they never took him seriously. He gave you to know, though, that, if ever a girl *had* taken him seriously, he might have made a fool of himself in her boudoir but he would have known exactly what to try to do. Langdon was infantile.

Ladies pursued him. He not only didn't know what was expected of him, he didn't even know they were after him. Everything from sex to money was college algebra to Langdon.

Like Charlie, Harry was a slow starter. Even after we learned how to use him—I mean, saw what his essential character was for screen purposes—we had to give him a hundred feet of film or so to play around in, do little bits of business, and introduce himself. The two were the same in their universal appeal. They were the little guys coping with a mean universe, and, since motion-picture audiences are seldom made up 100 percent of tycoons, heroes, or millionaires, a majority of people managed to identify themselves with these comedians. Charlie Chaplin, I suppose, carried out this appeal to the heights in the great pictures he made after he left me. But wonderful as Charlie was, or is, he didn't invent being a little man.

Being a little man was being laughed at and sympathized with long before Charlie, or Langdon, or Turpin arrived in the public eye. Like the fall of dignity, it is one of the essences of comedy. We didn't invent it any more than we invented those two other reliable stock characters, little David with his slingshot and little Cinderella with her pumpkin.

Langdon was as bland as milk, a forgiving small cuss, an obedient puppy, always in the way, exasperating, but offering his baby mannerisms with hopeful apology. Frank Capra's enormous talents first showed themselves when he saw all this as something that would photograph. Chaplin was a waif, but an adult waif who thumbed his nose at anything.

Under Frank's easy guidance Harry soon became a Keystone star in two-reel comedies. His salary went up to several thousand dollars a week. Langdon became important and unfortunately realized it. Suddenly he forgot that all his value lay in being that baby-witted boy on the screen. He decided he was also a businessman. His cunning as a businessman was about that of a backward kindergarten student and he complicated this by marital adventures, in which he was about as inept as he was on screen. He was soon behind in alimony payments.

He decided that if Harry Langdon pictures could make so much money for Mack Sennett, they could make all that money for Harry Langdon. He heard about the wonderful grosses of big pictures like *The Miracle Man* and *The Birth of a Nation* and concluded that this kind of enterprise was for him.

Other companies were always ready to grab my stars after they had been tested and proved profitable. Soon enough Langdon had an offer from First National. It was a wonder, too. First National offered him $6,000 a week and 25 per cent of the net provided he would make six pictures in two years with a limit of $150,000 production cost per picture.

Langdon was delighted by these fat figures, hired Harry Edwards as director at $1,000 a week, Capra at $750 a week, and Bill Jenner as his personal manager at $500 a week.

Then he forgot all this outgoing money was actually his own, merely his advance from First National. He blew the entire $150,000 production budget before he got his first story written.

Poor Langdon failed wretchedly as a producer, and lived brokenhearted and in near-poverty around Hollywood for many years. He did his last work at Columbia, where he attempted to dance in a musical comedy. But working and rehearsing all day exhausted the little fellow. He went into a coma and died of a stroke after lingering for about eight days.

He was bankrupt and neglected, forlorn and forgotten. His shy charm and his gentle humor have yet to be matched on the screen. I wish he had stayed with me. He was a quaint artist who had no business in business. He was hurt and bewildered at the end and he never understood what had happened to him.

Ben Turpin, the cross-eyed man, was an artist too, but another breed of cat.

All comedians, as I keep saying, are sensitive, egotistical persons. They require audiences, applause, security, and reassurance. Some are tender and some are tough. Some are both, but the combination of clown-poet-intellectual is a rare bird and occurs only once in a lucky generation, as in Chaplin.

Turpin came to us from the circus and the vaudeville stage. One of his demands on the studio as soon as his face became known all over the world was that we take out an insurance policy with Lloyd's of London which would pay him one million dollars if his eyes ever came uncrossed. It took only the simplest examination by an honest oculist to assure Lloyd's their money was safe. Ben's eyes were permanently fixed and so were his notions.

This skinny, strutting little man with a Polish piano player's mane of hair and a neck like a string was obsessed by money and by the conviction that he couldn't be funny after 5 P.M. He had a five-o'clock quitting time in his contract. When the bell rang he left no matter what it cost the studio.

Mr. Turpin had several wives. I was not acquainted with all of them, but he brought one to the studio and introduced her around. She was the one who was stone-deaf.

"Mr. Sennett," he said, "I want you to meet my wife. I got the old bag in trouble and had to marry her."

The deaf Mrs. Turpin smiled graciously and acknowledged the introduction.

Ben went on to find Mabel Normand.

"Mabel, I want you to meet the wife," he said. "She used to be a tattooed woman in a honky-tonk. Don't have anything to do with her. She's a blackmailer and a dope smuggler."

Mrs. Turpin beamed fondly on Ben and was delighted to meet his friends.

We paid Turpin $1,500 a week at the height of his powers. He invested all his money, bought apartment houses, and became a rich man. He always saved a few dollars a week by personally doing the janitor work at all his apartment houses.

He seldom drove an automobile—a frantic thought at that: who knows how many directions he would have tried to drive at once? He preferred to save money by traveling by streetcar. As he would enter the trolley, he would draw his wrenlike physique up to full strut and squeak at the top of his voice:

"I'm Ben Turpin! Three thousand dollars a week!"

Before taking a seat he would treat the passengers to a 108.

A 108 is an acrobat's term for a comic fall which only the most skillful athletes can perform without lethal results. One foot goes forward, the other foot goes backward, the comedian does a counter somersault and lands flat on his back.

I've seen Turpin perform the 108 not only on streetcars but on concrete sidewalks—if there was an audience handy to whom he could announce himself as three-thousand-dollars-a-week Ben Turpin.

Turpin was an emotional little man, especially under the influence of money or the bottle. Once when we had leased a special train to take a company to Lake Tahoe, scheduled to leave at seven in the evening, Del Lord found Mr. Turpin hitting crescendo in the throes of a crying jag. On such occasions Turpin demanded the attentions of his attorney, his business manager, and his priest.

When Del arrived at the roaring Turpin establishment, Ben had decided that *he* was all right, but that for reasons obscure to everyone else, his wife (the deaf one) was dying.

Since Mrs. Turpin was blooming with health, Del dismissed the lawyer and business manager, took the priest home, and called up Tommy Lofthaus, chief of the Los Angeles Motor Patrol. Mr. Lofthaus was a good friend because we often gave his cops jobs on off-duty days.

Turpin arrived at the station under full siren, delighted with his police escort. He dashed into his drawing room, belted down a scotch and soda, and went through the entire train announcing himself as Ben Turpin, $3,000 a week. He performed a 108 in each car.

We got him to Lake Tahoe in fancy fettle, but Turpin immediately become victim of a new terror. We had a scene in which the giant Kalla Pasha, wearing a black fur suit, worked interchangeably with a live bear which closely resembled him. The script called for Turpin to hop into bed with the fur-bearing Pasha. Ben winced and keened over this idea, said it was frightening enough to send a valuable actor to the looney bin just to think of getting into bed with Kalla Pasha, let alone a dangerous, man-eating critter. Anyway, Turpin complained, he had no faith whatsoever in the integrity or the human kindness of anybody connected with Keystone and Mack Sennett. He was dead sure he was being framed and would wind up in the embrace of the bear.

During this tantrum our bear got his teeth into his trainer's arm and almost chawed it off. This upset all of us to some extent. The accident was particularly dismaying to Turpin.

As things came out, we had to do away with that bear as a safety measure, but it seemed a shame to waste him. We put the warm corpse in Kalla Pasha's bed and inserted Mr. Turpin. Ben's histrionics made a notable scene for a few seconds. He never forgave us.

It is honorable to give credit where credit is due. It was Mabel Normand who connived the bedding of Ben Turpin and the bear.

Turpin seldom invited guests into his home. On the few special occasions when he did you knew immediately how you stood with him the moment you entered his parlor. Unless you were an extremely welcome guest you never got to see his furniture. He kept every piece draped with white cloths which he removed only as a delicate compliment of friendship.

Ben could fall, tumble, and prank with the best of my roughnecks, but his special and universal appeal was, of course, like Langdon's and Chaplin's, the appeal of all undersized gents who stand up against Fate *anyway.* Ridiculous to everyone, yes, but never to himself. In Von Stroheim breeches and monocle Turpin reduced Von Stroheim and all domineering Prussians to absurdity. With cross-eyes batting with passion he could lie on a tiger-skin rug and make the heaving sultriness of Theda Bara (or all pretentious love-making) a silly joke.

The thing was, he seemed to take himself with utter seriousness. You never felt sorry for him no matter how you laughed. You had to see that Mr. Turpin was very, very brave.

This was true also of Buster Keaton. Keaton carried out comic courage to its ridiculously logical absurdity. He never batted an eye or changed an expression, no matter what catastrophies threatened him. "Fatty" Arbuckle brought him to me. The two worked funnily together for several pictures. But these films were so hilarious that Keaton was immediately swamped with offers of more money than I could pay him.

He went to Metro-Goldwyn-Mayer, where he became, in my opinion, the greatest comedian the greatest studio ever had. His pictures eventually cost $200,000 to make and always brought in at least a couple of million dollars—a long cry from our cut-rate productions. Keaton married Natalie Talmadge, sister of Norma, Metro's biggest star at that time.

I fondly claim Buster Keaton. We could have done improbable things together. But the Great Stone Face was cut out for larger works than we had to offer. He was one of the first to set the pattern that kept me in trouble the rest of my life: start with Sennett and get rich somewhere else!

Ben Turpin died rich and having fun. After his retirement it was his hobby to direct traffic at the intersection of Santa Monica Boulevard and Western Avenue. With eyes crossed and arms flailing he engineered some of the most outrageous automotive jams in the history of congested Los Angeles.

He yelled to every motorist, "Ben Turpin, three thousand dollars a week!"

David Wark Griffith
THE MOVIES 100 YEARS FROM NOW

D. W. Griffith is acknowledged as America's first great motion picture director. Called the "Father of Cinematographic Art," Griffith is remembered for epic films such as Birth of a Nation, Intolerance, Broken Blossoms, *and* Way Down East. *In an age when many viewed the camera as a toy, Griffith realized its enormous artistic possibilities and social ramifications.*

THEY say I am a realist—a man who functions best when reproducing in the films life as he sees it or knows it. Whereupon the editor promptly assumes that fantasy will be perfectly easy for me, and propounds a question that scarcely can be answered by anything other than a dream. Fortunately, I have my fancies.

"What," asks the editor in substance, "will be the status of the motion pictures one hundred years hence?"

I have wondered that very thing many times myself, and since I am one of those persons who sometimes respond to their own imagery with answers, I can at least give an opinion. I may qualify this by adding that it is the opinion of one who has devoted a large part of his life to the subject.

In the year 2024 the most important single thing which the cinema will have helped in a large way to accomplish will be that of eliminating from the face of the civilized world all armed conflict. Pictures will be the most powerful factor in bringing about this condition. With the use of the universal language of moving pictures the true meaning of the brotherhood of man will have been established throughout the earth. For example, the Englishman will have learned that the soul of the Japanese is, essentially, the same as his own. The Frenchman will realize that the American's ideals are his ideals. All men are created equal.

It is not to be presumed that I believe one hundred years from now the pictures will have had time to educate the masses away from discord and unharmony. What I do mean to say is, by that time war, if there is such a thing, will be waged on a strictly scientific basis, with the element of physical destruction done away with entirely. My theory is that conflict, if and when it arises, will find itself governed by scientific rules and regulations to which both sides of the controversy will subscribe. Armies outfitted with boxing gloves, man to man, may, I think, go into "battle" to determine the victor. I am not smiling with you now. I am quite sincere. It will be a matter of science and fair play to the last letter. I am just as sincere when I predict that after the "battle" the warriors will repair to a prearranged cold-drink canteen and have grape juice. Just as the old English debtors' prison was wiped out by education, so will armed conflict be wiped out by education.

There is little question that a century ahead of us will find a great deal more of the so-called intimate drama presented on the screen, although there will always be a field set apart for the film with a vast background such as *The Birth of a Nation* and *America*.

You will walk into your favorite film theatre and see your actors appearing in twice the size you see them now, because the screens will be twice as large, and the film itself twice as large also. With these enlargements, "close-ups" will be almost eliminated, since it will be relatively easy to picture facial expression along with the full figure of the performer. It will always be necessary to picture the face in pictures. It is the face which reflects the soul of a man.

Our "close-ups," or "inserts," as I call them, are sometimes cumbersome and disconcerting. I invented them, but I have tried not to overuse them, as many have done. It is a mechanical trick, and is of little credit to anyone.

We shall say there are now five elaborate first-run picture theatres on one New York street, Broadway. In 2024 there will be at least forty. Cities of 1,000 will average at least six. Cities of 20,000 and thereabout will have over a hundred. By virtue of its great advantage in scope, the motion picture will be fitted to tell certain stories as no other medium can. But I must add that the glory of the spoken or written word in the intimate and poetic drama can never be excelled by any form of expression.

In the year 2024 our directors of the better order will be men graduated from schools, academies, and colleges carrying in their curriculum courses in motion-picture direction. Our actors and actresses will be artists graduated from schools and colleges either devoted exclusively to the teaching and study of motion-picture acting or carrying highly specialized courses in acting before the camera. This is inevitable.

I am well aware of the fact that the present cumbersome and haphazard method by which screen talent is selected (and by screen talent I mean to say directors, designers, actors, and cameramen) will not endure long. Time will find this matter adjusted upon a basis of merit and equipment.

Probably on an average of a dozen times each week persons ask me if I think color photography in the motion pictures will be perfected and made practical. Most assuredly, I do think so. Certainly all color processes and tint methods at present in use are wrong. They are not arrived at with any degree of inventiveness, and they cannot last. At present the colored pictures we see are made by the use of gelatines on the film or by the use of varicolored lenses which fly before the film. Thus we find a great lack of harmony and accuracy. I am willing to confess that I have tried them. But I should be the last to speak of my color effects seriously. We have been merely exploring and speculating.

Only through one method will color be naturally and properly given to objects and persons in the motion pictures. This is a method which will develop a film so sensitive that it will record the natural tints and colors as the picture is being photographed.

Of course, to the man or woman untrained in these lines, this seems remote and hardly possible. Still, consider the conquering of the air—the discovery of a means whereby the human voice may be projected through air three thousand miles! When we realize what has been done in the wireless it seems utter folly to suppose that color photography—natural, permanent color photography—may not be found for the films. One hundred years from now the color of a woman's eyes and hair, the tint of the sea, the hues of the rainbow itself will be a natural part of every motion-picture play.

On the other hand, I am quite positive that when a century has passed, all thought of our so-called speaking pictures will have been abandoned. It will never be possible to synchronize the voice with the pictures. This is true because the very nature of the films foregoes not only the necessity for but the propriety of the spoken voice. Music—fine music—will always be the voice of the silent drama. One hundred years from now will find the greatest composers of that day devoting their skill and their genius to the creation of motion-picture music.

There will be three principal figures in the production of a picture play—the author first, the director and music composer occupying an identical position in importance.

We do not want now and we never shall want the human voice with our films. Music, as I see it within that hundred years, will be applied to the visualization of the human being's imagination. And, as in your imagination those unseen voices are always perfect and sweet, or else magnificent and thrilling, you will find them registering upon the mind of the picture patron, in terms of lovely music, precisely what the author has intended to be registered there. There is no voice in the world like the voice of music. To me those images on the screen must always be silent. Anything else would work at cross purposes with the real object of this new medium of expression. There will never be speaking pictures. Why should there be when no voice can speak so beautifully as music? There are no dissonant r's and twisted consonants and guttural slurs and nasal twangs in beautiful music. Therefore the average person would much prefer to see his pictures and let the voice which speaks to him be the voice of music—one of the most perfect of all the arts.

I seem a little emphatic on this particular point, and I mean to be.

In the year 2024 we shall have orchestras of many kinds playing for the pictures. Each motion-picture theatre will have several orchestras of diversified character. The big, robust, outdoor pictures will have more than one orchestra in attendance at all times. String quartets will play for the mood of a string quartet; sighing guitars and thumpety banjos will play for their mood in the picture play; symphonic orchestras of greater proportions than we now dream of will be employed for moods to fit the sublime and the grand.

We have scarcely an inkling of what the development of music is going to be in the film play.

It really seems to me a little bit humorous now to realize how narrow a place in our everyday life the film is playing, despite the great rise in attendance in the last few years. One hundred years hence, I believe, the airplane passenger lines will operate motion-picture shows on regular schedule between New York and Chicago and between New York and London. Trains, which will be traveling twice or three times as fast as they do now, will have film theatres on board. Almost every home of good taste will have its private projection room where miniatures, perhaps, of the greater films will be shown to the family, and, of course, families will make their albums in motion pictures instead of in tintypes and "stills." Steamships will boast of first runs, which will be brought to them in mid-ocean by the airplanes, and I may add that almost all subjects in our schools will be taught largely with the use of picture play and the educational animated picture.

By the time these things come to pass, there will be no such thing as a flicker in your film. Your characters and objects in pictures will come upon the screen (which by then may not even be white, and certainly may not be square, or look anything like what it does now), and they will appear to the onlookers precisely as these persons and objects appear in real life. That much-discussed "depth" in pictures, which no one as yet has been able to employ successfully, will long since have been discovered and adopted. The moving canvas will not appear flat, but if a character moves before a fireplace you will recognize the distance as between the character and the fireplace. Likewise, in landscapes, you will feel the proper sense of distance. Your mountain peaks will not appear to rise one on top of another, but will appear exactly as if you stood and looked at them. Of course these are merely details that will require long and intense study and experiment, but they will come. In other words, from the standpoint of naturalness, motion pictures one hundred years from now will be so nearly like the living person or the existing object pictured that you will be unable, sitting in your orchestra seat, to determine whether they are pictures or the real thing.

By a perfection of the studio lighting system, film will be as smooth before the eye as if it were a stationary lighted picture. By that time the studios will have changed greatly, and instead of actors being forced to work before great blinding lights, which now at times register 117 degrees of heat, we shall have "cold" lights. We are experimenting in these already. Our studios will be great spreading institutions, as large as many of the cities surrounding New York. I think that one hundred years from now there will be no concentrated motion-picture production such as our Hollywood of today. Films will be made in various cities, most of which will be located near to New York.

It nettles me at times when I am asked if I do not think that in time the popularity of the motion pictures will subside. It seems to me ridiculous. As ridiculous as to assume that the popularity of music, or painting, or acting on our spoken stage will go out.

No. I not only do not think the popularity of motion pictures will decrease; I am already on record as predicting that the popularity of pictures will increase and keep on increasing. Consider my own *Birth of a Nation.* It was revived two years ago, after having been off for ten years, and it was as great a success in revival as in the original. The popularity of motion pictures (which are a natural form of dramatic expression) will ride higher and higher as the quality of motion pictures rises higher and higher. One hundred years from today we shall have novelists devoting all their energies toward creating motion-picture originals. By this I mean that the novelists giving their exclusive time to the films will create characters and situations and dramatic plots in terms of pictures. Motion-picture historians will have been developed, and they will be a great help to production. Motion-picture artists of all kinds will have grown up. It will all make for a more natural, dignified, sincere result because we shall have all our different branches devoting their time and efforts toward the completion of a single object —a motion picture.

I have no hesitancy in saying that the radio has claimed its share of amusement audiences. Unquestionably it has kept many persons away from both the films and the spoken stage. It is a great, useful discovery —a glorious medium. One hundred years from now there will be no confusion as between the radio and the motion picture. There cannot possibly be a connection nor a conflict. It is just possible there may be a conflict as between radio and spoken stage, but never between radio and film. Each occupies its own exclusive place in our lives.

Now let us prepare for a small-sized shock. One hundred years from today it will cost perhaps twice as much as it costs today to see the really first-class cinema. It is perfectly proper that it should. Time, effort, energy, and preparation put into pictures at that time will have advanced greatly. I am just honest enough to say that I do not at the moment understand how more time, effort, energy, and preparation could have been put into my own pictures; but, then, for the average large picture play this will hold true. The average supposedly high-class film play in 2024 will be on view at not less than $5 a seat.

In looking into the crystal I have seen many things which I have not touched upon here. Perhaps they would be too tedious to bring out and discuss. But of one thing I may place myself on record plainly and without qualification. The motion picture is a child that has been given life in our generation. As it grows older it will develop marvelously. We poor souls can scarcely visualize or dream of its possibilities. We ought to be kind with it in its youth, so that in its maturity it may look back upon its childhood without regrets.

Irving Thalberg
THE MODERN PHOTOPLAY

For twelve years, from 1924 until his death in 1936 at the age of thirty-seven, Irving Thalberg was the most powerful producer in Hollywood. As head of Metro-Goldwyn-Mayer, he was responsible for a series of box-office successes that included The Good Earth, Mutiny on the Bounty, *and* The Barretts of Wimpole Street. *It was his belief that "entertainment is the purpose and end of the photoplay." To that belief both he and Hollywood remained true.*

IN ORDER to understand the modern photoplay, in my opinion, which is based on about twelve years of experience during which time I have made fifty or more pictures in each of those years, one must understand the meaning of the word, entertainment, for entertainment is the purpose and end of the photoplay. The definition of the word, entertainment, as given in the dictionary, is that something which engages and holds the attention agreeably. There seem to be two essential points in this definition—that entertainment engages the attention of people, and that it brings about a pleasing response in them. Entertainment is the objective of the photoplay and we must keep in mind that as entertainment it must appeal to the varied tastes of all people. Other arts generally appeal to a selected group, but the motion picture art, and it is an art, must have universal appeal. This is fundamental, for the motion picture industry, with its investment of hundreds of millions of dollars, is based on the hope that it will appeal to the people of a nation and of a world, and if it did not have this appeal, it could not have reached its present state of development.

We have seen that the foundation upon which the whole motion picture industry is built is the desire to provide entertainment. Therefore, when we are judging or criticizing what we see on the screen, we must first consider it from the standpoint of entertainment value. We can also judge it from an artistic or technical viewpoint as well, but its entertainment value must be the first criterion.

■ ■ ■

We have seen that motion picture audiences are interested in pictures, movement, and changes in form, but even more important than these is the necessity of having the subject matter of photoplays correspond closely to current thinking—they must be topical. One of my chief functions is to be an observer and sense and feel the moods of the public. When I am asked to pass on the expenditure of huge sums of money and decide whether one kind of picture should be made or another kind, the greatest problem to be settled is that of judging whether or not the subject matter of the story is topical. What is accepted by the public today may not be accepted tomorrow. One of the finest examples I can give you of this is that war pictures in one period and another, in order to be successful, have had to be presented in an entirely different flavor.

During the war, various patriotic pictures were produced with success, showing war as a glorified thing in which no sacrifice was too great to make for your country, and having all the various forms of patriotism that could be gotten into a picture, including titles such as "The Kaiser, the Beast of Berlin." The people were stirred up and were thinking along those lines, and war photoplays capitalized on that thought. After the war, however, the war pictures were not successful, at least that was the common belief. However, we produced a picture called "The Big Parade" which to a great extent has made history along the lines of pictures, and the only difference between it and the other war pictures was the different viewpoint taken in the picture. We took a boy whose idea in entering the war was not patriotic. He was swept along by the war spirit around him and entered it but didn't like it. He met a French girl who was intriguing to him, but he wasn't really serious about her. The only time he was interested in fighting was when a friend, who was close to him, was killed. It was a human appeal rather than a patriotic appeal, and when he reached the German trenches and came face to face with the opportunity to kill, he couldn't do it. In other words, a new thought regarding the war was in the minds of most people and that was the basis of its appeal.

. . . Close attention to what the public is thinking about at the moment cannot be applied to the stage because stage audiences are not the normal audiences that the picture ones are. They are a centralized group of people, exotic, as a rule far better educated than the masses, and a different form of psychology and attention must be applied to them than to the picture audiences. The great successful plays never made any attempt to carefully correspond to the current thought of the moment and we find some that have run for generations. However, the spirit of modern life, the attitude of modern life, the attitude of children toward parents, the family life or the lack of it, is so quickly and so normally and clearly brought out in pictures. Of course, in each picture of the kind in which one thought is given the predominating position, there is an exaggeration, but nevertheless, there is a resemblance to the current thought of the day.

The motion pictures present our customs and our daily life more distinctly than any other medium and, therefore, if we were to come back a thousand years from today and tried to find some form of expression that would more clearly, more perfectly explain how we live today, it would have to be the motion picture, because there is no medium of today that so universally must please as great a number of people, and to do this it must be current in its thinking and in the processes by which its heroes and heroines do things. It couldn't be the magazines or the newspapers because they only use unusual subjects; and our literature appeals to an exotic or a sentimental group.

Right there is another side to this question. I have often been asked, "Do you think that the modern pictures, the great pictures, will endure forever?" While no one can state with any authority what will happen; in my opinion, the modern picture will not live forever as an artistic production, because one of the most important features of pictures is currency—the immediate fitting in with current thought. Now, of course, there are exceptions and at all times, a great story, a great work of genius will overcome any obstacle. We have the work of a master artist like Emil Jannings. At times he has been successful in overcoming all obstacles of ordinary standards of acceptance by the public. A great director like Ernest [*sic*] Lubitsch, through his cleverness and his genius will and has at times overcome the general lack of acceptance of his type of thinking. In short, I believe that although the modern picture will not live forever as a work of art, except in a few instances, it will be the most effective way of showing posterity how we live today.

H. L. Mencken
THE MOVIES

For four decades H. L. Mencken, the "Sage of Baltimore," roared his opinions on every aspect of American life. With vigor and acidity, he pursued pretentiousness and hypocrisy wherever he found it. Writing of movies in the thirties, Mencken revealed an amazing prescience. Today there are, as he predicted, "idiotic movies for the mob" as well as "movies made by artists."

AT SHORT intervals, one hears news that the movies are about to be uplifted. Does it ever actually happen? It does not.

The movies today, if the accounts of those who frequent them are to be believed, are as bad as they have ever been, and in more than one way they grow worse.

Has the threat of censorship purged them of their old frank carnality? Perhaps. But in place of it there is only imbecility. Of late, unable to endure the actual films, I have been reading some movie scenarios—that is, the scenarios of movies currently on view, and most of them successes. What I found in those scenarios, at the best, was precisely what the servant girls of my youth used to find in the *Fireside Companion.*

In other words, what I found there was simply mawkish and maudlin bilge.

There are, to be sure, films of a better sort, but how many? Certainly not enough to give any color to the general run. In that general run one finds only fodder for halfwits. The transactions depicted all lie upon the level of kitchen wench romance. That play of rational and amusing ideas which one encounters occasionally in the drama, and very frequently in the novel, is simply not there.

The best movie ever heard of, put beside the worst play by a Bernard Shaw or the worst novel of a Cabell, becomes sheer idiocy. The worst sinks so low that no other art, not even that of the architect of suburban filling stations, can show a parallel to it.

Where do the authors come from who concoct such depressing drivel? Some of them seem to be recruited from the ranks of the dramatists, and others are novelists of more or less dignity in their own craft. But when they write for the movies, something seems to happen to them—or, at all events, something happens to what they write. It may start out, for all I know, as plausible stuff, even as charming stuff. By the time it gets to the movie parlor, it is only garbage.

No author of any decent position has ever written a movie that added an inch to his stature as an artist. But many an author, going into the movies, has been ruined.

Why should this be so?

I can discern no sound reason in the nature of things. It is perfectly easy to imagine an intelligent and amusing movie, with an idea in it at least as sound as that in the average stage play, and enough ingenuity in its details to hold the attention of a civilized spectator. The technique of the movie, true enough, is still a bit stiff and unnatural, but so is the technique of the opera. Yet there are plenty of operas that do not insult the intelligence. They have true beauty in them; they conceal the clumsiness of their own form; they have intellectual dignity. One may endure them without throwing one's self into the mood of a hotel chambermaid on a holiday. Slightly intoxicated, one may even enjoy them.

But the movies never rise to that level. In order to enjoy them without treason to the higher cerebral centers, one must take on so vast a dose of stimulants that one cannot see them at all.

Why?

If the experts who profess the subject are to be credited, it is because every movie, before it gets to the screen, must be filtered through a dozen intelligences—and many of them are not intelligences at all, but simply vacuums. It is because the confection of movies is not entrusted to artists, but to gangs of blacksmiths. These blacksmiths decide what is to be played, and then they decide, in detail, precisely how it is to be played. The result is the aforesaid garbage.

No art, however sturdy, could conceivably survive such murderous sabotage. If any opera librettist had to submit his work to a committee of trolley conductors, and the composer had to write every note under the eye of a church choir tenor and an auctioneer, and if the resultant composition had to be produced by a designer of hot dog stands and the singers rehearsed by an oyster shucker, then opera would be what the movies are today.

In brief, they are idiotic because their production is mainly in the hands of idiots—with a few cynics interspersed to watch for the times when even idiots show some sense.

The bondage of the movies to men wholly incapable of grasping the nature of a fine art and of no more native taste or intellectual dignity than so many curve greasers or congressmen—this bondage is not due to the movies themselves, but simply to a chain of perfectly obvious natural causes.

The movie business, starting out on a shoestring, quickly plunged, like most new enterprises, into an era of wildcatting. Any man with money enough to hire a loft above a livery stable could set up a movie parlor, and any man who could borrow a secondhand camera and induce a few jobless actors to trust him was ready to make films. The result was a saturnalia of speculation and roguery. Patents were worth nothing to the wildcatters; copyrights were worth nothing; contracts were worth nothing. To take the word of a movie man, in those gay days, was like believing the oath of a Prohibition agent.

But among them were some men of greater rectitude and, what is more, of greater talent for business—mainly men who had been petty tradesmen, but still fellows with some grasp of business principles. They tried to reorganize and stabilize the movie industry, and after long and desperate struggles, they succeeded. The trade today, so its leaders boast, is as sound as the steel business and even has its code of honor. There are movie men in Rotary; there will be a movie window in the Cathedral of St. John the Divine.

But the bookkeeper of an opera house, alas, is seldom competent to select its repertory or to rehearse its caterwaulers. The movies, today, suffer from that profound and inconvenient fact. The men who organized them as an industry now attempt to operate them as an art—and the result is exactly the same as that which follows when a rich hog fattener, having decided to retire to the county seat, designs his own house, including the wallpaper and the steeple, and loads a fowling piece to make sure that the workmen carry out his plans.

In other words, the movies languish as a fine art because the men who determine what is to get into them haven't the slightest visible notion that such a thing as a fine art exists. Having learned by experience that certain classes of imbecilities fetch the mob and make a great deal of money, they conclude that such imbecilities are somehow worthy and laudable, and so admire them themselves.

Hence, their honest wonder when the movies are denounced; they can no more imagine than you could that what pleases them should be disgusting to other persons. And hence their vigorous, paralyzing policing of the authors, scenario writers, directors, and actors who are their slaves. The ideas of these gentry alarm them, as they would alarm a Baptist evangelist or a policeman. They prefer their own.

But soon or late the authors, scenario writers, directors and actors—that is, those among them who have any intelligence, which will not be many—will have to revolt against this bondage.

Soon or late the movie as an art will have to emancipate itself from the movie as a vast, machinelike, unimaginative, imbecile industry.

Soon or late the artist must get his chance. He is halted today by a delusion borrowed from his enemy—that movies are possible only on a great scale, that they must inflame the morons or have no being at all.

This is nonsense.

The theatre, once beset by the same folly, has been liberated by the so-called Little Theatre—that is, by the amateur. The movie, I suspect, will be liberated in much the same way. Some day someone with an authentic movie mind will make a cheap and simple motion picture that will arrest the notice of the civilized minority as it was arrested by the early plays of Eugene O'Neill.

When the day comes, the movies will split into two halves, just as the theatre has split. There will be huge, banal, maudlin, idiotic movies for the mob, and no doubt the present movie magnates will continue to produce them. And there will be movies made by artists, by and for people who can read and write.

Rudolf Arnheim
FILM AND REALITY

Does film merely "reproduce reality mechanically"? If so, can it legitimately be viewed as art? Revolutionary questions for 1933. Rudolf Arnheim, distinguished teacher, critic, and author of Film as Art *and* Art and Visual Perception, *discusses film and reality in this pioneering article. With clarity and insight, Arnheim anticipates those contemporary directors who have assured film "a place in the temple of the Muses."*

FILM resembles painting, music, literature, and the dance in this respect—it is a medium that may, but need not, be used to produce artistic results. Colored picture post cards, for instance, are not art and are not intended to be. Neither are a military march, a true confessions story, or a strip tease. And the movies are not necessarily film art.

There are still many educated people who stoutly deny the possibility that film might be art. They say, in effect: "Film cannot be art, for it does nothing but reproduce reality mechanically." Those who defend this point of view are reasoning from the analogy of painting. In painting, the way from reality to the picture lies via the artist's eye and nervous system, his hand and, finally, the brush that puts strokes on canvas. The process is not mechanical as that of photography, in which the light rays reflected from the object are collected by a system of lenses and then directed onto a sensitive plate where they produce chemical changes. Does this state of affairs justify our denying photography and film a place in the temple of the Muses?

It is worth while to refute thoroughly and systematically the charge that photography and film are only mechanical reproductions and that they therefore have no connection with art—for this is an excellent method of getting to understand the nature of film art.

With this end in view, the basic elements of the film medium will be examined separately and compared with the corresponding characteristics of what we perceive "in reality." It will be seen how fundamentally different the two kinds of images are; and that it is just these differences that provide film with its artistic resources. We shall thus come at the same time to understand the working principles of film art.

THE PROJECTION OF SOLIDS UPON A PLANE SURFACE

Let us consider the visual reality of some definite object such as a cube. If this cube is standing on a table in front of me, its position determines whether I can realize its shape properly. If I see, for example, merely the four sides of a square, I have no means of knowing that a cube is before me, I see only a square surface. The human eye, and equally the photographic lens, acts from a particular position and from there can take in only such portions of the field of vision as are not hidden by things in front. As the cube is now placed, five of its faces are screened by the sixth, and therefore this last only is visible. But since this face might equally well conceal something quite different—since it might be the base of a pyramid or one side of a sheet of paper, for instance—our view of the cube has not been selected characteristically.

We have, therefore, already established one important principle: If I wish to photograph a cube, it is not enough for me to bring the object within range of my camera. It is rather a question of my position relative to the object, or of where I place it. The aspect chosen above gives very little information as to the shape of the cube. One, however, that reveals three surfaces of the cube and their relation to one another, shows enough to make it fairly unmistakable what the object is supposed to be. Since our field of vision is full of solid objects, but our eye (like the camera) sees this field from only one station point at any given moment, and since the eye can perceive the rays of light that are reflected from the object only by projecting them onto a plane surface—the retina—the reproduction of even a perfectly simple object is not a mechanical process but can be set about well or badly.

The second aspect gives a much truer picture of the cube than the first. The reason for this is that the second shows more than the first—three faces instead of only one. As a rule, however, truth does not depend on quantity. If it were merely a matter of finding which aspect shows the greatest amount of surface, the best point of view could be arrived at by purely mechanical calculation. There is no formula to help one choose the most characteristic aspect: it is a question of feeling. Whether a particular person is "more himself" in profile than full face, whether the palm or the outside of the hand is more expressive, whether a particular mountain is better taken from the north or the west cannot be ascertained mathematically—they are matters of delicate sensibility.

Thus, as a preliminary, people who contemptuously refer to the camera as an automatic recording machine must be made to realize that even in the simplest photographic reproduction of a perfectly simple object, a feeling for its nature is required which is quite beyond any mechanical operation. We shall see later, by the way, that in artistic photography and film, those aspects that best show the characteristics of a particular object are not by any means always chosen; others are often selected deliberately for the sake of achieving specific effects.

REDUCTION OF DEPTH

How do our eyes succeed in giving us three-dimensional impressions even though the flat retinae can receive only two-dimensional images? Depth perception relies mainly on the distance between the two eyes, which makes for two slightly different images. The fusion of these two pictures into one image gives the three-dimensional impression. As is well known, the same principle is used in the stereoscope, for which two photographs are taken at once, about the same distance apart as the human eyes. This process cannot be used for film without recourse to awkward devices, such as colored spectacles, when more than one person is to watch the projection. For a single spectator it would be easy to make a stereoscopic film. It would only mean taking two simultaneous shots of the same incident a couple of inches apart and then showing one of them to each eye. For display to a larger number of spectators, however, the problem of stereoscopic film has not yet been solved satisfactorily—and hence the sense of depth in film pictures is extraordinarily small. The movement of people or objects from front to back makes a certain depth evident—but it is only necessary to glance into a stereoscope, which makes everything stand out most realistically, to recognize how flat the film picture is. This is another example of the fundamental difference between visual reality and film.

The effect of film is neither absolutely two-dimensional nor absolutely three-dimensional, but something between. Film pictures are at once plane and solid. In Ruttmann's film *Berlin* there is a scene of two subway trains passing each other in opposite directions. The shot is taken looking down from above onto the two trains. Anyone watching this scene realizes, first of all, that one train is coming toward him and the other going away from him (three-dimensional image). He will then also see that one is moving from the lower margin of the screen toward the upper and the other from the upper toward the lower (plane image). This second impression results from the projection of the three-dimensional movement onto the screen surface, which, of course, gives different directions of motion.

The obliteration of the three-dimensional impression has as a second result a stronger accentuation of perspective overlapping. In real life or in a stereoscope, overlapping is accepted as due merely to the accidental arrangement of objects, but very marked cuts result from superimpositions in a plane image. If a man is holding up a newspaper so that one corner comes across his face, this corner seems almost to have been cut out of his face, so sharp are the edges. Moreover, when the three-dimensional impression is lost, other phenomena, known to psychologists as the constancies of size and shape, disappear. Physically, the image thrown onto the retina of the eye by any object in the field of vision diminishes in proportion to the square of the distance. If an object a yard distant is moved away another yard, the area of the image on the retina is diminished to one-quarter of that of the first image. Every photographic plate reacts similarly. Hence in a photograph of someone sitting with his feet stretched out far in front of him the subject comes out with enormous feet and much too small a head. Curiously enough, however, we do not in real life get impressions to accord with the images on the retina. If a man is standing three feet away and another equally tall six feet away, the area of the image of the second does not appear to be only a quarter of that of the first. Nor if a man stretches out his hand toward one does it look disproportionately large. One sees the two men as equal in size and the hand as normal. This phenomenon is known as the constancy of size. It is impossible for most people—excepting those accustomed to drawing and painting, that is, artificially trained—to see according to the image on the retina. This fact, incidentally, is one of the reasons the average person has trouble copying things "correctly." Now an essential for the functioning of the constancy of size is a clear three-dimensional impression; it works excellently in a stereoscope with an ordinary photograph, but hardly at all in a film picture. Thus, in a film picture, if one man is twice as far from the camera as another, the one in front looks very considerably the taller and broader.

It is the same with the constancy of shape. The retinal image of a table top is like the photograph of it; the front edge, being nearer to the spectator, appears much wider than the back; the rectangular surface becomes a trapezoid in the image. As far as the average person is concerned, however, this again does not hold good in practice: he *sees* the surface as rectangular and draws it that way too. Thus the perspective changes taking place in any object that extends in depth are not observed but are compensated unconsciously. That is what is meant by the constancy of form. In a film picture it is hardly operative at all—a table top, especially if it is near the camera, looks very wide in front and very narrow at the back.

These phenomena, as a matter of fact, are due not only to the reduction of three-dimensionality but also to the unreality of the film picture altogether—an unreality due just as much to the absence of color, the delimitation of the screen, and so forth. The result of all this is that sizes and shapes do not appear on the screen in their true proportions but distorted in perspective.

LIGHTING AND THE ABSENCE OF COLOR

It is particularly remarkable that the absence of colors, which one would suppose to be a fundamental divergence from nature, should have been noticed so little before the color film called attention to it. The reduction of all colors to black and white, which does not leave even their brightness values untouched (the reds, for instance, may come too dark or too light, depending on the emulsion), very considerably modifies the picture of the actual world. Yet everyone who goes to see a film accepts the screen world as being true to nature. This is due to the phenomenon of "partial illusion" (see p. 72). The spectator experiences no shock at finding a world in which the sky is the same color as a human face; he accepts shades of gray as the red, white, and blue of the flag; black lips as red; white hair as blond. The leaves on a tree are as dark as a woman's mouth. In other words, not only has a multicolored world been transmuted into a black-and-white world, but in the process all color values have changed their relations to one another: similarities present themselves which do not exist in the natural world; things have the same color which in reality stand either in no direct color connection at all with each other or in quite a different one.

The film picture resembles reality insofar as lighting plays a very important role. Lighting, for instance, helps greatly in making the shape of an object clearly recognizable. (The craters on the surface of the moon are practically invisible at full moon because the sun is perpendicular and no shadows are thrown. The sunlight must come from one side for the outlines of the mountains and the valleys to become visible.) Moreover, the background must be of a brightness value that allows the object to stand out from it sufficiently; it must not be patterned by the light in such a way that it prevents a clear survey of the object by making it appear as though certain portions of the background were part of the object or vice versa.

These rules apply, for example, to the difficult art of photographing works of sculpture. Even when nothing but a "mechanical" reproduction is required, difficulties arise which often puzzle both the sculptor and the photographer. From which side is the statue to be taken? From what distance? Shall it be lighted from the front, from behind, from the right or left side? How these problems are solved determines whether the photograph or film shot turns out anything like the real object or whether it looks like something totally different.

DELIMITATION OF THE IMAGE AND DISTANCE FROM THE OBJECT

Our visual field is limited. Sight is strongest at the center of the retina, clearness of vision decreases toward the edges, and, finally, there is a definite boundary to the range of vision due to the structure of the organ. Thus, if the eyes are fixed upon a particular point, we survey a limited expanse. This fact is, however, of little practical importance. Most people are quite unconscious of it, for the reason that our eyes and heads are mobile and we continually exercise this power, so that the limitation of our range of vision never obtrudes itself. For this reason, if for no other, it is utterly false for certain theorists, and some practitioners, of the motion picture to assert that the circumscribed picture on the screen is an image of our circumscribed view in real life. That is poor psychology. The limitations of a film picture and the limitations of sight cannot be compared because in the actual range of human vision the limitation simply does not exist. The field of vision is in practice unlimited and infinite. A whole room may be taken as a continuous field of vision, although our eyes cannot survey this room from a single position, for while we are looking at anything our gaze is not fixed but moving. Because our head and eyes move we visualize the entire room as an unbroken whole.

It is otherwise with the film or photograph. For the purpose of this argument we are considering a single shot taken with a fixed camera. We shall discuss traveling and panorama shots later. (Even these aids in no sense replace the natural range of vision nor are they intended to do so.) The limitations of the picture are felt immediately. The pictured space is visible to a certain extent, but then comes the edge which cuts off what lies beyond. It is a mistake to deplore this restriction as a drawback. I shall show later that on the contrary it is just such restrictions which give film its right to be called an art.

This restriction (though also the lack of any sense of the force of gravity, see p. 77) explains why it is often very difficult to reproduce intelligibly in a photograph the spatial orientation of the scene depicted. If, for example, the slope of a mountain is photographed from below, or a flight of steps from above, the finished picture surprisingly will often give no impression of height or depth. To represent an ascent as descent by purely visual means is difficult unless the level ground can somehow be shown as a frame of reference. Similarly there must be standards of comparison to show the size of anything. To show the height of trees or of a building, for instance, human figures may be introduced beside them. A man in real life looks all round him when he is walking; and even supposing he is going up a mountain path with his eyes fixed on the ground at his feet, he still has a sense of the general lie of the surrounding country in his mind. This perception comes to him chiefly because his muscles and his sense of balance tell him at every instant exactly in what relation his body stands to the horizontal. Hence he can continually assess correctly the visual impression of the slanting surface. In contrast to such a man is one who is looking at a photograph or screen picture. He must depend upon what his eyes tell him without any assistance from the rest of his body. Moreover, he has only that part of the visual situation which is included within the confines of the picture to help him get his bearings.

The range of the picture is related to the distance of the camera from the object. The smaller the section of real life to be brought into the picture, the nearer the camera must be to the object, and the larger the object in question comes out in the picture—and vice versa. If a whole group of people is to be photographed, the camera must be placed several yards away. If only a single hand is to be shown, the camera must be very close, otherwise other objects besides the hand will appear in the picture. By this means the hand comes out enormously large and extends over the whole screen. Thus the camera, like a man who can move freely, is able to look at an object from close to or from a distance—a self-evident truth that must be mentioned inasmuch as from it is derived an important artistic device. (Variations of range and size can also be obtained by lenses of different focal lengths. The effects are similar but involve no change of the distance from the object and, therefore, no change of perspective.)

How large an object appears on the screen depends partly on the distance at which the camera was placed from it, but partly also on how much the picture is enlarged when the finished film is projected. The degree of enlargement depends on the lens of the projection machine and on the size of the theater. A film may be shown in whatever size is preferred—as small as the pictures in a child's magic lantern or gigantic as in a movie palace. There is, however, an optimum relationship between the size of the picture and its distance from the spectators. In a motion-picture theater the spectator sits relatively far away from the screen. Hence the projection must be large. But those watching pictures in a living room are quite close to the screen and therefore the projection may be much smaller. Nevertheless, the range of sizes used in practice is wider than is altogether desirable. In large theaters the projection is larger than in small ones. The spectators in the front rows naturally see a much larger picture than those in the back rows. It is, however, by no means a matter of indifference how large the picture appears to the spectator. The photography is designed for projection of a particular relative size. Thus in a large projection, or when the spectator is near the picture, movements appear more rapid than in a small one, since in the former case a larger area has to be covered than in the latter. A movement which seems hurried and confused in a large picture may be perfectly right and normal in a smaller one. The relative size of the projection, moreover, determines how clearly the details in the picture are visible to the spectator; and there is obviously a great difference between seeing a man so clearly that one can count the dots on his tie, and being able to recognize him only vaguely—more especially since, as has been pointed out, the size in which the object is to appear is used by the film director to obtain a definite artistic effect. Thus by the spectator's sitting too near or too far away a most disagreeable and obvious misrepresentation of what the artist intended may arise. Up to the present it is impossible to show a film to a large audience so that each member of it sees the picture in its right dimensions. After all, spectators must, as far as possible, be placed one behind the other; because when the rows of seats extend too far sideways, those sitting at the ends will see the picture distorted—and that is even worse.

ABSENCE OF THE SPACE-TIME CONTINUUM

In real life every experience or chain of experiences is enacted for every observer in an uninterrupted spatial and temporal sequence. I may, for example, see two people talking together in a room. I am standing fifteen feet away from them. I can alter the distance between us; but this alteration is not made abruptly. I cannot suddenly be only five feet away; I must move through the intervening space. I can leave the room; but I cannot suddenly be in the street. In order to reach the street I must go out of the room, through the door, down the stairs. And similarly with time. I cannot suddenly see what these two poeple will be doing ten minutes later. These ten minutes must first pass in their entirety. There are no jerks in time or space in real life. Time and space are continuous.

Not so in film. The period of time that is being photographed may be interrupted at any point. One scene may be immediately followed by another that takes place at a totally different time. And the continuity of space may be broken in the same manner. A moment ago I may have been standing a hundred yards away from a house. Suddenly I am close in front of it. I may have been in Sydney a few moments ago. Immediately afterward I can be in Boston. I have only to join the two strips together. To be sure, in practice this freedom is usually restricted in that the subject of the film is an account of some action, and a certain logical unity of time and space must be observed into which the various scenes are fitted. For time especially there are definite rules which must be obeyed.

Within any one film sequence, scenes follow each other in their order of time—unless some digression is introduced as, for example, in recounting earlier adventures, dreams, or memories. Within such a flashback, again, time passes naturally, but the action occurs outside the framework of the main story and need not even stand in any precise time relationship ("before" or "after") to it. Within individual scenes the succession of separate events implies a corresponding sequence of time. If, for example, a "long shot" of a man raising a revolver and firing it is shown, the raising and firing cannot be shown again afterward as a close-up. To do so would be to make a sequence of events that were in fact simultaneous.

That things are happening simultaneously is of course most simply indicated by showing the events in one and the same picture. If I see someone writing at a table in the foreground and someone else in the back playing the piano, the situation is self-explanatory as far as time is concerned. This method is, nevertheless, often avoided for artistic reasons and the situation composed of separate shots.

If two sequences of the action are to be understood as occurring at the same time they may simply be shown one after the other, in which case, however, it must be obvious from the content that simultaneity is intended. The most primitive way of giving this information in a silent film is by printed titles. ("While Elise was hovering between life and death, Edward was boarding the liner at San Francisco.") Or something of this sort: A horse race has been announced to begin at 3:40. The scene is a room full of people who are interested in the race. Someone pulls out a watch and shows the hands pointing to 3:40. Next scene—the racecourse with the horses starting. Events occurring simultaneously may also be shown by cutting up the various scenes and alternating the sections so that the progress of the different events is shown by turns.

Within the individual scenes the time continuum must never be disturbed. Not only must things that occur simultaneously not be shown one after the other, but no time must be omitted. If a man is going from the door to the window, the action must be shown in its entirety; the middle part, for example, must not be suppressed and the spectator left to see the man starting from the door and then with a jerk arriving at the window. This gives the feeling of a violent break in the action, unless something else is inserted so that the intervening time is otherwise occupied. Time may be dropped in the course of a scene only to produce a deliberately comic effect—as, for instance, when Charlie Chaplin enters a pawnbroker's shop and emerges instantly without his overcoat. Since to show complete incidents would frequently be dull and inartistic, because superfluous, the course of the action is sometimes interrupted by parts of scenes taking place simultaneously somewhere else. In this way it can be arranged to show only those moments of each event which are necessary for the action without patching together things that are incoherent in time. Apart from this, each scene in a good film must be so well planned in the scenario that everything necessary, and only what is necessary, takes place within the shortest space of time.

Although the time continuum within any individual scene must remain uninterrupted, the time relationship between scenes that occur at different places is undefined in principle so that it may be impossible to tell whether the second scene takes place before, during, or after the first. This is very clearly shown in many educational films where there is no connection in time but only in subject. As, for example: ". . . not only rabbits but also lions may be tamed." First picture—performing rabbits. Within this scene the continuity of time must be observed. Second picture—lion taming. Here too the continuity of time must not be broken. These two scenes, however, have no sort of time connection. The lion taming may go on before, during, or after the performance with the rabbits. In other words, the time connection is of no consequence and therefore does not exist. Similar situations arise occasionally in narrative films.

If sequences are meant to follow each other in time, the content of the film must make this relationship clear, precisely as in the case of simultaneity; because the fact that two sequences follow each other on the screen does not indicate in itself that they should be understood as following each other in time.

Film can take far greater liberties with space and time, however, than the theater can. To be sure, in the theater it is also permissible to have one scene occur at quite a different time and place from the preceding scene. But scenes with a realistic continuity of place and time are very long-drawn-out and allow of no break. Any change is indicated by a definite interruption—the curtain is lowered or the stage darkened. It might, nevertheless, be imagined that an audience would find it disturbing to see so many disconnected events on one and the same stage. That this is not so is due to a very curious fact: the illusion given by a play (or film) is only partial. Within any particular scene value is laid on naturalism. The characters must talk as people do in real life, a servant like a servant, a duke like a duke. (But even here we have this restriction: the servant and the duke are to talk clearly and sufficiently loudly, that is really, too clearly and loudly.) An ancient Roman lamp must not be put to light a modern drawing room nor a telephone by Desdemona's bed. Yet the room has only three walls—the fourth, the one that should intervene between the stage and the audience, is missing. Any audience would laugh if a piece of scenery fell down and revealed the wall of the room to be nothing but painted canvas, or if the crack of a shot were heard some seconds before the revolver was fired. But every audience takes it for granted that on the stage a room has only three walls. This deviation from reality is accepted because the technique of the stage demands it. That is to say, the illusion is only partial.

The stage is, so to speak, in two different but intersecting realms. It reproduces nature, but only a part of nature—separate in time and space from the actual time and space of the "house," where the audience is located. At the same time, the stage is a showcase, an exhibit, the scene of action. Hence it comes into the domain of the fictitious. The component of illusion is relatively strong in theater because an actual space (the stage) and an actual passage of time are given. The component of illusion is very slight when we are looking at a picture—for example, a photograph lying on the table in front of us. The photograph, like the stage, represents a particular place and a particular time (a moment of time), but it does not do this as is done in the theater with the aid of an actual space and an actual passage of time. The surface of the picture *signifies* a pictured space; and that is so much of an abstraction that the picture surface in no way gives us the illusion of actual space.

Film—the animated image—comes midway between the theater and the still picture. It presents space, and it does it not as on the stage with the help of real space, but, as in an ordinary photograph, with a flat surface. In spite of this, the impression of space is for various reasons not so weak as in a still photograph. A certain illusion of depth holds the spectator. Again, in contrast with the photograph, time passes during the showing of a film as it does on the stage. This passage of time can be utilized to portray an actual event, but is, nevertheless, not so rigid that it cannot be interrupted by breaks in time without the spectator feeling that these breaks do violence to it. The truth is that the film retains something of the nature of a flat, two-dimensional picture. Pictures may be displayed for as long or short a time as one pleases, and they can be shown next to one another even if they depict totally different periods in time.

Thus film, like the theater, provides a partial illusion. Up to a certain degree it gives the impression of real life. This component is all the stronger since in contrast to the theater the film can actually portray real—that is, not simulated—life in real surroundings. On the other hand, it partakes strongly of the nature of a picture in a way that the stage never can. By the absence of colors, of three-dimensional depth, by being sharply limited by the margins on the screen, and so forth, film is most satisfactorily denuded of its realism. It is always at one and the same time a flat picture post card and the scene of a living action.

From this arises the artistic justification for what is called montage. It was pointed out above that film, which records real situations on strips of celluloid that may be joined together, has the power of placing in juxtaposition things that have no connection at all in real time and space. This power was, however, primarily a purely mechanical one. One might expect the spectator to be overcome by a physical discomfort akin to seasickness when watching a film that had been composed of different shots. For example: In Scene 1 a man is discovered ringing the front doorbell of a house. Immediately following appears a totally different view—the interior of the house with a maid coming to answer the door. Thus the spectator has been jerked violently through the closed door. The maid opens the door and sees the visitor. Suddenly the viewpoint changes again and we are looking at the maid through the visitor's eyes—another breakneck change within the fraction of a second. Then a woman appears in the background of the foyer and in the next moment we have bridged the distance separating us from her, and we are close beside her.

It might be supposed that this lightning juggling with space would be most unpleasing. Yet everyone who goes to the movies knows that actually there is no sense of discomfort, but that a scene such as the one just described can be watched with perfect ease. How can this be explained? We have been talking as though the sequence had actually taken place. But it is not real and—which is of the greatest important—the spectators have not the (complete) illusion of its reality. For, as has already been said, the illusion is only partial and film gives simultaneously the effect of an actual happening and of a picture.

A result of the "pictureness" of film is, then, that a sequence of scenes that are diverse in time and space is not felt as arbitrary. One looks at them as calmly as one would at a collection of picture post cards. Just as it does not disturb us in the least to find different places and different moments in time registered in such pictures, so it does not seem awkward in a film. If at one moment we see a long shot of a woman at the back of a room, and the next we see a close-up of her face, we simply feel that we have "turned over a page" and are looking at a fresh picture. If film photographs gave a very strong spatial impression, montage probably would be impossible. It is the partial unreality of the film picture that makes it possible.

Whereas the theater stage differs from real life only in that the fourth wall is missing, the setting of the action changes, and the people talk in theatrical language, the film deviates much more profoundly. The position of the spectator is continually changing since we must consider him located at the station point of the camera. A spectator in the theater is always at the same distance from the stage. At the movies the spectator seems to be jumping about from one place to another; he watches from a distance, from close to, from above, through a window, from the right side, from the left; but actually this description, as has been said, is altogether misleading, because it treats the situation as physically real. Instead, pictures taken from the most various angles follow one another, and although the camera position had to be changed continually when they were taken, the spectator is not obliged to duplicate all this commotion.

Many people who are accustomed to clear thinking will feel that this theory of "partial illusion" is vague and equivocal. Is not the very essence of illusion that it should be complete? Is it possible, when one is surrounded by one's own friends and sitting in a chair at home in New York, to imagine oneself in Paris? Can one believe that one is looking at a room when a moment ago a street was there? Yes; one can. According to an outdated psychology that is still deeply rooted in popular thought, an illusion can be strong only if it is complete in every detail. But everyone knows that a clumsy childish scribble of a human face consisting of two dots, a comma, and a dash may be full of expression and depict anger, amusement, or fear. The impression is strong, though the representation is anything but complete. The reason it suffices is that in real life we by no means grasp every detail. If we observe the expression on somebody's face, we are far from being able to say whether he had blue eyes or brown, whether he was wearing a hat or not, and so on. That is to say, in real life we are satisfied to take in essentials; they give us all that we need to know. Hence if these essentials are reproduced we are content and obtain a complete impression that is all the more artistic for being so strongly concentrated. Similarly, in film or theater, so long as the essentials of any event are shown, the illusion takes place. So long as the people on the screen behave like human beings and have human experiences, it is not necessary for us to have them before us as substantial living beings nor to see them occupy actual space—they are real enough as they are. Thus we can perceive objects and events as living and at the same time imaginary, as real objects and as simple patterns of light on the projection screen; and it is this fact that makes film art possible.

ABSENCE OF THE NONVISUAL WORLD OF THE SENSES

Our eyes are not a mechanism functioning independently of the rest of the body. They work in constant coöperation with the other sense organs. Hence surprising phenomena result if the eyes are asked to convey ideas unaided by the other senses. Thus, for example, it is well known that a feeling of giddiness is produced by watching a film that has been taken with the camera traveling very rapidly. This giddiness is caused by the eyes participating in a different world from that indicated by the kinesthetic reactions of the body, which is at rest. The eyes act as if the body as a whole were moving; whereas the other senses, including that of equilibrium, report that it is at rest.

Our sense of equilibrium when we are watching a film is dependent on what the eyes report and does not as in real life receive kinesthetic stimulation. Hence certain parallels which are sometimes drawn between the functioning of the human eye and the camera—for instance, the comparison between the mobility of the eyes and that of the camera—are false. If I turn my eyes or my head, the field of vision is altered. Perhaps a moment ago I was looking at the door; now I am looking at the bookcase; then at the dining-room table, then at the window. This panorama, however, does not pass before my eyes and give the impression that the various objects are moving. Instead I realize that the room is stationary as usual, but that the direction of my gaze is changing, and that that is why I see other parts of the motionless room. This is not the case in film. If the camera was rotated while the picture was being shot, the bookcase, table, window, and door will proceed across the screen when the picture is projected; it is they which are moving. For since the camera is not a part of the spectator's body like his head and his eyes, he cannot tell that it has been turned. He can see the objects on the screen being displaced and at first is led to assume that they are in motion. In Jacques Feyder's *Les Nouveaux Messieurs,* for example, there is a scene in which the camera passes rapidly along a long wall covered with posters. The result is that the wall seems to move past the camera. If the scene that has been photographed is very simple to understand, if it is easy to get one's bearings in it, the spectator corrects this impression more or less rapidly. If, for instance, the camera is first directed toward a man's legs and if it then pans slowly up toward his head, the spectator knows very well that the man did not float feet first past a stationary camera. Film directors, however, often turn or shift the camera for taking pictures that are not so easy to grasp, and then a sensation of drifting supervenes which may be unintentional and may easily make the audience feel dizzy. This difference between the movements of the eyes and those of the camera is increased because the film picture has, as was said above, a fixed limit whereas the field of vision of our eyes is practically unbounded. Fresh objects are continually appearing within the frame of the picture and then disappearing again, but for the eyes there is an unbroken space-continuum through which the gaze wanders at will.

Thus there is relativity of movement in film. Since there are no bodily sensations to indicate whether the camera was at rest or in motion, and if in motion at what speed or in what direction, the camera's position is, for want of other evidence, presumed to be fixed. Hence if something moves in the picture this motion is at first seen as a movement of the thing itself and not as the result of a movement of the camera gliding past a stationary object. In the extreme case this leads to the direction of motion being reversed. If, for example, a moving car is filmed from a second one which is overtaking the first, the finished picture will show a car apparently traveling backward. It is, however, possible to make clear which movement is relative and which absolute by the nature and behavior of the objects shown in the picture. If it is obvious from the picture that the camera was standing on a moving car, that is, if parts of this car are seen in the picture, and, contrary to the landscape, they stay in the same place in the picture, the car will be perceived as moving and the surrounding landscape as stationary.

There is also a relativization of spatial coördinates—above, below, and so forth. To this are partly due the phenomena we described above in the section on the "Delimitation of the Image." A photograph of a slanting surface may not give an appearance of slope because there is no sensation of gravity to help the spectator realize "up and down." It is impossible to feel whether the camera was standing straight or was placed at an angle. Therefore, as long as there is nothing to indicate the contrary, the projection plane is perceived as vertical. If the camera is held over a bed to show from above the head of a man lying in it, the impression may easily be given that the man is sitting upright and that the pillow is perpendicular. The screen is vertical, although since the camera was turned downward it actually represents a horizontal surface. This effect can be avoided only by showing enough of the surroundings in the picture to give the spectator his bearings.

As regards the other senses: No one who went unprejudiced to watch a silent film missed the noises which would have been heard if the same events had been taking place in real life. No one missed the sound of walking feet, nor the rustling of leaves, nor the ticking of a clock. The lack of such sounds (speech, of course, is also one of them) was hardly ever apparent, although they would have been missed with a desperate shock in real life. People took the silence of the movies for granted because they never quite lost the feeling that what they saw was after all only pictures. This feeling alone, however, would not be sufficient to prevent the lack of sound being felt as an unpleasant violation of the illusion. That this did not happen is again connected with what was explained above: that in order to get a full impression it is not necessary for it to be complete in the naturalistic sense. All kinds of things may be left out which would be present in real life, so long as what is shown contains the essentials. Only after one has known talkies is the lack of sound conspicuous in a silent film. But that proves nothing and is not an argument against the potentialities of silent film, even since the introduction of sound.

It is much the same with the sense of smell. There may be people who if they see a Roman Catholic service on the screen imagine that they can smell incense; but no one will miss the stimulus. Sensations of smell, equilibrium, or touch are, of course, never conveyed in a film through direct stimuli, but are suggested indirectly through sight. Thence arises the important rule that it is improper to make films of occurrences whose central features cannot be expressed visually. Of course a revolver shot might occur as the central point of a silent film; a clever director could afford to dispense with the actual noise of the shot. It is enough for the spectator to see the revolver being fired and possibly to see the wounded man fall. In Josef von Sternberg's *The Docks of New York* a shot is very cleverly made visible by the sudden rising of a flock of scared birds.

Alfred Hitchcock
DIRECTION

Often called the "Master of Suspense," Alfred Hitchcock has directed films such as The Lady Vanishes, Lifeboat, Spellbound, Dial M for Murder, *and* Psycho. *Contending that films frequently "suffer from their own power of appealing to millions," Hitchcock has managed nevertheless to create films, which though indeed appealing to millions, also appeal to film buffs throughout the world.*

MANY people think a film director does all his work in the studio, drilling the actors, making them do what he wants. That is not at all true of my own methods, and I can write only of my own methods. I like to have a film complete in my mind before I go on the floor. Sometimes the first idea one has of a film is of a vague pattern, a sort of haze with a certain shape. There is possibly a colourful opening developing into something more intimate; then, perhaps in the middle, a progression to a chase or some other adventure; and sometimes at the end the big shape of a climax, or maybe some twist or surprise. You see this hazy pattern, and then you have to find a narrative idea to suit it. Or a story may give you an idea first and you have to develop it into a pattern.

Imagine an example of a standard plot—let us say a conflict between love and duty. This idea was the origin of my first talkie, *Blackmail.* The hazy pattern one saw beforehand was duty—love—love versus duty—and finally either duty or love, one or the other. The whole middle section was built up on the theme of love versus duty, after duty and love had been introduced separately in turn. So I had first to put on the screen an episode expressing duty.

I showed the arrest of a criminal by Scotland Yard detectives, and tried to make it as concrete and detailed as I could. You even saw the detectives take the man to the lavatory to wash his hands—nothing exciting, just the routine of duty. Then the young detective says he's going out that evening with his girl, and the sequence ends, pointing on from duty to love. Then you start showing the relationship between the detective and his girl: they are middle-class people. The love theme doesn't run smoothly; there is a quarrel and the girl goes off by herself, just because the young man has kept her waiting a few minutes. So your story starts; the girl falls in with the villain—he tries to seduce her and she kills him. Now you've got your problem prepared. Next morning, as soon as the detective is put on to the murder case, you have your conflict—love versus duty. The audience know that he will be trying to track down his own girl, who has done the murder, so you sustain their interest: they wonder what will happen next.

The blackmailer was really a subsidiary theme. I wanted him to go through and expose the girl. That was my idea of how the story ought to end. I wanted the pursuit to be after the girl, not after the blackmailer. That would have brought the conflict on to a climax, with the young detective, ahead of the others, trying to push the girl out through a window to get her away, and the girl turning round and saying: "You can't do that—I must give myself up." Then the rest of the police arrive, misinterpret what he is doing, and say, "Good man, you've got her," not knowing the relationship between them. Now the reason for the opening comes to light. You repeat every shot used first to illustrate the duty theme, only now it is the girl who is the criminal. The young man is there ostensibly as a detective, but of course the audience know he is in love with the girl. The girl is locked up in her cell and the two detectives walk away, and the older one says, "Going out with your girl to-night?" The younger one shakes his head. "No. Not to-night."

That was the ending I wanted for *Blackmail,* but I had to change it for commercial reasons. The girl couldn't be left to face her fate. And that shows you how the films suffer from their own power of appealing to millions. They could often be subtler than they are, but their own popularity won't let them.

But to get back to the early work on a film. With the help of my wife, who does the technical continuity, I plan out a script very carefully, hoping to follow it exactly, all the way through, when shooting starts. In fact, this working on the script is the real making of the film, for me. When I've done it, the film is finished already in my mind. Usually, too, I don't find it necessary to do more than supervise the editing myself. I know it is said sometimes that a director ought to edit his own pictures if he wants to control their final form, for it is in the editing, according to this view, that a film is really brought into being. But if the scenario is planned out in detail, and followed closely during production, editing should be easy. All that has to be done is to cut away irrelevancies and see that the finished film is an accurate rendering of the scenario.

Settings, of course, come into the preliminary plan, and usually I have fairly clear ideas about them; I was an art student before I took up with films. Sometimes I even think of backgrounds first. *The Man Who Knew Too Much* started like that; I looked in my mind's eye at snowy Alps and dingy London alleys, and threw my characters into the middle of the contrast. Studio settings, however, are often a problem; one difficulty is that extreme effects—extremes of luxury or extremes of squalor—are much the easiest to register on the screen. If you try to reproduce the average sitting-room in Golders Green or Streatham it is apt to come out looking like nothing in particular, just nondescript. It is true that I have tried lately to get interiors with a real lower-middle-class atmosphere—for instance, the Verlocs' living-room in *Sabotage*—but there's always a certain risk in giving your audience humdrum truth.

However, in time the script and the sets are finished somehow and we are ready to start shooting. One great problem that occurs at once, and keeps on occurring, is to get the players to adapt themselves to film technique. Many of them, of course, come from the stage; they are not cinema-minded at all. So, quite naturally, they like to play long scenes straight ahead. I am willing to work with the long uninterrupted shot: you can't avoid it altogether, and you can get some variety by having two cameras running, one close up and one farther off, and cutting from one to the other when the film is edited. But if I have to shoot a long scene continuously I always feel I am losing grip on it, from a cinematic point of view. The camera, I feel, is simply standing there, *hoping* to catch something with a visual point to it. What I like to do always is to photograph just the little bits of a scene that I really need for building up a visual sequence. I want to put my film together on the screen, not simply to photograph something that has been put together already in the form of a long piece of stage acting. This is what gives an effect of life to a picture—the feeling that when you see it on the screen you are watching something that has been conceived and brought to birth directly in visual terms. The screen ought to speak its own language, freshly coined, and it can't do that unless it treats an acted scene as a piece of raw material which must be broken up, taken to bits, before it can be woven into an expressive visual pattern.

You can see an example of what I mean in *Sabotage.* Just before Verloc is killed there is a scene made up entirely of short pieces of film, separately photographed. This scene has to show how Verloc comes to be killed—how the thought of killing him arises in Sylvia Sidney's mind and connects itself with the carving knife she uses when they sit down to dinner. But the sympathy of the audience has to be kept with Sylvia

Sidney; it must be clear that Verloc's death, finally, is an accident. So, as she serves at the table, you see her unconsciously serving vegetables with the carving knife, as though her hand were keeping hold of the knife of its own accord. The camera cuts from her hand to her eyes and back to her hand; then back to her eyes as she suddenly becomes aware of the knife making its error. Then to a normal shot—the man unconcernedly eating; then back to the hand holding the knife. In an older style of acting Sylvia would have had to show the audience what was passing in her mind by exaggerated facial expression. But people to-day in real life often don't show their feelings in their faces: so the film treatment showed the audience her mind through her hand, through its unconscious grasp on the knife. Now the camera moves again to Verloc—back to the knife—back again to his face. You see him seeing the knife, realising its implication. The tension between the two is built up with the knife as its focus.

Now when the camera has immersed the audience so closely in a scene such as this, it can't instantly become objective again. It must broaden the movement of the scene without loosening the tension. Verloc gets up and walks round the table, coming so close to the camera that you feel, if you are sitting in the audience, almost as though you must move back to make room for him. The the camera moves to Sylvia Sidney again, then returns to the subject—the knife.

So you gradually build up the psychological situation, piece by piece, using the camera to emphasise first one detail, then another. The point is to draw the audience right inside the situation instead of leaving them to watch if from outside, from a distance. And you can do this only by breaking the action up into details and cutting from one to the other, so that each detail is forced in turn on the attention of the audience and reveals its psychological meaning. If you played the whole scene straight through, and simply made a photographic record of it with the camera always in one position, you would lose your power over the audience. They would watch the scene without becoming really involved in it, and you would have no means of concentrating their attention on those particular visual details which make them feel what the characters are feeling.

This way of building up a picture means that film work hasn't much need for the virtuoso actor who gets his effects and climaxes himself, who plays directly on to the audience with the force of his talent and personality. The screen actor has got to be much more plastic; he has to submit himself to be used by the director and the camera. Mostly he is wanted to behave quietly and naturally (which, of course, isn't at all easy), leaving the camera to add most of the accents and emphases. I would almost say that the best screen actor is the man who can do nothing extremely well.

One way of using the camera to give emphasis is the reaction shot. By the reaction shot I mean any close-up which illustrates an event by showing instantly the reaction to it of a person or a group. The door opens for someone to come in, and before showing who it is you cut to the expressions of the persons already in the room. Or, while one person is talking, you keep your camera on someone else who is listening. This over-running of one person's image with another person's voice is a method peculiar to the talkies; it is one of the devices which help the talkies to tell a story faster than a silent film could tell it, and faster than it could be told on the stage.

Or, again, you can use the camera to give emphasis whenever the attention of the audience has to be focussed for a moment on a certain player. There is no need for him to raise his voice or move to the centre of the stage or do anything dramatic. A close-up will do it all for him—will give him, so to speak, the stage all to himself.

I must say that in recent years I have come to make much less use of obvious camera devices. I have become more commercially-minded; afraid that anything at all subtle may be missed. I have learnt from experience how easily small touches are overlooked.

The other day a journalist came to interview me and we spoke about film technique. "I always remember," he said, "a little bit in one of your silent films, *The Ring.* The young boxer comes home after winning his fight. He is flushed with success—wants to celebrate. He pours out champagne all round. Then he finds that his wife is out, and he knows at once that she is out with another man. At this moment the camera cuts to a glass of champagne; you see a fizz of bubbles rise off it and there it stands untasted, going flat. That one shot gives you the whole feeling of the scene." Yes, I said, that sort of imagery may be quite good: I don't despise it and still use it now and then. But is it always noticed? There was another bit in *The Ring* which I believe hardly any one noticed.

The scene was outside a boxing-booth at a fair, with a barker talking to the crowd. Inside the booth a professional is taking on all-comers. He has always won in the first round. A man comes running out of the booth and speaks to the barker: something unexpected has happened. Then a cut straight to the ringside: you see an old figure 1 being taken down and replaced by a brand-new figure 2. I meant this single detail to show that the boxer, now, is up against someone he can't put out in the first round. But it went by too quickly. Perhaps I might have shown the new figure 2 being taken out of a paper wrapping—something else was needed to make the audience see in a moment that the figure for the second round had never been used before.

The film always has to deal in exaggerations. Its methods reflect the simple contrasts of black-and-white photography. One advantage of colour is that it would give you more intermediate shades. I should never want to fill the screen with colour: it ought to be used economically—to put new words into the screen's visual language when there's a need for them. You could start a colour film with a board-room scene: sombre panelling and furniture, the directors all in dark clothes and white collars. Then the chairman's wife comes in, wearing a red hat. She takes the attention of the audience at once, just because of that one note of colour. Or suppose a gangster story: the leader of the gang is sitting in a café with a man he suspects. He has told his gunman to watch the table. "If I order a glass of port, bump him off. If I order green chartreuse, let him go."

This journalist asked me also about distorted sound—a device I tried in *Blackmail* when the word "knife" hammers on the consciousness of the girl at breakfast on the morning after the murder. Again, I think this kind of effect may be justified. There have always been occasions when we have needed to show a phantasmagoria of the mind in terms of visual imagery. So we may want to show someone's mental state by letting him listen to some sound—let us say church bells—and making them clang with distorted insistence in his head. But on the whole nowadays I try to tell a story in the simplest possible way, so that I can feel sure it will hold the attention of any audience and won't puzzle them. I know there are critics who ask why lately I have made only thrillers. Am I satisfied, they say, with putting on the screen the equivalent merely of popular novelettes? Part of the answer is that I am out to get the best stories I can which will suit the film medium, and I have usually found it necessary to take a hand in writing them myself. . . .

I choose crime stories because that is the kind of story I can write, or help to write, myself—the kind of story I can turn most easily into a successful film. It is the same with Charles Bennett, who has so often worked with me; he is essentially a writer of melodrama. I am ready to use other stories, but I can't find writers who will give them to me in a suitable form. . . .

To-day you can put over scenes that would have been ruled out a few years ago. Particularly towards comedy, nowadays, there is a different attitude. You can get comedy out of your stars, and you used not to be allowed to do anything which might knock the glamour off them.

In 1926 I made a film called *Downhill,* from a play by Ivor Novello, who acted in the film himself, with Ian Hunter and Isabel Jeans. There was a sequence showing a quarrel between Hunter and Novello. It started as an ordinary fight; then they began throwing things at one another. They tried to pick up heavy pedestals to throw and the pedestals bowled them over. In other words I made it comic. I even put

Hunter into a morning coat and striped trousers because I felt that a man never looks so ridiculous as when he is well dressed and fighting. This whole scene was cut out; they said I was guying Ivor Novello. It was ten years before its time.

I say ten years, because you may remember that in 1936 M.G.M. showed a comedy called *Libelled Lady.* There is a fishing sequence in it: William Powell stumbles about in the river, falls flat and gets soaked and catches a big fish by accident. Here you have a star, not a slapstick comedian, made to do something pretty near slapstick. In *The Thirty-nine Steps,* too, a little earlier, I was allowed to drag Madeleine Carroll over the moors handcuffed to the hero; I made her get wet and untidy and look ridiculous for the purpose of the story. I couldn't have done that ten years ago.

I foresee the decline of the individual comedian. Of course, there may always be specially gifted comedians who will have films written round them, but I think public taste is turning to like comedy and drama more mixed up; and this is another move away from the conventions of the stage. In a play your divisions are much more rigid; you have a scene—then curtain, and after an interval another scene starts. In a film you keep your whole action flowing; you can have comedy and drama running together and weave them in and out. Audiences are much readier now than they used to be for sudden changes of mood; and this means more freedom for a director. The art of directing for the commercial market is to know just how far you can go. In many ways I am freer now to do what I want to do than I was a few years ago. I hope in time to have more freedom still—if audiences will give it to me.

Michelangelo Antonioni
REFLECTIONS ON THE FILM ACTOR

Michelangelo Antonioni, for the past decade one of the world's most controversial film-makers, is best known for abstract films such as L'Avventura, La Notte, Blow-Up, *and* Zabriskie Point. *In the following article, Antonioni discusses the delicate relationship inherent between actor and director.*

THE film actor need not understand, but simply be. One might reason that in order to be, it is necessary to understand. That's not so. If it were, then the most intelligent actor would also be the best actor. Reality often indicates the opposite.

When an actor is intelligent, his efforts to be a good actor are three times as great, for he wishes to deepen his understanding, to take everything into account, to include subtleties, and in doing so he trespasses on ground which is not his—in fact, he creates obstacles for himself.

His reflections on the character he is playing, which according to popular theory should bring him closer to an exact characterization, end up by thwarting his efforts and depriving him of naturalness. The film actor should arrive for shooting in a state of virginity. The more intuitive his work, the more spontaneous it will be.

The film actor should work not on the psychological level but on the imaginative one. And the imagination reveals itself spontaneously—it has no intermediaries upon which one can lean for support.

It is not possible to have a real collaboration between actor and director. They work on two entirely different levels. The director owes no explanations to the actor except those of a very general nature about the people in the film. It is dangerous to discuss details. Sometimes the actor and director necessarily become enemies. The director must not compromise himself by revealing his intentions. The actor is a kind of Trojan horse in the citadel of the director.

I prefer to get results by a hidden method; that is, to stimulate in the actor certain of his innate qualities of whose existence he is himself unaware—to excite not his intelligence but his instinct—to give not justifications but illuminations. One can almost trick an actor by demanding one thing and obtaining another. The director must know how to demand, and how to distinguish what is good and bad, useful and superfluous, in everything the actor offers.

The first quality of a director is to see. This quality is also valuable in dealing with actors. The actor is one of the elements of the image. A modification of his pose or gestures modifies the image itself. A line spoken by an actor in profile does not have the same meaning as one given full-face. A phrase addressed to the camera placed above the actor does not have the same meaning it would if the camera were placed below him.

These few simple observations prove that it is the director—that is to say, whoever composes the shot—who should decide the pose, gestures, and movements of the actor.

The same principle holds for the intonation of the dialogue. The voice is a "noise" which emerges with other noises in a rapport which only the director knows. It is therefore up to him to find the balance or imbalance of these sounds.

It is necessary to listen at length to an actor even when he is mistaken. One must let him be mistaken and at the same time try to understand how one can use his mistakes in the film, for these errors are at the moment the most spontaneous thing the actor has to offer.

To explain a scene or piece of dialogue is to treat all the actors alike, for a scene or piece of dialogue does not change. On the contrary, each actor demands special treatment. From this fact stems the necessity to find different methods: to guide the actor little by little to the right path by apparently innocent corrections which will not arouse his suspicions.

This method of working may appear paradoxical, but it is the only one which allows the director to obtain good results with nonprofessional actors found, as they say, "in the street." Neorealism has taught us that, but the method is also useful with professional actors—even the great ones.

I ask myself if there really is a great film actor. The actor who thinks too much is driven by the ambition to be great. It is a terrible obstacle which runs the risk of eliminating much truth from his performance.

I do not need to think I have two legs. I have them. If the actor seeks to understand, he thinks. If he thinks, he will find it hard to be humble, and humility constitutes the best point of departure in achieving truth.

Occasionally an actor is intelligent enough to overcome his natural limitations and to find the proper road by himself—that is, he uses his innate intelligence to apply the method I have just described.

When this happens, the actor has the qualities of a director.

Ingmar Bergman
WHAT IS "FILM MAKING"?

Perhaps more than any other individual, Ingmar Bergman has been responsible for raising film to the level of high art. His brooding, allegorical studies of the human condition have appealed to intellectuals and aesthetes the world over. In "What Is 'Film Making'?" he discusses the compulsions and conflicts that engross the director as artist.

"FILM-MAKING" is for me a necessity of nature, a need comparable to hunger and thirst. For some, self-expression involves writing books, climbing mountains, beating one's children or dancing the samba. In my case, I express myself in making films.

In *The Blood of a Poet,* the great Jean Cocteau shows us his alter ego stumbling down the corridors of a nightmare hotel and gives us a glimpse, behind each one of the doors, of one of the factors of which he is composed and which form his ego.

Without attempting here to equate my personality with Cocteau's, I thought I would take you on a guided tour of my internal studios where, invisibly, my films take form. This visit, I am afraid, will disappoint you; the equipment is always in disorder because the owner is too absorbed in his affairs to have time to straighten it up. Furthermore, the lighting is rather bad in certain spots, and on the door of certain rooms, you will find the word "Private" written in large letters. Finally, the guide himself is not always sure of what is worth the trouble of showing.

Whatever the case may be, we will open a few doors a crack. I won't guarantee that you will find precisely the answer to the questions you are wondering about, but perhaps, in spite of everything, you will be able to put together a few pieces of the complicated puzzle that the forming of a film represents.

If we consider the most fundamental element of the cinematographic art, the perforated film, we note that it is composed of a number of small, rectangular images—fifty-two per meter—each of which is separated from the other by a thick, black line. Looking more closely, we discover that these tiny rectangles, which at first glance seem to contain exactly the same picture, differ from each other by an almost imperceptible modification of this picture. And when the feeding mechanism of the projector causes the images in question to succeed each other on the screen so that each one is seen only for a twentieth of a second, we have the illusion of movement.

Between each of these small rectangles the shutter closes and plunges us into total darkness, only to return us to full light with the next rectangle. When I was ten years old and working with my first apparatus, a shaky lantern made of sheet metal—with its chimney, its gas lamp and its perpetual films which repeated themselves indefinitely—I used to find the above-mentioned phenomenon exciting and full of mystery. Even today, I feel myself quiver as I did when I was a child when I think of the fact that, in reality, I am creating illusion; for the cinema would not exist but for an imperfection of the human eye, namely its inability to perceive separately a series of images which follow each other rapidly and which are essentially identical.

I have calculated that if I see a film that lasts an hour, I am in fact plunged for twenty minutes in total darkness. In making a film, therefore, I am making myself guilty of a fraud; I am using a device designed to take advantage of a physical imperfection of man, a device by means of which I can transport my audience from a given feeling to the feeling that is diametrically opposed to it, as if each spectator were on a pendulum; I can make an audience laugh, scream with terror, smile, believe in legends, become indignant, take offense, become enthusiastic, lower itself or yawn from boredom. I am, then, either a deceiver or—when the audience is aware of the fraud—an illusionist. I am able to mystify, and I have at my disposal the most precious and the most astounding magical device that has ever, since history began, been put into the hands of a juggler.

There is in all this, or at least there should be, the source of an insoluble moral conflict for all those who create films or work on them.

As for our commercial partners, this is not the place to bring out the mistakes they have made from year to year, but it would certainly be worthwhile someday for a scientist to discover some unit of weight or measure which one could use to "calculate" the quantity of natural gifts, initiatives, genius and creative forces that the film industry has ground through its formidable mills. Obviously, anyone entering into the game must accept the rules in advance, and there is no reason why work in the cinematographic branch should be more respected than anywhere else. The difference is due to the fact that, in our specialty, brutality is manifested more overtly, but this is actually rather an advantage.

Loss of balance offers consequences that are even more grave for the film-maker than for a tightrope walker or an acrobat who performs his tricks beneath a circus tent and without a net. For the film-maker as well as for the equilibrist, the danger is of the same order: falling and being killed. No doubt you think I am exaggerating; making a film isn't as dangerous as all that! I maintain my point, however; the risk is the same. Even if, as I mentioned, one is a bit of a magician, no one can mystify the producers, the bank directors, the movie-theatre owners or the critics when the public abstains from going to see a film and from paying out the obol from which producers, bank directors, movie-theatre owners, critics and magicians must draw their subsistence!

I can give you as an example a very recent experience, the memory of which still makes me shudder—an experience in which I myself risked losing my balance. A singularly bold producer invested money in one of my films which, after a year of intense activity, appeared under the title of *The Naked Night (Gycklarnas afton).* The reviews were, in general, destructive, the public stayed away, the producer added up his losses, and I had to wait several years before trying again.

If I make two or three more films which fail financially, the producer will quite justifiably consider it a good idea not to bet on my talents.

At that point, I will become, suddenly, a suspect individual, a squanderer, and I will be able to reflect at my leisure on the usefulness of my artistic gifts, for the magician will be deprived of his apparatus.

When I was younger, I didn't have these fears. Work for me was an exciting game and, whether the results succeeded or failed, I was delighted with my work like a child with his castles of sand or clay. The equilibrist was dancing on his rope, oblivious and therefore unconcerned about the abyss beneath him and the hardness of the ground of the circus-ring.

The game has changed into a bitter combat. The walk on the rope is now performed in full awareness of the danger, and the two points where the rope is attached are now called "fear" and "incertitude." Each work to be materialized mobilizes all of the resources of one's energy. The act of creation has become, under the effect of causes that are as much interior as they are exterior and economic, an exacting duty. Failure, criticism, coldness on the part of the public today cause more sensitive wounds. These wounds take longer to heal and their scars are deeper and more lasting.

Before undertaking a work or after having begun it, Jean Anouilh has the habit of playing a little mental game in order to exorcise his fear.

He says to himself, "My father is a tailor. He intimately enjoys creating with his hands, and the result is a beautiful pair of pants or an elegant overcoat. This is the joy and the satisfaction of the artisan, the pride of a man who knows his profession."

This is the same practice I follow. I recognize the game, I play it often and I succeed in duping myself—and a few others—even if this game is in fact nothing but a rather poor sedative: "My films are fine pieces of work, I am enthusiastic, conscientious and extremely attentive of details. I create for my contemporaries and not for eternity; my pride is the pride of an artisan."

I know, however, that if I speak this way, it is in order to deceive myself, and an irrepressible anxiety cries out to me, "What have you done that can last? Is there in any of your movies a single foot of film worthy of being passed on to posterity, a single line of dialogue, a single situation which is really and indisputably true?"

And to this question I am forced to answer—perhaps still under the effect of a disloyalty which is ineradicable even in the most sincere people—"I don't know, I hope so."

You must excuse me for having described at such length and with so much commentary the dilemma which those who create films are forced to confront. I wanted to try to explain to you why so many of those who are devoted to the realization of cinematographic works give in to a temptation which cannot really be expressed and which is invisible; why we are afraid; why we sometimes lose our enthusiasm for the works we are doing; why we become fools and allow ourselves to be annihilated by colorless and vile compromises.

I would still, however, like to dwell a bit longer on one of the aspects of the problem, the aspect that is the most important and difficult to comprehend—the public.

The creator of films is involved in a means of expression which concerns not only himself but also millions of other people, and more often than not he feels the same desire as other artists: "I want to succeed today. I want celebrity now. I want to please, to delight, to move people immediately."

Midway between this desire and its realization is found the public, who demands but one thing of the film: "I've paid, I want to be distracted, swept off my feet, involved; I want to forget my troubles, my family, my work, I want to get away from myself. Here I am, seated in the darkness, and, like a woman about to give birth, I want deliverance."

The film-maker who is aware of these demands and who lives on the money of the public is placed in a situation which is difficult and which creates obligations for him. In making his flim, he must always take the reaction of the public into account. On my part, personally, I am forever asking myself this question: "Can I express myself more simply, more purely, more briefly? Will everybody understand what I want to say now? Will the simplest mind be able to follow the course of these events? And, even more importantly, this question: up to what point do I have the right to admit compromise and where do my obligations to myself begin?"

Any experimentation necessarily involves a great risk, for it always keeps the public at a distance, and keeping the public at a distance can lead to sterility and to isolation in an ivory tower.

It would be quite desirable, then, for producers and other technical directors of the cinema to put laboratories at the disposition of the creators. But this is scarcely the case today. The producers have confidence only in the engineers and stupidly imagine that the salvation of the film industry depends on inventions and technical complications.

Nothing is easier than frightening a spectator. One can literally terrify him, for most people have in some part of their bearing a fear that is all ready to blossom. It is much more difficult to make people laugh, and to *make them laugh* in the right way. It is easy to put a spectator in a state worse than the one he was in when he entered the theatre; it is difficult to put him in a better state; it is precisely this, however, that he desires each time he sits down in the darkness of a movie-theatre. Now, how many times and by what means do we give him this satisfaction?

This is the way I reason; but at the same time I know with an absolute evidence that this reasoning is dangerous, since it involves the risk of condemning all failures, of confusing the ideal with pride, and of considering as absolute the frontiers that the public and the critics establish, whereas you neither recognize these frontiers nor consider them your own, since your personality is perpetually in the process of becoming. On the one hand, I am tempted to adapt myself and to make myself what the public wants me to be; but on the other hand, I feel that this would be the end of everything, and that this would imply a total indifference on my part. Thus, I am delighted to have not been born with exactly as many brains as feelings, and it has never been written anywhere that a film-maker must be contented, happy, or satisfied. Who says you can't make noise, cross frontiers, battle against windmills, send robots to the moon, have visions, play with dynamite or tear pieces of flesh from one's self or others? Why not frighten film producers? It is their job to be afraid, and they are paid to have stomach ulcers!

But *"film-making"* is not always confronting problems, dilemmas, economic worries, responsibilities and fear. There are also games, dreams, secret memories.

Often it begins with an image: a face which is suddenly and strongly illuminated; a hand which rises; a square at dawn where a few old ladies are seated on a bench, separated from each other by sacks of apples. Or it may be a few words that are exchanged; two people who, suddenly, say something to each other in a completely personal tone of voice—their backs are perhaps turned from me, I can't even see their faces, and yet I am forced to listen to them, to wait for them to repeat the same words which are without any particular meaning but which are pregnant with a secret tension, with a tension of which I am not yet even fully conscious but which acts like a crafty potion. The illuminated face, the hand raised as if for an incantation, the old ladies at the square, the few banal words, all of these images come and attach themselves like silvery fish to my net, or more precisely, I myself am trapped in a net, the texture of which I am not aware of—fortunately!

Quite rapidly, even before the motive has been entirely designed in my mind, I submit the game of my imagination to the test of reality. I place, as if I'm playing a game, my sketch, which is still very rough and fragile, on an easel in order to judge it from the point of view of all the technical resources of the studios. This imaginary test of "viability" constitutes for the motive an effective ferruginous bath. Will it suffice? Will the motive keep its value when it is plunged into the daily, murderous routine of the studios, far from the shadows of sunrises, which are quite propitious for the games of the imagination?

A few of my films mature very quickly and are finished rapidly. These are the ones that meet the general expectations, like children that are still undisciplined but in good health and about whom one can predict immediately: "They are the ones who will support the family."

And then there are other films, films which come slowly, which take years, which refuse to be imprisoned in a formal or technical solution, and which, in general, refuse any concrete solution. They remain in a shadowy zone; if I want to find them, I have to follow them there and find a context, characters and situation. There, faces that are turned aside begin to speak, the streets are strange, a few, scattered people glance out through window-panes, an eye glistens at dusk or changes into a carbuncle and then bursts with a noise of breaking crystal. The square, this autumn morning, is a sea; the old ladies are transformed into ancient trees and the apples are children building cities of sand and stone near the foam of the waves.

The tension is there, ever present, and it appears again, either in the written word, or in the visions, or in the excess of energy, which bends like the arch of a bridge, ready to rise up by its own forces, by these forces which are the most important element, once the manuscript is finished, in setting in motion the immense wheel which the work required in shooting a film represents.

What is "shooting a film," then? If I were to ask this question of everybody, I would no doubt obtain quite different responses, but perhaps you would all agree on one point: shooting a film is doing what is necessary in order to transport the contents of the manuscript onto a piece of film. In doing so, you would be saying quite a lot and yet not nearly enough. For me, shooting a film represents days of inhumanly relentless work, stiffness of the joints, eyes full of dust, the odors of make-up, sweat and lamps, an indefinite series of tensions and relaxations, an uninterrupted battle between volition and duty, between vision and reality, conscience and laziness. I think of early risings, of nights without sleep, of a feeling keener than life, of a sort of fanaticism centered about a single task, by which I myself become, finally, an integral part of the film, a ridiculously tiny piece of apparatus whose only fault is requiring food and drink.

It sometimes happens—in the middle of all this excitement, when the studios are humming with a life and a labor that seem as if they should make the studios explode—that, suddenly, I find the idea for my next film. You would be wrong, however, if you thought that the activity of a film-maker supposes, at this moment, a kind of ecstatic vertigo, an uncontrolled excitement and a frightening disorganization. To shoot a film is to undertake the taming of a wild beast that is difficult to handle and very valuable; you need a clear mind, meticulousness, stiff and exact calculations. Add to this a temper that is always even and a patience that is not of this world.

Shooting a film is organizing an entire universe, but the essential elements are industry, money, construction, shooting, developing and copying, a schedule to follow but which is rarely followed, a battle plan minutely prepared where the irrational factors occur the most often. The star has too much black around her eyes—a thousand dollars to start the scene over again. One day, the water in the pipes has too much chlorine in it and the negatives get spotted—let's start again! Another day, death plays a dirty trick on you by taking away an actor—let's start with another—and there are several thousand more dollars swallowed up. It starts to thunder, the electric transformer breaks down, and there we are, all made up and waiting in the pale light of the day, the hours flying by and money with them.

Idiotic examples, chosen at random. But they have to be idiotic, since they touch that great and sublime idiocy, the transforming of dreams into shadows, the chopping up of a tragedy into five hundred small pieces, the experimentation with each of these pieces, and finally the putting back together of these pieces so that they constitute again a unity which will once more be the tragedy. It is the idiocy of fabricating a tapeworm 8,000 feet long which will nourish itself on the life and mind of the actors, producers, and creators. Shooting a film is all that, but it is still something else, and it is much worse.

Film-making is also plunging with one's deepest roots back into the world of childhood. Let's descend, if you wish, into this interior studio, located in the most intimate recesses of the life of the creator. Let's open up for a moment the most secret of these rooms so that we can look at a painting of Venice, an old window-blind, and a first apparatus for showing "action films."

At Upsala, my grandmother had a very old apartment. While I was there, I once slipped beneath the dining-room table; I was wearing an apron with a pocket in front of it; from my vantage point I listened to the voice of the sunbeams which entered through the immensely high windows. The rays moved continually; the bells of the cathedral chimed out; the rays moved, and their movement generated a sort of special sound. It was one of those days between winter and spring; I had the measles and I was five years old. In the neighboring apartment, somebody was playing the piano—it was always waltzes—and on the wall hung a big painting of Venice. While the rays of sun and the shadows were passing like waves across the painting, the water of the canal began to flow, the pigeons flew up from the pavement of the square, people spoke to each other noiselessly, making movements with their hands and heads. The sound of the bells wasn't coming from the cathedral but rather from the painting, as were the strains from the piano. There was something very strange about this painting of Venice. Almost as strange as the fact that the sunbeams in my grandmother's living-room were not silent but had a sound. Perhaps it was all those bells—or perhaps the enormous pieces of furniture which were conversing uninterruptedly.

I seem to remember, however, an experience even more distant than the one of the year I had measles: the perception—impossible to date—of the movement of a window-blind.

It was a black window-blind of the most modern variety, which I could see, in my nursery, at dawn or at dusk, when everything becomes living and a bit frightening, when even toys transform into things that are either hostile or simply indifferent and curious. At that moment the world would no longer be the everyday world with my mother present, but a vertiginous and silent solitude. It wasn't that the blind moved; no shadow at all appeared on it. The forms were on the surface itself; they were neither little men, nor animals, nor heads, nor faces, but *things for which no name* exists. In the darkness, which was interrupted here and there by faint rays of light, these forms freed themselves from the blind and moved toward the green folding-screen or toward the bureau, with its pitcher of water. They were pitiless, impassive and terrifying: they disappeared only after it became completely dark or light, or when I fell asleep.

Anyone who, like myself, was born in the family of a pastor, learns at an early age to look behind the scenes in life and death. Whenever

Father has a burial, a marriage, a baptism, a mediation, he writes a sermon. You make an early acquaintance with the devil and, like all children, you need to give him a concrete form. Here is where the magic lantern comes in, a little sheet-metal box with a gas lamp (I can still smell the odor of the heated metal) and which projected colored pictures. Among others, there was Little Red Ridinghood and the wolf. The wolf was the devil, a devil without horns but with a tail and vivid red mouth, a curiously palpable and yet elusive devil, the emissary of evil and persecution on the flowered wallpaper of the nursery.

The first film I ever owned was about ten feet long and brown. It pictured a young girl asleep in a prairie; she woke up, stretched, arose and, with outstretched arms, disappeared at the right side of the picture. That was all. Drawn on the box the film was kept in was a glowing picture with the words, "Frau Holle." Nobody around me knew who Frau Holle was, but that didn't matter; the film was quite successful, and we showed it every evening until it got torn so badly we couldn't repair it.

This shaky bit of cinema was my first sorcerer's bag, and, in fact, it was pretty strange. It was a mechanical plaything; the people and things never changed, and I have often wondered what could have fascinated me so much and what, even today, still fascinates me in exactly the same way. This thought comes to me sometimes in the studio, or in the semidarkness of the editing room, while I am holding the tiny picture before my eyes and while the film is passing through my hands; or else during that fantastic childbirth that takes place during the recomposition as the finished film slowly finds its own face. I can't help thinking that I am working with an instrument so refined that with it, it would be possible for us to illuminate the human soul with an infinitely more vivid light, to unmask it even more brutally and to annex to our field of knowledge new domains of reality. Perhaps we would even discover a crack that would allow us to penetrate into the *chiaroscuro* of surreality, to tell tales in a new and overwhelming manner. At the risk of affirming once more something I cannot prove, let me say that, the way I see it, we film-makers utilize only a minute part of a frightening power—we are moving only the little finger of a giant, a giant who is far from not being dangerous.

But it is equally possible that I am wrong. It might be that the cinema has attained the high point of its evolution, that this instrument, by its very nature, can no longer conquer new territory, that we are stuck with our noses to the wall, since the road ends in a dead end. Many people are of this opinion, and it is true that we are treading water in a marsh, our noses just rising above the surface of the water, and paralyzed by economic problems, conventions, stupidity, fear, incertitude and disorder.

I am asked sometimes what I am trying to attain in my films, what my *goal* is. The question is difficult and dangerous, and I usually answer it by lying or hedging: "I am trying to tell the truth about the condition of men, the truth as I see it." This answer always satisfies people, and I often wonder how it happens that nobody notices my bluff, because the true response should be, "I feel an incoercible need to express through film that which, in a completely subjective way, takes form some place in my consciousness. This being the case, I have no other goal but myself, my daily bread, the amusement and respect of the public, a kind of truth that I feel precisely at that moment. And if I try to sum up my second answer, the formula I end up with is not terribly exciting: 'An activity without much meaning.'"

I am not saying that this conclusion doesn't distress me inordinately. I am in the same situation as most artists of my generation; the activity of each one of us doesn't have much meaning. Art for art's sake. My personal truth, or three-quarters of a truth, or no truth at all, except that it has a value for me.

I realize that this way of looking at things is quite unpopular, particularly today. Let me hasten, then, to form the question in a different way: "What would be your goal in making your films?"

The story is told that, a long time ago, the cathedral of Chartres was struck by lightning and burned from top to bottom. It is said that thousands of people rushed there from the four corners of the world, people of all conditions; they crossed Europe like lemmings in migration; together, they began to rebuild the cathedral upon its old foundations. They stayed there until the immense edifice was completed, all of them, architects, workers, artists, jugglers, nobles, priests and the bourgeoisie, but their names were unknown, and, even today, nobody knows the names of those who built the cathedral of Chartres.

Without letting that give you any preconceived ideas about my beliefs or doubts—which, furthermore, have nothing to do with what we are discussing here—I think that any art loses its essential potency the moment it becomes separated from the "cult." It has cut the umbilical cord and it lives its own separate life, a life that is astonishingly sterile, dim, and degenerate. Creative collectivity, humble anonymity are forgotten and buried relics, deprived of any value. Little wounds of the ego and moral colics are examined under a microscope *sub specie aeternitatis.* The fear of the dark which characterizes subjectivism and scrupulous consciences has become quite stylish, and ultimately we are all running around in a big enclosure where we argue with one another about our solitude without listening to each other or even noticing that we are pushing ourselves mutually to the point of dying of suffocation from all this. It is in such a way that individualists look each other in the eye, deny the existence of those they see and invoke omnipotent obscurity without ever having once felt the saving force of the joys of community. We are so poisoned by our own vicious circles, so closed in by our own anguish that we are becoming incapable of distinguishing true from false, the ideality of gangsters and sincere unaffectedness.

To the question concerning the goal of my films, I could therefore answer: "I want to be one of the artists of the cathedral that stands above the plains. I want to occupy myself making from stone a dragon's head, an angel or a devil, or perhaps a saint, it doesn't really matter; I feel the same enjoyment in each case. Whether I am a believer or an unbeliever, a Christian or a pagan, I am working along with everybody else to construct a cathedral, because I am an artist and an artisan, and because I have learned to extract faces, limbs, and bodies from stone. I never have to worry about the judgment of posterity or of my contemporaries; my first and last names are engraved nowhere, and they will disappear with me. But a small part of my self will survive in the anonymous and triumphant totality. A dragon or a devil, or perhaps a saint, what does it matter!"

Ken Kelman

THE REALITY OF NEW CINEMA

Describing himself as "first of all a playwright," and "secondly a semi-retired film critic," Ken Kelman has written film criticism for Film Culture, Moviegoer, *and* The Nation. *In this article he notes the contributions of the "New American Cinema" to traditional cinema and to the entire concept of film reality.*

TRADITIONAL cinema made clear distinctions between the "real" and "subjective" (content) on the one hand, and between the "real" and "abstract" (form) on the other. Perception—the seeing or hearing of things—came through either the "filter" of characters who were understood as sharing their experience with the audience; or through the "impersonal" camera which was understood as presenting phenomena "objectively," with mechanical fidelity (that is, in recognized customary ways, the machine itself having been invented and developed to reproduce our *standard* perceptions). Psychological states were generally shown from the outside looking in. But when the converse treatment was attempted, when the material was presented to indicate mental processes directly, as most classically in *The Cabinet of Dr. Caligari,* it was "framed" by "reality" (standardized *par excellence* in Hollywood's "dream sequence" technique) so there would be no confusion, no misunderstanding that the world of dream, vision, or hallucination could be accepted as a "real" one. Similarly, abstraction was very clearly "abstract," distanced from "reality" by the use of geometric shapes (Richter, Fischinger), or, when "real" objects were edited in "abstract" patterns, by the marked fantasy and whimsy of their treatment (Man Ray, McLaren).

What has been occurring with increasing clarity in recent years, chiefly in the New American Cinema, is the crossing of these well-established and confining boundaries. The stages of this revolutionary process follow, not in their strictly chronological development, but in order of departure, more and more radical, from conventions of old cinema.

(1) A breakthrough of prime importance is implicit in the conscious articulation and exposure of filmic illusion. This is exemplified in the work of Bruce Conner, with his use of scratchy old newsreel and cartoon footage, and numbered "leader" (the "10-9-8-7 . . ." that begins reels of film) at various places in his movies, as well as repetition of the same shots until they seem more *film* than illusion. Such devices have sporadically cropped up in other avant-gardes and Nouvelles Vagues, but never before were united to such purposeful and concentrated effect. The most full-fledged instance yet of the anti-illusion film is Stanton Kaye's feature *Georg,* in mock *cinéma-vérité style,* where the "reality" (or illusion) of cinema ironically interplays with that of life itself (or the subject); during the course of which various fancy film techniques are subtly mishandled to call attention to themselves, the camera's shadow appears in the picture, lettering appears between reels, etc.

(2) An even more striking change is implicit in the way in which some of today's film artists handle the concept of reality. Conventional film has established traditions of "reality" which, even in documentary, preclude its being too "real." Sheer undiluted "reality" has always been associated with "primitive" style, and a maxim of popular art has been that too much "reality" will bore, stupefy, cease indeed to have the impact of the "real." The *effect* of "reality," or rather, the use of "realistic" materials to entertain or make points, has been the traditional goal of filmmakers. To show life in all its nuance and detail (with no arrangement or abridgement for purposes of theme or drama) is to show life in its infinite richness *and* poverty, with all its surprise *and* dullness. This is what Andy Warhol has done in his unedited, "straight" versions of sleeping (*Sleep*), eating (*Eat*), and more complex matters *(Screen Test, The Chelsea Girls).* Warhol's approach is the denial of contrivance, of spurious appeals, the presentation of "reality" for its own sake and no other. And the very fact that no "realistic" *effects* are striven for gives to Warhol's hyperrealism an illusionistic quality, that which life itself gives when contemplated with absolute unwavering focus; an undeviating concentration that old cinema never conceived, since such purity is indeed a negation of the "reality" (illusion) principle. In short, the border between illusion and "reality" is not clear enough either in life or in the cinema of absolute realism to satisfy the old standards.

(3) The converse of the ultimate "objectivity" of Warhol is the "subjectivity" of Stan Brakhage or Carl Linder, a yet more extreme departure from normal movies. Here perceptions and mental states *are* the norm, the "reality"—as validly as conventional images (with the *cus-*

tomary focus, perspective, angle, of "recognizable" objects) themselves only externalize *ideas* of "reality." Brakhage is aware of "reality" as conditional, as dependent on, indeed existing, in the mind and its eye. His world is not constructed of the rigid preconceived "truths" without which standard movies would be lost (e.g., for him a mountain may be a breast, a blood corpuscle, a creature struggling up a mountain); and, rather, consists of images correlative to immediate personal perceptions (e.g., he has handpainted patterns over the birth of his child, patterns which he actually did see, does see at times of emotional stress, visions which were an absolute "reality" for him at the time, and which thus complete the truth of the situation—what the conventionally trained eye perceives *plus* what the inner ancient eye experiences). The visionary and hallucinatory worlds of Brakhage and Linder are not "framed" in another, more conventional world (as in *Caligari* or *Dead of Night,* or even, more subtly, in *Un Chien Andalou*), but are projected directly, immediately and unmediated, without any "explanatory notes," seeking no justification in the eyes of the "regular" world.

(4) Finally, and most recently, there has emerged film dispensing entirely with figurative imagery, whether "real" or "abstract"; film consisting absolutely of light; black-and-white in Tony Conrad's *The Flicker,* pure basic colors plus white in a remarkable section of John Cavanaugh's *Acid Man.* Here there is hardly even any question of "real," "illusory," "abstract," "subjective," "objective"; there are no images to interpret. The vision shown is that of sheer light, light as the medium and power, light as the substance and subject. And traditional realism is made practically absurd (in its assumption of verisimilitude as basic truth) by the stark undeniable "reality" of perception itself—not of preconceived images we have been taught to see in certain ways, as "real," as "abstract," as "fantastic"—of nothing more than the very light, the light upon the eye.

The four new ways of handling cinematic illusion that are noted above display a progressive tendency toward richness and flexibility of meaning, away from the calculations of specific emotional effect, toward liberation of the senses, away from insistence on the credibility or "reality" of a particular illusion. The art, not of anti-illusion or anti-realism, but of conscious illusion and conscious realism, is hardly out of its infancy in film, compared to other media; but by the same token, in film it is growing at the greatest rate of all.

Jonas Mekas
WHERE ARE WE—THE UNDERGROUND?

Founder and publisher of Film Culture, *cinema critic for* The Village Voice, *film-maker, Jonas Mekas is one of the strongest voices in the "new cinema" movement. In recognition of his contribution in "directing people's attention to the avant-garde arts," the Philadelphia College of Art honored him with its highest award. Responding to that award, Mekas delivered the following remarks at the College's commencement exercises in June, 1966.*

WHEN I was asked to accept the highest award of the Philadelphia College of Art, I hesitated for a moment. I said to myself: Who am I? Really, I haven't done much in my life. Everything I want to do, all my dreams, are still in the future. Then I thought again. What the College is really doing by awarding this honor to me, is directing people's attention to the avant-garde arts. This award doesn't, really, go to me; it goes to the new cinema—to all those avant-garde artists who are trying to bring some beauty into a world full of sadness and horror.

What are we really doing? Where are we—the Underground? What's the meaning of it all? I will try to answer, or to indicate, some of the meanings connected with our work—meanings that are closely connected with all of us.

There was a time, when I was sixteen or seventeen, when I was idealistic and believed that the world would change in my own lifetime. I read about all the suffering of man, wars, and misery that took place in the past centuries. And I somehow believed that in my own lifetime all this would change. I had faith in the progress of man, in the goodness of man. And then came the war, and I went through horrors more unbelievable than anything I had read in the books, and it all happened right before my eyes—before my eyes the heads of children were smashed with bayonets. And this was done by my generation. And it's still being done today, in Vietnam, by my generation. It's done all over the world, by my generation. Everything that I believed in shook to the foundations—all my idealism, and my faith in the goodness of man and progress of man; all was shattered. Somehow, I managed to keep myself together. But, really, I wasn't one piece any longer; I was one thousand painful pieces.

It's really from this, and because of this, that I did what I did. I felt I had to start from the very beginning. I had no faith, no hope left. I had to collect myself again, bit by bit. And I wasn't surprised when, upon my arrival in New York, I found others who felt as I felt. There were poets, and filmmakers, and painters—people who were also walking like one thousand painful pieces. And we felt that there was nothing to lose any more. There was almost nothing worth keeping from our civilized inheritance. Let's clean ourselves out, we felt. Let's clean out everything that is dragging us down—the whole bag of horrors and lies and egos. The Beat Generation was the outgrowth, the result of this desperation; the mystical researches came out of this desperation. No price was too high, we felt, to pay for this cleaning job, no embarrassment too big to take. Let them laugh at us and our shabby appearances; let them spit into our beards. Even if we had nothing—some of us still have nothing to put in the cleared place—we couldn't remain as we were. We had to clean out not only the present but, through the drug experience or through meditation, to go back by several generations, to eliminate our egos, our bad faith, our mistrust, our sense of competition, of personal profit—so that if there was anything beautiful and pure, it would find a clear place and would settle in us and would begin to grow. It was a painful search, and it still is. We are still in the beginning of this search and growth, and many minds get broken to pieces. We are going through a dramatic end of the Christian Era and the birth of what we begin to call the Aquarian Age, and there are violent happenings taking place in man's spirit and they aren't always in our control. But it's a little bit easier because there are today many of us in various places of the country, of the world; we keep meeting each other, and we recognize each other; we know we are the traveling pioneers of the new age. We are the transitional generations. My generation, your generation, we have been marked by the sign of travel. We kept going and searching (we still do) in constant movement, from one side of the continent to another, between San Francisco and New York, between India and Mexico, and through all the inner journeys of the psychedelics and yoga systems, and macrobiotics. No generation since Columbus has traveled more than the current two generations of America. Yes, other generations have also traveled, but they always traveled as conquerors, to conquer the others, to teach them their own way of life. Our parents are still traveling through Vietnam as conquerors; they travel, yes—but how useless and unreal all their journeys and their conquerings seem to us today! For we are traveling, collecting the broken bits and pieces of knowledge, of love, of hope, of old ages; not the wisdom of our parents, nor our mothers' wisdom, but that wisdom which is as old as the earth, as the planets, as man himself—the mystical, the eternal—collecting, gathering ourselves bit by bit, having nothing to offer to others but taking gladly whatever is invested with love and warmth and wisdom, no matter how little that may be.

In cinema, this search is manifested through abandoning of all the existing professional, commercial values, rules, subjects, techniques, pretensions. We said: We don't know what man is; we don't know what cinema is. Let us, therefore, be completely open. Let us go in any direction. Let us be completely open and listening, ready to move to any direction upon the slightest call, almost like one who is too tired and too weary, whose senses are like a musical string, almost with no power of their own, blown and played by the mystical winds of the incoming Age, waiting for a slightest motion or call or sign—let's go in any direction to break out of the net that is dragging us down. Our mothers' wisdom! Don't get tied down to any of the establishments; they will go down and they will drag us down. The sun, that is our direction. The beauty, that is our direction—not money, not success, not comfort, not security, not even our own happiness, but the happiness of all of us together.

We used to march with posters protesting this and protesting that. Today, we realize that to improve the world, the others, first we have to improve ourselves; that only through the beauty of our own selves can we beautify the others. Our work, therefore, our most important work at this stage is ourselves. Our protest and our critique of the existing order of life can be only through the expansion of our own being. We are the measure of all things. And the beauty of our creation, of our art, is proportional to the beauty of ourselves, of our souls.

You may be wondering, sometimes, why we keep making little movies, underground movies, why we are talking about Home Movies, and you hope, sometimes, that all this will change soon. Wait, you say, until they begin making big movies. But we say, No, there is a misunderstanding here. We *are* making real movies. What we are doing comes from the deeper needs of man's soul. Man has wasted himself outside himself; man has disappeared in his projections. We want to bring him down, into his small room, to bring him home. We want to remind him that there is such a thing as home, where he can be, once in a while, alone and with himself and with a few that he loves close to him, and be with himself and his soul—that's the meaning of the home movie, the private visions of our movies. We want to surround this earth with our home movies. Our movies come from our hearts—our little movies, not the Hollywood movies. Our movies are like extensions of our own pulse, of our heartbeat, of our eyes, our fingertips; they are so personal, so unambitious in their movement, in their use of light, their imagery. We want to surround this earth with our film frames and warm it up—until it begins to move. We could continue expressing our own surroundings, being mirrors of the dirty cities, the black dailiness. But we have done that job already. There is pain in the arts of the last few decades. The whole period of so-called modern art is nothing but the pain of our ending civilization, the last decades of the Christian Era. Now we are looking, we are being pulled by a desire for something joyful deep within us, deep in the stars, and we want to bring it down to earth so that it will change our cities, our faces, our movements, our voices, our souls—we want an art of light. You'll see more and more of luminous colors and heavenly sounds coming through our art. The brush strokes will be charged with a different energy, not to express our egos, not to promote ourselves "as artists" (that is gone, all that is gone and gone), but to bring down the whispers of heaven to serve as strings, as instruments of ethereal winds, with our own personalities almost disappearing. I see it all over the country, and humble, unknown artists keep coming from various and distant countries, passing the town like monks stopping on their way somewhere, showing glimpses brought down from heaven. There is a renaissance, a spiritual renaissance coming upon us, and it's through artists that this new age is bringing to us its first voices and visions; it's through their intuition that the eternity communicates with us, bringing a new knowledge, new feelings. Let us then be very open to our art, to this new art, and to our work as artists. This isn't time for lowering ourselves, but for being ready to sing the most beautiful note.

I was talking in the beginning about my own disillusionment after the war. Today, for the first time in a long time, I suddenly again begin to see the broken pieces of myself coming together. I am listening, very openly, with all my senses, with my eyes and ears open, and I begin to hear and see a new man emerging. After fifteen years of disillusionment, slowly, during the last few months, I have gained again the belief and trust in man, and the knowledge that this is the generation that is building the bridge from horror to light. You, me—we are the one thousand painful pieces that are beginning to come together in one beautiful note. As if a completely new race of man were emerging on earth. Do you know what the rock 'n' roll group called *The Byrds* do with their money? They are making huge signs and putting them all along the roadsides of California, and the signs say one word: Love. But our parents would say: This is crazy, you should put your money into the bank. That's the difference. That's what I mean. That's where we stand in 1966 and midsummer.

2

AUDIENCE AND EFFECT

Mervyn LeRoy
WHAT MAKES A GOOD SCREEN STORY?

What does the public want in its films? "What Makes a Good Screen Story?" Mervyn LeRoy, who began directing in 1927, is responsible for films such as Anthony Adverse, No Time for Sergeants, Quo Vadis, *and* Little Caesar. *His movies, he contends, are for the public, not for the critics.*

WHAT baffles the makers of movies and the writers of stories is that public taste is not so lofty and cosmopolitan as is generally believed. This is a fact that has long since failed to surprise the pollsters. What the average person says he likes and what he really pays his money to see are two different things.

Question: What kind of movies do you like?

Answer: Good, meaty pictures with dramatic impact, such as *Death of a Salesman.*

Question: Did you see *Death of a Salesman?*

Answer: I just happened to miss that one, but I heard it was great.

Question: What pictures *did* you see last month?

Answer: Well, just for laughs, you know, *Ma and Pa Kettle.* And a Betty Grable picture—I forget the name.

Question: Did you ever see *The Heiress,* the picture that won Olivia de-Havilland the Academy Award for the best performance of 1949?

Answer: I never got around to that one; but that's the kind I mean—dramatic.

It's like the boy who *says* he wants to marry a good, strong person, like his mother, but who really marries the blonde who swings her hips when she walks down the street.

It's a matter of public record by now that *The Heiress* was not a big financial success. Yet everyone kept telling the industry that we should make more pictures just like it. We can't make more pictures like *The Heiress* if they don't justify their cost. It's like the book-publishing business. A well-written, artistic success can be a commercial failure. The publisher who doesn't pay for his artistic flops with commercially successful books that will pay the printer's bill isn't going to be publishing *any* books, great or small, very long. Of course, in the book world the biggest artistic successes often do very well. It's the little artistic successes that are commercial flops. The same is true of motion pictures.

As for movies just for the intelligentsia, these so-called critics' pictures rarely make money, and I'll tell you why. Anyone who makes a picture for a critic is out of his mind. A critic isn't representative. I have never found a bad picture any critic could help and I've never found a good one any critic could hurt. *Another Part of the Forest,* for instance, was a critics' picture. It was beautifully done, *but it was not a picture most people wanted to see.*

If you saw *Francis,* the movie about the talking mule, you saw a really enjoyable picture. The people in it were great and the people who made it were great, *and it was a picture everyone wanted to see.* They needed a talking mule in *Another Part of the Forest.* Because it's this way: *The Blue Boy* is a beautiful picture, but comparatively few people have seen it. The *Mona Lisa* is one of the greatest pictures the world has ever known, but more people have seen Lana Turner. My answer to that is: people want entertainment. If The Blue Boy sang like Jolson, they'd go to see him. Or if Mona Lisa looked like Hedy Lamarr, more people would go to the Louvre. Hollywood was crazy to have made a picture like *Mourning Becomes Electra.* That was a great play and beautifully written, but who the devil wants to see it as a picture? You might want to see *Quo Vadis.* Or *Ivanhoe.* Or *Bend of the River.* But who wants to see a movie whose basic theme is incest? There is nothing inspirational about such a story. At best, its appeal is to a limited sophisticated, cosmopolitan audience. Owing to Breen Office restrictions, the same honesty of characterization and motivation as was shown on the stage could not be shown in the picture. Therefore it didn't come off. There were a lot of heavy dramatics over a theme that was never brought out or clarified.

This isn't to say that we ever set out to make a bad movie. We all set our sights on the highest goal. But the fact is that the would-be motion-picture writer cannot begin his writing career with too arty an approach. There has to be the perfect blend. Maybe your story is it. Maybe it falls short. The point is that you'll be more successful in cracking a brand-new field if you will remember certain basic box-office-proved points.

You have to remember that the majority of people who go to movies go because they want to forget their worries for a while. Movies are escape. In the main, people don't want to go to be reminded of the troubles and tragedies they must face the next day unless the story is extremely inspirational. They want to leave the theater happier than when they went in. For example, though musicals may be only fantasy, they also take us away from life as it is lived from day to day.

The cynics are always with us—those who say Hollywood cannot face reality, that everything must be glossed over and made unreal. What the cynics do not realize is that dreams are often more real than reality. There is a reality beyond that which we see and touch and feel. There exists within man a groping toward an idealistic extension of himself: an undefeatable belief that life can be pleasanter than it may be at the moment, a stanch conviction that there are possibilities beyond his own narrow horizons. The movie with the fairytale, Cinderella, happy-ending plot brings joy because it also brings hope.

Dudley Nichols
THE WRITER AND THE FILM

Author of memorable screen plays such as The Informer, The Lost Patrol, Stagecoach, *and* The Long Voyage Home, *Dudley Nichols provided the words that directors and cameramen turned into striking images. While recognizing the importance of the screen writer, Nichols never forgot that in the film "it is the audience which is in motion."*

1

OURS is the age of the specialist. In older times, before the Machine, men did specialize of course in the various arts and crafts—but those arts and crafts were not themselves subdivided into specialized functions. The man who painted did the whole job himself: he was a painter. So with the silversmith and the shoemaker and the sculptor. But the Machine changed all that. The painter today has his materials prepared by other people, by specialized craftsmen or tradesmen, and only wields those materials in the final function of creating pictures. The etcher buys his copper plates already prepared and seldom pulls his own prints. The sculptor models in clay and leaves to others the pouring of the mold or the work of the pointing machine. The writer no longer turns out beautiful manuscripts that may be passed from hand to hand: he pounds out a script on the typing machine and passes it on to his publisher's printing factories. In science and art we have become specialized, narrowing our fields of study and work because those fields have grown too enormous for the single mind to embrace. We are all specialized, for better or worse, and it is only natural that the one new art form which the Machine has produced should be the most highly specialized of all. For the motion picture *is* an art form, whether it be so regarded or not.

By rights this new art form should be controlled by individuals who include all functions in themselves. They should be film-makers. But the functions are too diversified and complex to be handled by the creative energy of one individual. So we break them down into separate crafts—writing, directing, photography, scenic designing, optical printing and camera effects, cutting and assembly of film, composing music, recording, mixing and re-recording, the making of *dissolves* and *fades* and other transitions—into an immense field of works which require the closest and most harmonious collaboration to produce excellent results.

This in effect is a detriment to film as an art form and an obstacle to the development of artists who wish to work in film. It is too much the modern factory system—each man working on a different machine and never in an integrated creation. It tends to destroy that individuality of style which is the mark of any superior work of art. Individual feeling gets lost in the complicated process, and standardized products come off the assembly line. I make these remarks by way of preface to point out that there is only one way to overcome the impediments—and that is to learn the whole process, to be a master craftsman within the factory system; to be, in short, a film-maker first and a writer or director or whatever-you-will afterwards.

Of course, this poses a dilemma: one cannot under our present system make films without first learning to make films: and the only way to learn film-making is by making films. Hence by subterfuge of one sort or another one must enter the field as a specialized apprentice and try to learn all the other specialized functions, so that the individual may return to his specialty with the full equipment of an artist. A screenwriter should have knowledge of direction, of cutting, of all the separate functions, before his imagination and talent can be geared effectively and skillfully to his chosen line of work. Unfortunately we are none of us so competent as we might be, if for no other reason than that Hollywood is too bent on turning out films to take the time to train its artisans to the top of their bent. As a result, there is always room for the interested new worker. A writer can find a place, even without knowing much about film-making, and if he has a secret star he may glitter into sudden prominence even without knowing the slightest thing about film-making.

Hollywood is used to taking works of fiction in other forms and translating them into film; and for this and other reasons the talented writer does not feel encouraged to write directly for the screen. This is to be regretted because the screenplay might easily become a fascinating new form of literature, provided the studio heads acquired sufficient taste to recognize and desire literary quality. Yet there have been, there are, and there will continue to be written, screenplays of quality and sincerity—if only because of the dogged efforts of writers and directors who set themselves high goals and persist frequently against their own material interests.

There is one other circumstance which makes it difficult for the screenplay to be enjoyed as a literary form in itself: It is not and never can be a finished product. It is a step, the first and most important step, in the process of making a film. One might also say that a play is not a finished product for the theatre; yet a play relies entirely on the word; idea, character, and action are projected by means of the word; and a skillful playreader can enjoy wonderful performances within the theatre of his own imagination. The screenplay is far less a completed thing than the play, for the skilled screenwriter is thinking continuously in terms of film as well as the word. The filmwriter must be a film-maker at heart, and a film-maker thinks and lives and works in film. That is the goal, the end result—eight or ten thousand feet of negative patched together to reproduce, upon its unreeling, an illusion of a particular kind and quality. It is that illusion which the film-maker—and in this instance the filmwriter—is pursuing when he begins to gather together his first nebulous conception.

The truth is that a motion picture undergoes a series of creations. First it is a novel, a short story, or a conception in the mind of the screenwriter. That is the point of departure. Next the filmwriter takes the first plunge toward the finished negative by building the story in screenplay form. This rough draft, at least in the case of the present writer, will undergo two or three revisions, each nearer to the peculiar demands of cinema. With luck the director, who must have an equal sympathy for the drama to be unfolded, will be near at hand during the groundwork, contributing cinematic ideas here and there, many of which will not appear in the script but will be remembered or recorded in other notes to be used when the time comes.

Ordinarily, when all ideas of cinematic treatment have been unearthed and the final draft completed, the writer's work is ended and the creation of the projected film moves on into the hands of the director and other specialists; this is most unfortunate for the writer, for his education ceases in the middle of an uncompleted process. Let us, however, follow along with the writer who is able to follow the progress toward film. The second creation of the film is in its casting, which can help or hinder the designed illusion. The novelist is a fortunate artist who creates his characters out of the flesh and spirit of his own imagination; they need never be distorted by being embodied by living beings who necessarily have other traits and characteristics. But the playwright and the filmwriter must have real people to present their characters—and identity is not to be found. There have been ideal casts, but even the most perfect will alter indefinably the shape and mood and meaning of an imagined drama. Now each of the actors chosen must create his part of the film; and the sum of their parts create another phase of the film. Implicated in this is the personality of the director, who creates the film by combining (in his own style, which may not be the style of the writer) the contributions of the writer and actors.

It is at this point that a peculiar thing occurs, which must be understood to discriminate between the stage and screen. I have never seen this pointed out before, even by film-workers, and it needs to be set down: Stage and screen are entirely different media because the audience participates in quite opposite ways. The theatre—and I use the term to embrace both stage and screen—demands an audience. It is not complete without its audience and even derives much of its power from its audience. Every stage actor knows this and has experienced it. The audience identifies itself with the actor, its collective emotions rush out in sympathy or buffet against him with antipathy like an unseen electric discharge—which increases the actor's potential, so to speak, permitting him to give back his feelings with increased power, which again returns to him, like the oscillating discharge of an electric machine. It is these heightened moments that create unforgettable experiences in the theatre when the drama is great both in its literary power and in its acting. Here the relationship between the actor and the audience is direct and the intelligent actor can grow by what he experiences, just as the audience does.

Now, curiously, this phenomenon does not exist at all in the cinema; but it does exist at the stage of cinema-making we are discussing. On the stage of a film studio the actor still has an audience, though a small one: the half-hundred people who comprise "the crew"—grips, juicers, cameramen, script girl, and all the familiar others. But if he acts in such a style as to affect this audience solely he is lost, for his actual audience is miles away and they will see him only through the uncaring single eye of the camera that looks on like a tripod man from Mars. The significant thing is that at this point there is an invisible transition taking place that will break all the rules of the stage and impose new ones of the screen.

The actors are creating a film, not a stageplay, even though it appears they are making a stageplay. We are not cameras, we are living beings, and we cannot see things with the detachment of a lens. In the early days of sound-film I observed many failures because this was not understood. The action seemed good on the sound-stage, but it did not come off on the screen.

The reason is that the audience, the film-theatre audience, participates in an entirely different way with the projected images of a film. This is not so strange if we remember that a motion-picture film will give just as good a performance in an empty theatre as in a full one. It will not, of course, be so moving or so amusing to a single spectator as it will to that same spectator in a crowded theatre: Members of an audience need each other to build up laughter, sorrow, and joy. But the film is unaffected; it does not in itself participate as do the actors on a stage. It is a complete illusion, as in a dream, and the power of identification (which you must have in any form of theatre) must be between audience and the visually projected re-actor.

Unthinking people speak of the motion picture as the medium of "action"; the truth is that the stage is the medium of action while the screen is the medium of reaction. It is through identification with the person *acted upon* on the screen, and not with the person acting, that the film builds up its oscillating power with an audience. This is understood instinctively by the expert film-makers, but to my knowledge it has never been formulated. At any emotional crisis in a film, when a character is saying something which profoundly affects another, it is to this second character that the camera instinctively roves, perhaps in close-up; and it is then that the hearts of the audience quiver and open in release, or rock with laughter or shrink with pain, leap to the screen and back again in swift-growing vibrations. The great actors of the stage are actors; of the screen, re-actors.

If anyone doubts this, let him study his own emotions when viewing a good film; an experienced film-maker can do this automatically at the first showing of a film, but very likely others will have to go a second time, or check it over in mental review. I once did this with some lay friends after a showing of Noel Coward's *In Which We Serve,* and it was illuminating to find out that they had been most deeply moved by reactions, almost never by actions: the figure of a woman when she gets news her husband has been lost at sea, the face of an officer when told his wife has died. (And how cunningly Noel Coward had that officer writing a letter to his wife when the radioman entered with the news; the reaction then was continued to the point where the officer goes on deck and drops the letter into the sea, a reaction extended into action, so to speak.) In the same film one of the most affecting scenes was the final one where the captain bids good-by to the remainder of his crew; and while this appears to be action, the camera shrewdly presented it as reaction: It is the faces of the men, as they file past, that we watch, reaction to the whole experience even in their laconic voices in the weary figure of the captain.

It is because the film can, at any moment of high emotional tension, pull an entire audience close to the faces of the actors, that reaction exerts more powerful effects on the screen than on the stage. Thus, in the final climax of *The Bridge on the River Kwai* (to name a more recent film), we *see* the anguished bewilderment of the Colonel, played by Alec Guinness, as he realizes what is actually occurring; and this reaction goads him to the final enigmatic action which blows up the bridge. The intention behind this final act remains ambiguous, but the dramatic moment is the Colonel's realization of his terrible dilemma, which realization we read in his face. On the stage, this mental process would have to be projected in speech. On the screen, where nothing is so eloquent as the silent image, any utterance would be fatal.

Despite the importance of reaction in cinema, the film is regarded as a medium of action, or at least of motion, and we fail to perceive that *it is the audience which is in motion.* In the stage-theatre (the so-called legitimate theatre), each member of the audience sits in a fixed chair and is free to observe this character or that, or the ensemble; he is free to make his own montage or accumulation of impressions; in short, he sees through his own untrammeled eyes. But in the film-theatre, though he sits in a seemingly fixed chair, he can see only *through the roving eye of the camera* and must continually shift his position and point of view at the command of the camera.

Paradoxically, it is not so much the actors on the screen who are in motion as the viewer, comfortably seated and quite unaware of riding this witch's broom, which darts him in at one instant to peer into an actor's face or at some person or object at which the actor looks, the next instant jerking him far back to look at the ensemble, or racing him along in airplane, train, or car to watch the actions and reactions of actors and share their emotions and excitement. The viewer of a film is no longer an autonomous individual as in the stage-theatre. He can see only what the film-maker commands. It is this absolute control over the audience which makes the cinema essentially different from the traditional theatre and its plays. It is also, triumphantly, the very source of the art of the film.

This is not to say that the two theatre forms, stage and screen, are opposed. Stagecraft has borrowed many things (the flashback, for instance) from cinema, just as filmcraft has borrowed from the stage. And long before film was dreamed of, the Elizabethan stage, by leaving location and background to the imagination and continually shifting scenes, anticipated aspects of the technique of film. In any case, bearing these fundamental principles of film-writing and direction in mind, we initiate a film, working first with the pen and next with the camera.

This brings us to the next phase in the making of a film, or next "creation" if you prefer. I have said that a film ensues from a series of consecutive creations, which were enumerated from the first stage of concept to the point where the first recording on film is made. The director, the actors, the art director, the cameraman, the whole crew in fact, have followed after a fashion (but with many inevitable departures in which the writer, if he is fortunate, has collaborated) the final draft of the screenplay. Now you have perhaps a hundred thousand feet of film, the negative of which is safely tucked away in the laboratory while you have for your study a "work print." Now the film is in the cutting room, in a thousand strips or rolls, some strips perhaps only a few feet long, some four or five hundred. Every foot-and-a-half is a second of time in the projection room, and you do not want your finished film to be one second longer than is determined by dramatic necessity. Every good artist, every good workman, has a passion for economy; if you can do a thing in one stroke, don't use two; if a certain mood or atmosphere is essential to the illusion you are after and it requires a hundred strokes, use them. By elimination and rough assembly the cutter patches together a work print, say, fourteen thousand feet long: two or three miles of strips of film, assembled consecutively on seventeen or eighteen reels. That is the first creation of the cutter.

Now another job begins, one of the most delicate and sensitive jobs of all. Rough cutting was determined by the screenwriter, but this did not and could not include the interior cutting of the director and cameraman. Since terminology is not yet standardized in film-making, I designate the cutting of the director on the set the "montage," using a word which the Russians apply for all cutting or editing. It is determined by the style of the director, his feeling for photographed images, the way he rests the eye of the audience or gives it sudden pleasures, moving in at different angles on his scenes and characters. Had the writer attempted to anticipate the director and set down all this montage on paper, his script would have become a useless mess, for this interior cutting cannot be determined precisely (though many attempt to do so) before arriving on the set. The manner of shooting and handling the camera must be guided by spontaneous feeling and by discoveries made on the set. I for one have no patience with the growing method of having every camera shot sketched beforehand so that director, cameraman, and actors can work by rote. It destroys that spontaneity of feeling which is the essence of film art; though of course many films are so unimportant that it does not matter how they are shot: they never were alive at any moment.

To continue following our film through to its finish, you now have a rough assembly which is far overlength, the cutting of which was largely determined by the script and direction. But this is only a provisional arrangement. Everything depends on the final cutting, elimination, and rearrangement. And the only compass to guide you in this final orchestration of images is your own feeling. The final test is to project the film on the screen and see how the arrangement you have made affects you. By this time you have grown weary of every foot of the film but you doggedly keep your feeling fresh as the only touchstone, until you have wearily said, "That's the best we can make of it." And I promise you disappointment in every film, for it is far removed from the perfection of imagination, as is everything that is realized.

Yet you have not finished with this scratched and tattered work print, which now looks as tired as yourself. There are two final stages, sound and music recording, and finally the re-recording of the whole thing. Sound is a magic element, and part of your design as a screenwriter or director has been the effect of sound. In the case of *This Land Is Mine,* which was directed by a great film-maker, Jean Renoir, one of the focal points of the drama was a railroad yard, and as we could not shoot the action in an actual railroad yard we determined to create it largely by sound. We spent endless days gathering sound tracks and trying to orchestrate our sounds as carefully as if they were music. And finally came the scoring of the music itself, not a great deal of it but every bar important: choosing Mendelssohn here, Méhul there, original composition for the rest, and getting it re-recorded in a harmonious whole.

At last you have, say, nine or ten thousand feet of image film and a second sound film of the same length synchronized to the split second. Every frame of both films is numbered, corresponding with the thousands of feet of negative in the laboratory. You send your final work prints to the laboratory, the negative is cut, the sound track printed alongside—and you receive your first composite print. And, if the composite print checks, your work is finished and the negative is shipped, ready for countless prints to be made and released through the theatres of the world. This is what you set out to make—or rather help to make—when you began writing your rough draft of a screenplay. And this is what you had to keep in mind all the wearisome while.

2

. . . screen plays are . . . not complete works in themselves; they are blueprints of projected films. Many factors may have intervened to make the finished films different from the designed illusion, for better or worse.

The most noticeable feature of a skillful screenplay is its terseness and bareness. This is because the eye is not there, the eye which fills and enriches. Nor does the screenwriter waste time with much descriptive matter or detailing of photographic moods. These have all been discussed at length with the director, art director, and others. It is the writer's job to invent a story in terms of cinema or to translate an existing story into terms of cinema. He creates an approximate continuity of scenes and images, suggesting cinematic touches where he can. He will write "close-up" of a character without setting down the most important thing, which is what that character is feeling during that close-up, because the text clearly shows what the character is supposed to be experiencing. The director will take care of that. If he is an artist, the director will submit the actor to that experience while photographing the close-up, by playing the actual scene out of range of the camera.

Writing for the screen, if long practiced, also seduces one to write dialogue in a synoptic fashion, which may show itself to the eye when printed on a page, but should never reveal itself to the ear when spoken from the screen. Stage dialogue, no matter how wonderful in quality, cannot be directly shifted to the screen; it must be condensed, synopsized. The reason is obvious: on the stage the actor depends for projection upon the word; on the screen he relies upon visual projection. And it is hard to describe visual projection in a screenplay; that must be left to the director and cast. . . .

. . . almost everyone who is seriously interested in the cinema has seen *The Informer* on the screen, and as the film projects the screenplay with great fidelity I am prompted by Mr. Gassner to explain the method by which I translated Mr. O'Flaherty's novel into the language of film. In 1935 this was in a certain sense an experimental film; some new method had to be found by which to make the psychological action photographic. At that time I had not yet clarified and formulated for myself the principles of screenwriting, and many of my ideas were arrived at instinctively. I had an able mentor as well as collaborator in the person of John Ford and I had begun to catch his instinctive feeling about film. I can see now that I sought and found a series of symbols to make visual the tragic psychology of the informer, in this case a primitive man of powerful hungers. The whole action was to be played out in one foggy night, for the fog was symbolic of the groping primitive mind; it is really a mental fog in which he moves and dies. A poster offering a reward for information concerning Gypo's friend became the symbol of the evil idea of betrayal, and it blows along the street, following Gypo; it will not leave him alone. It catches on his leg and he kicks it off. But still it follows him, and he sees it like a phantom in the air when he unexpectedly comes upon his fugitive friend.

So it goes all through the script; some of the symbolism is obvious, much of it concealed except from the close observer. The officer uses a stick when he pushes the blood money to Gypo at headquarters, symbolic of contempt. The informer encounters a blind man in the dark fog outside and grips his throat in sudden guilt. The blind man is a symbol of the brute conscience, and Gypo releases him when he discovers the man cannot see. But as Gypo goes on to drown his conscience in drink, the tapping of the blind man's stick follows him; we hear it without seeing the blind man as Gypo hears his guilt pursuing him in his own soul. Later, when he comes face to face with his conscience for a terrifying moment, he tries to buy it off—by giving the blind man a couple of pounds, a lordly sum. . . . But I shall not continue this account of a screenplay that cannot be presented in this book. Sufficient to say that the method of adaptation in this instance was by a cumulative symbolism, to the very last scene where Gypo addresses the carven Christ, by which the psychology of a man could be made manifest in photographic terms. In this case I believe the method was successful. I might add that I transferred the action of the drama from its original, rather special setting to a larger and more dramatic conflict which had national connotations. Whether that was any gain I do not know. Size of conflict in itself I hold to be unimportant. It is the size of characters within a conflict and how deeply they are probed that matters.

So much for an adaptation. For the problems of writing an *original* screenplay I can only rely on my personal experiences. It is not easy to trace the origin of a story. It is easier to say that a work of fiction happens. But that is not exact, for a story comes into existence because of some inner necessity of the individual. Every human being contains creative energy; he wants to make something. A man may make a chair, or a pair of shoes, a masterpiece of painting, or a pulp-magazine story; precisely what he makes is dictated by his imagination, temperament, experience, and training. But the act of creation is dictated by desire. I should imagine this runs through the universe as a law, since it is so with man, and man is a part of the universe. If the Supreme Will desires to build a Universe, the Universe will "happen." It is all a matter of the degree of intensity of desire. A storyteller is passionately interested in human beings and their endless conflicts with their fates, and he is filled with desire to make some intelligible arrangement out of the chaos of life, just as the chairmaker desires to make some useful and beautiful arrangement out of wood. Frustrate those creative desires in man, and his forces will be turned toward destruction; for energy cannot remain unexpended, it is not static, it must swing one way or another.

Stories for the purpose of entertainment alone are commonplace fiction and can be redeemed only by a dazzling style, a sheer delight in the materials of storytelling, a touch of the poet. The cinema is only in its infancy as an art form, and its usual fate so far has been to be used only for entertainment and making money. Because it is a very costly medium it will continue to be employed for making money until money ceases to be the great desire of the people of the world. Most motion pictures are mere entertainment, and accordingly the screenwriter can work with only half of himself; his satisfaction must usually be in artistry of manner, skill in the way he accomplishes his work, without much regard for the content of the film. For this reason the story of serious intention can rarely be written within a film studio; and for this reason serious writers in other fields, novelists and dramatists, have given great aid to the development of the cinema. For the powers-that-be will buy the film rights of a serious novel if it seems to have enough readers, and though the contents of the novel are sometimes perverted by film censorship or bad taste, enough remains to make a notable motion picture. But the screenwriter who desires to make an original story has no readers, at least not for the projected story. If the story proposes to make a serious statement beyond mere entertaining, it will seem off the beaten track and the writer will very likely meet opposition. It is for this reason and this reason alone that so few stories of any account *originate* within Hollywood. In France, before World War II, the film-makers were largely their own entrepreneurs and for this reason produced many brilliant original works. They were storytellers functioning freely in the new medium of film.

Nevertheless the serious film-writer cannot resign himself to Hollywood's barriers against original work designed for the screen. The average Hollywood entrepreneur is an intelligent man, and it is up to writers and directors to prove to him that films which probe into the chaos of life can be successful. John Ford made *The Informer* in spite of studio resistance; even after its completion it was held to be a failure and a waste of money by certain entrepreneurs. But the film did go out and make a profit. There *was* an audience for the realistic film. In spite of this and other instances I will say in all fairness that usually the studio heads have been right and the film-makers wrong—because usually the film-makers have not measured up to their task and their responsibilities when granted freedom. They have not measured up or they have wanted both money and freedom, which are incompatible. It is an axiom that no one will pay you to be a free artist. You are hired for profit—that is common sense. Very well, then, you must stop working for salary; you must devote yourself to the task in hand as do the novelist and dramatist, and only be recompensed if the film makes a profit. Economically I believe the writer and director will fare even better with this arrangement than under the salary system. Spiritually they will become whole men and work with integrity.

I have not attempted to explain the secrets of screenwriting—because there are no secrets. There are certain prescribed forms, but the forms are not final. Others will come along and do better work as we come to understand more clearly the peculiar demands of cinema. Meanwhile, those people who may become interested in screenwriting as a vocation must study the best examples of screenplays available and then have a try at it themselves. I do not touch on technical jargon, such as *fade, lap dissolve, dolly,* or *pan,* because they are quite unnecessary to the craft. And no matter where you write them into your script, the completed film will make its own demands in the cutting room and very likely change your imagined plan. This terminology can safely be ignored; it is merely a convenience.

We try to formulate a classical form for the cinema but there are no final rules. Film continuity can be as broken and erratic as a dream, if it is a potent dream and by some inner need requires that sort of continuity. There are really no rules, in spite of what Hollywood will tell you. A film in its continuity is a stream of images, and if they combine into an exciting, intelligible whole you have accomplished your purpose. Most film technique today is very imperfect, as we are still groping for the pure form. The cinema is still a giant in chains, and a giant who has not even yet stood up and shaken his chains. Those chains are censorship, commercialism, monopoly, specialization—all the faults that are indigenous to industrial society and not just characteristic of the cinema. If control of film production should fall into the hands of government, any government, the old chains will be struck off only to be replaced by heavier ones. And because of the potent propaganda effect of film, that is a danger. No art, including the wonderful medium of sound film, can serve one set of ideas—it must be free or perish.

In conclusion, I hope that in sketching the successive steps of making a film I have not underrated the importance of the screenplay. It is, in my opinion, pre-eminent in the field of film-making. It is the writer who is the dreamer, the imaginer, the shaper. He works in loneliness with nebulous materials, with nothing more tangible than paper and a pot of ink; and his theatre is within his mind. He must generate phantoms out of himself and live with them until they take on a life of their own and become, not types, but characters working out their own destinies. If the ultimate film is to have any significant content, throwing some new glint of light on life, it is the writer who will have to create it. Yet it is the director who has always dominated the field and will no doubt continue to dominate it, for various good reasons. It is the director who must *realize* the imagined people on film, who must know all the technological processes, and command the extravagantly costly tools of film art. Writing costs are negligible by comparison. The film-writer can afford to bow to the director; and if it be one of the world's few great directors, he can do so with pride and gratitude. For there are few satisfactions to match seeing a story you have created, or even re-created in terms of film, come to a powerful life on the screen—a new creation with all the writing washed invisibly away.

Richard Schickel
THE MOVIES ARE NOW HIGH ART

Richard Schickel, film critic for Life *magazine and author of numerous books on cinema, examines today's moviegoer. His findings and observations reveal much, not only about the moviegoer but about the nation as well. No longer simply entertainment for the masses, the film is today playing a vital role "in the shaping of our century's culture."*

CULTURAL cliché: "Movies are the central art of our time." Or the most relevant of the arts. Or the one that most efficiently reveals ourselves to ourselves. Or, more simply, the one we like best.

All rise . . .

Be seated.

This Sunday's sermon attempts to analyze this particular tidbit of the conventional wisdom, and it begins, as all good sermons should, with a *mea culpa.* Like everyone who makes his living around movies, I have indulged in this particular form of egocentricity; we all like to feel that we're operating at the red-hot center of things. Indeed, together with the *New Leader*'s John Simon, I recently edited a little symposium* in which a dozen film critics addressed themselves to the question of film's centrality to modern experience and, not surprisingly, the majority of us more or less unquestioningly agreed that film was The Thing. To be sure, Newsweek's Joseph Morgenstern suggested that it would probably continue to take second place to "the mother art of weaponry." And the redoubtable Andrew Sarris of The Village Voice raised some good caveats, pointing out the pot scene was better reflected in pop music than in pop movies, that a cinematic equivalent of "Pale Fire" is an impossibility, that TV has taken over many of the social func-

* [Editors' note: This symposium appears on pages 293–312]

tions the movies used to perform. But most of us went along with the proposition, and it is probably right that we did. It would be a poor lot of critics who believed the art with which they perforce live is an insignificant or meaningless thing. Only the masochist—or a Dwight Macdonald—engages himself critically and regularly with an art for which he has no fundamental affection or at least respect.

Still, we are obviously prejudiced witnesses, and I am beginning to wonder if this prejudice—necessary to us if we are to maintain our sanity as we trudge from one screening room to another in midtown Manhattan—is necessary or sensible or desirable for the audience. I am beginning to think that the movies now bear a heavier weight of cultural ambition—and anxiety—than they were intended to bear. The very notion that they are as important to us as the centrality doctrine implies raises our expectations, as we approach each film, to heights unprecedented even a decade ago, which means that the letdown, when the film fails to live up to those expectations—as inevitably most will—is all the greater.

Why, one wonders, have movies—humble, once-despised movies—become so important to us? The beginning of the answer lies, I think, in carefully defining that little word, "us." Who are we, those of us who care so much about the movies? Well, a recent survey taken at the behest of the Motion Picture Association of America discovered that some 50 per cent of the movie audience is under 24 and that 75 per cent of it is under 40. The moguls also discovered that the regulars, the people who go to the movies once a month or more, tend to be college students and college graduates. And it is reasonable to guess that, had they pressed their inquiry a little further, they would have found that among high school kids it is the ones who plan to go on to college who most regularly flick out.

Now, of course, from the vantage point of a writer for this magazine, or one of its readers, that means that everybody who is anybody is going to the movies—our friends, our co-workers, our kids. But really it only seems that way. The fact is that for the majority of Americans moviegoing is not even a peripheral, let alone a central, concern. Back before that great watershed date in our cultural history, 1948 (when television networking began), that was probably not the case. In that year some 3.4 billion admissions to the movies were sold. Since 1963 the number of tickets sold annually has stabilized around 1.1 billion—and this in a period of population growth. The industry's prosperity, thanks to increased ticket prices and the sale and production of films for TV, is now booming, but the fact is that it sells only 21 million tickets a week, meaning that all the movies on view in such a period attract an audience no greater than that of the weekly episode of a television show that is close to the peril point in the ratings.

So it turns out that Mr. Nixon's army of silent citizens—the factory worker and the farmer, the aged and the middle-aged, the people whose incomes range from poor to middle-middle class—besides grousing about taxes, worrying about law and order and flirting with the Wallace fantasy complete their misery by generally shunning such solace as the movies might provide them. Typically, however, John Q. Silent takes a dim view of what he hears is going on these days down at the old Bijou, which a few years ago was renamed The Art—about the time they ripped out the popcorn counter and replaced it with an espresso bar. Sex and Violence, sex and violence, that is what is going on down there. And they call it culture.

O.K. Movies aren't movies any more. They are the playthings of The New Class, those who are custodians (or, perhaps, prisoners) of the technostructure. This is, I think, no small point, for it means there has been a fundamental reordering of film's place and function in our society. In the beginning, in the days of the nickelodeon, movies—because of their brevity, their cheapness and their silence—were truly an art of the masses and, as experience if not art, truly central to the lives of many people. They imposed no language barrier, no intellectual hurdles not easily surmountable by the illiterate (or the merely uncultivated), whether he was child, immigrant or rube. Even the addition of sound did not fundamentally change that basic relationship between film and audience.

As we have seen, it required television—free, damnably convenient, even less challenging than the typical pre-1948 film—to break up the longstanding love affair between the movie medium and its traditional audience. To put it simply, the new medium freed the older one from its thrall to the 12- or 13-year-old mentality for which, in the past, the moguls cheerfully admitted they aimed. Though it seems, on the face of it, preposterous to regard any form of art or entertainment that attracts over a billion customers a year as anything less than a mass medium, that is precisely what movies have become: Something Less than a Mass Medium. Indeed, it seems to me that everything that is not television is, given that medium's potency, Something Less than a Mass Medium today.

What, then, are the movies? Is there some positive definition of them? I think they are best defined in terms of a process rather than in a single word or phrase. Film is a form that is now about halfway toward creating a conscious definition of itself as an art. It has yet to sever completely its ties to its folkish past. It has yet to fasten firmly to its future, which is, alas, as a high art, a thing to be savored more or less exclusively by what will pass as an élite—a new class—in the quite radically different society we are, willy-nilly and without malice aforethought, building in this country.

Now, two quick explanations must be appended to the foregoing. First, there is nothing unique about the development of movies in the direction I have outlined. All the arts—poetry, prose fiction, the graphic arts, music, the dance—had popular roots and developed, finally, into élite affairs over fairly long historical spans. The only difference between them and the movies is that the latter are an industrial art born in an age of rapidly accelerating industrial change, which means that they are going to complete this evolution much more quickly than the other arts did. It has taken them only a little more than a half-century to reach the mid-point in this development; it should take them no more than another 25 years to complete it.

Second, the élite to which films will soon be more or less exclusively directed will, obviously, be much larger, much less homogeneous, than any previous cultural élite the world has ever known. It will be an élite less sure of itself, less intensively educated, more panicky about its status than any we have ever known. But an élite it will be, for as journalist William A. McWhirter has put it, "The world is not so much divided between classes, races and religions as it is between those who *know* and those who don't; between Them and Us."

That little word again. For "us" the movies are, comparatively speaking, an easy art to appreciate. Even the very greatest films require only a couple of hours to consume, to get yourself in a position where you can claim to have "seen" them. The great novels, in contrast, demand far greater commitments of time in order merely to claim that one has "read" them. They also demand, as do the other traditional arts, a heavy investment in effortful study, not only of the texts themselves but of the vast body of critical literature that surrounds them. Filmic literacy is much more easily and pleasurably acquired; indeed, a fairly good grasp of film techniques is to be obtained more easily than is a good technical understanding of music, dance or even painting. In short, movies are an almost ideal medium for half-baked intellectuals and, the population and educational explosions being what they are, we are very shortly going to have more of them than any other class of people. If the notion that the film is the central art of our time has any validity, it lies simply in the fact that this New Class is the most significant socioeconomic group of our time. They are the great consumers, not only of culture but of all the other doodads of affluence—notably such items as foreign food, foreign cars, foreign travel.

And foreign movies. In this, they recapitulate the special kind of provincialism of the wives and daughters of the industrial statesmen (or robber barons, as we used to know them) who established the institutions of our formal culture in the late 19th and early 20th centuries and who would not buy a painting or go to a concert unless the artist were European or, at the least, European-trained. The value of the

Continental cachet has largely disappeared in the traditional arts, but, for the moment, it is very potent in film.

There is no question that much of the interest in foreign films is esthetically justifiable. Those that have been released here have generally been more interesting, more liberated and liberating, than the best American products. It should, however, be remembered that we have seen only the crest of sundry new waves; we are rarely allowed to sport in the troughs, except, of course, when it comes to exploitable sex films, which are to our time what French postcards were to other epochs.

On the other hand, one observes a lack of critical spirit in our approach to many of these films, a certain faddishness—even cultishness—in the enthusiasm for them. Moreover, there is a great lack of historical perspective in our appreciation of the European film. The directors who created the French New Wave and the young Czech directors who have lately so excited us have been quite careful to note their debt to the great American directors whose work has profoundly influenced them; but, excepting the *auteur* critics, who hold that the director is the author of a film, few in this country have responded by taking a serious interest in these men or in the younger American directors who might, in time, achieve a comparable status in world cinema. In fact, it generally remains for the critics associated with the Parisian magazine, Cahiers du Cinéma, to point out to us the merits of people like Nicholas Ray, Don Siegel and Sam Peckinpah, which does not seem to help them get work.

Of course, these three, along with many other equally underrated American directors, are more or less committed to genre films, and Hollywood, though it continues to turn out Westerns and crime films and musicals, no longer has its heart in these matters. The New Yorker's Pauline Kael recently and rightly observed that since blacklisting and the breakup of the big studios (whose B pictures were the training ground for young directors) we have lost several generations of young moviemaking talent, men who were not perhaps destined for greatness, but for the kind of professional competence that is the bedrock on which a vital film industry is built. Unable or unwilling to tell good from bad among the European directors, afraid of entrusting large investments to young American directors, the industry has turned to what Miss Kael calls "the mediocrities and the bunglers of England"—a nation whose culture has always seemed very classy to us, but whose filmmakers (although they may not quite be "the sad joke" she says they have always been) are certainly joyless, imitative squares and have been (with a few great exceptions) since the earliest days of the movies. To hire these people to superintend the production of films on classic *American* themes is preposterous on the face of it, especially when someone like Peckinpah has not made a theatrical film in almost four years.

Miss Kael attributes this state of affairs to the "classic acumen" of our producers, and that is certainly a factor. But there is, I think, more to it than that. The people now in charge in Hollywood are, like their basic audience, members of the New Class. As such, they are bright, bright, bright in their shallow little ways. They sense that they—that we—have lost something, some set of commonly held, virtually unconscious beliefs that helped the individual to define himself, that prevented the society from flying apart at the seams.

That something was recently defined by psychoanalyst Rollo May as "the myth of the mythless society." Like all the nations of the Western world since the 18th century, the United States has been energized by a belief in progress, both personal and social, through rationalism and individualism. However, as May is by no means the first to observe, both of these beliefs are, today, in a state of crisis, and nowhere is that crisis more deeply felt than among the New Class, which, of course, prides itself on getting news of this kind first. As a result all of our culture is in a state of anxiety that borders on the frantic. There is a legitimate feeling that none of the traditional cultural forms—including the traditional film genres—truly reflects the unpleasant day-to-day psychological reality that all of us experience. It is for this reason that we have turned, rather desperately, to Warhol and McLuhan, to "Futz" and "Hair," to Happenings and light shows. Never in history—at least in American history—has each sneeze, cough and burp of the avant-garde been so earnestly and intensively studied by so many for (*a*) clues to cultural salvation and (*b*) portents of a happier future and (*c*) escape. It is for this reason that we are presently putting such heavy pressure on the movies to grow up, to get serious, to be art.

But, as social critic David T. Bazelon pointed out some years ago, serious moviegoing has always involved a conflict "between one's desire to dream and one's desire to have a firmer relationship with high culture." In other words, there is a part of us that remains a child before the larger-than-life figures on the screen, figures that, in the darkness, inevitably have a magical, mythical quality about them. There is also a part of us that resents this reversion, that sternly calls us back to duty, "to relevance."

Now, back in the days when we really believed in the myth of the mythless society, there actually were, according to Dr. May, two integrating myths that had a peculiar hold on us—the one which dealt with the frontiersman and the one which dealt with the Horatio Alger figure. They were, if you will, a country myth and a city myth, and each figure, in his way, embodied those qualities of individualism and rationalism in which all of us held an implicit, unspoken faith. Much has been written, of course, about the movie Westerner and the movie gangster (who was merely Alger's boy grown up and grown rancid because no one else believed, as he still did, in really free enterprise). When these two characters were very well done, as they so often (indeed, routinely) were in the films of the nineteen-thirties and forties, conflict between the desire to dream and the desire for relevance was elegantly resolved by the simple expedient of satisfying both. These were "the good old-fashioned *movie* movies" that sentimental critics are always mourning for these days (and which, thank God, they still occasionally find). These were, as Bazelon said, "the heart of movies as cultural events [and] as release of dreams."

And now, I think, the heart has gone out of them—and out of our comedies and musicals which also revolved around familiar archetypes. Some producers try desperately to revivify the old forms, mostly by adding strong doses of very explicit sex and violence to them. (I am convinced that the outcry against S-and-V is an expression of cultural shock, not genuine moral outrage, by people who just don't expect to find such material in genre films where, not long ago, even a discreet kiss between cowpoke and schoolmarm was frowned upon and where death, when it came, was a bloodless "drilling.") Occasionally, we get an attempt at self-conscious purification of these forms, the sort of arty reactionaryism that made "Shane" and "High Noon" middle-brow bywords in the postwar years, when, in fact, anybody who really cares about the Western could name a half-dozen films (including, currently, "The Stalking Moon") that were considerably more interesting variations on the standard themes. Most often these days, one sees campy parodies of all the genres because, very simply, most of us simply can't believe in them anymore or, at the very least, don't want to be caught seeming to believe in them.

The desperation of movie people confronted by this cultural phenomenon is beautifully exemplified by the new Kirk Douglas gangster film, "The Brotherhood," which the star caused to be produced under the direction of the heavy-handed Martin Ritt. Its ineptitude would do credit to perfidious Albion, but there is a special kind of moral blindness about it that I found intriguing. Douglas plays an old-style Mafia hood, running an assortment of labor and, one assumes, vice and protection rackets in the crude, small-timey way of his forefathers. He is still content to have his gunmen take care of stool pigeons in the old, vulgar fashion—they are seen taking one for a ride to the city dump and, when he is bumped off, stuffing the corpse's mouth with a symbolic canary. "No, no, no, Kirk," cry the leaders of his gangland family, "you don't understand. Times have changed. We're going into electronics, defense contracts, the big time." He turns out to be stubborn, unable to shift with the times and, ultimately, he must receive, from his own brother, the kiss of death.

Clearly, there is little to choose morally between the old-style and the new-style mobster. But the movie does choose. It actually gets very sentimental, almost lyrical, about the type Douglas portrays. In effect, it is a last hurrah for the *little* Caesars of our movie past, nostalgia for the small-scale, free-enterprise crook of our movie childhoods now invoked (simple-mindedly, to be sure) to divert us from his true nature, a diversion that no maker of the much more humble progenitors of "The Brotherhood" would have thought necessary or wise.

What is comes to is this: we have run out of myths. In the early forties, Albert Camus wrote: "The whole effort of Western art is to provide our imagination with types. . . . In desperation, it has invented the movie hero." But now the movies are full of antiheroes, and the institution of movie stardom, which was based on a system of heroic typology, is in total decline. Dr. May tells us, as many have, that the preferred life-style of our new age emphasizes cooperation, subjectivity and collectivism, and who can doubt that he is right. And who is genius enough to make a satisfactory mythical hero out of a cooperative, subjective central figure whose aim is a harmonious collective society? Perhaps it can be done, and surely there will continue to be an atavistic place for the old stories and characters in television, which is aimed at those primitive souls who still think that we live in a highly competitive, individualistic and more or less rational society, poor dears.

There are, of course, citizens of our world who might make very suitable mythic heroes for movies—revolutionary leaders, for example, foreign and domestic, black and white, young and old, though it is possible that they represent threats to the *status quo* too potent for comfortable assimilation into fiction. In any case, it is certain—as films like Jules Dassin's "Up-Tight" prove—that there is very little intelligent understanding of the type among professional filmmakers and thus small hope of their soon becoming the source of a new mythic richness in film. It is also possible that over a longish period of time an interaction between the underground and the aboveground moviemakers will produce a style of film-making so radically different from any we have known up to now that none of what we have been discussing will be germane. That, however, seems unlikely. The avant-garde produces a very abstract form of film, a thing of lovely surfaces, and stylistically exciting, but with none of the psychological resonance of either truly great art or, oddly, of the best popular movies.

For the moment, one imagines, the balance in our films will remain tipped in favor of our yearning for a firmer relation with high culture, away from the desire to dream—although Bazelon argues persuasively that the desire to dream at the movies remains very much alive. The audience that snobbishly refuses to attend American movies but goes religiously "to every lousy French film" is, he says, also looking for a dream—"It's just that you're not dreaming about this country." The implication—that we can no longer live psychologically in the United States—is interesting and more than a little frightening, and although this makes it very difficult for an excellent movie like the recent "Pretty Poison" to find its audience here, I do think that over the long run this, too, shall pass.

Meantime, if the new, more or less restricted film audience has yet to achieve the connection with high culture that they want and seem to need on a more than intermittent basis, there nevertheless has been one substantial gain in the content of our movies. They are, finally, beginning to examine, with an unprecedented degree of truthfulness, with a fine eye for accuracy of detail in setting and decor, a fine ear for language, some of the common issues of middle-class life. This year "Pretty Poison," "Petulia," "Rachel, Rachel" and, most notable of all, John Cassavetes's "Faces," have all, one way and another, plunged exploratory scalpels into the quivering flesh of the very culture that now supports the movies. All are about bourgeois yearnings—for love, for existential meaning—in the midst of affluence. All deal with various attempts to trick shallow life into making some sort of satisfying sense.

It seems to me, too, that since post-industrial societies are so much alike, we are not always escaping America when we go to see a foreign film. "Blow-Up," for instance, was a profound metaphorical examination of how technology as art fails us when we confront the timeless, universal mysteries of existence. Ingmar Bergman, whose stubborn insistence on making very difficult movies has rendered him unfashionable with the in-crowd lately, deals brilliantly in his latest films with the silencing effect of modern life on the humanistically oriented artist. Godard keeps probing in his infuriating, fascinating way at the half-formed revolutionary spirit of middle-class youth the world over.

In short, though we may have lost something quite valuable since movies became the "central art" of the "central people" of our time, we have also gained something. Or, more properly, we have gained a potential (still too often unrealized) for a greater, more direct understanding of the quality of our inner lives and of the external world of both things and ideas which we inhabit.

That is—to re-emphasize my basic point—some of us have made a gain. There is a part of me that dislikes and distrusts this business of taking over what was once an art (or was it, then, merely a medium?) that belonged to everyone and making it into a semiprivate preserve. To put it very simply, the movies have their historical roots in the mass, and anything that is cut off from its roots is in danger. The experience of such a detachment may be exhilarating, but the risks should not be minimized.

To take just one example, whole generations learned to love movies in their preteen years, when they represented a very special kind of escape, when they were among the first, and the few, experiences one was allowed to engage in alone, free of parental supervision. In those days, when all movies were allegedly made for that conventionalized 12-year-old mentality, that was perfectly feasible. Now, people find it impossible to allow their young children such freedom, and the kids are condemned to the generally wretched films made expressly for them and to a handful of more expensive—but generally no better—pictures that are advertised for family consumption. Worse, the movies have now formalized this style of censorship and, under the new classification system, theater managers will become moral cops, barring kids under 17 from "X" category films. It is hard to see how, under these ground rules, a new generation will regard films as a "central" experience; absence may make the heart grow fonder, but one must first experience the presence for that cliché really to work.

What it all comes to is this: the first art (or quasi-art or presumptive art or whatever it is) that was entirely the creation of modern industrial society, the only art in living memory that operated, however crudely, on the basis of a kind of participatory democracy (with tickets the equivalent of ballots) is in the process of exchanging its broad-based democratic status for a more prestigious social and intellectual status, and one must measure the obvious gains that are accruing to it against the less obvious but no less real losses implicit in its new role. No one who believed, however fleetingly, however warily, in the movies' potential as a genuine art of the masses, one which appealed to all classes, one which could serve an invaluable function as a kind of social cement, can be anything but saddened by the alienation that very large numbers of people now feel about the movies, an alienation that is imperfectly expressed by the protests against sex and violence now so common. This shrinkage in the audience, this slippage in the general interest in movies, the indignant, hurt and puzzled tone that pervades the letters any critic with a large audience receives, are all cause for alarm.

One is tempted to fear for the future of theatrical film, especially with cable television, pay TV and the possibility of home film libraries which can be played through a television set now technologically feasible and therefore inevitable. Movies truly will not be movies anymore if we do not share them in public, in large groups before a large screen in theaters. We do not need more socially fragmenting experiences; we do need more integrative ones.

And yet the fear is controllable. There is—at least for a sizable number of people—something mysteriously fascinating and basically resistant to analysis about the attraction of film. Andrew Sarris put it very nicely in that symposium of ours: "I happen to derive more pleasure from film than from any other art, but that is *my* sensibility speaking, not necessarily modern sensibility. I enjoyed movies before they were intellectually fashionable, and I shall enjoy them long after they have gone out of fashion. I can no more renounce movies than literary men can renounce books."

Precisely. As he says, there is no way of knowing how history will regard the role of films in the shaping of our century's culture. All one knows, finally, is that for some of us, no matter what our general views about the broad trends in film and filmmaking, the movies are the only game in town; and if all they were showing in the theaters was Warhol's "Sleep," we would probably drag ourselves to see it, mourning the while for the good old days and wondering whatever became of Randolph Scott. I suspect—no, I am absolutely certain—that there will always be a few million of us around. Enough to form some kind of audience for some kind of movies. For us, they will always be the central art of our time.

Walter Kerr
THE MOVIES ARE BETTER THAN THE THEATER

Highly influential drama critic for the New York Times, *Walter Kerr is the author of numerous books on the theater. In this article he compares the intrinsic nature of the stage and of film and reaches some surprising conclusions.*

A MAN can be loyal to the theater and still tell himself the truth: nowadays he goes to the theater out of loyalty and to the movies out of interest. In the theater he knows exactly what to expect; he hopes he will get a good example of the expected, but he does not really look to be electrified. At the movies he has a fair, lively hope of having his eyes pop.

And this is so, now, for those of us who have been around for a while —not just for all of those buzzing arts majors in the incredibly equipped universities, clamoring for time with the camera equipment, time with the projection machines, time with the viewers and splicers. It is true for those of us for whom it shouldn't be true: those who have lived through the earliest, never-quite-to-be-recaptured excitements of films when Chaplin and Keaton and Ernst Lubitsch were yearly promises, lived through René Clair and the whole discovery of the European sound film, lived through Hitchcock when Hitchcock was something to be accompanied by popcorn rather than a devout and dazzling running commentary by Truffaut. *Our* appetite should be sated; in point of fact we can remember where most of the new techniques came from; film should not seem so new, the theater not so threatened.

But there we are in one or another art house that is no longer called an art house, safely past the vending machines or in more discreet environments the free coffee, straight up in our seats built for lounging, agog with discovery. The film seems to skid at us, take us off tracks we thought we knew, whistle past our ears dangerously, squirt color at us with a spray-gun and erase it before it has stuck, stare at us in long silences that suggest too much light has been let in. We are jarred. We are alerted. And we jump. It is in the theater that we fish for mints to pass the time.

How come? Film is way out front these days, I think, for a very simple reason. It knows that it is film. The theater doesn't know that it is theater.

The strongest sensation I have whenever I go to a new movie is one of fingers. Fingers holding up a short, curled stretch of celluloid near a naked light bulb. Fingers pressing film into the sprockets of a cutter and bearing down sharply with one thumb. Fingers running like a tarantula's leg across racks from which 8 or 10 or 20 strips of film can be snatched and simply hurled at one another, hoping the glue holds. Fingers, not story, making the rhythm. Fingers flinging blank or black snips of leader at us to remind us that it is all patched together, fingers so enamored of the *work* they do—and the material they play with—that they want us to share the crazy joy of the work and the tactile pleasure of the material. Fingers tampering with the film, running it at too fast or too slow speeds or suddenly turning it a solid blue, to call explicit attention to the fact that film is manipulable.

Narrative is rarely in our eye. We are three-quarters through "A Man and a Woman" before we realize that until now the narrative has contained no thread and therefore wasn't really a narrative at all. Defined character is not much in our eye. "Persona" is about two women who are each other. The film opens and closes with utterly empty celluloid churning through the machine; between these two points images are impressed upon the celluloid but we are to remember that these are only impresses and that the celluloid is by nature empty, open; the film has something to do with the proposition that the women *are* film. Sustained atmosphere is not in our eye, as it always was with the old fade-out, fade-in picture; the faster atmosphere can be reversed or in some way violated the better. A finger is in our eye.

But montage has always been with us, hasn't it? Indeed, montage—the rapid juxtaposition of separate pieces of film and separate camera angles to make a single intelligible mosaic—was the sacred cow of the earliest film exegetes. Nothing new here to account for such startling vitality. Long ago Eisenstein assembled shocking counterpoints for everyone to admire and virtually no one to imitate. If we find the unannounced juggling of five bands of time the only thing of real interest in "Two for the Road" (the film is five separate journeys through time treated as a single journey without respect for time) why should we find it interesting at all? D. W. Griffith kept four bands of time hopping in "Intolerance," putting them neck to neck in the final reels, and earned no more than apathy and parody for his pains. The movies have been here before and not been so lucky.

There is a difference. Griffith failed with "Intolerance" because he failed to interest the audience in the film as film. He wasn't even trying to do that. This was a new way of doing things, all right, rubbing-ancient Babylon up against Model-T Fords. But the thing being done, the essential thing, was old: Griffith was primarily trying to interest the audience in history as history, in spectacle as spectacle, in morality as morality. There was no necessary relationship between the material at hand and the material *in* hand. The cutting in no way controlled, or even struck up a special relationship with the content. The whole thing could have been done as an outdoor pageant somewhere, under religious auspices, and Griffith finally managed to recoup some of his losses by extracting one time-thread from his kaleidoscope and releasing it as a straightforward, strictly sequential, narrative (a trick that could not possibly be pulled off with "Two for the Road"; that film either stands on its fingering of time or falls altogether).

Even Eisenstein, who has surely played some part in reawakening filmmakers to the stuff they hold in their hands and whose individual images were often so brilliant that they are still locked in our skulls (the woman with the smashed eyeglasses, the dead horse slipping through the slowly opening bridge), was not fundamentally concerned with making the audience conscious of film. *He* was conscious of film; they were to become conscious of historical necessity, of horror, of a people. His audiences were in no way in the laboratory with the film editor; they were on the Odessa steps.

The montages we admire most did not dictate the over-all shape, or any part of the meaning, of the film; they were way stops, stunning small explosions, in an essentially linear document. They were, in effect, absorbed into an experience not very much different from the experience of reading a novel or seeing a play. They were stylistic devices, not the control panel itself. Film had not yet insisted on growing the meaning out of the medium. It insisted less—if at all—as Hollywood took charge in the twenties and thirties. Instead of pointing a finger at the finger that was playing with slices of life as though they were so many slices of celluloid (because they *were* so many slices of celluloid), Hollywood steadily suppressed what was peculiar, arbitrary and unique about film and did its level best to persuade the audience that it was coasting along as cozily as at novel-pace, as directly as at stage-pace. It often deliberately hid its own innate artifice. The transitional fade-out, fade-in that became standard in the period was, after all, a soothing effort to conceal the splice.

Now we want the splice, quick, jagged, breathless, bewildering, appropriate. (I have always been astonished that we did not want it sooner. I think I first saw a jump-cut in a Sacha Guitry film in the early thirties, and it was exciting then; but this sort of clobbering of time at the hands of a technician who literally held time curling up in his hands had to wait its turn, no doubt because Hollywood thought it had plenty of time.)

We want film to do what it can do that no other medium can—rip time assunder, let space lurch, wipe the face of the world red or blue, tangle the threads like a computer already God, show its sprocket holes proudly. We want the *what* of its meaning to be made out of the *what* film is. It is negative, subject to impress. "Persona." It is a spool, subject to speed change. "Bonnie and Clyde." "Tom Jones." It is a labwash, a filter. "Elvira Madigan." "A Man and a Woman." It is a cropping, a blow-up. "Blow-up" (Interchange as many as you like.) Becoming conscious of itself, becoming *interested* in itself, film has become more completely itself. We're all happy.

There's more to it than that, naturally. I'm overstating the case for the man in the lab. Something in the world was waiting for just this uprush and outblast, if only Marshall McLuhan and his electronic circuitry. Notice, though, that there's virtually no difference in fundamental content between stage and film today. Whatever advantages the screen may have does not really lie in its subject matter. Both media have been up to their ears in the same thematic preoccupations: ruthless investigations of the antihero, dissections of fragmented personality, explorations of the existentialist void, simple but truth-telling genre studies, sex with the shirt off. "Alfie" was a play before "Alfie" was a film, and Harold Pinter works both sides of the street.

If anything, the stage stays a bit ahead of the screen where *material* is concerned: Mr. Pinter's work for the stage is more radical than his work for film, and I haven't yet seen the cunnilingual sex of "The Beard" in my neighborhood movie house (or have I missed it?). Where content is concerned, about the only thing the stage lacks is automobiles; I sometimes come from films thinking they're no longer about people, they're about cars. But cars are right for film, of course. They do destroy time and dissolve landscapes. And as everyone knows, they invite tinkering. I suspect that the act of looking in the mirror to see where its teeth were, the fact of facing up to its face, was for film the single most important step toward all the unleashing, and all the plugging-in, that has come after.

The theater, lagging and lonely? Let's back into it through a piece of film. In 1924 Buster Keaton, who in his instinctive way was one of the first serious analysts of film, made a comedy called "Sherlock Jr."

In it he played a film projectionist. Falling asleep at his machine, he dreamed himself leaving the projection booth, wandering down the center aisle of the theater, climbing onto the stage, and walking into the film. Once he was in the film, the film of course cut around him, wildly, unpredictably. But he didn't cut with it; he maintained continuity. This was dangerous. He might start to sit on what was plainly a garden bench and wind up sitting on a rock in mid-ocean. He might then dive into what was plainly water and wind up stuck in a snowbank.

To this day the sequence is a small marvel of technical ingenuity. Keaton possessed such physical dexterity that he was able to place himself precisely in separately shot landscapes with dissolve, telltale lapover, or any break in his own "outside" continuity. But the sequence is more than a stunt. It is film criticism. Keaton is pointing out to his audience how films are made, how they alter habits of perception, how they differ from experienced life. He is showing us that cutting is one thing and continuity another by letting us see both at once, in conflict.

There is a conflict here. Keaton doesn't belong in the sequence. He can't cut. He belongs back on the stage where he came from. And one of the things he is telling us, or at least one of the things that can be deduced from the risky conjunction, is what life back on the stage is all about. It is about continuity, about an eye-to-eye, toe-to-toe relationship between character and audience that is maintained without interruption of any sort until it becomes exhaustive and even unendurable, about intimacy so absolute that only a figurative death will relieve it (*all* plays must end in death, the Player King of "Rosencrantz and Guildenstern" insists), about a line that can't be broken until the hero or audience is.

The stage is defined by, and lives on, the pressure that comes of this closeness, of the fact that no one can get out of there, cannot change his mind or even his angle of vision, not for a moment. (The primitive instinct that first made the playing area circular was a right one: the ring was meant to surround, to enclose, to prevent escape.) Film is like being bombarded. The stage is like being handcuffed. We are locked to the man up there, he is locked to us, and neither of us can make a move without moving the other. (I have developed a curious tic over the years of playgoing. Whenever an actor on stage shrugs, I shrug. I can't help it, it just happens. But it never happens at the movies, only in the theater.)

Literally, we are bound hand and foot; our ankles chafe; our nerves may scream; any satisfaction we get is going to have to come from enduring our total exposure to one another until we have got past irritation into anguished, groaning, final and helpless commitment. The relationship *is* linear, which is why it may be out of vogue at the moment.

Second by second, hour by hour, we are going to be with one another: time can't be shaken off, or space evaded. When, say, Hal Holbrook invites us in to spend an evening with Mark Twain, we are not to be allowed any more relief than he is. There are only so many places he can go: to a table to pick up a book, to a humidor to pick up a cigar, to a chair. We watch him track his way, the same way, across the carpet he doesn't dare leave (he can't vanish; that would end everything) until he seems to have dug a trench in the carpet.

He *is* digging a trench, but he is digging it in us—in our skins, in our retinas, in our brain-cells. He is never out of our sight, we are never out of his, and finally the two sights become so cemented that he can doze off for a catnap and we won't budge. We'll wait. Imprisoned by the continuity of the performance, we have no alternative.

At higher levels we can't escape Phèdre or Oedipus or Lear, either; they are *at* us, they have invaded and are now occupying us, they won't shut up, won't take their clammy hands off our arms. The power of the theater is a particular kind of power: it is *staying* power, in every possible sense of the term.

This power isn't easily or randomly generated; it comes into being through specific means. These means aren't primarily visual (though all theater has visual elements, sometimes thoroughly monotonous ones.) Marcel Marceau can transfix an audience by visual means alone, but he does so in short takes; when he attempts to press mime toward the duration and the complexity of an hour-long playlet, the pressure evaporates. Obviously—though not so obviously in contemporary theater practice—if we are going to endure the awful intensity of being bound hand and foot, minute by minute and mile by mile, to an alter ego we cannot escape even by closing our eyes, we must speak or go mad. Theater eases the pressure by expressing the pressure. Words are its out. It opens its mouth and howls its confinement. In so doing it also intensifies the closeness, completes it.

But not just any old words will do. Ordinary words, banal words, prosaic words, the humdrum words of our everyday experience are not adequate to the task. No one wants to be chained to a bore who can't express himself, or who says the same thing all the time. The time is the same, the place is the same, the words don't dare be. They are the discovery that comes of the closeness, its climax, its purpose, its definition, its reward. Only language at its maximum intensity, displaying maximum revelation, generating maximum heat can satisfy the awful demands of the situation, and that language, of course, is poetry.

Not poetry of movement, which belongs to ballet, or poetry of mood, which may belong to the short story, or poetry of pause. Poetry of word, meter; language thumping like heartbeat. Of course, Sophocles isn't at work now. Too bad. But the theater can still inch toward total outcry: the stir of imagery inside the prose of Tennessee Williams, the crackle of wit that polarizes our attention in "A Man for All Seasons" (more riveting on the stage because of our undeflected concentration on a mind), the undisguised rhetoric of Shaw and the onrushing epithetry of Albee and Osborne at their best, all intimate the compulsion we have toward speech that sears, and, in the searing, seals. We hear where we are going, or at least want to go.

Whenever we do get there, whenever the words flung in our faces persuade us that we have grasped the man facing us whole, we say that we have come through an experience of theater as theater to an experience of drama as drama. Theater placed us in position; drama spelled out the sensation. One has grown out of the other, each has needed the other. That is what the stage is about. It is about a binding of bodies that demands a loosing of tongues.

But that is not what the stage has thought it was about lately. While film has been leaping up and down proclaiming its very special nature, pockmarks and all, the stage has sheepishly been pretending to be half a dozen other things, including film. It has splintered its image, done its damnedest to splinter time and space, struggled, really, to diffuse the only pressure that will ever make it work. Look at a stage today, laboring to move as rapidly and as frequently as film: scenery flying away before our eyes, houses dropping in from the heavens, benches coming up through the floorboards, landscapes projected on white walls (are we ever *out* of the movie theater?), dissolve, dissolve, dissolve. Or, since stage machinery is rather sluggish, fade-out, fade-in. With a soundtrack.

Instead of competing by asserting what is distinctive about it, the stage has failed to compete by vainly aping the enemy's lively discontinuity. The effort is vain, always was. No matter how fast the turntables turn or the treadmills roll (they had those in "Ben Hur," for heaven's sake), they can never catch the coattails of film. If we're going to have a foot-race, film will win. Playing it this way, the stage is bound to seem laggard, effortful, antiquated and not itself.

In the rush, in the gasp, it naturally has no time to create the particular pressure that demands language. A cliché, a routine epithet, a mere marker will do in the scurry. Current stage language is not necessarily bad, mind you: it often has wit, in a quiet way it may have style, it can echo street sounds accurately. But—and this is the dead giveaway—it feels no need to be better than, or different from, the language used in film. (The closer the better; we'll get a movie sale.)

I call this a dead giveaway because it says, perfectly plainly, that what is happening on stage does not call for any higher or more intense level of speech. There is nothing unique in its requirements, the pressure cooker isn't cooking. Language is only an accessory of film, not the dynamite that blows the bridge up; so long as the stage uses its essential tool as though it were a handy hairpin, a mere substitute for the master shot, it is going to be taken at its own valuation. Verbally it is no stronger than films; visually it is weaker. How should it hold its head up, or have a name worth asking for twice?

Indifference to language as the indispensable means of releasing and at the same time realizing the peculiar hothouse powers of the stage is not just a current accident, an absence of writers. It is an attitude. A few weeks ago in The Times Magazine Bruce Jay Friedman was quoted about his plans for the future. Mr. Friedman is a novelist who has just had his first success in the theater, a far-out, immensely funny comedy called "Scuba Duba." It is undoubtedly proper of him, now that he is *in* the theater, to give its special nature some attention. But when he turns to the theater as theater, what does he make of it? Moving toward his next play, Mr. Friedman says, "This time I think I'll trust the medium more. With 'Scuba Duba' I didn't trust the medium. I kept going straight to my trump, language."

No one thinks of language—a special kind of language under a special kind of pressure—as the theater's own trump any longer. Even a novelist riding on a stage success that is successful *because* of the run-on blare and tumble of its words is thinking of getting rid of some of the words. He's in the theater now.

It's almost a death wish, and widespread. Why the stage should have struggled for so long to be less than itself, why it should have breathlessly tried to overtake a camera it could never claim as its own or why it should still feel compelled to lower its voice to accommodate the prosy ear of the scriptgirl, would require separate and extended analysis, and perhaps a short course in the psychology of the defense mechanism. Fundamentally, I think, it has been intimidated for a hundred years by the onrushing sciences: by the social sciences that demanded documentary evidence, by the physical sciences that gave birth to so many means of literal reproduction. If literalness was to be the new vein, the one trustworthy vein, how could the stage not go along—even if going along meant tagging after?

Actually, it was quite a trick for film to make lively visual poetry out of literal pictures; film did it by defying its own literalness, by running the pictures out of rational or linear sequence. The stage couldn't manage that. Its own only means of escape lay in the flexibility of speech, in the power of nonliteral, nonrational, nonlinear combinations of words of penetrate and to ravage the subconscious. But in the new circumstances the stage didn't wish to seem out of step, out of touch. It decided to hold its tongue. Holding its tongue, it became superfluous. It is still standing there waiting for a reawakening of the verb.

My own simple belief is that, somewhere short of eternity, the stage is going to deliver more that is powerful and more that is profound than the film can hope to do: the dispersed image, the essentially visual image, the busy image has in the end less concentration. It is an exciting, often beautiful, surface, and I love it. (I grew up on it.) I like being so constantly distracted. But when I feel like digging in and staying there, when I want an intensive rather than a panoramic experience, when I want to get under the blanket instead of being tossed in it, to be pulled centripetally instead of being exploded centrifugally, I go home to "Hamlet" or "Heartbreak House."

The stage can command all of us home again (at least for its fair share of the nights). Ironically, it can do it by learning from film the only thing it has not tried to learn from film. It can ask itself, "What am I really?" and act on the answer.

Stanley Kauffmann
THE FILM GENERATION

"To have great poets, there must be great audiences, too," wrote Walt Whitman many years ago. So also claims Stanley Kauffmann, distinguished film critic for the New Republic, *there must be great audiences for the movies of the "Film Generation." Can the audience and the artist keep pace to seize the present opportunity?*

SOME of the following remarks were included, in different forms, in talks delivered recently at several universities, colleges and seminars. In one of the audiences were a distinguished poet and a critic of the graphic arts. Afterward, the critic came up to me and said, "You destroyed us. You wiped out our professions. You rendered my friend and me obsolete." I said that I neither believed nor intended that. Then he said wryly, stroking his chin, "On the other hand, if I were twenty years younger, I know I'd go into films."

His dismal reaction had been prompted by my assertion that film is the art for which there is the greatest spontaneous appetite in America at present, and by my reasons for thinking so. I must be clear that this is not to say that it is the art practiced at the highest level in this country; the film public depends more on imports today than does any other art public. But observation and experience, and the experience of others, make me believe that this uniquely responsive audience exists.

Or, in another phrase, there exists a Film Generation: the first generation that has matured in a culture in which the film has been of accepted serious relevance, however that seriousness is defined. Before 1935 films were proportionately more popular than they are now, but for the huge majority of film-goers they represented a regular weekly or semiweekly bath of escapism. Such an escapist audience still exists in large number, but another audience, most of them born since 1935, exists along with it. This group, this Film Generation, is certainly not exclusively grim, but it is essentially serious. Even its appreciations of sheer entertainment films reflect an over-all serious view.

There are a number of reasons, old and new, intrinsic and extrinsic, why this generation has come into being. Here are some of the older, intrinsic reasons.

1. In an age imbued with technological interest, the film art flowers out of technology. Excepting architecture, film is the one art that can capitalize directly and extensively on this century's luxuriance in applied science. Graphic artists have used mechanical and electronic elements, poets and painters have used computers, composers use electronic tapes. These are matters of choice. The film-maker has no choice: he must use complicated electronic and mechanical equipment. This fact helps to create a strong sense of junction with his society, of membership in the present. American artists have often been ashamed of—sometimes have dreaded—a feeling of difference from the busy "real" American world around them. For the film-maker the very instruments of his art provide communion with the spirit of his age. I think that the audience shares his feeling of union, sometimes consciously (especially when stereophonic sound, special optical effects, or color processes are used). The scientific skills employed are thus in themselves a link between the artist and the audience, and are a further link between them all and the unseen, unheard but apprehended society bustling outside the film theater.

There is a pleasant paradoxical corollary. In an era that is much concerned with the survival of the human being as such, in an increasingly mechanized age, here a complicated technology is used to celebrate the human being.

2. The world of surfaces and physical details has again become material for art. Just as the naturalistic novel seems to be sputtering to a halt, overdescribed down to the last vest button, the film gives some of its virtues new artistic life. A novelist who employs the slow steamroller apparatus of intense naturalism these days is asking for an extra vote of confidence from the reader, because the method and effects are so familiar that the reader can anticipate by pages. Even when there is the interest of an unusual setting, the reader is conscious that different nouns have been slipped into a worn pattern. The "new" French novel of Robbe-Grillet, Duras, Sarraute attempts to counteract this condition by intensifying it, using surfaces as the last realities, the only dependable objective correlatives. Sometimes, for some readers, this works. But both the old and the latter-day naturalisms must strain

in order to connect. Rolf Hochhuth, the author of *The Deputy*, has said:

> When I recently saw Ingmar Bergman's *The Silence*, I left that Hamburg movie house with the question, "What is there left for the novelist today?" Think of what Bergman can do with a single shot of his camera, up a street, down a corridor, into a woman's armpit. Of all he can say with this without saying a word.

Despite Hochhuth's understandable thrill-despair, there is plenty left for the novelist to say, even of armpits, but the essence of his remark rightly strips from fiction the primary function of creating material reality. The film has not only taken over this function but exalted it: it manages to make poetry out of doorknobs, breakfasts, furniture. Trivial details, of which everyone's universe is made, can once again be transmuted into metaphor, contributing to imaginative act.

A complementary, powerful fact is that this principle operates whether the film-maker is concerned with it or not. In any film except those with fantastic settings, whether the director's aim is naturalistic or romantic or symbolic or anything else, the streets and stairways and cigarette lighters are present, the girl's room is at least as real as the girl—often it bolsters her defective reality. Emphasized or not, invited or not, the physical world through the intensifications of photography never stops insisting on its presence and relevance.

This new life of surfaces gives a discrete verity to many mediocre films and gives great vitality to a film by a good artist. Consciously or not, this vitality reassures the audience, tangentially certifying and commenting on its habitat. Indeed, out of this phenomenon, it can be argued that the film discovered pop art years ago, digested this minor achievement, then continued on its way.

3. The film form seems particularly apt for the treatment of many of the pressing questions of our time: inner states or tension or of doubt or apathy—even (as we shall see) doubts about art itself. The film can externalize some psychical matters that, for example, the theater cannot easily deal with; and it can relate them to physical environment in a manner that the theater cannot contain nor the novel quite duplicate. The film can dramatize post-Freudian man, and his habitat—and the relation between the two. One does not need to believe in the death of the theater or the novel—as I do not—in order to see these special graces in the film.

4. Film is the only art besides music that is available to the whole world at once, exactly as it was first made. With subtitles, it is the only art involving language that can be enjoyed in a language of which one is

ignorant. (I except opera, where the language rarely needs to be understood precisely.)

The point is not the spreading of information or amity, as in USIA or UNESCO films, useful though they may be. The point is emotional relationship and debt. If one has been moved by, for instance, Japanese actors in Japanese settings, in actions of Japanese life that have resonated against one's own experience, there is a connection with Japan that is deeper than the benefits of propaganda or travelogue. No one who has been moved by *Ikiru* can think of Japan and the Japanese exactly as he thought before.

Obviously similar experience—emotional and spiritual—is available through other arts, but rarely with the imperial ease of the film. As against foreign literature, foreign films have an advantage besides accessibility in the original language. The Japanese novelist invites us to recreate the scene in imagination. The Japanese film-maker provides the scene for us, with a vividness that our minds cannot equal in a foreign setting. Thus our responses can begin at a more advanced point and can more easily (although not more strongly) be stimulated and heightened.

This universality and this relative simultaneity of artistic experience have made us all members of a much larger empathetic community than has been immediately possible before in history.

5. Film has one great benefit by accident: its youth, which means not only vigor but the reach of possibility. The novel, still very much alive, is conscious of having to remain alive. One of its chief handicaps is its history; the novelist is burdened with the achievements of the past. This is also true of poetry. It flourishes certainly; as with fiction, the state of poetry is far better than is often assumed. But poetry, too, is conscious of a struggle for pertinent survival. In painting and sculpture, the desperation is readily apparent; the new fashion in each new season makes it clear. But the film is an infant, only begun. It has already accomplished miracles. Consider that it was only fifty years from Edison's camera to *Citizen Kane,* which is rather as if Stravinsky had written *Petrouchka* fifty years after Guido d'Arezzo developed musical notation. Nevertheless the film continent has only just been discovered, the boundaries are not remotely in sight. It is this freshness that gives the young generation—what I have called the Film Generation—not only the excitement of its potential but a strong proprietary feeling. The film belongs to them.

These, I think, are some of the reasons for the growth of that new film audience. But they raise a question. As noted, these reasons have been valid to some degree for a long time, yet it is only in about the last twenty years that the Film Generation has emerged. Why didn't this happen sooner? Why have these reasons begun to be strongly operative only since the Second World War?

In that period other elements have risen to galvanize them. Some of these later elements come from outside the film world: the spurt in college education; political and social abrasions and changes; moral, ethical, religious dissolutions and resolutions. All these have made this generation more impatient and more hungry. But, since the Second War, there have also been some important developments within the film world itself.* These developments have been in content, not in form. Three elements are especially evident: increased sexuality, an increase in national flavor, and an increased stress on the individual. The latter two are linked.

As for the first, sex has been important currency in the theater since *The Agamemnon,* and with the first films came the first film idols. In fact there are scenes in many silent films that would have censor trouble today. But apart from sexual display or the sex appeal of any actor or actress, there is now—in many foreign films and some American ones—a sexual attitude that can be respected: an attitude closer to the realities of sexual life than the mythology that is preached by clergy of every faith, by mass media, by parents. This relative sexual freedom, long established in fiction and the theater, has been slower to arrive in films because of their wider availability to all ages and mentalities, and the consequent brooding of censors. Now, in a more liberal time, this freedom makes films even more pertinent to this generation. The mythology that still passes for sexual morality is prescriptive, these films are descriptive; but there is more to their merit than verisimilitude. Not by nudity nor bedroom calisthenics nor frank language but by fidelity to the complexities of sexual behavior, these films provide more than recognition. By accepting and exploring complexities, they provide confidence in the fundamental beauty of those complexities, in the desirability of being human, even with all the trouble it involves.

The second element, national flavor, has been described by the English critic Penelope Houston in *The Contemporary Cinema* (1963):

> However partial or distorted an image one gets of a society through its cinema, it is still possible to discern the national face behind the screen. It is difficult to conceive of a neorealist idealism [in Italy] without the jubilant preface of the

* These do not include linguistic developments. Nothing has changed the language of film as, for example, electronics has changed music or abstract expressionism has altered the vision of painting. There have been many technical film developments—wide screens, stereophonic sound, color refinements—but so far they have largely been peripheral to the art itself. They, and the improved hand-held camera and recorder, may affect the basic language of film in future; they have not yet markedly done so. This fact can be taken as an implied strength. Experiments in artistic technique are usually a sign that a boundary has been reached with old techniques. In film there is no hint of exhaustion in the techniques that were known to Griffith and Eisenstein forty years ago.

liberation of Rome; or to look at Britain's films of the past few years without reference to our redbrick radicalism; or to ignore the effect of the political climate on a French cinema which declares its awareness of strain in the very insistence with which it puts private before public life and creation for creation's sake before either.

It would be easy to add a similar sentence for almost every major film-producing country. Japanese films are concerned with contemporary unrest, directly and indirectly. Many of their costume pictures about samurai swordsmen are set in the 1860s when the feudal system was crumbling and immense social metamorphosis was taking place. The Soviet film has deepened in lethargy as revolutionary fervor wore off, as Stalinist despotism made it nervous, as some subsequent economic and scientific successes made it smug. It has become, with a few exceptions, either war glory or the ideologic equivalent of the petty bourgeois confection. As for America, the poor boy and rich girl story (or rich boy and poor girl) which was the staple of the popular film before the Second War has disappeared. Money as romance, the Gatsby dream, has receded, not because everyone is now rich but because the middle-clase image has replaced both the poor image and the rich image. What American would now relish the ancient compliment "poor but honest"? And what is the difference *in appearance* between the clerk's car and the boss's? The much-mooted ascendancy of the middle class has reached the point where it is strong enough to control cultural forms, to magnify its own image in art.

With this ascendancy we have seen the emergence of a new romantic hero, posed against this bourgeois background, since all such heroes must contrast with their societies. The new romantic is the liberated prole, with a motorcycle or a Texas Cadillac, seeking his life by assaulting convention and morality, rather than by striving for success in accepted modes, either with money or with women. This hero scoffs at ideals of excellence and aspiration at the same time that he wants to dominate. There are signs that this hero may have run his course, but in the last twenty years or so he was pre-eminent.

A lesser companion of his still continues: the Frank Sinatra-Dean Martin figure, the smart, cool operator just inside the law, a philanderer righteously resentful of any claims on him by women. His casual *persona* derives in part from the night-club microphone, which was first a necessity, then became a prop, then a source of power and ease for those who had little power and could achieve nothing but ease. The invisible hand-held microphone accompanies the crooner-as-hero wherever he goes. His oblique, slithering solipsism seems likely to persist after the Brando figure, more directly descended from the proletarian rebel and Byronic individualist, has passed. Mere "coolness" persists; purposeful rebellion fades.

All the national colors described above apply both to popular and serious films. If we concentrate on serious film—film made primarily as personal expression, not as contractual job or money-spinner—then we often find, besides intensified national color, an intensified introspection. This is the third of our elements: a concern with the exploration of the individual as a universe. It is not a novelty in films. No more introspective films have ever been made than Wiene's *The Cabinet of Dr. Caligari* (1919) or Pabst's *Secrets of a Soul* (1926). But merely to mention such names as Bergman, Antonioni, Fellini, Ozu, Torre Nilsson, Olmi, Truffaut is to see that, for many outstanding directors, there has lately been more reliance on inner conflict than on classic confrontation of antagonists. These men and others, including some Americans, have been extending the film into the vast areas of innermost privacy, even of the unconscious, that have been the province of the novel and of metaphysical poetry. Saul Bellow has complained that the modern novelist doesn't tell us what a human being *is* today. Bellow is a notable exception to his own complaint; but whether we agree or not, we can see that many contemporary film-makers have tried to answer that question, with a more consistent application than ever before in the history of the art.

These two elements—national color and the exploration of the individual—are obviously inseparable. Society and the man affect each other, even if it is in the man's withdrawal. These elements are further linked in a curious contradictory motion against our time. In an age when internationalism is promulgated as a solution to political difficulties, national colors have become more evident in films. In an age when social philosophers have begun to question the durability of individualism—which is, after all, a fairly recent concept in history and almost exclusive to the West—the film is tending to cherish the individual. Does this indicate a time lag between the film and the advances of political and social philosophy? On the contrary, I believe it indicates a perverse penetration to truth. The truth of art sometimes runs counter to what seems politically and intellectually desirable; that is always a risk of art. I think the film is showing us that nationalism, in the purely cultural sense, is becoming more necessary to us as jet plane and Telstar threaten to make us one world. I think that just at the time when technological and power structures challenge individualism, our own minds and souls have become more interesting to us. Up to now, technology has outraced self-discovery. Only now—in this postreligious, self-dependent age—are we beginning to appreciate how rich and dangerous each one of us is.

These elements have led, directly and by implication, to the phenomenon we are examining; the historical moment for the rise of the Film Generation, a surge of somewhat nostalgic revolution; a reluctance to lose what seems to be disappearing, accompanied by an impulse to disaffection, an insistence on an amorphous cosmos. ("Stay loose." "Swing.") Doubtless that nostalgia is sentimental, an unwillingness to be banned from an Eden of individualism that in fact never existed. But much of the revolution is clearheaded; not so much an attempt to halt change as to influence it; a natural and valuable impulse to scratch on the chromium fronts of the advancing tanks of factory-society "Kilroy was here."

The divided attitude toward social change leads to another, crucial polarity. This generation has an ambivalent view of cultural tradition. On the one hand there is a great desire for such tradition, admitted or not. Everyone wants to know that he came from somewhere; it's less lonely. But this desire is often accompanied by a mirror attitude that looks on the past as failure and betrayal. It is of course a familiar indictment, the young accusing the old of having made a mess, but now the accusation is more stringent and more general because of the acceleration of change and the diminutions of choice.

This ambivalence toward tradition—this polarity that both wants and rejects it—has created a hunger for art as assurance of origins together with a preference for art forms that are relatively free of the past. Outstanding among these is film. Even though it has been on hand for sixty-five years or so, the film seems much more of the present and future than other forms. It has its roots—of content and method—in older arts: drama, literature, dance, painting; yet it is very much less entailed by the past than these arts. It satisfies this generation's ambivalent need in tradition.

So far, this inquiry has been almost all celebration; now a concern must be raised. So far, we have discussed certain phenomena as cultural dynamics and social facts: now a word must be said in value judgment of the revolutionary standards involved. Not all the films that the Film Generation venerates seem worth its energy and devotion. It is not my purpose to lay down an artistic credo: I could always think of too many exceptions. Taste is a matter of instances, not precepts. One forms an idea of another's taste—or of one's own—from the perspective of many instances of judgment and preference, and even then, general deductions must be drawn delicately. But, drawing them as delicately as I am able, I am left with a concern to posit against the foregoing celebration.

There are enthusiasms of this Film Generation that I do not share, there are many enthusiasms of mine that they seem not to share. For the most part this is nobody's fault and probably nobody's virtue. But there is one enthusiasm in particular that has taken many members of this generation—not all, but a large proportion—that seems potentially deleterious and therefore to need discussion.

On college campuses around the country, in some film societies and small theaters (there are at least three in New York at this writing), much is being made of certain experimental films. The passion for experiment, as such, is eternal and necessary, but out of disgust with much commercial and fake-serious fare, there is a strong tendency to value experiment for its own sake, to regard it as a value instead of a means to value. And since, at this period in social and political affairs, a passion for these films has been taken to have other significances as well, the phenomenon is especially important.

The films to which I refer are often called underground films. In America a large proportion of them come from a group centered in New York but not confined there, variously called New American Films or the Film-maker's Cooperative. It is an association of dedicated film-makers and dedicated apostles. (The apostles carry the word widely. Two minutes after I met Federico Fellini in Rome, he asked me whether I had seen Jack Smith's *Flaming Creatures.*) The group also has a circle of apostolic critics.

Predictably, this group considers itself the element of poetry in an otherwise prosaic film situation in this country and the world. Also predictably, its works are difficult to describe because it is not a school like neorealism or surrealism. It includes these and many more styles. It welcomes anyone who uses film as a form of personal expression. The most lucid general statement about this group that I know was written by Ken Kelman (*The Nation,* May 11, 1964). He divides their works into three main categories. First, "outright social criticism and protest" (Dan Drasin's *Sunday,* Stan Vanderbeek's *Skullduggery*). Second, "films which suggest, mainly through anarchic fantasy, the possibilities of the human spirit in its socially uncorrupted state" (Jack Smith's *Flaming Creatures* and *Normal Love*). The third group "creates, out of a need to fill our rationalistic void, those actual inner worlds which fall within the realm of myth" (Kenneth Anger's *Scorpio Rising,* Stan Brakhage's *Anticipation of the Night* and *Window Water Baby Moving*).

Kelman's article, like others on the subject, is a ringing statement written with inner consistency and a fire that outstrips mere sincerity. The difficulty is that, when one sees these films (I have seen all those cited and numerous others), one finds small consonance between the descriptions and the works. Not to belabor individual films, one can say that most of them represent the attitudes and intents that Kelman describes but that their acceptance as accomplishment reflects a deliberate disconnection from cultural and social history. For me, most of the "new" techniques are dated, most of the social criticism is facile or vacuous, the mythic content undernourishing, the general quality of inspiration tenuous, strained, trite. Much of the work seems made for a young audience that insists on having its *own* films, at any critical or cultural price.

One of the grave liabilities in the situation is that writing like Kelman's and the attitudes it promotes tend to encourage the symbiotic state that exists today in the graphic arts. There is not much direct relation between film and audience, nothing so simple as the audience coming to the theater and being affected, or not, by what it sees. The audience exists jointly with these films in a highly verbalized critical environment; its preformed attitudes are eager dramatizations of credos and exegeses. Much of modern painting—op, pop, collage, latter-day abstraction—seems to have its life almost as much in what is written about it as on canvas. Indeed many of the paintings seem to have been made to evoke aesthetic disquisition, to exist verbally and in viewers' attitudes. The underground film has entered this territory—of art as "position"—a position sustained as much by the polemic-conscious audience as by the material on the screen. It has long been an indictment of Broadway and Hollywood hits that the audience is preconditioned, whipped into line by newspaper raves. Here is very much the same situation at a higher intellectual altitude.

Another grave liability is the pressure brought to bear by the underground movement for disconnection from cultural history. Generally, as has been noted, the Film Generation has at least an ambivalent attitude toward tradition: this underground movement pushes—by implication and otherwise—for complete rejection of the standards that have been continuingly evolved through some centuries of Western art. They are not to be evolved further, they are to be discarded. It is easy to chuckle patronizingly at this belief as one more instance of the perennial artistic rebellion of the young, but current social upheavals give it a momentum that takes it out of the sphere of mere youthful high spirits—or low spirits. And the morning or the year or the decade after the excitements of rebellion have passed, it may be discovered that a valuable continuum in culture has been seriously injured—to the detriment of the very aims for which the action was taken.

I do not argue against change, including radical change. I do argue against nihilism as a necessary first step for progress. Besides, this film nihilism contains a bitter contradiction. It is often a manifestation in art of discontents elsewhere, of anger at older generations' betrayal of certain ideals. But the best art of the past—in all fields—is expression of those ideals, often despite society's apathy toward them. In discarding that inheritance of art, the rebels discard much of the best work that the human race has done for the very ideals that galvanize this new rebellion.

There is a parallel between this devotion to the underground film in many of the Film Generation and an element in the "new left," the new political radicalism. Some of radical youth are engaged in genuinely creative action: antimilitarism, antidiscrimination, support of various economic programs. But many of them equate radicalism with personal gesture and style—revolt consummated by bizarre hair and dress, unconventional sexual behavior, flirtations with drugs. One who is aware of the valid basis for disaffection can still regret the introversions and futilities of these gestures. Likewise, one hopeful for the invigoration of the American film can doubt the pertinence of comparable gestures in this field: the exaltation of meaninglessness in film as a statement of meaninglessness in the world: the praise of juvenile irreverence—perennial in art—as a new formulation of myth; the approval of a social criticism that is devoid of intellectual foundation and political belief.

I dwell on the partiality to these experimental films not to counterbalance the happy fact of the Film Generation's existence but precisely because of its existence. Art has never been well created for long independently of an audience; in fact, history shows that audience response feeds great eras of art (painting in Renaissance Italy, the drama in Elizabethan England and neoclassic France, the sudden, ravenous world-wide appetite for silent-film comedy).

Speaking in the large, I believe that the Film Generation has the power to evoke the films that it wants, even though that generation is a minority and despite the harsh conditions of production and exhibition around the world. *All* films will not alter, nor should they, but if the dynamics of cultural history still obtains, an insistent group of art takers can—sooner or later, one way or another—have an effect on art makers. The effect is circular. The audience obviously cannot do it alone; there have to be talented artists. But talent is a relative constant in the human race; it is sparked by response and, even at its best, can be dampened by neglect. (Think of Herman Melville's twenty years in the Customs House.)

Thus, by a logical progression, we can see that the Film Generation has extraordinary powers. If it is true (as I have claimed) that film is the most pertinent art at present; if it is true that the young generation is closer to the film than to other arts; if it is also true that audience appetite can evoke art; then, it follows that the Film Generation has the opportunity to help bring forth the best and most relevant art of our age. And it is the possible impediment to this opportunity that makes a devotion to culturally baseless, essentially sterile films seem wasteful.

I am aware that the above puts an almost ludicrously large burden on this Film Generation. In effect, it is almost to ask them to solve the problems of cultural transition, to define what culture will become. The problem is not to be solved in any one locus, even when the locus —film and its audience—has come into being quite naturally. It is never to be solved; it is only to be confronted continually, particularly in an age that is *not* an age, that is a rapid series of continually shifting points. But the size of the conclusion does not diminish the opportunity.

There is not much question among the thoughtful that we live in a time of the most profound cultural change, when the very purposes of art, as well as its content, are being transformed. The New American Cinema is one manifestation of that upheaval. In my view, most of its films that I have seen are of minuscule importance, but the implication in most of them is important: the implication that what's past is quite dead. The art of the future may be divorced from present concepts of humanism; it may find its pertinences in modes that, to most eyes, now look cold or abstract or even antihuman. But they will have been made by men who would not be what they are, whatever that may be, without the precedents of culture; and if that new art, whatever it may be, is to be held to its highest standards, the best of the past needs to be brought forward with us. The real *use* of our inheritance in the contemporary situation would throw a good deal of illumination on much of the new that is now adulated. The Kelmans tell us that an Antonioni is only seemingly free, that he is trapped by attempting to renovate the past. But, to take Antonioni as an example, it is precisely the effort to alter in an altered cosmos without returning Western culture to Year One that may keep a cultural future possible; may sustain us as we travel from a terrain that once was fruitful to one that has not yet been sighted. We don't want to starve en route.

As an important part of this process—this rescue operation, if you like—the Film Generation can demand a new film from the serious film-maker that is more than a gesture of denial. Such a generation, joined with the past and therefore truly equipped to outgrow it, may eventually get in its films what the Kelmans have prematurely claimed: a new social cohesion, a new fertile and reassuring mythos. If these come, they will manifest their presence, not so much by the blown prose of rhapsodists as by an irony: middle-of-the-road art will imitate the new film. That film will certainly not be ignored, as the majority now ignore underground efforts. When the imitation begins, then authentically progressive artists and audiences will know that they have thus far succeeded, and will know it is again time to move forward.

So the Film Generation, flaws and all, represents both a circumstance and an opportunity. On the whole it is, I believe, the most cheering circumstance in contemporary American art. That generation can be a vital force, or it can twiddle its strength and chances away in irrelevant artistic nihilism, in engorged social petulance. One does not ask them to "save" film forever. In the long run, the history of the film will be the same as that of all arts: a few peaks, some plateaus, many chasms; but the present chance—a rare one—could save much time in the development of this young medium. The foreseeable future is all that, reasonably, we can have hopes or anxieties about in art. The Film Generation can help to make the foreseeable future of film interesting and important. Let us see.

Arthur Knight
ENGAGING THE EYE-MINDED

The "eye-minded generation," contends Arthur Knight, professor in the Cinema Department at the University of Southern California and author of numerous articles and books on film, seeks in its movies the "now" look—"a swift-moving, constantly shifting surface that suggests rather than reveals depths."

WHEN one unkind critic, writing of Stanley Kramer's *Guess Who's Coming to Dinner,* dubbed it "the best film of 1956," he was in effect capsulizing the enormous change that has come over pictures in the past ten years. In 1956, everyone was still urging the movies to "say something," to be about something that mattered to our society. Today, such sociological concerns are being met one way or another in an astonishing number of films. But what has changed even more significantly is the *style* of storytelling on the screen. Incredibly enough, ten years ago Kramer's approach to *Guess Who's Coming to Dinner* was virtually the only one open to a film-maker, unless he was aiming specifically for an art house release. Ten years ago, for example, the flat, abrupt transitions in Stankey Kubrick's *Paths of Glory* seemed downright revolutionary. Today, new styles and new techniques are proliferating on every hand—and woe to the director who ignores them.

It requires no vast research to discover how and where this new syntax and vocabulary entered the cinematic language. The change was going on throughout much of the Fifties, and under our very noses. There were the films of Ingmar Bergman, the enigmatic Swede, whose *Wild Strawberries* flashed from present to past on the swift wings of free association, and whose *Magician* never left us certain of what was real and what was hallucination. There was Antonioni who, in films like *L'Avventura, La Notte,* and *L'Eclisse,* slowed down life with his camera to reveal the meaning behind each nuance and gesture of his tortured, middle-class characters; and, far more volatile, there was his compatriot Fellini, who, in *La Dolce Vita*—and even more impressively in *8½*—seemed to capture the contemporary scene in all its intensity, using his camera as a prism to reveal its many facets. Most of all, beginning late in the Fifties, there was the impetus of the French "new wave"—Godard, Resnais, Truffaut—that swept before it all the rules, all the conventions, all the accepted standards for theatrical moviemaking. Most of the youthful "new wave" directors, incidentally, had begun as film students and film critics. Because they knew their medium so well, they knew what was safe—and perhaps even necessary—to smash.

What started in France spread swiftly to England, where a whole new generation of film-makers—headed by Lindsay Anderson, Karel Reisz, and Tony Richardson—operating under the banner of "free cinema," drastically altered the leisurely pace and well bred air of most British pictures. With such titles as *Room at the Top, Saturday Night and Sunday Morning, The Sporting Life,* and *The Loneliness of the Long Distance Runner,* they moved the British film out of the drawing room into the kitchen and introduced a taut, elliptical narrative style. Curiously, these pictures, although originally booked into the art houses, began to attract considerably wider audiences—especially youthful audiences. (Father John Culkin now calls *The Loneliness of the Long Distance Runner* "the *Silas Marner* of high school study groups.") With the appearance of Richard Lester's free-form, free-wheeling *A Hard Day's Night* and *Help!,* all previous distinctions between art house pictures and mass-appeal movies completely broke down. What had started out in the art houses had suddenly swept into the mainstream of film-making, and with such force, such impact, as to demolish any picture made in the more traditional or conventional modes.

Of inestimable importance in preparing audience acceptance for the new look in films was, ironically, television. It has often been said that TV's moronic situation comedies, crime shows, and Westerns—not to forget the commercials—were what drove people back to the movie houses in the first place. But when they got there, they brought with them a new way of seeing. As the McLuhanites are so fond of pointing out, television—and particularly the commercials—had accustomed them to seeing more, and faster. It is no coincidence that Richard Lester first made his reputation in England as a director in this field, now that what might be called the "now" look in movies has all the zip, speed, and visual excitement of a picture that has to deliver its entire message in just sixty seconds.

For the fact is that we are watching a new kind of storytelling on the screen today. Consider the recent *Bullitt* as an example. In the old days of the murder mystery, after the killer had been tracked down and disposed of, the detective would generally assemble the entire surviving cast and patiently explain, clue by clue, how he had solved the case and, motive after motive, what had caused the killings in the first place. In *Bullitt,* on the other hand, the criminal is simply pursued, unmasked, and shot down in cold blood, whereupon our hero returns home, washes his hands, and pops into bed (with his lady friend). No explanations are forthcoming. If anyone wants to try to figure out who did what to whom, and why, that is strictly up to him.

Bullitt, I find, is completely typical of the "now" look in American movies—a swift-moving, constantly shifting surface that suggests rather than reveals depths. If the surface is made particularly intriguing, then perhaps the viewer will want to plunge beneath it, will see the film again and again—as do the devotees of *The Graduate,* for example —until they have plumbed it to their satisfaction. I suspect that neither director Mike Nichols nor Buck Henry and Calder Willingham, the writers of *The Graduate,* were quite prepared for the quantities of intensive analysis that their little comedy occasioned; and I am quite certain that Richard Benton and David Newman, the youthful authors of *Bonnie and Clyde,* had no idea of the comtemporary implications that today's audiences would discover in their retelling of a particularly sordid episode from the early Thirties. (Perhaps Arthur Penn, the film's director, knew, but not Benton and Newman.) Similarly, Antonioni's *Blow-Up* owes its unanticipated success at least as much to the bafflements of its story as to its nude teen-agers tussling with David Hemmings on that purple paper. The very best film-makers may aim to engage the minds of their audiences—generally, either by piquing their curiosity or by shocking them out of their apathy—but they are becoming increasingly aware that first they must catch their eye.

For television has made this a particularly eye-minded generation. And what it sees, often in the briefest of flashes (the "clues" in *Mission Impossible,* for example), it retains and seeks relationships for. It was a young film student who pointed out to me the presence of a tiny red Volkswagen in the final shot of *Finian's Rainbow* as Astaire dances off toward the horizon. Was it there, he asked, because the director wanted to make some sly reference to the contemporary scene in what was otherwise a thoroughly uncontemporary musical? The car was there, I subsequently learned from Francis Ford Coppola, the director in question, because he had tried a dozen times to get an effective shot of a rainbow, and just on this one, which came out beautifully, "that damned Volks happened along." Coppola was delighted with my student's rationalization, commended him on his sharp eyesight, but still wished that the driver could have waited a few minutes.

It is this kind of visual alertness, however, that has enforced a change of pace on those film-makers who hope to stay "with it." *A Hard Day's*

Night, Help!, and, currently, *Head* are perhaps extreme examples of how willingly the producers will forego any semblance of plot today in favor of sheer momentum and the attractions of the unanticipated—qualities, not coincidentally, that characterize many of television's most successful commercials. But even the plotted film has been affected by the new speed of perception. Pictures such as *The Knack, Point Blank,* and *Bullitt* waste little time on dialogue scenes. Not only are the words pared to a minimum, but lines are frequently carried over into the next shot, when visually we have already moved to a new location and the start of a new scene. In *Charly,* director Ralph Nelson avoided the ping-pong effect of cutting back and forth between two characters talking together by placing them side by side, angled toward each other on a split screen, and letting us look at both at the same time. In one of the most effective sequences from *The Boston Strangler,* Richard Fleischer showed us on one side of his split screen the feet of a dead woman in a darkened room; on the other side, two neighbors wonder why she has not collected her mail. As they cautiously push open the door on the right panel, we see it simultaneously opening into the death room on the left. The audience, miraculously in two places at once, can only confirm the neighbor's apprehensions.

Not only are we seeing faster than ever these days, but apparently we can see more—if the film-makers will give us more to look at. The experience at Expo 67, less than two years ago, has provided ample confirmation of this, particularly in the Ontario pavilion's *A Place to Stand,* with its exciting innovation of the fragmented screen. Instead of merely one image to the frame, it may contain six, a dozen, two dozen of all shapes and sizes. But if the techniques of *A Place to Stand* have already been imitated in at least half a dozen pictures since their first appearance, so far only the makers of *The Boston Strangler* have grasped the fact that they have added a whole new dimension to storytelling. Where other films have used the device merely as an extension of the montage, a transitional means of hurrying through an awkward time lapse, Fleischer saw that it could be a functional part of his exposition, revealing in a single glance what half a dozen police units were doing at a given moment, or portraying the panic fear of sudden death spreading through an entire community. Watching it, as Joseph Morgenstern had written earlier of *A Place to Stand,* "is to learn how to read whole sentences instead of individual words."

These new techniques, however, cannot be forced upon traditional subject matter. Content and form are not separable; and nowhere is this more evident than in pictures that attempt to engraft Expo's multiple screen effects, or Resnais's swift flashbacks and flash-forwards, onto stories that follow a conventional formula. Thus, earlier this year, Richard Boone's *Kona Coast,* a straight-forward adventure yarn, looked both pretentious and preposterous as it proceeded to mix up time in the *Marienbad* manner. Similarly, the split screens of *Grand Prix, The Thomas Crown Affair,* and the psychedelic sequence of *Charly* were all too obviously an affectation. On the other hand, the flat cutting of *Bullitt* (there is only one dissolve in the entire picture, and no fade-out until the final shot), the adroit use of multiple images in *The Boston Strangler,* and the swift, abrupt, discontinuous bits and pieces of *Petulia* and the current *Joanna* were all enormously effective precisely because they gave a fresh visual style to material that had a fresh, contemporary feel to it. More conventional techniques would have been as inappropriate as doing *Yellow Submarine* in the manner of *Snow White and the Seven Dwarfs.*

For large factions of Hollywood, I fear, the impulse is to borrow a technique rather than to create a style, to use an idea that has already won acceptance rather than to encourage new modes of expression. Consequently, today's audiences—and particularly the young audiences—are frequently considerably ahead of them. Many have chosen Godard as their cinematic deity because, as far back as *Breathless,* he has been breaking all the careful rules of picture-making and splotching the screen with only those moments where he feels that his story, his characters, or his ideas have achieved their fullest intensity. For much the same reason, Richard Lester has been accorded a high place in the young people's pantheon. *A Hard Day's Night,* with its exuberant disregard for logic—as when Beatle George Harrison races down the corridor of a train, then a moment later is glimpsed through a window running alongside the train—has already been raised to the status of a contemporary classic. And both the aural and visual trickery of Antonioni's *Blow-Up*—such as his climactic, enigmatic tennis game in which the camera follows, and the microphone hears, a nonexistent tennis ball—somehow turn on its youthful viewers as surely as a capsule of LSD.

Does this mean that today's screen has become a showcase for brainless, purely sensory delights? Not at all. Just as Herman Melville interrupted the narrative of *Moby Dick* for what he deemed significant dissertations on whales, whaling, and the sea (or, perhaps even more apt, just as Henry Miller generously larded his Tropical philosophizing with gobs of scatological storytelling), so Godard is not at all unwilling to punctuate his pictures with long passages in which the camera functions as little more than a tape recorder while characters recite their—or Godard's—views on world affairs. The point is that in these sequences, the words have become all-important to Godard, and therefore he has quite consciously de-emphasized the visuals.

On another plane entirely, in my view, is Ingmar Bergman, who has made of the camera an ideal instrument for the expression of his metaphysical concepts of the multifaceted nature of man, the artist, and

God. In both *Persona* and *Hour of the Wolf,* characters speak directly into the camera, while Bergman deliberately introduces devices—the tearing film in *Persona,* the sound-stage noises in *Hour of the Wolf* —to keep audiences ever conscious that they are actually looking at a movie, creating thereby the filmic equivalent of a Brechtian distancing. And, to choose yet another extreme, Satyajit Ray has successfully combined the poetic, documentary approach of Robert Flaherty with the humanistic concerns of a Jean Renoir to re-create on the screen small, personal drama—from the past in his famed *Apu* trilogy, from the present in his more recent *Mahanagar*—that must someday be recognized as among the finest anthropological studies ever created.

For film does not move in only one direction, much as that might simplify life for the heads of studios—and perhaps for movie critics as well. But the conventional story well told in a conventional manner, such as *Lawrence of Arabia,* will no doubt always remain with us, as will such conventional movie musicals as *Finian's Rainbow,* or such artfully cinematized plays as *A Man for All Seasons* and *The Lion in Winter.* But these are for audiences who prize the security of the familiar, who enjoy the experience of having been there before. For the "now" audience, there are the face-to-face encounters provided by *cinéma verite,* which may take the form of a close-up of Stravinsky, or a harrowing tour of a state mental institution (*The Titicut Follies*), or a two-hour interview with a Negro male prostitute (*Portrait of Jason*). For the "now" audience, the "personal" film-makers, some of them still in the film schools now proliferating throughout the nation, are opening up new worlds of subject matter and new techniques to explore them with. Ed Emshwiller's *Relativity,* for example, is an erotic poem created out of the free association of bold, startling, yet familiar images viewed at strange angles through distorting lenses. Bruce Conner's collage films, with their swift, artful cutting together of outrageously disparate snippets of old movies set against "hard rock" scores, manage a social commentary that is at once bitter and hilarious. And like it or not, Andy Warhol's marathon "happenings," despite—or perhaps because of—their technical crudities, convey a frighteningly accurate picture of the twilit, drug-fogged world of today's "mod" underground artists.

Significantly, these film-makers are also exploring the potential of the multiple image. Warhol designed his *Chelsea Girls* and the twenty-six-hour **** to be shown two reels at a time, side by side on the same wide screen; for the finale of *Chelsea Girls,* a Cinemascope lens placed over one projector completely engulfs and saturates the image from the other. Underground film-maker Barbara Rubin also designed her *Christmas on Earth* to be shown two reels at a time, but with one superimposed upon the other. And Stan Vanderbeek, one of the wittiest and most inventive of the personal film-makers, designed his own version of the Cinerama dome at Stony Point, New York, with multiple images bounding about the ceiling while viewers recline on the floor.

"Involvement" is perhaps the key word to all that is happening in movies today. Whether it be the environmental involvement of the light shows that have been sweeping the country during the past year, the intellectual involvement of Bergman and Godard, the multiple-image excitements of *The Boston Strangler,* or merely the surface tensions of *Point Blank* and *Bullitt,* the "now" audience has outgrown the passivity of the past. Watch 'em and forget 'em is no longer good enough; the neat, happy ending that sends the viewer out into the night with the cinematic equivalent of a Chinese dinner no longer suffices. Unquestionably, such films will continue to be made, all looking as "modern" and as "with it" as *Guess Who's Coming to Dinner.* True, they may be gimmicked up a bit, but they will still be based on past formulas. And if the critics—and the kids—prefer *The Graduate* or *Blow-Up,* well, what do they know about the movie business anyway? Did they ever *make* a picture? While such complacency may suffice for a studio dining room conversation, it can no longer bolster the status quo. For, as the song says, the times they are a-changing—and the brightest, and most realistic, of the film-makers today are those who are learning to change along with them.

Judith Crist
MOVIES: MORALS, VIOLENCE, SEX—ANYTHING GOES

"Our eyes have opened to film," states Judith Crist, film critic for New York *magazine. And with that opening has come the "rip-roaring explosion that has shattered any delusions about which is the liveliest of the arts and where the cultural action is today—and tomorrow."*

FADE IN . . . lone stranger . . . mean, ugly, handsome-ugly, lonely stranger . . . skyline . . . mean, ugly, handsome-ugly, lonely skyline . . . out of shadows comes a man . . . pow, bam, sock . . . four-letter words . . . smash to the groin . . . pow, bam, sock . . . lone stranger pulls a gun . . . pow . . . man bites the asphalt . . . bam, sock . . . lone stranger walks on . . . mean, ugly, handsome-ugly, lonely lone stranger . . . out of shadows comes a girl, beautiful-anonymous, big-bosomed boy-body, all hair and mouth, no forehead, no hips . . . pow, bam, sock . . . five-letter words . . . smooch to the groin . . . pow, bam, sock . . . pop-art penthouse . . . bare shoulders, bare thighs, bare everything . . . pow . . . beautiful-anonymous bites the bed sheets . . . bam, sock . . . lone stranger walks on . . . mean, ugly, handsome-ugly, lonely lone stranger . . . wham, crash . . . op-art penthouse . . . six dead bodies and six beautiful anonymouses, and you can't tell the bodies from the anonymouses without six-letter words . . . discotheque . . . writhing, swaying, hyper-hipping and some tripping . . . psyche my delic and call me Vanessa . . . seven-letter words and eight more nudes . . . nine-letter words and ten-letter words and bingo! . . . ALIENATION!!! . . . zowie . . . camp and noncommunication and every man a lone stranger with two cars in every garage and pot in the pot . . . noncommunication . . . hallelujah . . . incoherence . . . FADE OUT.

Thus the age of film has come full century in the sixties, and the optimists among us choose to think that films have come of age as well. *Blow-Up* has exploded in the worlds of Kirche, Kuche and Kinder alike; but we need not despair, because *The Sound of Music* is still the all-time record holder, and throughout the past year, *To Sir, with Love* had the kids in thrall, and *A Man and a Woman* let everyone wallow in a world of *Ladies Home Journal* fiction while keeping *Réalités* on the coffee table. Above all, *Gone with the Wind* is back in contemporary format to reassert the all-time cinematic values that seemed uncertain a while back when the woe-betiders were worrying that Andy Warhol might be the Griffith of our day, and the local art house, the stag-movie showcase of our neighborhood. The nicest thing you can say about Lee Marvin is that he has the Humphrey Bogart magnetic meanness, and there are those who maintain that Julie Andrews might well be Mary Pickford with hair-straightener. So who's America's Sweetheart now?

Doris Day isn't, and Rock Hudson isn't, not anymore, and that's what separates the fifties from the sixties, wherein the fuse was finally lit for the rip-roaring explosion that has shattered any delusions about which is the liveliest of the arts and where the cultural action is today —and tomorrow.

The speed of the explosion, even in this age of hypersonics, is amazing. Was it indeed only yesterday—1960—that *Hiroshima, Mon Amour* burst forth with those embarrassment-evoking bare shoulders and intertwined thighs to suggest to the American movie audience that perhaps not every woman went to bed, Hollywood-star fashion, with a long-sleeved nightie that tied at the neck and a bow in her carefully coifed curls, and not every man wore pajamas, all two pieces? (We're left to ponder, those of us who are not unaware of the industrial aspects of the "art form" known as movies, whether it was American morality that kept even married folk at sleeptime well clad and in twin beds or whether it was the nightwear and furniture manufacturers.)

Some of us encountered Godard's hand-held camera in 1961's *Breathless,* and Truffaut's sensations-of-Sennett the next year in *Jules and Jim.* But for the non-art-house-oriented among us, the changes in form and rhythm and content really came with *Tom Jones* and *8½* and *Dr. No* in 1963; *Dr. Strangelove* and *The Servant* and *A Hard Day's*

Night in 1964; *Darling* and *Mickey One* and *The Ipcress File* in 1965; *Georgy Girl* and *Dear John* and *Who's Afraid of Virginia Woolf?* in 1966–1967—and, with the sizzling and sputtering of a fuse, *Ulysses* and *Blow-Up* and *I, a Woman* and *The Chelsea Girls* and the shattering impact of *Bonnie and Clyde* and *Portrait of Jason.* Above all, there was Expo '67 to demonstrate the excitement of form, the infinite variety of projection and the endless possibility therein.

Well, the more it changes, the more it is of the same old thing. This movie-minded generation, set agog by Expo's films, is much in the position of the pot smoker who encounters De Quincey's *Confessions of an English Opium-Eater* and wonders how long this sort of thing has been going on. Expo offered Labyrinth, more than a year in construction, longer in conception, millions in expenditure, with its wall and floor projection, its mini-lights and music pause for meditation, its five-screen-cross finale; a 360-degree projection for a trans-Canada trip (another version of the trans-U.S.A. trip offered at Disneyland); projection on moving geometrics; multi-multi-multiscreens; and finally, the circle completed at the Ontario pavilion, where a brilliant film was projected in 70mm on a single screen to give one the illusion of multi-screen projection.

The wonder and stimulation are there for the movie-minded, if not for the movie-history-minded. Let James Card, curator of motion pictures at George Eastman House in Rochester, N.Y., point to another Expo, the great Paris Exposition of 1900, where the results of the first two decades of moviemaking were demonstrated. By then, Mr. Card notes, there were sound films, trick films with stop-motion effects and multiple exposures, news features, story films and movies in color, even Cineorama and a sixty-nine-foot-wide screen. At that other exposition, he reports, Sarah Bernhardt and Coquelin spoke from the screen; Raoul Grimon-Sanson's Cineorama, more than twice the size of today's Cinerama, used ten synchronized cameras and projectors (versus today's single projector) and a screen thirty feet high that completely surrounded the spectators with a gigantic color movie. Today's Cinemascope? The Lumière brothers showed their color films on a 48 x 69-foot screen, with twenty-five thousand viewers (four times a Radio City Music Hall full house) seated at a session.

Why, then, the explosion sixty-seven years later? The wonders of film form and shape were tucked away until they became "commercially" feasible or essential for survival. When the public began staying home to listen to radio for free in the twenties, sound (and sound-on-film had been developed as early as 1908) was added for talkies. When the public began staying home to watch television for free in the forties and fifties, out came the expanding screens, the 3-D experiments, the new shapes and forms. And new generations of filmmakers and filmgoers saw a wondrous world unfolding. Certainly, the explosive nature of the Expo films is to be attributed to the entire audiovisual orientation of our society, our growing literacy and awareness of the aspects of the medium, our perhaps diminishing awareness of the importance of the message.

Our eyes have opened to film. In an age of affluence, ten-year-olds make 8mm movies replete with cuts, miniatures and judiciously applied catsup blood to out-Bond Flint; and teen-agers turn out animations that make middle-Disney look like the filmstrip artistry that elementary-school youngsters turn out daily in more progressive art classes. The long-haired lad who, in a recent *New Yorker* cartoon, approached his father at the breakfast table with, "Dad, could I have twenty thousand dollars to make a film?" was speaking for his generation. Where mine intended to write the Great American Novel, today's plans exclusively on making the Great American Movie—that will, of course, be far ahead of the now slightly aging New Wave boys but pay tribute, naturally, to those great camp artists of Hollywood's Magnificent Thirties. Above all, it will have the Truth that one finds in *Blow-Up* and *Bonnie and Clyde* and that audiences will be finding this year in Shirley Clarke's *Portrait of Jason,* Dusan Makavejev's *Love Affair . . . or the Case of the Missing Switchboard Operator* and Frank Simon's *The Queen,* on the arthouse and campus circuits, and hopefully, in Bergman's *Shame* or Harold Pinter's *The Birthday Party* of John Frankenheimer's *The Fixer* or Mike Nichols's *Catch-22.*

The Truth, of course, is where you find it—and you can find it on occasion in form, but always in content. And so we can go back to Expo and discover how far form without content sticks with us, how much of the freak-show aspect vanishes, how little of substance does evade us. From Labyrinth one recalls vividly the surprising splash of the bread the little girl throws from shore on the wall screen into the water on the floor screen; but how much more vivid is recollection of the eyes of the savage in search of the diabolic crocodile, the eyes of the woman searching for herself in front of her makeup mirror. And these last are on small, square screens, the art in the humanity on both sides of the camera lens, the Truth in the content of the vision. And Labyrinth stays in memory not because of its meditation room and galleries but because, in the midst of a jubilant world exposition, in the midst of affluence and arty sales pitches for the material wonders of the world, one cinematic voice and vision said to us, "Hey, hold on, maybe what's wrong with the world is inside you." And despite all its beautiful and imaginative use of triple screens, the Francis Thompson-Alexander Hammid *To Be Alive!* provided as memorable an experience at Expo as it had at the New York World's Fair, because it had something to say and voiced the truth that life in the world around us is wondrous and good, but only the very young and the very old take the time to observe it.

What, then, of the content of films that are taking every shape and form that technology permits? Without question, almost every film—from the television-oriented quickie (i.e., *Games,* which fades in and out almost by the clock to adapt its piecemeal plotting to the requirements of commercials and station breaks) to the grind-audience special (i.e., *I, a Woman,* a sexploitation film that became socially acceptable because it was foreign-made and boasted English subtitles)—has beautiful scenes or values in musical scoring or film editing. A Hollywood mogul has rightly said that "It's easy to *take* a good picture—the hard part is to *make* a good picture."

Obviously, and to the horror of the puritans and Neanderthals among us, we're in a no-holds-barred era as far as the content of film is concerned. Inveterate moviegoers (and who more inveterate than a see-'em-all movie critic?) are hard-pressed to think of any human aberration, let alone practice, that has not been put on film, with almost as much remaining in the mind, if not the eye, of the beholder (i.e., *Bonnie and Clyde,* wherein, much as in Bergman's *The Silence,* only those who know of certain practices will see them). Sadism? We've graduated from the recurrent spreadeagle torture scenes of the Bond movies to where, in *Point Blank,* for example, Lee Marvin can deliver a karate chop to a chap's groin. "A first for that one," I remarked to a colleague. "Guess you're right," he replied after a moment's consideration. "After all, in *St. Valentine's Day Massacre,* the gal only kneed George Segal." All the varieties of bloodletting have been explored in full and blazing color, and the body beautiful exposed in repose and in motion in a manner to make *Hiroshima*'s shoulders seem wondrously decorous. We're growing up, as are our movie stars. In *The Family Way,* little Hayley Mills, bless 'er 'eart, not only exposed her scrumptious little derriere but did so in a film devoted exclusively to a young couple's difficulties in "consummating" their marriage. Heavens, when we think of what Doris and Rock used to go through just so Doris could emerge *intacta* at fadeout time!

But is it really the nudity *à trois* that made *Blow-Up* perhaps the most talked about if not the best film of the past twelve months? I think not, no more than that the violence was a come-on aspect of *Bonnie and Clyde.* Both films demonstrate the ultimate in cinematic skill, in establishing a milieu, in editing and romanticizing reality for artistic purpose. More important is that young people—and the young lead us more often than not in movie matters, and I do mean far beyond their inspiring the grown-up world to take that reluctant first look at the Beatles—have found their time of day and their message. To the seasoned and sophisticated aficionado, *Blow-Up* is Antonioni at his most watchable, with cinema style derived from Stanley Donen, but the same old Antonioni on alienation and noncommunication in his refusal to come to grips with the flesh and blood of life. To younger and/or fresher eyes, new to this Italian filmmaker, it is "now," in a world of surface living and sensual self-indulgence, where the fine line between reality and illusion is blurred, and you can blow your mind in the coping therewith. *Bonnie and Clyde* is amazing in its morality, its thesis that those who live by violence shall die thereby, its demonstration that the rewards of crime are nil, its depiction of the empty, shallow young psychopaths who captured the imagination of a Depression-ridden countryside. But young people catch its rhythm as a purely American folk ballad underlining and snowballing of wrongdoing, the inability to stop short once one has set out on a path in that fruitless endeavor to "be" somebody, the interdependence of law-breakers and of lawmen, the sordid depravity of two folk "heroes."

Thus the films we are getting and that are to come have no holds barred as far as sex and violence and language go. Shocking? It's time we faced the fact that films, much like literature and drama, come out of our society and mirror it, and that beyond matters of clothing and interior decoration, movies reflect and do not set patterns. At this point, *Virginia Woolf's* "hump the hostess" sounds meek and mild next to the fond exchange of "bitch" and "bastard" between no lesser stars than Albert Finney and Audrey Hepburn, reverberating from no less a screen than that of Radio City Music Hall in no less a film than Stanley Donen's *Two for the Road.* And there was no bowdlerization of Molly Bloom's soliloquy from the screen version of *Ulysses,* thanks to the wise judge's conclusion more than thirty years ago, in the course of freeing the American publication of the James Joyce classic, that no girl had ever been raped by a book. Or, he might have added, by a movie—albeit rape and seduction and variations of both may be viewed at leisure at your neighborhood theater. And violence. And bloodshed.

But we are grown-ups, and we have seen a man murdered in our living rooms via television (the Oswald-Ruby murder), and we are ready to face the reality on the wide screen that all is not happy endings and twin beds and ultimate virginity. We're ready, then, for Shirley Clarke's *Portrait of Jason,* a 105-minute near-monologue by a Negro male prostitute (with off-screen "interviewing" by the director and needling by a friend or two), a film that demonstrates the difference between an artist (i.e., Miss Clarke) and a commercialist (i.e., Andy Warhol and other recorders of the boring prurience that evolves on the screen in freak-show terms as *The Chelsea Girls*). Jason talks and does his "act" and his "bit"; and through the completely frank and therefore shocking exposure of a desperate human, we get a throbbing and horrifying and compassionate understanding of what society can make of a man.

And because the world is our cinematic oyster, the new year offers us a film "collage" by a young Yugoslav, Makavejev's *Love Affair,* an ironic commentary, via the recounting of a fatal romance between a serious man and a surface maid, on the tragic trivia of all lives, let alone on life behind the Iron Curtain. And very much in the tradition of the New Wave, let alone the internationalism of today's moviemaking, we can revel in *Le Départ,* directed by a young Pole, made in Belgium with a sparkling French cast (headed by Jean-Pierre Léaud, the boy of *The 400 Blows* grown to manhood and stylish comedy), and learn to our delight how a young hairdresser can switch his passions from fast cars to one lovely girl.

What we as grown-ups are willing, let alone ready, to face in the name of adulthood is one thing, however, and what the purveyors of films are offering in the name thereof is quite another. Lip service and sign service to the generation gap—the "suggested-for-mature-audiences" bit, the "persons-under-eighteen-not-admitted-unless-accompanied-by-their-parents" dichotomy, the "adults-only" blurb—serve at most to advise the semiconscientious parent that the film so labeled is not a family film. (A "family" film is all too often one designed for the family that is glued together by sentimentality, simplemindedness and a set of values as distinguished by its banality as its vulgarity; but thank goodness we can take grandma and the kids—there are no bare, though bulgy, bosoms and nothing more lecherous than an eight-year-old ogling Brigitte Bardot, Daddy slapping Mommy gaily on the rump or Mommy comically suspecting Daddy of instant adultery with every female within fifty feet of her own split level.) More often than not, however, the adults-only label serves to alert the thrill-seeker and, on rare occasion, deprive the mature adolescent of cinematic experiences that he may be far better equipped to appreciate than are many of his elders.

But how stringent or restrictive indeed is the adult label when just about every film is destined for television, that massest of the media? The purveyors of *The Penthouse,* which epitomizes the current sex-and-sadism-for-voyeurs product, got well ahead of the game in their publicity. Under the title in tiny letters was "s.m.a.," catering to the production code's "suggested-for-mature-audiences" labeling restriction. But in caps as large as the title was the titillating news that this was "THE PICTURE YOU WILL NOT SEE ON TELEVISION." But who's kidding whom? If there were qualitative safeguards on television films, we might not see on the home screen the sick and sickening and utterly pointless ninety-seven minute depiction of two madmen torturing a slobbish adulterer and taking bedroom turns with his sluttish doxy. But quality is not the test; and morally, there are getting to be fewer and fewer holds barred even on the small screen—with forty million viewers on hand for even the dullest of offerings. Let's just say that we may not be seeing *The Penthouse* on television this year. I'd hedge my bets as far as next year is concerned.

This is, after all, the television season that has brought us *Never on Sunday* on a network prime-time basis, so that the kiddies who weren't abed by nine P.M. could get a gander at the happiest prostitute in Piraeus and consider Jules Dassin's dubious thesis that the life of the flesh and the instincts has it all over the intellectual one in any clime. It's the season that's promising us *Tom Jones,* a bawdy, lusty romp no matter how you slice it—and slice and splice the feature films the networks and local stations do to eliminate that bit of breast or bottom that under mixed-up morality may be seen in the flesh at home but not in the film that is watched there. But oddly enough, on occasion, the slicing and splicing is done with taste and forethought, and, because great and even good films can manage to survive the interruptions for commercials and station breaks, throughout the country, we've been able, courtesy of local stations, to have such truly adult films as *Room at the Top* and *The Pawnbroker* and *La Dolce Vita* come to us with their guts and basic artistry intact.

This year, feature films will make even further encroachments on prime time that television should ideally devote to its own creations, with seven instead of the current six network movies a week on the agenda. The factories are hard at work to provide the product, with filmmakers and, as *Variety* so jazzily put it on one occasion, "video execs" reaching prior agreement "on moral requirements that would clear the film for homescreen viewing and still bring out sex-happy filmgoers in prior theatrical release." But we can rely on television to serve its sex-happy video viewers as well, what with tailored-for-television films (produced directly for television, with no exhibition in theaters beforehand) going on about homosexuality, adultery, drug trips and the other major divertissements of our day. The "moral requirements" of the home or theater screen seem to be getting broader by the season.

Time to view with alarm? Not really. The more it changes . . . We have *Doctor Dolittle* and *Half a Sixpence* for the high-class family trade for the new year, and Claude Lelouch's successor to *A Man and a Woman,* his *Live for Life,* to permit us to wallow again in some schmaltz *à la française* and feel sophisticated about our sentimentality. And lurking offscreen, ready to pop on—beyond the bare bones of Jane Fonda that are getting to be a cinematic staple, beyond the much-anticipated screen debut of Barbra Streisand, beyond the black comedies and sick comedies and tough-guy dramas—there is the great moviemaker. He's a man of any or all nationalities, age or background. It doesn't matter. What does matter is that he is a man with something to say that can and must be said only through film in his very own way and on his own terms. He is the man to move us and the movies up a few rungs of the ladder in our climb to maturity.

We're readier than ever, perhaps, certainly willing and anxiously waiting for him. Let's hope that sixty-eight will be his year. After all, the greatest movie is still unmade.

Anthony Schillaci

FILM AS ENVIRONMENT

The Reverend Anthony Schillaci, a member of the National Film Study Program at Fordham University, is a teacher of Mass Media and respected critic in the field. For him and for the generation with which he is concerned, "film is an environment which you put on, demanding a different kind of structure, a different mode of attention than any other art."

THE better we understand how young people view film, the more we have to revise our notion of what film is. Seen through young eyes, film is destroying conventions almost as quickly as they can be formulated. Whether the favored director is "young" like Richard Lester, Roman Polanski, and Arthur Penn, or "old" like Kubrick, Fellini, and Buñuel, he must be a practicing cinematic anarchist to catch the eye of the young. If we're looking for the young audience between sixteen and twenty-four, which accounts for 48 per cent of the box office today, we will find they're on a trip, whether in a Yellow Submarine or on a Space Odyssey. A brief prayer muttered for Rosemary's Baby and they're careening down a dirt road with Bonnie and Clyde, the exhaust spitting banjo sounds, or sitting next to The Graduate as he races across the Bay Bridge after his love. The company they keep is fast; Belle de Jour, Petulia, and Joanna are not exactly a sedentary crowd. Hyped up on large doses of *Rowan and Martin's Laugh-In,* and *Mission: Impossible,* they are ready for anything that an evolving film idiom can throw on the screen. And what moves them must have the pace, novelty, style, and spontaneity of a television commercial.

All of this sounds as if the script is by McLuhan. Nevertheless, it is borne out by the experience of teaching contemporary film to university juniors and seniors, staging film festivals for late teens and early adults, and talking to literally hundreds of people about movies. The phenomenon may be interesting, and even verifiable, but what makes it important is its significance for the future of film art. The young have discovered that film is an environment which you put on, demanding a different kind of structure, a different mode of attention than any other art. Their hunger is for mind-expanding experience and simultaneity, and their art is film.

Occasionally a young director gives us a glimpse of the new world of film as environmental art. The optical exercise known as *Flicker* came on like a karate chop to the eyes at Lincoln Center's Film Seminar three years ago. One half-hour of white light flashing at varied frequency, accompanied by a deafening sound track designed to infuriate, describes the screen, but not what happened to the audience. As strangers turned to ask if it was a put-on, if they had forgotten to put film in the projector, they noticed that the flickering light fragmented their motions, stylizing them like the actions of a silent movie. In minutes, the entire audience was on its feet, acting out spontaneous pantomimes for one another, no one looking at the flashing screen. The happening precipitated by *Flicker* could be called the film of the future, but it was actually an anti-environment that gives us an insight into the past. By abstracting totally from content, the director demonstrated that the film is in the audience which acts out personal and public dramas as the screen turns it on. The delight of this experience opened up the notion of film as an environmental art.

Critics have noted the trend which leaves story line and character development strewn along the highways of film history like the corpses in Godard's *Weekend.* The same critics have not, in general, recognized that the growing option for nonlinear, unstructured experiences that leave out sequence, motivation, and "argument" is a vote for film as environment. Young people turn to film for a time-space environment in which beautiful things happen to them. The screen has, in a sense, less and less to do with what explodes in the audience. This new scene could mean either that film is plunging toward irrelevant stimulation, or that there is a new and unprecedented level of participation and involvement in young audiences. I prefer to think the latter is the case. Young people want to talk about Ben's hang-up, why Rosemary stayed with the baby, or what it feels like to be in the electronic hands of a computer like Hal. They do not forget the film the minute they walk out of the theater.

The attention given the new style of film goes beyond stimulation to real involvement. A generation with eyes fixed on the rearview mirror tended to give film the same attention required for reading—that is, turning off all the senses except the eyes. Film became almost as private as reading, and little reaction to the total audience was experienced. As the Hollywood dream factory cranked out self-contained worlds of fantasy, audiences entered them with confidence that nothing even vaguely related to real life would trouble their reveries. As long as one came and left in the middle of the film, it was relatively non-involving as environment. When television brought the image into the living room, people gave it "movie attention," hushing everyone who entered the sacred presence of the tube as they would a film patron who talked during a movie. One was not allowed to speak, even during commercials. It took post-literate man to teach us how to use television as environment, as a moving image on the wall to which one may give total or peripheral attention as he wishes. The child who had TV as a baby-sitter does not turn off all his senses, but walks about the room carrying on a multiplicity of actions and relationships, his attention a special reward for the cleverness of the pitchman, or the skill of the artist. He is king, and not captive. As McLuhan would put it, he is not an audience, he *gives* an audience to the screen.

The new multisensory involvement with film as total environment has been primary in destroying literary values in film. Their decline is not merely farewell to an understandable but unwelcome dependency; it means the emergence of a new identity for film. The diminished role of dialogue is a case in point. The difference between *Star Trek* and *Mission: Impossible* marks the trend toward self-explanatory images that need no dialogue. Take an audio tape of these two popular TV shows, as we did in a recent study, and it will reveal that while *Mission: Impossible* is completely unintelligible without images, *Star Trek* is simply an illustrated radio serial, complete on the level of sound. It has all the characteristics of radio's golden age: actions explained, immediate identification of character by voice alone, and even organ music to squeeze the proper emotion or end the episode. Like *Star Trek,* the old film was frequently a talking picture (emphasis on the adjective), thereby confirming McLuhan's contention that technologically "radio married the movies." The marriage of dependence, however, has gone on the rocks, and not by a return to silent films but a new turning to foreign ones. It was the films of Fellini and Bergman, with their subtitles, that convinced us there had been too many words. Approximately one-third of the dialogue is omitted in subtitled versions of these films, with no discernible damage—and some improvement—of the original.

More than dialogue, however, has been jettisoned. Other literary values, such as sequential narrative, dramatic choice, and plot are in a state of advanced atrophy, rapidly becoming vestigial organs on the body of film art as young people have their say. *Petulia* has no "story," unless one laboriously pieces together the interaction between the delightful arch-kook and the newly divorced surgeon, in which case it is nothing more than an encounter. The story line wouldn't make a ripple if it were not scrambled and fragmented into an experience that explodes from a free-floating present into both past and future simultaneously. *Petulia* is like some views of the universe which represent the ancient past of events whose light is just now reaching us simultaneously with the future of our galaxy, returning from the curve of outer space. Many films succeed by virtue of what they leave out. *2001: A Space Odyssey* is such a film, its muted understatement creating gaps in the action that invite our inquiry. Only a square viewer wants to know where the black monolith came from and where it is going. For most of the young viewers to whom I have spoken, it is just there. *Last Year at Marienbad* made the clock as limply shapeless as one of Salvador Dali's watches, while *8½* came to life on the strength of free associations eagerly grasped by young audiences. The effect of such films is a series of open-ended impressions, freely evoked and enjoyed, strongly inviting inquiry and involvement. In short, film is freed to work as environment, something which does not simply contain, but shapes people, tilting the balance of their faculties, radically altering their perceptions, and ultimately their views of self and all reality. Perhaps one sense of the symptomatic word "grooving," which applies to both sight and sound environments, is that a new mode of attention—multisensory, total, and simultaneous—has arrived. When you "groove," you do not analyze, follow an argument, or separate sensations; rather, you are massaged into a feeling of heightened life and consciousness.

If young people look at film this way, it is in spite of the school, a fact which says once more with emphasis that education is taking place outside the classroom walls. The "discovery" that television commercials are the most exciting and creative part of today's programing is old news to the young. Commercials are a crash course in speed-viewing, their intensified sensations challenging the viewer to synthesize impressions at an ever increasing rate. The result is short films like one produced at UCLA, presenting 3,000 years of art in three minutes. *God Is Dog Spelled Backwards* takes you from the cave paintings of Lascaux to the latest abstractions, with some images remaining on the screen a mere twenty-fourth of a second! The young experience the film, however, not as confusing, but as exuberantly and audaciously alive. They feel joy of recognition, exhilaration at the intense concentration necessary (one blink encompasses a century of art), and awe at the 180-second review of every aspect of the human condition. Intended as a put-on, the film becomes a three-minute commercial for man. This hunger for overload is fed by the television commercial, with its nervous jump cuts demolishing continuity, and its lazy dissolves blurring time-space boundaries. Whether the young are viewing film "through" television, or simply through their increased capacity for information and sensation (a skill which makes most schooling a bore), the result is the same—film becomes the primary environment in which the hunger to know through experience is satisfied.

Hidden within this unarticulated preference of the young is a quiet tribute to film as the art that humanizes change. In its beginnings, the cinema was celebrated as the art that mirrored reality in its functional dynamism. And although the early vision predictably gave way to misuse of the medium, today the significance of the filmic experience of change stubbornly emerges again. Instead of prematurely stabilizing change, film celebrates it. The cinema can inject life into historical events by the photoscan, in which camera movement and editing liberate the vitality of images from the past. *City of Gold,* a short documentary by the National Film Board of Canada, takes us by zoom and cut into the very life of the Klondike gold rush, enabling us to savor the past as an experience.

Education increasingly means developing the ability to live humanly in the technological culture by changing with it. Film is forever spinning out intensifications of the environment which make it visible and livable. The ability to control motion through its coordinates of time and space make film a creative agent in change. Not only does film reflect the time-space continuum of contemporary physics, but it can manipulate artistically those dimensions of motion which we find most problematic. The actuality of the medium, its here-and-now impact, reflects how completely the present tense has swallowed up both past and future. Freudian psychology dissolves history by making the past something we live; accelerated change warps the future by bringing it so close that we can't conceive it as "ahead" of us. An art which creates its own space, and can move time forward and back, can humanize change by conditioning us to live comfortably immersed in its fluctuations.

On the level of form, then, perhaps the young are tuned in to film for "telling it like it is" in a sense deeper than that of fidelity to the event. It is film's accurate reflection of a society and of human life totally in flux that makes it the liberating art of the time. We live our lives more like Guido in *8½*—spinners of fantasies, victims of events, the products of mysterious associations—than we do like Maria in *The Sound of Music,* with a strange destiny guiding our every step. Instead of resisting change and bottling it, film intensifies the experience of change, humanizing it in the process. What makes the ending of *The Graduate* "true" to young people is not that Ben has rescued his girl from the Establishment, but that he did it without a complete plan for the future. The film may fail under analysis, but it is extraordinarily coherent as experience, as I learned in conversations about it with the young. The same accurate reflection of the day may be said of the deep space relativity of *2001,* the frantic pace of *Petulia,* or the melodramatic plotting of *Rosemary's Baby.* Whether this limitless capacity for change within the creative limits of art has sober implications for the future raises the next (and larger) questions of what young people look for and get out of film.

When the question of film content is raised, the example of *Flicker* and other films cited may seem to indicate that young people favor as little substance as possible in their film experiences. A casual glance at popular drive-in fare would confirm this opinion quickly. Nevertheless, their attitude toward "what films are about" evidences a young, developing sensitivity to challenging comments on what it means to be human. The young are digging the strong humanism of the current film renaissance and allowing its currents to carry them to a level deeper than that reached by previous generations. One might almost say that young people are going to the film-maker's work for values that they have looked for in vain from the social, political, or religious establishments. This reaction, which has made film modern man's morality play, has not been carefully analyzed, but the present state of evidence invites our inquiry.

As far as the "point" of films is concerned, young people will resist a packaged view, but will welcome a problematic one. The cry, "Please, I'd rather do it myself!" should be taken to heart by the film-maker. It is better to use understatement in order to score a personal discovery by the viewer. Such a discovery of an idea is a major part of our delight in the experience of film art. A frequent answer to a recent survey question indicated that a young man takes his girl to the movies so that they will have something important to talk about. It is not a matter of pitting film discussion against "making out," but of recognizing that a rare and precious revelation of self to the other is often occasioned by a good film. The young feel this experience as growth, expanded vitality, more integral possession of one's self with the consequent freedom to go out to others more easily and more effectively.

Very little of the business of being human happens by instinct, and so we need every form of education that enlightens or accelerates that process. While young people do not go to films for an instant humanization course, a strong part of the pleasure they take in excellent films does just this. Whether through a connaturality of the medium described earlier, or because of a freer viewpoint, young audiences frequently get more out of films than their mentors. It is not so much a matter of seeing more films, but of seeing more in a film. The film-as-escape attitude belongs to an age when the young were not yet born; and the film-as-threat syndrome has little meaning for the sixteen to twenty-four group, simply because they are free from their elders' hang-ups. A typical irrelevance that causes youthful wonder is the elderly matron's complaint that *Bonnie and Clyde* would teach bad driving habits to the young.

The performance of youthful audiences in discussions of contemporary film indicates their freedom from the judgmental screen which blurs so many films for other generations. In speaking of *Bonnie and Clyde,* late high school kids and young adults do not dwell upon the career of crime or the irregularity of the sexual relationship, but upon other things. The development of their love fascinates young people, because Clyde shows he knows Bonnie better than she knows herself. Although he resists her aggressive sexual advances, he knows and appreciates her as a person. It is the sincerity of their growing love that overcomes his impotence, and the relationship between this achievement and their diminished interest in crime is not lost on the young audience. The reversal of the "sleep together now, get acquainted later" approach is significant here. These are only a few of the nuances that sensitive ears and eyes pick up beneath the gunfire and banjo-plucking. Similarly, out of the chaotic impressions of *Petulia,* patterns are perceived. Young people note the contrasts between Petulia's kooky, chaotic life, and the over-controlled precision of the surgeon's existence. The drama is that they both come away a little different for their encounter. Instead of a stale moral judgment on their actions, one finds open-ended receptivity to the personal development of the characters.

Youth in search of identity is often presented as a ridiculous spectacle, a generation of Kierkegaards plaintively asking each other: "Who am I?" Nevertheless, the quest is real and is couched in terms of a hunger for experience. SDS or LSD, McCarthy buttons or yippie fashions, it is all experimentation in identity, trying on experiences to see if they fit. The plea is to stop the world, not so that they can get off, but so they can get a handle on it. To grasp each experience, to suck it dry of substance, and to grow in the process is behind the desire to be "turned on." But of all the lurid and bizarre routes taken by young people, the one that draws least comment is that of the film experience. More people have had their minds expanded by films than by LSD. Just as all art nudges man into the sublime and vicarious experience of the whole range of the human condition, film does so with a uniquely characteristic totality and involvement.

Ben, *The Graduate,* is suffocating under his parents' aspirations, a form of drowning which every young person has felt in some way. But the film mirrors their alienation in filmic terms, by changes in focus, by the metaphors of conveyor belt sidewalk and swimming pool, better than any moralist could say it. The satirical portraits of the parents may be broad and unsubtle, but the predicament is real and compelling. This is why the young demand no assurances that Ben and the girl will live happily ever after; it is enough that he jarred himself loose from the sick apathy and languid sexual experimentation with Mrs. Robinson to go after one thing, one person that he wanted for himself, and not for others. Incidentally, those who are not busy judging the morality of the hotel scenes will note that sex doesn't communicate without love. Some may even note that Ben is using sex to strike at his parents —not a bad thing for the young (or their parents) to know.

Emotional maturity is never painless and seldom permanent, but it can become a bonus from viewing good films because it occurs there not as taught but experienced. Values communicated by film are interiorized and become a part of oneself, not simply an extension of the womb that parents and educators use to shield the young from the world. Colin Smith, in *The Loneliness of the Long Distance Runner,* IS youth, not because he did it to the Establishment, but because he is trying to be his own man and not sweat his guts out for another. The profound point of learning who you are in the experience of freedom, as Colin did in running, is not lost on the young who think about this film a little. Some speak of Col's tragedy as a failure to realize he could have won the race for himself, and not for the governor of the Borstal. Self-destruction through spite, the pitfalls of a self-justifying freedom, and the sterility of bland protest are real problems that emerge from the film. The values that appeal most are the invisible ones that move a person to act because "it's me" (part of one's identity), and not because of "them." Because they have become an object of discovery and not of imposition, such values tend to make morality indistinguishable from self-awareness.

It should be made clear, however, that it is not merely the content, but the mode of involvement in the film experience that makes its humanism effective. In terms of "message," much of contemporary film reflects the social and human concerns that Bob Dylan, the Beatles, Simon and Garfunkel, and Joan Baez communicate. But the words of their songs often conceal the radical nature of the music in which they appear. The direct emotional appeal of the sound of "Eleanor Rigby," "Give a Damn," "I Am a Rock," or "Mr. Businessman" communicates before we have the words deciphered. Films with honest human concern, similarly, change audiences as much by their style as their message. *Elvira Madigan*'s overpowering portrait of a hopeless love, *A Thousand Clowns'* image of nonconformity, *Zorba*'s vitality, and *Morgan*'s tragedy are not so much the content of the images as the outcome of their cinematic logic. If these films change us, it is because we have done it to ourselves by opening ourselves to their experiences.

Expo 67 audiences were charmed by the Czech Kinoautomat in which their vote determined the course of comic events in a film. Once again, we find here not a peek into the future, but an insight into all film experience. In one way or another, we vote on each film's progress. The passive way is to patronize dishonest or cynical films, for our box-office ballot determines the selection of properties for years to come. We have been voting this way for superficial emotions, sterile plots, and happy endings for a generation. But we vote more actively and subtly by willing the very direction of a film through identification with the character, or absorption into the action. The viewer makes a private or social commitment in film experience. He invests a portion of himself in the action, and if he is changed, it is because he has activated his own dreams. What happens on the screen, as in the case of *Flicker,* is the catalyst for the value systems, emotional responses, and the indirect actions which are the by-products of a good film. Film invites young people to be part of the action by making the relationships which take the work beyond a mere succession of images. The reason why young people grow through their art is that they supply the associations that merely begin on the screen but do not end there. When parents and educators become aware of this, their own efforts at fostering maturity may be less frantic, and more effective.

It is not only the films that please and delight which appeal to the young, but also those which trouble and accuse by bringing our fears into the open. The new audience for documentary films highlights a new way of looking at film as an escape *into* reality. From *The War Game* to *Warrendale,* from *The Titicut Follies* to *Battle of Algiers,* young audiences are relishing the film's ability to document the present in terms of strong social relevance. *Portrait of Jason* is more than a voyeuristic peek into the psyche of a male whore; it is a metaphor for the black man's history in America, and this is what young people see in that film. Even the most strident dissenters will appreciate the ambiguities of *The Anderson Platoon,* which leaves us without anyone to hate, because it is not about Marines and Vietcong, but about men like ourselves. In these as in other films, the social content is intimately wed to the film experience, and together they form a new outlook. Ultimately, we may have to change our views on what film art is about.

The foregoing analysis of how young people look at film will appear to some to constitute a simplistic eulogy to youth. For this reason, we may temper our optimism by a hard look at real problems with this generation. There is a desperate need for education. Although they cannot all be structured, none of the better youthful attitudes or responses described came about by chance. Mere screening of films, for example, whether they be classics or trash, does little good. Colleges can become places where the young are taught hypocrisy, being told they "should" like Fellini, Bergman, Antonioni, or Godard. They can accept these film-makers just as uncritically as their parents adulated movie stars. Unless there is encouragement to reflect on film experience, its impact can be minimal and fleeting. Most of the responses I have mentioned came from students who were well into the habit of discussing film. These discussions are best when they flow from the natural desire we have to communicate our feelings about a film. Nonverbalization, the reluctance to betray by treacherous abstractions the ineffable experience of the film, arises at this point. Real as it is, there must be found some middle ground between a suffocatingly detailed dissection of a film, and the noncommunicative exclamation, "like WOW!" Reflecting on one's experience is an integral part of making that experience part of one's self. Furthermore, one can see an almost immediate carry-over to other film experiences from each film discussed.

A problem more crucial than lack of reflection is the poverty of critical perspective. The young can plunge into their personal version of the *auteur* theory and make a fad or fetish out of certain films and directors. Roman Polanski has made some bad films, that is, films which do not reflect his own experience and feelings honestly as did *Knife in the Water.* Fascinating as *Rosemary's Baby* is, it suffers from an uncertain relationship of the director to his work. Some directors are adulated for peripheral or irrelevant reasons. Joseph Losey is a good film-maker, not because of a cynical preoccupation with evil, but because, like Hitchcock and Pinter, he makes us less certain of our virtue. And Buñuel, far from being a cheerful anarchist attacking church and society with abandon, is a careful surgeon, excising with camera the growths of degenerate myth on the cancerous culture.

In their own work, young people can celebrate bad film-making as "honest" and voyeuristic films as "mature." Criticism of poor films is not "putting down" the director for doing his own thing, especially if his thing is trite, dishonest, or so personal that it has no meaning accessible to others. Criticism means taking a stand on the basis of who you are. The current preference of spoof over satire is not just another instance of cool over hot, but is symptomatic of a noncritical stance. *Dr. Strangelove* makes comic absurdity out of the cold war from a certain conviction about what mature political action should be. The *Laugh-In* has no convictions but a lot of opinions. If it is accused of favoring an idea or cause, it will refute the charge by ridiculing what it holds. The cynical, sophisticated noninvolvement of the "won't vote" movement in the recent election has its counterpart in film viewing.

A question that should perhaps have been asked earlier is: Why should we be concerned with asking how young people look at film? Tired reasons, citing *Time's* Man of the Year, the under-twenty-five generation, or the youth-quake menace of *Wild in the Streets* (they'll be taking over!) are not appropriate here. Anyone who is interested in the direction taken by cinema, and its continued vitality in the current renaissance of the art, will have to take the young into account as the major shaping force on the medium. If the age group from sixteen to twenty-four accounts for 48 per cent of the box office, it means that this eight-year period determines the success or failure of most films. Fortunately, there has not yet appeared a formula for capturing this audience. *Variety* described the youth market as a booby trap for the industry, citing the surprise success of sleepers such as *Bonnie and Clyde* and *The Graduate,* as well as the supposed youth-appeal failures *(Half a Sixpence, Poor Cow, Here We Go Round the Mulberry Bush).* The list may suggest a higher level of young taste than producers are willing to admit. In any case, if the young have influenced the medium this far, we cannot ignore the fact. It is for this reason that we are encouraged to speculate on the future in the form of two developments revolutionizing the young approach to film: student film-making and multi-media experiences.

More and more, the answer to how young people look at film is "through the lens of a camera." In coming years, it will be youth as film-maker, and not simply as audience, that will spur the evolution of the cinema. Students want a piece of the action, whether in running a university, the country, or the world; in terms of our question, this means making films. There is a strong resonance between film-making and the increasingly sophisticated film experience. Young people delighted by a television commercial are tempted to say: "I could do that!" Considering the cost and artistry of some commercials, this is a pretty naïve statement, but it doesn't stop the young from taking out their father's Super-8 or buying an old Bolex to tell their story on film. Today, anyone can make a film. Although Robert Flaherty's longed-for parousia, when film is as cheap as paper, has not yet arrived, the art has come into the reach of almost everyone. The Young Film-Makers Conference held by Fordham University last February drew 1,200 people, 740 of them student film-makers below college age. On a few week's notice, some 120 films were submitted for screening. Kids flew in from Richmond, California, and bussed in from Louisville, Kentucky, with twenty-seven states and Canada represented. Numbers, however, do not tell the story. One of the notable directors and actors present sized up the scene by saying: "My God, I'm standing here in the middle of a revolution!" It was the quality of the films that caused Eli Wallach to remark, only half in jest, that some day he'd be working for one of these film-makers. The young look at film as potential or actual film-makers, and this fact raises participation to an unprecedented critical level. The phenomenon also removes the last residue of passive audience participation from the Golden Forties box-office bonanza.

Foolhardy though it may be, one can predict that the new interest in film will take the direction of multi-media experimentation. Expo 67, it seems, is *now.* Our new and growing capacity to absorb images and synthesize sounds demands a simultaneity that cannot be met by traditional forms of film-making. The response so far has been the half-hearted multiple screens of *The Thomas Crown Affair,* not part of the conception of the film, but inserted as fancy dressing. The object of multiple images is not so much to condense actions as to create an environment such as the Ontario pavilion film, *A Place to Stand.* My own students have begun to relegate location shots such as street scenes or mood sequences to peripheral attention on side screens and walls, while the action takes place on the main screen.

It is symptomatic that the staged novelty of the Electric Circus is giving way to a new and interesting experiment in Greenwich Village, Cerebrum—where for a modest fee parties can set up their own media platforms equipped with projectors, tape recorders, and lights to stage their own happening. The idea being developed here is central to multimedia art, that is, the orchestration of contemporary media instruments. Young people are not afraid to carry a running projector around, spraying the images on walls and ceilings for distortions which communicate. An older generation is inclined to think of the media hardware as "machines" to be screwed to the floor or locked in a booth while they "produce" images and sounds. The young, in contrast, recognize this hardware as part of the information environment of electronic technology, and they use it accordingly. Spontaneity, the chance synchronization, overload that leads to breakthrough—these are all part of the excitement that draws people to media rather than film alone.

The young look at film is a revolutionary one, motivated more by love of the medium than hatred of the Establishment. In a sense, the new taste is liberating film for a free exploration of its potential, especially in the area of humanizing change. The hunger for a relativity of time and space will extend to morality, producing films that explore problems rather than package solutions. Nevertheless, the very intensity of young involvement gives promise of profound changes in the youth audience as people open themselves to the reality of the medium. Whether as young film-maker or multi-media entrepreneur, the young will have their say. If we take the time to cultivate their perspective, we may learn an interesting view of the future of media, and a fascinating way to stay alive.

Tom Wolfe
LOVERBOY OF THE BOURGEOISIE

"Look at you! I just had to come over here and touch you!" Hollywood created the gods and the American public worshipped. Through the Jazz Age, the Depression and the war years, our film stars reigned. The star system made Hollywood and, in the process, altered the manners and mores of America. Tom Wolfe, whose writing appears frequently in Esquire *and other magazines, examines the magic of one of our most durable gods—Cary Grant.*

ON THEIR way into the Edwardian Room of the Plaza Hotel all they had was that sort of dutiful, forward-tilted gait that East Side dowagers get after twenty years of walking small dogs up and down Park Avenue. But on their way out the two of them discover that all this time, in the same room, there has been their dreamboat, Cary Grant, sitting in the corner. Actually, Grant had the logistics of the Edwardian Room figured out pretty well. In the first place, the people who come to the Plaza for lunch are not generally the kind who are going to rise up and run, skipping and screaming, over to some movie star's table. And in the second place, he is sitting up against the wall nearest the doorway. He is eating lunch, consisting of a single bowl of Vichyssoise, facing out the window towards three old boys in silk toppers moseying around their horses and hansoms on 59th Street on the edge of Central Park.

Well, so much for logistics. The two old girls work up all the courage they need in about one-fourth of a second.

"Cary Grant!" says the first one, coming right up and putting one hand on his shoulder. "Look at you! I just had to come over here and touch you!"

Cary Grant plays a wonderful Cary Grant. He cocks his head and gives her the Cary Grant mock-quizzical look—just like he does in the movies

—the look that says, "I don't know what's happening, but we're not going to take it very seriously, are we? Or are we?"

"I have a son who's the spitting image of you," she is saying.

Cary Grant is staring at her hand on his shoulder and giving her the Cary Grant fey-bemused look and saying, "Are you trying to hold me down?"

"My son is forty-nine," she's saying. "How old are you?"

"I'm fifty-nine," says Cary Grant.

"*Fifty-nine!* Well, he's forty-nine and he's the spitting image of you, except that he looks *older* than you!"

By this time the other old girl is firmly planted, and she says: "I don't care if you hate me, I'm going to stand here and *look* at you."

"Why on earth should I hate you?" says Cary Grant.

"You can say things about me after I'm gone. I don't care, I'm going to stand here and look at you!"

"You poor dear!"

Which she does, all right. She takes it all in; the cleft chin; this great sun tan that looks like it was done on a rotisserie; this great head of steel-gray hair, of which his barber says: "It's real; I swear, I yanked it once"; and the Cary Grant clothes, all worsteds, broadcloths and silks, all rich and underplayed, like a viola ensemble.

"Poor baby," says Cary Grant, returning to the Vichyssoise.

"She meets some one for the first time and already she's saying, 'I don't care if you hate me.' Can you imagine? Can you imagine what must have gone into making someone feel that way?"

Well, whatever it was, poor old baby knows that Cary Grant is one leading man who, at least, might give it a second thought. Somehow Cary Grant, they figure, is the one dreamboat that a lady can walk right up to and touch, pour soul over and commune with.

And by the time Grant's picture, "Charade," with Audrey Hepburn, had its première at the Radio City Music Hall, thousands turned out in lines along 50th Street and Sixth Avenue, many of them in the chill of 6 A.M., in order to get an early seat. This was Grant's 61st motion picture and his 26th to open at Radio City. He is, indeed, fifty-nine years old, but his drawing power as a leading man, perhaps the last of the genuine "matinee idols," keeps mounting toward some incredible, golden-aged crest. Radio City is like a Nielsen rating for motion pictures. It has a huge seating capacity and is attended by at least as many tourists, from all over the country, as New Yorkers. Grant's first 25 premiers there played a total of 99 weeks. Each one seems to break the records all over again. Before "Charade," "That Touch of Mink," with Doris Day, played there for 10 weeks and grossed $1,886,427.

And the secret of it all is somehow tied up with the way he lit up two aging dolls in the Edwardian Room at the Plaza Hotel. In an era of Brandoism and the Mitchumism in movie heroes, Hollywood has left Cary Grant, by default, in sole possession of what has turned out to be a curiously potent device. Which is to say, to women he is Hollywood's lone example of the Sexy Gentleman. And to men and women, he is Hollywood's lone example of a figure America, like most of the West, has needed all along: a Romantic Bourgeois Hero.

One has only to think of what the rest of Hollywood and the international film industry, for that matter, have been up to since World War II. The key image in film heroes has certainly been that of Marlon Brando. One has only to list the male stars of the past 20 years—Brando, Rock Hudson, Kirk Douglas, John Wayne, Burt Lancaster, Robert Mitchum, Victor Mature, William Holden, Frank Sinatra—and already the mind is overpowered by an awesome montage of swung fists, bent teeth, curled lips, popping neck veins, and gurglings. As often as not the Brandoesque hero's love partner is some thryoid hoyden, as portrayed by Brigitte Bardot, Marilyn Monroe, Jayne Mansfield, Gina Lollobrigida or, more recently, Sue Lyons and Tuesday Weld. The upshot has been the era of Rake-a-Cheek Romance on the screen. Man meets woman. She rakes his cheek with her fingernails. He belts her in the chops. They fall in a wallow of passion.

The spirit of these romances, as in so many of the early Brando, James Dean and Rock Hudson pictures, has been borrowed from what Hollywood imagines to be the beer-and-guts verve of the guys-and-dolls lower classes. Undoubtedly, the rawness, the lubricity, the implicit sadism of it has excited moviegoers of all classes. Yet it should be clear even to Hollywood how many Americans, at rock bottom, can find no lasting identification with it. The number of American men who can really picture themselves coping with a little bleached hellion who is about to rake a cheek and draw blood with the first kiss is probably embarrassingly small. And there are probably not many more women who really wish to see Mister Right advancing toward them in a torn strap-style undershirt with his latissimae dorsae flexed.

After all, this is a nation that, except for a hard core of winos at the bottom and a hard crust of aristocrats at the top, has been going gloriously middle class for two decades, as far as the breezeways stretch. There is no telling how many millions of American women of the new era know exactly what Ingrid Bergman meant when she said she loved playing opposite Cary Grant in "Notorious" (1946): "I didn't have to take my shoes off in the love scenes."

Yet "Notorious," one will recall, was regarded as a highly sexy motion picture. The Grant plot formula—which he has repeated at intervals for 25 years—has established him as the consummate bourgeois lover: consummately romantic and yet consummately genteel. Grant's conduct during a screen romance is unfailingly of the sort that would inspire trust and delight, but first of all trust, in a middle-class woman of any age. Not only does Grant spare his heroines any frontal assault on their foundation garments, he seldom chases them at all at the outset. In fact, the Grant plot formula calls for a reverse chase. First the girl—Audrey Hepburn in "Charade," Grace Kelly in "To Catch a Thief," Betsy Drake in "Every Girl Should Be Married"—falls for Grant. He retreats, but always slowly and coyly, enough to make the outcome clear. Grant, the screen lover, and Grant, the man, were perfectly combined under the escutcheon of the middle-class American woman—"Every Girl Should Be Married"—when Grant married Betsy Drake in real life.

During the chase Grant inevitably scores still more heavily with the middle-class female psyche by treating the heroine not merely as an attractive woman but as a witty and intelligent woman. And, indeed, whether he is with Katharine Hepburn or Audrey Hepburn or Irene Dunne or Doris Day, both parties are batting incredibly bright lines back and forth, and halfway through the film they are already too maniacally witty not to click one way or another.

Because of the savoir faire, genial cynicism and Carlyle Hotel lounge accent with which he brings it all off, Grant is often thought of as an aristocratic motion picture figure. In fact, however, the typical Grant role is that of an exciting bourgeois. In "Charade" he is a foreign service officer in Paris; in "Bringing Up Baby" he was a research professor; in "Mr. Blandings Builds His Dream House" he was an enthusiastic suburbanite; and in countless pictures—among them "Crisis," "People Will Talk," "Kiss and Make Up"—he was in the most revered middle-class role of them all, exploited so successfully by television over the past three years: the doctor. Seldom is Grant portrayed as a lower-class figure—he did not make a good beatnik Cockney in "None But the Lonely Heart"—and rarely is he anything so formidable as the trucking tycoon he played in "Born To Be Bad" in 1934. The perfect Grant role is one in which he has a job that gives him enough free time so that he does not have to languish away at the office during the course of the movie; but he has the job and a visible means of support and highly visible bourgeois respectability all the same.

Grant, of course, has had no Hollywood monopoly on either savoir faire or gentility on the screen. Many suave, humorous gentlemen come to mind: Jimmy Stewart, David Niven, Fred Astaire, Ronald Colman, Franchot Tone. None of them, however, could approach Grant in that other part of being the world's best bourgeois romantic:

viz., sex appeal. It was Cary Grant that Mae West was talking about when she launched the phrase "tall, dark and handsome" in "She Done Him Wrong" (1933), and it was Cary Grant who was invited up to see her sometime. Even at age fifty-nine, the man still has the flawless squared-off face of a comic strip hero, a large muscular neck and an athletic physique which he still exhibits in at least one scene in each picture. Every good American girl wants to marry a doctor. But a Dr. Dreamboat? Is it too much to hope for? Well, that is what Cary Grant is there for.

So Cary Grant keeps pouring it on, acting out what in the Age of Brando seems like the most unlikely role in the world: the loverboy of the bourgeoisie. The upshot has been intriguing. In 1948, at the age of forty-four he came in fourth in the box-office poll of male star popularity, behind Clark Gable, Gary Cooper and Bing Crosby. By 1958, when he was fifty-four, he had risen to No. 1. This fall—when he was fifty-nine—the motion picture Theater Owners Association named him as the No. 1 box-office attraction, male or female.

Well, the two old dolls had left, and the next crisis in the Edwardian Room was that an Italian starlet had walked in, a kind of tabescent bijou blonde. Old Cary Grant knows he has met her somewhere, but he will be damned if he can remember who she was. His only hope is that she won't see him, so he has his head tucked down to one side in his Cary Grant caught-out-on-a-limb look.

He can't keep that up forever, so he keeps his head turned by talking to the fellow next to him, who has on a wild solaro-cloth suit with a step-collared vest.

"Acting styles go in fads," Cary Grant is saying. "It's like girls at a dance. One night a fellow walks in wearing a motorcycle jacket and blue jeans and he takes the first girl he sees and embraces her and crushes her rib cage. What a man!' all the girls say, and pretty soon all the boys are coming to the dances in motorcycle jackets and blue jeans and taking direct action. That goes on for a while, and then one night in comes a fellow in a blue suit who can wear a necktie without strangling, carrying a bouquet of flowers. Do they still have bouquets of flowers? I'm sure they do. Well, anyway, now the girls say, 'What a charmer!' and they're off on another cycle. Or something like that.

"Well, as for me, I just keep going along the same old way," says Cary Grant with his Cary Grant let's-not-get-all-wrapped-up-in-it look.

But now that the secret is out, the prospects are almost forbidding. Think of all those Actors Studio people trussed up in worsted, strangling on Foulard silk, speaking through the mouth instead of the nose, talking nice to love-stricken old ladies in the Edwardian Room of the Plaza Hotel. The mind boggles, baby.

Richard S. Randall
FREEDOM OF SPEECH IN A MASS MEDIUM

How far can a mass medium push the boundaries of free speech? No longer is it a legal question—that battle appears to have been won. It is rather, as Richard Randall, in the concluding chapter from his study, Censorship of the Movies: The Social and Political Control of a Mass Medium, *points out, "recognition that censorship is in large measure a social and political problem. . . ."*

MOTION pictures can hardly avoid being a major object of censorship in a mass democratic society that is officially dedicated to realizing as wide a freedom of speech as possible. The censorship interest in the medium seeks to keep from the screen that which it perceives to be threatening or offensive, and in attempting to do so, operates through a number of controls—governmental, nongovernmental, legal and extra-legal—which vary in frequency and effectiveness of sanction. This interest is rooted sociologically in a disequilibrium between the content of films and their audience. In the past, such imbalance was held to a minimum by governmental boards of censors, the film industry's own self-regulatory apparatus, and Roman Catholic pressure. This triad of controls successfully enforced a common denominator of content called the "family" film, though the extraordinary profit in such movies made the censorship task an easier one. When this pattern of control was eventually broken up by the decline of the censor boards and industry self-regulation, on the one hand, and the arrival of television, on the other, the content of movies underwent a radical change that, until now at least, has far outpaced changes in the audience pattern. Today, as in the past, the movies are a mass medium playing to a largely undifferentiated mass audience in which youth is especially well-represented. At the same time, unchecked by advertisers, they have come to deal in sex and manners with a freedom traditionally reserved for the elite media of hardcover books and the stage.* The resulting lack of balance arouses a censorship interest at the same time that traditional modes of control are less responsive to that interest. This has resulted in the partial frustration of censorial energies on the one hand, and the finding of new, often highly effective accommodation for some of these energies on the other.

Of the traditional controls, prior censorship administered by governmental licensing boards has been unquestionably the most controversial, even if not the most effective. Its form as a prior restraint has made it the target of libertarians, and, in fact, in much of the debate, this peculiar institution has been cast as the major obstacle to true freedom in films. Though it was clearly a highly restrictive and often abusive censorship at one time, it does not remain so today. Its reformation by the courts in the last fifteen years makes comparison with the past especially difficult. Gone are the vague substantive standards and the freewheeling procedures which so often gave the censors leverage far beyond their statutory powers. The governmental censors of today, subject to close judicial supervision, actually "control" motion pictures only in the first instance. Moreover, elimination of almost all censorial standards except obscenity, and the liberalization of obscenity doctrine itself, have completely altered the substance of prior censorship.

Today the boards are faced with the question of, not whether the camera should play upon a woman's face as she is presumably having intercourse with her lover *(Ecstasy),* but whether entire bodies should be shown in intercourse *(A Stranger Knocks);* not whether a heroin needle should be shown entering a man's arm *(The Man with the Golden Arm),* but whether a man's leg should be shown after he has been drawn and quartered *(Two Thousand Maniacs);* not whether a woman should be portrayed as finding happiness in adultery *(Lady Chatterley's Lover),* but whether she should be shown about to have sexual congress with a large dog *(491).* Today most nudist camp films, nudity in documentaries, run-of-the-mill "nudie" films, much sadomasochistic violence, and much that is suggestive in dances, dialogue, and situations is routinely passed, in most cases for viewing by a general audience. In fact, it can almost be said that anything censored as late as the early 1960's would be licensed today, and that almost anything censored today would not even have been produced for public exhibition as late as the early sixties.

* Some magazines and paperback books today are also marked by the same audience-content disequilibrium, and it is not surprising to find them subject to some of the same censorship interest and pressures. There is a difference in degree, however, with movies traditionally regarded as a far more powerful communicating device and, therefore, one having a special capacity for harm.

Though prior censorship is now more of a disadvantage in form than in substance, some film proprietors have maintained that it still sets movies apart in a kind of second class status among the media of speech. However, evidence indicates that the movies exercise an actual freedom of content that is far greater any of the other mass media—newspapers, magazines, radio, or television. Though free of governmental prior restraint, these media are all subject to very powerful internal restraints in the form of advertisers' influence, which is almost always exercised in the defense of conventional values and decencies. In the portrayal of erotica, control by advertisers actually functions as a kind of broker mechanism that adjusts the rigorous official free speech ethic prescribed by the First Amendment to the level of popular acceptability. It is just such a broker mechanism that the movies have never had. Hence control of the latter has always been more "public," inevitably involving government to a much greater degree than that of the other mass media.

A striking example of the relatively greater freedom exercised by movies can be seen in the 1962 censorship case involving the film *The Connection.* The New York Court of Appeals held that the word "shit," used several times in the sound track as slang for heroin, was not ground for denying an exhibition permit, and the film was then shown intact in the state. However, neither the trade nor the general press mentioned the word at all in their reporting of the decision, though some verbal gymnastics were necessary to avoid doing so.* Other examples of the freedom differential abound, not the least of which result from the widespread practice of newspapers and radio and television stations editing movie advertising copy, and in some cases rejecting it altogether.

This greater *de facto* freedom in the movies would be less remarkable if they had developed some kind of audience stratification. Yet, with few exceptions, this has not been the case. Some foreign, art, and exploitation films do play in selected theatres or to audiences with special interests, but this division is an unreliable one, since it tends to break down wherever there are strong proprietary economic temptations to enlarge the audience. Another possible stratification, that of classification, has been resisted by most of the film industry despite recent changes in the Motion Picture Code. In effect, then, the movies exercise a new freedom of content while remaining a mass medium without either the inhibition of functioning internal restraints or an

* *The New York Times* substituted "an Anglo-Saxon word" and "a four-letter word," leaving some doubt in the reader's mind about exactly what word was involved. *Variety,* the show business weekly which takes pride in a certain hardboiled sophistication and which has few, if any, youthful readers, was more informative if not less euphemistic, describing the word as "the second most tabooed in polite society."

established audience stratification. In these circumstances, the charge that today's highly limited prior censorship casts the movies as an underprivileged medium of speech appears to be a hollow one indeed.

Though partially blocked by the declining responsiveness of both the boards of censors and the industry's self-regulation, the censorship interest aroused by the new freedoms still exercises a coercive and often clandestine control on films. However, its energies have definitely not been channeled primarily through individual patron decision-making buttressed by advisory ratings, nor through use of the criminal process—the two methods of control preferred by film-makers and libertarians. On the one hand, advisory ratings (excluding Catholic ratings, which because of their coercive dimension and relation to organized group power are not merely advisory in character) are too diffused in their effect to win recognition as an important and realistic means for controlling movies. On the other hand, the prosecuting power, though invoked more often than in the past, is frequently frustrated on appeal by the liberalized obscenity doctrine, with the result that the power is probably used far more often to intimidate than to indict. Indeed, if advisory ratings, obscenity prosecutions, and prior censorship were the only controls on movies, partisans of free speech would have little need to fear. Libertarian and proprietary forces have managed to win one courtroom battle after another. But the real war over freedom of speech in the medium today is less one of a conventional set-piece struggle against boards of censors or prosecutors than one of an anti-guerilla campaign against scattered, frequently unseen, but often highly effective opposition.

Except for Catholic influence on production and distribution, most censorship of movies today is effected informally within the community against exhibitors. Its forms include a variety of extralegal acts by public officials at the demand of community groups, and direct action by groups themselves. Sometimes officials have also employed legal but noncensorship powers—such as that of occupational licensing—for censorial purposes. In many instances, informal censorship is or becomes self-operating through the exhibitor's anticipation of unwanted consequences. Whatever its form, the aim of informal censorship is to effect changes in motion picture exhibition as quickly, cheaply, and effectively as possible. Such censorship is almost totally lacking in anything resembling standards of due process and often comes close to being an *in rem* lynching. Proscriptive objectives invariably range far beyond the narrow legal standard of obscenity, and the informal censor is often an infrequent moviegoer or a non-moviegoer lacking the sophistication or experience necessary to distinguish the artful or merely unconventional from the exploitative or pornographic. It is not surprising, then, to find many films—such as the award-winning *Who's Afraid of Virginia Woolf?* which was routinely licensed by boards of censors—kept from exhibition at certain theatres, or in entire communities, by informal censorship.

Under these circumstances, the significant question about prior censorship today is not whether it is bad, but whether it does any good. The answer here would seem to depend on whether licensing can be further reformed and, more importantly, on whether it is a real alternative to informal censorship. Clearly, further improvements are needed to ease the burdens on the film proprietor and on free speech. For example, judicial review of censorship orders should be speeded up even more, so that it takes place in a matter of days rather than weeks; fees charged to film proprietors should be eliminated entirely; and fairly rigorous qualification standards, accompanied by an attractive pay scale, need to be developed for the selection of censors. These minor reforms added to the major ones already effected would leave prior censorship, from the submission of a film to a court order on it, a routinized control process offering a quick public review according to requirements of due process of law, in a proceeding in which the values of free speech are likely to receive an extraordinarily high priority.

If prior censorship and informal censorship are inversely related, as available evidence seems to suggest, then the former control probably functions to rechannel a large amount of censorship energy. On the other hand, though reconstructed within, licensing remains a censorship institution in form and can still be an effective limitation on films raising the question of obscenity.

For films approved, prior censorship actually functions as a form of insurance against other controls; issuance of a license has a kind of legitimating effect upon a film. This protection may not necessarily prevent all other censorial action, but it is likely to reduce the probability of such action and to increase a proprietor's will to resist where such action does occur. In this way, licensing may actually serve to insulate some nonobscene yet unconventional expression from community pressures or interdiction.

Finally, the systematic coverage of films, which distinguishes governmental licensing from the film industry's self-regulatory apparatus, could also mean that prior censorship might come to play an important role in any eventual stratification of the medium. Licensing is particularly well suited to the classification of films, should legislative bodies decide to require such audience restriction. Whether undertaken as a supplement to general licensing, as a substitute for it, or initiated without general licensing, an enforceable systematic rating of films according to their suitability for young persons appears to be a promising way of reducing censorship pressures in almost every community in the nation.

As the apparent utility of prior censorship today is an ironic testament to libertarian victories of the past, the entire problem of freedom in the mass medium raises a number of questions concerning the traditional libertarian approach to free speech. Among many libertarians and not a few film proprietors, there is an orthodoxy which not only considers prior censorship antithetical in its very form to free speech, but which views any compromises with the censorship interest at all as ignoble and unnecessary. This orthodoxy sees the free speech problem principally in philosophical, legal, and formal terms, rather than in its political, social, and informal aspects. The enemy is government itself, and the aim is to use the power of the law to deny the censorship interest. In the extreme, the orthodox approach takes an almost ideological turn. The struggle against censorship becomes a kind of crusade on behalf of an eternal verity against the forces of ignorance, fear, and evil. The extent to which freedom is threatened, the justifications offered for limitation, or other such pragmatically dispositioned considerations may be ignored or actually ruled out-of-bounds.

Such an orientation leads to certain misconceptions about the censorship interest itself. Classically, the libertarian orthodoxy battles against government, especially government formally arrayed. Officials themselves are looked upon as the main source of censorship energies. Yet, actually, speech involving sex and manners is the very sort which does *not* threaten the stability or existence of the government. On these issues government is likely to act as it acts on most others in a democratic polity—as an *agent* of marshaled interests perhaps themselves amounting to a majoritarian will.

Since the orthodox view often fails to see the popular character of censorship interest, it is apt to consider the censorship problem capable of legal solution, with a Comstockian censorship interest formally defeated in open battle. This view misconceives not only the nature of the enemy but also that of the war itself. Its formalism overestimates the efficacy of legal power, in the same fashion that another kind of formalism often overestimates the efficacy of military power, as applied to problems essentially social and political in character.

It is unlikely that any mass medium in the American mass democratic society today can be completely, or even nearly, free of control except at a tremendous potential cost to the political system itself. The censorship interest, however misguided it may be thought to be, is nevertheless political force; and though, as a practical matter, there is little chance that it can or will be completely frustrated, the consequences of such a development would be serious. Because the values censorship defends are often of an emotionally elemental character, their repeated denial could lead to a reaction of generalized intolerance or to some other pathological resolution, such as support for extremist politics already built upon tensions produced by group, class, race or individual insecurities, or to even a sense of alienation from the political system itself. In fact, from the standpoint of conflict management, the fact that censorship energy is essentially accommodated informally may itself be a signal of a systemic malfunctioning.

Finally, in the light of the present state of knowledge about the effects of motion pictures, the merits of the censorship interest—which have not been considered in this book—lay claim to a degree of legitimacy. Though much censorship interest is unquestionably irrational, some of the interest is reasonably and intelligently held. The ideal that some motion picture content may be harmful to viewers, especially youthful viewers, is not one that can be completely dismissed as the product of wild or morbid imaginings. The absence of conclusive evidence on one side or the other of this question adds a moral complexity to the entire censorship problem.

Two measures would go far toward an accommodation of opposing interests in the controversy over the movies. One is the establishment of some kind of double standard for proscribable erotica, among the media of speech, that would take the movies' unusual communicative power into account. The other is the development of a reliable stratification for the medium that would afford a more finely drawn audience—content balance. The first is a problem for the courts; the second, for the film industry in the first instance, though it is clearly unlikely to come about through the efforts of the industry alone. Developments such as these, though not of libertarian character in themselves, are, in the long run, likely to make freedom of speech in motion pictures more secure and allow its writ to run more widely than it does today.

The great victories already won for freedom of speech in the movies have resulted in much in their content that is beyond the level of acceptability of a large part of the population. These free speech victories have applied to the entire population a standard that, at least in terms of the tolerance it demands, is essentially elitist. To be sure, the popular threshold of acceptability is not static, and the "people," or at least large numbers of persons, can be led or educated to a higher degree of practicing tolerance. Yet where the issues involve fundamental emotional concerns like those of sex and morality, this process is apt to run by a far different clock than the one which has governed changes in the legal doctrine and in motion picture industry economics. The problem for freedom of speech in the movies today is not the winning of legal battles, which is easily enough done, but the winning of battles that are not later lost outside the courtroom. This involves recognition that censorship is in large measure a social and political problem and therefore one that is only partially curable through legal action, however forceful that may be.

Motion Picture Association of America
RATING CODE

In order to cope with the movies' new freedom on the one hand and rising parental protest on the other, the Motion Picture Association of America has recommended the following Rating Code to be used in determining a film's suitability for a given audience.

All ages admitted. General audiences.

This category includes motion pictures that in the opinion of the Code and Rating Administration would be acceptable for all audiences, without consideration of age.

All ages admitted. Parental guidance suggested.

This category includes motion pictures that in the opinion of the Code and Rating Administration would be acceptable to all audiences, without consideration of age, as to which because of their theme, content and treatment, parents may wish to obtain more information for their guidance.

Restricted. Under 17 requires accompanying parent or adult guardian.

This category includes motion pictures that in the opinion of the Code and Rating Administration, because of their theme, content or treatment, should not be presented to persons under 17 unless accompanied by a parent or adult guardian.

No one under 17 admitted. (Age limit may vary in certain areas.)

This category includes motion pictures submitted to the Code and Rating Administration which in the opinion of the Code and Rating Administration are rated [X] because of the treatment of sex, violence, crime or profanity. Pictures rated [X] do not qualify for a Code Seal. Pictures rated [X] should not be presented to persons under 17.

3
CRITICS AND CRITICISM

Pauline Kael
MOVIES, THE DESPERATE ART

Film reviewer for The New Yorker *magazine, Pauline Kael is a critic of critics as well as an observer of Hollywood and avant-garde films. In "Movies, the Desperate Art" she analyzes the current state of cinema, focuses on some inadequacies, and suggests some possible improvements in the evaluation and the production of films.*

THE film critic in the United States is in a curious position: the greater his interest in the film medium, the more enraged and negative he is likely to sound. He can assert his disgust, and he can find ample material to document it, but then what? He can haunt film societies and re-experience and reassess the classics, but the result is an increased burden of disgust; the directions indicated in those classics are not the directions Hollywood took. A few writers, and not Americans only, have taken a rather fancy way out: they turn films into Rorschach tests and find the most elaborate meanings in them (bad acting becomes somnambulism, stereotyped situations become myths, and so forth). The deficiency of this technique is that the writers reveal a great deal about themselves but very little about films.

SIZE

Hollywood films have attempted to meet the "challenge" of television by the astonishingly simple expedient of expanding in size; in the course of this expansion the worst filmic tendencies of the past thirty years have reached what we may provisionally call their culmination. Like a public building designed to satisfy the widest public's concept of grandeur, the big production loses the flair, the spontaneity, the rhythm of an artist working to satisfy his own conception. The more expensive the picture, the bigger the audience it must draw, and the fewer risks it can take. The big film is the disenchanted film: from the outset, every element in a multi-million-dollar production is charged with risk and anxiety, the fear of calamitous failure—the loss of "big" money. The picture becomes less imaginative in inverse ratio to its cost. But the idiot solution has worked: size *has* been selling, and Hollywood has learned to inflate everything, even romance *(Three Coins in the Fountain)* or murder mystery *(Black Widow)*—the various genres become indistinguishable. A "small" picture would probably seem retrogressive to Hollywood—as if the industry were not utilizing its full resources, and, indeed, when the CinemaScope screen contracts for an "old-fashioned"-size picture, the psychological effect is of a going *back.* Films must be big to draw the mass audience, but the heroes and heroines, conceived to flatter the "ordinary," "little" persons who presumably make up the audience, must be inanities who will offend no one.

The magic that films advertise is the magic of bloated production methods—it is no longer the pyramid the company photographed at Gizeh which is the selling point (that has become too easy) but the pyramid they have *built.* It is the "magic" of American industry—the feats of production presumed to be possible nowhere else (musical extravaganzas like *Easy to Wed* or *Latin Lovers* are incarnations of American speed and efficiency, vigor and abundance, held together by the conviction that all this is the good life). Abroad, especially, the glamour of American movies emanates from the wastefulness of Hollywood methods as much as from the land of plenty revealed in film stories.

Those who see the era of the wide screen and the traveling camera crew as encouraging evidence that movies will once again become magical and exciting recall their childhood when the wonder of film lay in the entraordinary scope of the camera. But the panoramic views of a CinemaScope or VistaVision production are about as magical as a Fitzpatrick travelogue, and the actors are not unlike the girls that travelogue makers love to place at the entrance to each glorious temple—commonplace, anachronistic and reassuring. In a film like *Soldier of Fortune* the story material and the exotic backgrounds do not support each other (as they do in Carol Reed's *The Outcast of the Islands*); the company goes to Hong Kong to tell a story that could just as easily be told in Southern California—the location shots are used to make the familiar seem unusual.

The split between background and foreground in pictures with foreign settings develops into schizophrenia in historical and Biblical spectacles. A reconstruction of Egypt (usually filtered through Maxfield Parrish) means authenticity; the audience is supposed to feel that the film is "real" and important because the background material has been thoroughly researched (the sets are real sets). But the heroes and heroines are not really intended to look of the period at all; the audience might lose its bearings if Susan Hayward or Alan Ladd did not hold them in the familiar present. Would *20,000 Leagues under the Sea* have been such a commercial success if Kirk Douglas had not been there to destroy the illusion of the nineteenth century? The emotions and actions recorded by novelists and historians might insult American tastes and mores; audiences rest easier when characters do only those things modern young men and women are supposed to do (Salome can dance, but she can't get the head). Accuracy (or what passes for accuracy) in background details becomes enormously important—it gives the shoddy, sexy films the sanction of educational and religious values. (The fantastic emphasis on accurate sets and costumes may indicate also a last desperate stand by the artists and technicians who have failed to grapple with the most restrictive censorship—the tastes of the national audience—but who still cling to some kind of pride in their work.) There is a crude appeal in Hollywood's "realism." Arliss made up to look like Disraeli was a living display of ingeniousness for the same public that appreciates a painted horse that looks real enough to ride. There is an instinct for what the public respects that works beneath film methods: the backgrounds of *Seven Brides for Seven Brothers* are painted to fool the audience into seeing real snow on real mountains. In proving that it can make things look real (reality rates higher with the mass audience than style and illusion) Hollywood comes full circle—back to before the beginnings of art.

Hollywood follows the mass audience and the mass audience follows Hollywood; there is no leader. The worst of the past is preserved with new dust. How many films that we once groaned at do we now hear referred to nostalgically? When the bad is followed by the worse, even the bad seems good. (Film addicts talk about *Grand Hotel* or Busby Berkeley's choreography, as if *those* were the days.) The hostility toward art and high-browism that infects much of our culture helps to explain the popularity of so many untrained and untalented screen performers. Richard Burton and Daniel O'Herlihy do not stimulate the fans; Tony Curtis, Tab Hunter, Janet Leigh, Jane Powell do. Fans like untrained actors; perhaps they like even the embarrassment of untrained actors (why should they tolerate the implied criticism of speech or gesture that derives from a higher culture?). The office girl says, "No, I don't want to go see Howard Keel—he was a professional singer, you know." The tastes of the mass audience belong to sociology, not aesthetics. Those who make big films do not consider primarily the nature of the medium and what they want to do with it, they try to keep ahead of the mass audience.

As the mass media developed, the fine points of democratic theory were discarded, and a parody of democracy became public dogma. The film critic no longer considers that his function is the formation and reformation of public taste (that would be an undemocratic presumption); the old independent critic who would trumpet the good, blast the bad, and tell his readers they were boobs if they wasted their money on garbage, gives way to the amiable fellow who feels responsible not to his subject matter but to the tastes of his stratum of the public. Newspaper critics are, in many cases, not free to attack big films (too much is at stake), but they are usually free to praise what they wish; yet they seem too unsure of themselves, too fearful of causing a breach with their readers, to praise what may be unpopular. It is astonishing how often they attack the finest European productions and the most imaginative American ones—safe targets. Attitudes become more important than judgments. The critic need not make any definite adverse comments; his descriptive tone is enough to warn his readers off. Praise which includes such terms as "subtle," "low-keyed" or "somber" is damnation; the critic saves his face but helps kill the movie.

There are people, lots of them, who take big pictures seriously. What is one to say to the neo-Aristotelianism of the salesgirl who reports, "I saw *The Student Prince* last night—it was so wonderful and so sad. I cried and cried, and when it was over, why, I just felt all cleaned out." Only snobs howl at *Duel in the Sun* ($11.3 million gross), and if you crawled out on *Quo Vadis* ($10.5 million gross) you not only showed your disrespect for heavy labor, you implied contempt for those who were awed by it. Hollywood productions are official parts of American life, proofs of technological progress; derision is subversive. You will be reproved with "What right have you to say *Samson and Delilah* is no good when millions of people liked it?" and you will be subjected to the final devastation of "It's all a matter of taste and one person's taste is as good as another's." One does not make friends by replying that although it *is* all a matter of taste (and education and intelligence and sensibility) one person's taste is *not* as good as another's.

Three or four years ago, films by Huston and Zinnemann and, at times, Mankiewicz, Kazan and a few others, stood out from the thick buttered-up products and showed the working of individual creative responsibility. The wide screen and the rediscovery of Christianity have restored films to their second childhood. In the thirties we thought Cecil B. De Mille passé; the American film of 1955 represents his full triumph. In the infancy of films there was promise and fervor; the absurdities were forgivable—we could find them amusing and primitive because we thought we saw the beginnings of a prodigy and we knew there were real obstacles ahead. But this synthetic infancy is monstrous—a retracing of the steps, not to discover the lost paths of development, but to simulate the charms of infancy—and, for all we know, there may be a return to each previous (and doomed) period of film. Something must be done to keep a huge film in motion—in desperation everything gets thrown in. *Grand Hotel* itself becomes a model: put in enough characters and stories and perhaps the huge screen will fuse what it encompasses (Mankiewicz' *The Barefoot Contessa,* Kazan's *East of Eden,* as well as *Violent Saturday, Soldier of Fortune, The Cobweb*). The biggest productions often look like a compendium of the worst filmic crimes of the past, achieving a really massive staleness. Some directors, feeling possibly that spectacles are a joke, attempt elaborate spoofs like *Athena* or *Jupiter's Darling.* But films have got so close to no conviction and no believability that there is very little difference when they cross the line into satire of themselves. If an audience can accept *Mambo* as a serious film, how is it to know, the next week, that *Many Rivers to Cross* is supposed to be funny? When the spectacular production scale is used for comedy, audiences may be too stunned by size and expense to see the humor.

One reason recent spectacles are so much worse than the earliest ones is the addition of sound; it was bad enough to look at the Saviour on the cross, now we must hear his gasps. And the wide screen, which theoretically expands filmic possibilities in certain areas of material, in general limits what can be done—while the areas in which it offers possibilities will probably never be explored. A master could use the vast medium; he could even find themes and dialogue adequate to it *(The Dynasts* or *Peer Gynt* perhaps—or *Road to Damascus),* but what master would be entrusted with the cost of such a venture? It was Michael Todd who enlisted the Yugoslav Army for *War and Peace* ("We're going to make this movie accurate down to the last bit of hairdress and harness") while David Selznick, the Civil War behind him, commands another *War and Peace* (even the legions and larders of Hollywood may be exhausted building the steppes of Russia). Selznick and his peers continue the worst heritage of Griffith, not the visual inventiveness which is his glory but the spread of his conceptions and the spliced sentiments and ideas which substituted for structure. Erich von Stroheim's synopses of *Walking down Broadway* and *Queen Kelly* (recently published in *Film Culture*) are extraordinary documents (as high-school themes they would be hilarious); is it possible that early film makers did not realize that they were heirs to *any* traditions, that because the film medium was new they thought it should be approached with an empty mind? The egotism of the self-taught, which is a practical, though often paranoid, defense against commercial pressure, has had considerable effect on film development. The megalomaniacs who make films can think of no bigger subject than *War and Peace* (Italians, Finns and Russians all race to complete their versions); what can they do next—recreate the creation of the world? All these companies but one will probably lose their shirts; if *all* lose their shirts, perhaps producers will heed the Tolstoyan lesson and learn to approach film making with the economy of a peasant.

ACTION

The best films of recent years have not been spectacles and they have not been geared to a large audience; they have made more and more demands on concentrated attention. The trained eye of an adult may find magic in the sustained epiphanies of *Day of Wrath,* the intricate cutting and accumulating frenzy of *La Règle du Jeu,* the visual chamber drama of *Les Parents Terribles.* American attempts in these directions have met with resistance not only from the public but from American film critics as well. The critics' admiration for "action" and "the chase" lead them to praise sleazy suspense films but to fret over whether *A Streetcar Named Desire* or *The Member of the Wedding* is really "cinematic."

For the gullible, advertising provides a rationale for spectacles (the duplication of big historical events is edifying, and the films themselves are triumphs comparable in status to the original events); a more sophisticated audience finds its own rationale for suspense films: crime and punishment suggest some connection with the anxieties and terrors of modern man. The police pursuing a mad killer in the most routine chase seems more "realistic" than a spectacle, and have not some film theorists decided that the chase is "pure cinema"? Suspense films may reflect modern anxieties but they don't deal with them; the genre offers the spring of tension, the audience recoils. For critics, the suspense film has been a safety valve: they could praise it and know themselves to be in accord both with high "technical" standards and a good-size audience.

But critics have been quick to object to a film with a difficult theme, a small camera range, or a markedly verbal content (they object even when the words are worth listening to). Because action *can* be extended over a wide area on the screen, they think it must be—or what they're seeing isn't really a movie at all. The camera is supposed to get outside, even when it has no place to go. According to *Time, The Member of the Wedding* "comes most vibrantly alive when it forsakes the one-set stage original and untrammeled by high-flown talk, roves through the neighborhood, e.g., Frankie's journey through blaring, glaring honky-tonk town." The drama, however, was in the "high-flown talk," and the excursion into town was the least dramatically interesting sequence in the film (and, as a matter of fact, the camera moved more fluidly within the room that it did outside). *Miss Julie* was a beautifully executed "cinematic" treatment of a play with the action extended over acres and generations. Yet when it was over one wanted to see the play itself—that confined, harrowing drama which had been dissipated in additional material and lyrical compositions from nature. The closed framework employed in *Les Parents Terribles* could have brought us *Miss Julie* as we could never see it on the stage, with the camera intensifying our consciousness of the human face and body, picking up details, and directing the eye toward the subtleties of performance. The film *Miss Julie* treats the play as if stage and screen were opposed media and the play had to be subjected to a chemical change. (What is chemically changed in the process is the material and meaning of the play.) But, of course, it was dramatists like Strindberg and Ibsen who reformed stage movement and acting technique and created the modern style—the style to which virtually all film directors are indebted. They are the dramatists who taught film how to behave.

Concerned to distinguish between the "proper" functions of stage and screen, critics tend to overlook that most important dramatic function which they share: the revelation of human character. Instead of asking, "Does the film mean anything?" they ask, "Does the film move?" It is not surprising that there should be many in the mass audience who can see action only in a cavalry charge, but it is surprising how many film critics have the same basic notion of action. (The idea that filmic action must be red-blooded turns up in surprising places. Why did Olivier as Hamlet feel it necessary to throw Ophelia down as if to break every bone in her body?) Most of the elements they condemn as "stagy" were taken over from films anyway—the theatrical devices of Tennessee Williams, for example. Kazan's transition from stage director to film director was so smooth because he had already been adapting film techniques to the stage. The most widely applauded "advanced" staging derives from films: revolving stages *(Lady in the Dark)* simulate rapid cutting, scrim sets *(Death of a Salesman)* conjure variable perspectives, unit sets *(Tea and Sympathy)* attempt a controlled panorama, light-plot sets *(The Trial)* imitate the whole process of the dissolve and montage. And to confound the issue, Griffith and the other film pioneers who developed these techniques extracted them in large part from Max Reinhardt—who was bursting the bounds of the stage frame. Few, if any, of the devices of film originated exclusively with film.

The giveaway in the critics' demand for action is that fine films in which the camera is brilliantly active over considerable terrain often disturb and displease them; they found *Miracle in Milan* too fantastic and imaginative, *Los Olvidados* too grim, *The Beggar's Opera* too contrived, *The Earrings of Madame De* too chic and decadent. When they asked for action they didn't mean action with intellectual content (they want the chase to be pure). One of the strongest critical terms of condemnation is that a film is *slow.* This is understood to mean dull, but what it may really indicate is complexity or subtlety. Renoir's lovely comedy *The Golden Coach* was described as "slow" (and died at the box office), though after sitting through it twice I still had not had time to catch up with everything in it. Those who are used to films which underscore and overscore every point for them are bewildered when they are required to use their own eyes and ears—nothing seems to be going on. Perhaps the effects of a few decades of radio have been underestimated: film audiences don't want images to carry the dramatic idea; they don't know what's happening unless there are words to tell them. And they want the same kind of words they are used to on the radio. When the simplest kind of visual image is added to the verbal plane of soap opera or radio humor, you have the style of Hollywood films. One of the reasons for their extraordinary popularity all over the world is that once the audience gets used to this visual-verbal redundancy (which is remarkably easy to understand) it dislikes the effort of adjusting to more complex types of film. The patrons of "action" houses, steady customers for the heroics of Jeff Chandler or Rory Calhoun, are displeased only when there is some content that slows up the "action." The speed of Hollywood films is a necessity; there is nothing for the eye to linger on and nothing verbal that requires thought.

So many film pedants have insisted that one portion "belongs" to the camera and one portion "belongs" to the stage that it has become a mark of culture to discuss movies in terms of their cinematic properties and their theatrical deviations. In place of this tug of war (which would split both film and stage down the middle) may one propose simple basic terms for the evaluation of film: does the frame of meaning support the body of photographic, directorial, and acting styles; and conversely, do these styles define the frame of meaning? Examples of this integrity are Keaton's *The Navigator* or *The General,* Guitry's *Les Perles de la Couronne, On Approval, The Fallen Idol, Rashomon.* There are other examples, where the meaning may vitiate our interest in the film, but where the film is obviously of a piece—*The Maltese Falcon* or *Sunset Boulevard.* The integration of meaning and style is almost always the result of the director's imaginative grasp of the story material and control over the production. A great film is one in which the range of meaning is so imaginatively new, compelling, or exciting that we experience a new vision of human experience *(Grand Illusion).* One might also call a film great because it triumphantly achieves a style (René Clair's *Le Million)* or because it represents a new method and approach *(Potemkin).* Only rarely does an American film, as a whole, sustain an interesting range of meanings, but frequently there are meaningful sections and efforts in a film. For example, the theme of *On the Waterfront* is inflated and the directorial style is overscaled, but certain sections of the film are more dramatically meaningful than anything else in recent American movies. When the latent meanings in the material are disintegrated in the photography, direction and acting, we have fiascoes like *The Caine Mutiny* and *The Bridges of Toko-*

Ri. When the meanings are too obvious and too absurd to support the body, we have the typical bloated film (*The Prodigal, Garden of Evil, Daddy Long Legs,* or that CinemaScope edition of *The Reader's Digest, A Man Called Peter*).

ACADEMIC "CRAFTSMANSHIP"

The serious, literate audiences share with the larger American audience the fear of being duped. Even the small audiences at cinema guilds and art houses are suspicious of new artists, who might be charlatans pulling tricks and willfully obscuring things. Americans are susceptible to the widespread democratic propaganda that the really great artists of history were simple and lucid; they don't want to be *had*. Music lovers who listen to nothing later than Mozart are saved from errors in taste; they are certain to consider themselves discriminating. The film audience dedicated to Pudovkin or von Stroheim or the early René Clair are playing it just as safe.

While it is not easy to recognize or understand new art, meticulous, ponderous craftsmanship—the emulation of already recognized art—can be appreciated at once. George Stevens used to direct some pictures with good moments *(Alice Adams, The More the Merrier);* now that he makes heavy, expensive pictures full of obese nuances *(I Remember Mama, A Place in the Sun, Shane)* he is highly regarded. Literate carefulness is the much advertised "quality" of Samuel Goldwyn productions (assemble "distinguished" writers, a costly story property, director and actors and technicians with artistic reputations, and you have a "prestige" picture—though the results may suggest the old Community Chest slogan "Suppose nobody cared . . ."). The production values of a Goldwyn picture *(The North Star, The Best Years of Our Lives, Hans Christian Andersen)* are not as banal and vulgar as those of *A Woman's World,* but crudity has often been the only sign of life in American movies; the prestige picture sacrifices even this feeble vitality for an impressive façade.

The look of solid, serious construction seems to be very important to the educated audience; they are fearful of approving the films of Cocteau—perhaps, like Gulley Jimson, he may be painting for pleasure on walls that are collapsing. Readers who put down *The Horse's Mouth* and ask anxiously if Gulley Jimson is really supposed to be a great painter are, no doubt, part of the same audience that feels reassured when George Stevens says, "I don't make films for pleasure." Work without joy is respectable; it doesn't raise doubts that it may not be serious. Cocteau, with his enigmas and ambiguities, is he not perhaps trying to put something over? His high style is suspicious; members of the serious audience don't want to go out on a limb for something that may turn out to be merely chic and fashionable. Though they are educated beyond the fat production values of routine pictures, they still want the fat of visible artistic effort. And there is something they want even more, something they value even higher than "artistic values"—the fat of "important ideas" and paraphrasable content (in the thirties, Warner Brothers was the chief purveyor; in the late forties, Stanley Kramer took over). While the less educated mass audience may be in awe of the man-hours and banker's dollars that go into a colossal production, the educated audience, uncertain and self-sacrificial, respects the good a movie will do for others.

PRESSURES

Our films are stuffed with good intentions. A *Life* editorial pointed out that "in 1951 Americans bought more tickets to symphony concerts than they did to baseball games. . . . The hunger of our citizenry for culture and self-improvement has always been grossly underestimated." Is it hunger or is it a nutritional deficiency? These educated people of conscience don't feel they should waste their time; they reserve their interest for films with praiseworthy aims. The themes favored by the serious audience in the thirties and forties—race relations and mob violence—are perfectly good themes, but treatment of them in conformity with the moral and social aims of conscientious people bleached the interest out. The morally awakened audience banished the early subhuman racial stereotypes from the screen; they developed their own stereotypes—which they must know to be lies and yet feel are *necessary* lies. Could Melville's *Benito Cereno* be filmed, a century after it was written, without a barrage of protests from the educated audience—an audience that cannot admit to the dread and terror of Melville's white man held captive by Negroes?

It is the enlightened message, e.g., *Gentleman's Agreement,* that people must be educated into tolerance; prejudice is wrong. Any motives indicated for the prejudice must be superficial or wrongheaded, so that the prejudiced character can be exposed, if not to himself, at least to the audience. At the lowest level in *It's a Big Country* (a bottom-grade big picture) the Jewish soldier was the usual Hollywood boy next door, and the woman's hostility toward him was the product of sheer ignorance; we left her enlightened by the recognition that he was exactly like the boy next door, only better, and she was about to correspond with his mother. At a more complex level in *Crossfire* the Jew-hater was a fanatic who never learned; but what the audience saw was once again the liberal stereotype: the murdered Jew was a decorated war hero. (Suppose the murdered man was a draft dodger, or a conscientious objector, would the audience then feel no sting, would the fanatic have been justified in killing him?) In John Sturges' *Bad Day at Black Rock* (one of the few reasonably good films to come out of Hollywood this year) the pattern is the same: the period is 1945 and the victim of the townspeople is a murdered Japanese farmer—this time it is the victim's son (killed in action) who is the decorated war hero. By a quota system, war films admitted carefully selected minority representatives, clean-cut Jewish and Negro soldiers whose participation in the national defense apparently gave them a special claim to equality over and above mere membership in the human species. Can it be that even in liberal thinking there is a stigma which can be rubbed off only if minority characters behave heroically?

The fantasy structure is familiar: We have had countless movie heroines who sin (i.e., express sexual passion) and repent by way of almost automatic illegitimate births and various forms of social condemnation. Eventually they "work off" the sin by self-sacrifice, commonly the sacrifice of mother for child. This pleasure-pain bookkeeping (for which the production code, and hence the pressure groups, are partly responsible) tells you that you pay for pleasure by the sacrifice of all future pleasures. Can it be that for the middle classes, Jews and Negroes also need to work off something? Pinky gave up the white doctor and dedicated her life to her people; in what sense they were her people at all it was hard to say, but as a partly Negro heroine she was expected to behave sacrificially—like the escaped convict she had to return to prison to pay her debt to society.

How effective, one wonders, are the "necessary" lies of well-meaning people when the mass audience lives in a world full of the very people that the movies tell us are figments of prejudiced thinking—the Negroes of Harlem or the Fillmore, the Jews of Broadway and Central Park West, and the Hollywood producers of the Hillcrest Country Club, with its own gentleman's agreement (no Gentiles accepted). Films may "expose" anti-Semitism or anti-Negroism but they dare not deal with Semitism or Negroism (the existence of which they deny). Behind the pressures that destroy the thematic possibilities in race relations (and similar pressures obtain in sex relations) is the fear that some portions of the public are not intelligent enough to understand that if one Jew is pictured as aggressive, this does not mean that all are aggressive; or if one Negro pulls a knife in a fight, all will; or, for that matter, if one dentist overcharges, all do. This fear has been played upon by the leaders of minorities and pressure groups: Negroes or Jews are made to feel that because others might associate them with the actions of Josephine Baker or Walter Winchell, they are somehow responsible for those actions. Any Italian or doctor or psychiatrist on the screen is considered as a *representative* of the group, who might, by his action, discredit the whole group. In order to protect themselves, minorities act upon the premise which they ascribe to the ignorant public.

The situation is not simple. Art derives from human experience, and the artist associates certain actions and motivations with certain cultural and vocational groups because that is how he has observed and experienced them. Would Jews be so fearful of the depiction of Jewish characters as ostentatious and vulgar, aggressive and secretive, if they did not recognize that these elements often converge in "Jewishness"? Would Negroes be so sensitive to the images of sullen bestiality and economic irresponsibility if they did not feel the impact? It is the germ of observed truth that pressure groups fear a germ which infects only the individual but which the group treats as epidemic. The whole group becomes defensive under the guidance of pressuring leaders who inoculate them with false responsibilities. All these inoculations have produced a real democratic disease: a mass culture made up of stereotypes, models, whitewashes, smiles and lies. To allow the artist to treat his experience freely may be dangerous, but it is a step toward the restoration of individual responsibility. And how else can American indifference and cynicism be cured?

Truth is feared most of all in the visualization of sex relations. The presumption is that romantic models of happiness are less dangerous than truth, that if youngsters saw in films the same kind of problems they experience and see all about them, they would be "misled" into believing that human relations are often difficult, painful and unsatisfactory, that society is unwilling to consider the problems of adolescents, and that the impetus for divorce is not an absurd, unmotivated quarrel which will be patched up in the last reel *(Phfft!)* but a miserable impasse. These lies are certainly more dangerous than truth; the split between the romantic glorifications of love, marriage and family life and our actual mores adds to the perplexity and guilt of those whom the films seek to protect.

Films do not suffer from the pressure to do something; they turn into drivel because of the pressures not to do almost everything. One may suspect that there is something fundamentally corrupt in a concept of democracy which places safety, harmony and conformity above truth. The educated audience deplores the films offered to the less educated audience, but, in order to protect the ignorant, and in the cause of democracy, they effectively prevent an exploration of the living world. Art, perhaps unfortunately, is not the sphere of good intentions.

IS ANYTHING LEFT?

If there are almost no films (except the suspense variety) set in contemporary America, the reason is clear: there are almost no modern themes acceptable to the mass audience. The treatment of historical subjects generally reduces them to nothing *(Desirée),* but it is easier to dress up nothing in a foreign or period setting. The hollowness of the big productions is a direct result of the effort to please the public while doing nothing that might displease countless sections within the public. (A competent movie like *Blackboard Jungle* has to fight its way against pressure groups and legal action.) To a marked degree, the effort is self-defeating: when nothing is left to hang the *décor* on, audiences get bored. They were amazed and delighted when *On the Waterfront* and, before that, *From Here to Eternity* made contact with some areas in their experience; it's as if they had forgotten that movies could mean anything at all. It may be that such box-office successes as *The Robe* and *Quo Vadis* are among the last belches of the giant. Spectacles will cease to be events, and audiences can be more comfortably bored at home. Tony Curtis and Janet Leigh can easily transfer to television, which has inherited not only the worst of radio and vaudeville but the content of B movies as well (the dreary humors of family life). Americans do have some sort of taste: they will accept mediocrity, but they don't like to *pay* for it. Vaudeville died because people refused to support it in its decrepitude, but they were perfectly willing to listen to its ghost on the radio. They will suffer, on television, chopped-up, incoherent prints of bad movies—the very worst specimens of what destroyed their enthusiasm for going out to a theater. (David Riesman's suggestion that people over thirty may be staying away from theaters because "films are too mature, move too fast, for older people to catch on to and catch up with" is altogether remarkable. No doubt, Americans as they age do tend to lose the youngsters' lively interest in the world, but American movies show the same middle-aged spread. To a sociologist, movies can be a constant source of material on up-to-date habits and manners. But one interested in film as an art form finds these surface shifts about as significant as a sculptor finds the cosmetic lore of Forest Lawn. Riesman offers us possibilities of "mature" comedy. Documentary camera in hand, one would like to follow the proposed team of "humanists and social scientists" as they "come together to see what each set of skills might contribute to heighten the awareness of Americans of all ages for the imaginative qualities of their best films." The man who described for us the outlines of the American mousetrap now calls for mice to walk in. Skilled teamwork, having already destroyed movies, will now take over movie criticism.

Americans don't have to go to the movies at all. They spend as much money on equipment for fishing as they do at movie box offices; they spend as much on hunting and bowling. Sports not only invite participation, they provide suspense about the outcome (something which our movies have failed to do for a long time); sports are geared to leisure interests, travel, photography and a whole range of consumer goods—casual clothes, equipage. And sports comprise the proper interests for getting along and getting ahead in a sociable way.

Drama, on the other hand, posits intense interest in the character and destiny of the individual, and American culture is indifferent, and even hostile, to strong individuality. The American film is no longer concerned with characters of real dramatic stature; it gives the actor few chances for any interesting or full characterizations and often constricts acting possibilities to the barest minimum. Films do not center as much as they used to on one or two heroic individuals who were often engaged in a grand passion, or a drive toward money or power, or even in some struggle against society and conventions. The new heroes and heroines of film and television are dismaying—not because they're not attractive and presentable (often they're competently played), but because they represent the death of drama as we have known it. They are not protagonists in any meaningful sense; they represent the voice of adjustment, the caution against individuality, independence, emotionality, art, ambition, personal vision. They represent the antidrama of American life. Biblical spectacles convey magnitude of character by magnitude of close-up. Film versions of the lives of the "great" turn out to be success stories drawn from the mass media—Knute Rockne, Marty Mahrer, Glenn Miller, Eva Tanguay, Ruth Etting, Jackie Robinson, Houdini, Cole Porter, Rodgers and Hart, Sigmund Romberg, Jane Froman, "Crazy-Legs" Hirsch, Lou Gehrig, Joe Louis, etc. And with Valentino, Al Jolson, Eddie Cantor, and the projected Jean Harlow and Theda Bara, Hollywood feeds upon itself—a confection only for jaded palates. The heroism of Hollywood is the gift of itself to the world: *A Star Is Born* is the epic of Hollywood's self-sacrifice. The new path for success is to enact the success of someone else in the same field; when you have reached the summits, you re-enact your own success.

Other arts show an internal logic in their development, the constant solving of aesthetic challenges; films have changed simply by following the logic of the market. When one cycle was exhausted, a new personality (embodying some recognizable form of human experience and a new kind of sexual excitement) in a new type of picture usually set off another. Joan Crawford doing the Charleston on the table in *Our Dancing Daughters* incarnated a new youthful abandon for her period, just as Valentino had brought dark, exotic sensuality to his, and Fairbanks joy of life to his. Bette Davis introduced a more complicated sexual character—driving, neurotic. When the public interest in gangsters and the socially downtrodden was exhausted, and the war over, Hollywood lacked a social orientation. Kirk Douglas injected something new into melodrama: he represented a new type—the guy who's got the stuff, but who is really a wrong guy, the ambitious heel in a disoriented society. Now Marlon Brando breathes some life into films: he projects the tensions of displaced, alienated American youth—characters who reject the hypocritical society that denies their instincts. Refresher personalities don't, of course, stay fresh; their roles become stale; the public becomes satiated. Idolatry turns to mockery and boredom, and new idols appear. When his magic was gone, it didn't matter that Charles Boyer was an excellent actor. Sometimes the public gets the full spectacle of the fall: John Barrymore became a buffoon. And the public was more than willing to turn Garbo into a national butt of humor.

Though even the biggest stars have not remained at the zenith, we are now witnessing a desperately contrived effort to keep them there: waning stars provide the "big" names for the big productions. Clark Gable or Gary Cooper, Robert Taylor or James Stewart add size and importance, but do they have any vital star quality left? Advertising announces "the *new* Greer Garson" or "Lana as you've never seen her before"—obviously the public wasn't buying the old Greer or Lana. Can Hollywood manufacture the artificial asteroid? (Joan Crawford has come to represent the tenacity of a woman determined to remain a star: her survival power is the only drawing power she has left. She shows us her legs to prove that they are *still* good.) From time to time newspapers or the radio play upon the popular nostalgia about old favorites, but the public stopped buying a Norma Shearer or a Janet Gaynor long before they faded. The camera itself uses up an Esther Williams rapidly; her expressive resources are so limited that close-ups are like billboard ads—the image is constant, only the backgrounds vary. Can a new refresher find so much as a toe hold in the blubber of big films? The old big name or the actor who can impersonate a model American is safer than a challenging new personality; the studios are rather resentful of Brando's drawing power: what big pictures does he really fit into? He will, of course, be remade to fit.

When the remains of Christianity are returned to their caskets, Hollywood may delve into Buddhism or Mohammedanism (all gods are pretty much alike and resemblance to the Christian god will, no doubt, lend the others a certain respectability). This step is foreshadowed in *The Egyptian.* A clash of cymbals announces the name of Darryl F. Zanuck, but, with all modesty, the letters of fire are reserved for the postscript: "All these things happened thirteen centuries before the birth of Christ." (Obviously the producers would like to get precedence on *The Robe*—an estimated $19 million gross.) Why should Americans be offended by other religions when they can all be depicted as anticipation of the true faith? Hollywood will probably also "adjust" itself. *Rogue Cop* is a somewhat longer and bigger version of the typical glossy MGM melodrama of the thirties and forties. It is what might be called the "academic commercial" film—competently done, considering that it's not worth doing. Can films like this, over a period of time, draw people away from television and into theaters? It's more than doubtful—the material of television drama *is* old movie melodrama; when films recapitulate their past, they're in a deadlock with television. And the film becomes increasingly subject to pressure. That *Rogue Cop* has been banned in some states, at the insistence of police departments who argue that the crooked cop of the film might give some juvenile delinquents the wrong idea about policemen, suggests that there is almost no subject matter left for the mass-audience film. When everybody knows that there is widespread police corruption, the movies are not supposed to show even one cop who isn't a model (the police have good reason to be so sensitive). Obviously if one made a film about an incompetent teacher's effect upon a child, or dramatized the results of a doctor's mistaken diagnosis, one would be in trouble. (Artists, on the other hand, may be pictured as pathological cowards, cheats and murderers—they're not organized.) Every group wants glorification, but even glorification carries risks (audiences can be derisive about the discrepancies between film and fact), so perhaps it is safer to leave all subjects untouched. This feat is virtually accomplished in films like *White Christmas* and *The Long Gray Line.* Fear of offending someone—anyone—may help to account for the death of American film comedy. Films like *Roxie Hart, His Girl Friday, A Letter to Three Wives,* and the Preston Sturges comedies didn't seem so important when we had them; in retrospect, after a *Sabrina,* they acquire new luster. While serious drama is smothered by moral restrictions and the preordained ending (characters must get their "just desserts"), the verve and zest of comedy dribble away when you're half afraid to make a joke of anything.

WHO CARES ABOUT MOVIES?

It may be that in a few years the film situation will be comparable to the present stage situation. The few dozen Broadway plays a year are supplemented by thousands of little theaters and college groups. It would not be unlikely that a few hundred big houses showing big Hollywood productions would be surrounded by a swarm of small "art" houses, catering to a fairly limited audience and showing foreign films, revivals and new American films—experimental or, at least, inexpensive ones. The art houses might even be forced to help finance small new films. Good American films like *The Treasure of Sierra Madre* have often failed financially—possibly because they attempted to succeed in the wrong places; if Hollywood could make good pictures on a low-budget basis, book them into art houses, and give them months and even years to return the investment, they might show a modest profit.

Small houses cannot grow to a swarm on foreign films alone. After the initial enthusiasm for French, Italian and English films, Americans begin to lose interest. The acceptance of life in European films, the acceptance of joys and defeats, does not make vital contact with American experience. We do not live in those terms, and *our* terms are apparently somewhat incomprehensible to Europeans. Representations of Americans in foreign films always feel wrong to an American audience. It is true we are shallow, but we are not carefree and irresponsible, we are shallowly *serious.* Even the worst American films have often had more energy than the imports. English comedies, with their high level of craftsmanship, their quiet charm and their tiny scope, become almost as wearisome to us as the shoddy tasteless products of Hollywood. Success within such small limits is ultimately not very interesting, especially to Americans. *Genevieve* is delightful, but have you missed anything if you didn't see it? And just how many *Genevieves* do you want to see? The economy of the enterprise is so straitened; you can't accuse the English of not fulfilling large intentions because they don't aim very high. Where is the insolence that gives bite to comedy? The English have their own way of playing it safe. Not every moving picture can be great or even good, and there can be no objection to honest failure or modest success. But every work of art has a core of risk and it is around this core that the work takes form.

Our commercialized culture never integrates all the individuals with energy and talent. They constitute a reserve of independence and dissidence, and idiosyncrasy. And in this reserve there is, perhaps, a more vital hope for the American film.

There are people who can sit around for hours discussing early films, giving detailed accounts of dialogue, action, gesture, even costume, exchanging remembered reactions to Colin Clive, or what Nils Asther was like in *The Bitter Tea of General Yen,* or Bette Davis in *Cabin in the Cotton.* Sentiment and romance may be attached to the memories, but, more important, these people remember movies because they were alert to them. They were fascinated by what went on in the films —the personalities, the talents, the inadvertences, the reactions of the audience, the mélange of techniques, the actress working against hopeless material, the director injecting a clever bit of business, the glaring close-ups as in a strip tease revealing the human material. The people who love movies are a knowing audience; the early period of going to movies has not deadened their taste, it has cultivated it. They are capable of judging in advance just about what a given production will be like, though they may want to taste for themselves the precise flavor even of horseradish. Films are at the mercy of this knowing audience: it goes to see everything it can in a film, and often comes out with much more than it was intended to see. In a sense, every movie is a documentary: the actor is as exposed as the tenant farmer, the sets as exposed as the Aran Islands. In one way or another, everyone who goes to the movies knows this; when the film fails to hold the attention of the audience and when the theater situation permits, the disgruntled patrons comment on what is exposed to them.

Just as there are people alive to poetry but blind to painting, there are literate people who don't care for movies. The quality of most

Hollywood films has made it easy for them to say they are not interested, without even that nod at acknowledging a failing that usually accompanies the statement that one draws a blank on opera or poetry. They tend, in fact, to view lack of interest in films as evidence of superiority and to be contemptuous of the "low tastes" of those who go to films frequently (many of them *do* go to movies—in guilty secrecy). One is inclined to suspect that these people who dismiss movies as a lost cause and a circus for the masses never could tell a good picture from a poor one.

With all the waste and disappointment, growing up at the films was, for our generation, an extraordinary education of the senses. We were in almost at the beginning, when something new was added to human experience. In high school and college we formed friendships as much on the basis of film tastes as of literature or politics. When the commercialized Hollywood films could no longer satisfy our developing tastes, *Le Jour se Lève* and *La Grande Illusion* restored us. After more than fifteen years one still recalls the rage one felt toward the college boy who was so busy pointing out the biographical falsifications in *Beethoven* that he had no eyes for Harry Baur. Arguments about films were formative, and, by the logic of developing taste, those who cared enough to argue found that film-going resulted in disgust. It took a couple of decades for Hollywood films to wear us out; we wearied more quickly of the imports. While in the mass audience older people abandoned movies to the kids, we could not abandon film-going any more than we could give up other vital appetites.

Cocteau, after revivals of *Blood of a Poet,* emerged as the most important film maker, not necessarily because one especially liked the film, but because Cocteau suggested to us the shattering possibilities of an artist using the medium for his own ends, not just to make movies, but to say what he wanted to say in movies. Because of him, we began to look at films in a new way: we were no longer merely audience, we were potential film makers. And we discovered new ancestors. Searching through early film experiments, looking for the excitement that our senses told us the medium could produce, we found the early experimenters who had discovered the film medium for themselves. When we arrived at the infant beginnings of film art, we realized that we had grown up in a period of steady decline, scarcely aware of what films had started out to be.

From the beginning, American film makers have been crippled by business financing and the ideology it imposed: they were told that they had an obligation to entertain the general public, that this was a democratic function and a higher obligation than to give their best to a few hundred or a few million people. This "obligation" forced even the early innovators to lard their work with sentimentality. And this "obligation" has contributed to fear of the medium itself—they began to use titles and music to explain and add to what they were already doing with images; when sound became possible, they were fearful of imaginative or difficult speech and music. It is clear now that there is more than one audience, and that artists must judge their own obligations. The film artist knows what happened to the innovators; he knows he can't expect the banks and studios to finance him. Fortunately his experience at expensive movies should have surfeited him—his tastes need not be so extravagant. If he wants to make movies he must cadge and borrow and save and fill out fellowship forms and beg from foundations—like other American artists. And if he produces a squiggly little mess of abstract patterns or a symbolic drama full of knives, keys and figures receding in the night, at least the responsibility is where it should be.

The responsibility is on the artist, even when he tries to evade responsibility. If, so far, American experimental and "little" films haven't received much support, most of them haven't deserved it, either. All too frequently, after an evening of avant-garde cinema, one wants to go see a movie (at least a little fresh air comes in through the holes in Hollywood plots). Though avant-garde film makers don't always know what they're doing when they make a film, they demonstrate a marvelous talent for the post-factum scenario; often their greatest effort at composition is in explaining away the lack of it in their films. They become so adept at escaping consideration of their failures and limitations that they rarely develop at all; what they fail to put in they deride you for not seeing there. You're supposed to find a whole world of meaning in that three-minute cinepoem. The times are out of joint: the poisonous atmosphere of Hollywood premieres is distilled to pure pretension at avant-garde premieres. Object to the Hollywood film and you're an intellectual snob, object to the avant-garde films and you're a Philistine. But, while in Hollywood, one must often be a snob; in avant-garde circles one must often be a Philistine.

William Fadiman
SHOULD AMERICAN FILMS BE SUBSIDIZED?

Once Hollywood was truly the international capital of movies. But American productions in recent years have lost their monopoly. William Fadiman, motion picture producer, literary critic, and presently a vice-president of Seven Arts Associated Corporation, explores the complex reasons for this change and asks "Should American Films Be Subsidized?"

THE current artistic state of the film in America has evoked a condemnatory chorus from many sources. Accusations of intellectual sterility, slavish devotion to formulas, lack of imagination, indifference to esthetic values, degrading capitulation to commercialism, blatant disregard of discriminating tastes, deliberate pandering to vulgarity, and emphasis on arbitrary violence are familiar pejoratives to our Hollywood producers. Moreover, the recent *réclame* and popularity of the imported film as a new standard of comparison and contrast have given all these indictments fresh fuel. In a recent issue of *The New York Times,* Bosley Crowther, the *Times*'s film critic, epitomized this viewpoint by stating flatly, "Experience has long since prepared us to accept the uncomfortable fact that the best work in motion pictures—the most intelligent, progressive, astute, and alert to what is happening to people—is being done abroad."

Czechoslovakia, Mexico, India, Japan, France, Italy, England, etc., are lauded as producing motion pictures which achieve the quality and distinction conspicuously missing from our home product. Film festivals from Montevideo to Monte Carlo continually honor their artistic excellence, the philosophic profundity, the comic or tragic inventiveness, the fluid (or static—sometimes it does not seem to matter which) photography, the simplicity (this appears to be highly coveted) of the narratives, the preeminence of the performers, the genius of the editing, the technical virtuosity, and, of course, the masked or naked symbolism of the style.

It is true that the foreign films *we see* are indeed frequently superior in many ways to American films. But it is essential to realize that we are seeing only a small percentage of the hundreds of films produced abroad, all methodically culled and chosen especially for American viewers. And that, furthermore, even these selections are by no means made solely on the basis of their putative artistic value, but also for their appeal to the *voyeurs* in our audiences who derive vicarious satisfaction from the sight of bedroom activities not permitted in American films. It is not to be summarily assumed from this observation that foreign art films (the majority of imported films fall into this category) are deliberately fashioned to attract the prurient American moviegoer. This would be a serious distortion of the truth. It remains important to know, however, that we are seeing only those foreign films which are exhibited for two small segments of our population, the *cognoscenti* and the concupiscent.

■ ■ ■

It is perhaps fortunate for those critics who bewail our cinematic lot that the majority of European and Asian run-of-the-mill motion pictures are not shown in the United States. For it is a lamentable fact that the average commercial film made in Europe or India or Japan or Mexico is as trite, mindless, vapid, and jejune as any of our own offerings in an identical or parallel genre. Nor is there any validity to the happy assumption that all overseas studios are populated by a talented assembly of Fellinis, Bergmans, Kurosawas, Godards, Resnais, Buñuels, Rays, Polanskis, Demys, Truffauts, Reiszes, and Antonionis. The American cinema has no stranglehold on mediocrity; Europe and Asia have their own creative shortcomings.

But it is not my purpose to advance cinematic chauvinism or to demonstrate that the attacks on the sorry artistic condition of the film in America are mere canards. On the contrary, they are true. Gregory Peck, acting chairman of the recently formed American Film Institute, has publicly deplored "our concern with excessive commercialism," and he is not alone in his censure. Mr. Crowther was right when he stated that the best work in motion pictures is being done abroad.

But why is this so?

Does the fault lie with our moviemakers? Are we really uninventive, unoriginal, untalented, and imitative; are we truly artistically inferior to our European competitors; are our technicians wanting in ingenuity; are we afraid to be enterprising and challenging; do our writers and producers and directors and performers lack the mastery we applaud so unstintingly in their European and Asian colleagues? The answer to all of these charges is, of course, no. There is no cinema magic which is uniquely foreign; our creators and craftsmen are fully as gifted as their foreign rivals. Granting that premise, why is our film fare bereft of so many of the values we extol in foreign motion pictures? It may be worthwhile to examine some of the reasons for this situation, reasons which turn out to be differences—differences which effectually prevent the American film from achieving the deserved supremacy of the foreign films we admire.

In the first place, the cost of producing a film in many foreign countries is considerably lower than it would be in America. It has been proved again and again that the charges for a film production abroad compared to those for the identical film in the United States reveal a 10 to 15 percent difference in favor of the outlander country.

There are various explanations for this lower cost factor, some having to do with the price of the physical materials required, such as the raw stock. Another—and more substantial—is that of labor. Labor is cheaper outside of the United States. Unions exist, but their wage scale is less than ours, and in certain nations the film industry does not have to cope with unions at all, being granted exemptions or lowered rates.

■ ■ ■

As to stars' salaries, the gap is again in favor of the foreign producer. The extravagant sums paid to our leading players simply do not exist overseas, nor are there many duplications of the American system whereby performers share in the profits and even the grosses of their films. A few examples should suffice: Marlon Brando and Burt Lancaster both receive $750,000 plus a participation in the profits or gross receipts of their films; Elizabeth Taylor demands $1,000,000 in addition to a percentage of the film's revenue. Turning to Europe, one finds that the highest salary paid in Sweden to a performer of the first magnitude, Max von Sydow, is $10,000, whereas Mr. Sydow's remuneration for an American film is approximately $250,000.

Another economic variant is that the foreign film is planned to make its profit uniquely in the country of its origin. It is only the unusual foreign film that ventures beyond national borders. The converse is true of American motion pictures; more than 55 percent of the earnings from American pictures comes from outside the United States. Few American films can anticipate a substantial profit from their domestic showings alone. In fact, almost all our films do well abroad, irrespective of merit or mediocrity. (Is it possible that the alleged twelve-year-old audience level of appreciation could exist in Dijon, Gothenburg, Sapporo, Perugia, and San Miguel Allende exactly as it purportedly does in Kokomo, Indiana?)

The foreign film that is exported to the United States usually finds its acceptance in art houses rather than in ordinary neighborhood theaters. For the foreign film this is a supplementary income from an unanticipated quarter, a sizable bonanza which American films do not enjoy in foreign lands where art houses are not found in any quantity. American films, on the other hand, are almost never produced for the limited exposure offered by art houses. From time to time, avant-garde cinema makers create a modicum of films destined solely for art house consumption; these are known as underground films and in almost all instances are purely experimental. They are invariably undercapitalized, attract a very small coterie patronage composed mainly of loyal cultists, and realize negligible amounts in revenue.

Censorship is another sphere which affects foreign and domestic films in quite different ways. Although we are completely free of government restrictions such as prevail in many foreign countries, these restrictions are rarely applied to sexual behavior, which still remains the one outstanding universal ingredient of screen entertainment. In addition, it must be said that the treatment of sexuality in foreign films is invariably on a more penetrating, forthright, sophisticated, and adult plane than can be found in the most progressive of our films, hobbled as they are by taboos. For the American film faces multiple censorship interdictions ranging from its own self-regulatory Motion Picture Association of America and the National Catholic Office for Motion Pictures to literally hundreds of state, city, village, and hamlet prohibitions and proscriptions. Moreover, the American producer is continually harassed by powerful pressure groups and lobbies hampering and impeding any critical portrayals of various professions, industries, and minority groups. Consequently, we simply cannot present films with the same sexual or social freedom and candor that other nations sanction. The recently applied label for what our censor code calls adult pictures, "Recommended for Mature Audiences" (whatever that may mean), is a feeble attempt to solve this dilemma.

Television also exercises a critical and baleful influence on the American film, an influence which is barely existent in Europe and Asia thus far. For television wields a double-edged sword in the

American film industry. Primarily it functions as a competitor for audience attention. Secondarily, however, a strange phenomenon has occurred in which television has suddenly become our ally and our support. For television now pays stupendous fees for the privilege of one or two screenings of a motion picture. Hence, very few pictures are made nowadays without serious consideration of their potential sales value to this medium. I do not wish to belabor the inanities of American television; but when films are conceived within the framework of this unholy alliance they necessarily become debased and degraded. Here again is a factor and a force that foreign films do not have to either consider or counter.

A final problem confronting Hollywood films is that of multiple controls or committee-created productions, a situation which does not apply to such a marked degree in foreign films. It has been said that distinguished foreign films invariably bear the stamp and the imprint of a single man, the director, and that this individual control is a decisive reason for their high esthetic content. This is substantially correct. Why can't this be true in America? For the answer we must turn reluctantly but ineluctably to the financial syndrome which dominates our film industry.

American film companies are publicly owned organizations, while most foreign films are either owned by one man or a private corporation. (There are exceptions, but these are not numerous.) This does not mean that foreign film-makers are not interested in a profit; but it does mean that they do not have the responsibility and obligation to satisfy suspicious and cost-conscious stockholders. One-man supervision permits a wide latitude in the making and implementation of all decisions, whereas our motion picture companies are justifiably chary of allowing a single authority to arbitrarily dispose of millions of dollars. Once in a while a director of proven box-office competence is delegated such power. Historically, Chaplin and De Mille come to mind, and contemporaneously, Wilder and Wyler and Stevens and Hitchcock and Huston, but even these men are not granted the freedom of operation which obtains in Europe, where the very term "film-maker" often encompasses director and producer and writer in one person.

It seems clear that although these are meaningful contrasts between foreign and domestic films in creative autonomy as well as the pressures exerted by television and censorship, the fundamental difference is that of economics, and that brings us squarely to the subject of subsidization. This is by far the most basic, most influential, and most potent cause of the superiority of the better foreign films. For foreign films are frequently partially subsidized by outright money grants to encourage indigenous production. France, England, Italy, Sweden, Spain, etc.—all maintain institutions whereby the producer receives a sum of money which enables him to finance his product with fewer fiscal problems. His risk is calculably and importantly diminished at the outset, unlike that of the American producer who receives no such donation or lagniappe. These subsidies either come from the government directly or from organizations of a semiofficial nature.

▪ ▪ ▪

In France an annual fund is derived from the imposition of a fixed tax of a little less than a franc on every ticket sold at the box office. By utilizing a complicated disbursement pattern, each picture ultimately receives approximately 14 percent of the producer's share of the income collected from this taxation process. Therefore, that producer with a box-office success will receive more money than the one whose picture has failed to attain audience approval. The sum is given to the producer as a credit to be applied to his next production, thus assuring him of a continuity of plans for his succeeding efforts. Similar financial assistance is also accorded to short subjects (money prizes are awarded to a maximum of fifty each year), thus encouraging an area of film apprenticeship which has become a successful proving ground for such cinematic luminaries as Jean-Luc Godard, François Truffaut, Alain Resnais, and Louis Malle, to name but a few. It is irrefutable that the New Wave of French productions could never have come into being without this financial sponsorship.

England, too, supports its national film-makers under the aegis of a procedure known as the Eady Plan. The Cinematograph Film Act of 1957 expressly provides for the proceeds of a theater ticket tax to be used in subsidizing British films. This levy is administered by the British Film Fund Agency, which divides the money among producers in relation to the box-office potency of their respective productions. This has averaged 40 percent or more on earnings and has gone as high as 55 percent. In 1966, for example, a total of $12,357,117 was disbursed.

Japan likewise has a national subsidization program in which modest amounts of money are donated to those producers who sponsor films specifically designed for the taste and enlightenment of the younger generation, i.e., experimental films devoid of formulas. A study is now being undertaken of additional grants of $5,556,000 for the industry in the form of an annual subsidy for three years.

Spanish films are underwritten with a grant of 15 percent of the gross profits of national films, and the percentage occasionally goes as high as 30 percent for films of outstanding excellence. The Film

Aid Fund supervising these gifts also maintains a school for film trainees and dispenses annual awards to individual pictures ranging from 2,000,000 to 4,500,000 pesetas ($33,400 to $75,150)—sums which are often nearly equal to half the total cost of a Spanish film. There are also subsidies for directors who create films of "artistic interest."

Italy, too, offers assistance to its films. This aid amounts to 13 percent of the gross earnings of a film in the first five years it is shown. The Italians also finance a production school, the Centro Sperimentale, and distribute annual awards of 40,000,000 lire ($64,000) each to films demonstrating "special or artistic qualifications." Lesser sums are awarded to meritorious short subjects.

Holland's film fare is financed in part by the Netherlands Production Fund, controlled jointly by the Holland Cinema League and the government. A producer may receive $30,000 to $100,000, depending on the viability of the production he envisages and his own capital. This is a loan to be repaid from his box-office receipts, but with no penalty if such receipts are not forthcoming.

Sweden furthers films via the Swedish Film Institute, which awards a series of cash bonuses to "good" pictures selected by a committee of educators, psychologists, film critics, and industry representatives. Of the money collected from a levy of 10 percent of the box-office receipts from all pictures, one-third goes to the Swedish National Film School for experimental films and training of future film-makers, one-third to box-office winners in proportion to the number of tickets sold, and the last third to films which lost money but won recognition or awards for excellence.

■ ■ ■

Other countries which donate money to promote national film production include India and Denmark, the latter having donated 1,275,000 kroner ($184,720) for feature films and 225,000 kroner ($32,580) for short subjects in 1965. West Germany provides 4,000,000 marks ($1,000,000) annually in film subsidies supplemented by various Federal Film Prizes, and supports the Association for Young Film Makers. Iron Curtain countries such as Poland and Czechoslovakia likewise allot financial aid to films, principally to those which meet the demands for national propaganda, but also to pictures which are deemed to be cultural assets.

It is obvious that the intent of most of the subsidizations noted above is to foster film-making in general, whether commercial or artistic. It is patent, particularly in England and France, that such financial benefits accrue to the producer in direct proportion to his competence in pleasing mass audiences; but a welcome result of these dividends it that the truly creative foreign producer is thus enabled to gamble occasionally—and he does—on a film of quality (noncommercial) by virtue of having his investment partially protected. He has the privilege and opportunity of making a film, if not completely *con amore,* at least without total dependence on box-office returns for its and his survival.

From the foregoing, two conclusions may be reached: First, that many foreign films—especially those which cultivate the new and the progressive—are importantly aided by money grants, in addition to freedom from creative restraints; second, that the American motion picture industry cannot hope to exercise its full artistic resources and capabilities until it is independent of the necessity of catering to the lowest common denominator of audience acceptance for profitable returns. Putting it in other terms, foreign producers can strive for an artistically rewarding product without incurring a financial penalty if they fail; American films, quite obviously, cannot do so.

▪ ▪ ▪

Film-making in America is a business. Even though the end product is sometimes an art product and hence permits the production of films to be labeled an art-industry, the critical noun in that hyphenated description remains the word "industry." Like all industries, it survives on its ability to please the majority of its customers—a majority whose judgment and discrimination are of a substantially low order. If we wish to cater to the minority of filmgoers seeking products of a high artistic order, we cannot do so without suffering gigantic losses.

In any case, it is apparent that the vitriolic attacks on the quality of American films as compared to foreign productions have been based on little understanding of the differing circumstances under which each product is engendered and no consideration of the substantial fact that financial aid to our foreign confreres may be a significant cause of the discrepancy. As this discrepancy becomes more evident the question is being asked more and more impatiently: What can we do about this?

It seems highly probable that subsidization of some kind may be one, if not the primary, answer. This possibility has been seriously advanced by many members of the film community. Carl Foreman, one of America's most renowned producers, recently stated in an interview in *Variety,* "We are faced today with serious competition. Film-making is improving in all other countries . . . each country helps by giving a subsidy or a grant because they are faced with the same problems that face Hollywood: 1) competition and 2) the high cost of production. . . . Our problem in the United States, creatively, is to play it safe." Arthur Mayer, an eminent motion picture historian and a veteran exhibitor, wrote in the *Producer's Journal*, "Worthy people constantly complain about the low intellectual and artistic standard of a large percentage of our motion pictures. Unless we adopt a system of film subsidies as practiced by European governments, this condition will continue to exist."

■ ■ ■

The National Association of Theatre Owners, a powerful group of exhibitors, has established a special committee to investigate the feasibility of a film production subsidy. A formal and urgent recommendation by the Screen Actors Guild to all elements of the motion picture industry "to give immediate and sincere attention to the possibilities of establishing such a plan (subsidization) for American production within our geographical borders" has given the subject even greater currency.

The inauguration of the American Film Institute under the auspices of the National Foundation of the Arts and Humanities Act of 1965, with George Stevens, Jr., as its director, is the first institutional acknowledgment of America's delinquency in treating film as an art form. This is encouraging, to be sure, with its contemplated five-pronged program devoted to training, education, production, publications, and archival activities. Its operations, however, are limited to only three years, and its budget of $5,200,000, of which only $3,900,000 is currently available, is pathetically small for its grandiose aims. (The Ford Foundation gave United States symphony orchestras alone $85,000,000 in 1967.) Nor is the budget automatically renewable. It is a beginning, but little more than that, and most important, it does not encompass either the permanency or the proven value of the outright subsidization formulas existing outside of the United States.

One may well question the broaching of the question of subsidization for an industry which is far from ailing financially. Why should America be concerned with such an artificial and unnecessary stimulus when it is obviously not needed for commercial viability? The answer has to do with our role as citizens. The motion picture is (or could be) as important a contribution to our cultural climate as other forms of performing arts such as music, ballet, and the theater—all of which are the recipients of various grants and subsidies from public-spirited citizens, foundations, city or state funds, and cultural commissions. As responsible members of a community and of a nation, we are pleased and proud to subsidize such institutions as representative of our interest in the arts. Why should we not manifest equal pride and pleasure in the art of the cinema and consider similar subsidizations?

Perhaps government aid may not be the most desirable approach, since subvention could easily lead to subversion. But another avenue of assistance may be worthy of consideration. This would be from the American film industry itself. We might well reflect on the advisability of channeling a specific portion of our dollar gains from commercial (nonartistic) films into art ventures rather than to discuss or seek outside bounty. We could easily install a system of self-taxation, the proceeds to be utilized for the sponsorship and development of art films. It would be ironic if our very skill in producing and purveying mediocrity would provide us with the needed excess funds to abet film-making on an artistic level: Ironic, indeed, if we could be our own Maecenas.

The potential advantages of such an undertaking are self-evident, for it is only by experimentation—by trying the untried—that any art form remains vibrant and alive. To liberate our film-makers from continually reinforcing the low taste level of the mass audience would permit them to slowly but inevitably attract new and larger audiences as greater numbers of people are exposed to films of quality. This would not only be a step forward in our cultural progression, but might even become a profitable investment in the long run.

But whether such aid comes from the film industry or from any other source, it seems apparent that subsidization may be the only means for the American film industry to recapture its onetime undisputed leadership in the single new art form produced in the twentieth century. For as Mr. Stevens announced rather bleakly when accepting the stewardship of the American Film Institute, "Let's face it, the art of motion pictures [in America] has seen better times."

Ernest Callenbach

THE MOVIE INDUSTRY AND THE FILM CULTURE

Editor of Film Quarterly, *Ernest Callenbach traces his interest in cinema from his college days, when interest in films was "distinctly strange." Today in colleges throughout America the film is recognized and studied as an art. This change and its implications for the movie industry and the film culture form the subject of Callenbach's article.*

WHEN I first found out about films, it was through a kind of secret society known as the Documentary Film Group: a student film society at the University of Chicago. Unlike too many "student organizations" of today's multi-versities, which use student fees for their operations but are controlled by the administration, Docfilm was an independent affair, full of internecine disputes, struggles for succession, and the glories of self-propelled activity: it put on a taxing program of two double-features per week and focused serious interest in films (by no means only documentaries) on a campus not exactly surrounded by culture.

In those days, being interested in films was distinctly strange. Our president for a while beside being the dedicated kind of old red who lectured in a monotone about Film & Reality, was also a member of the campus Rocket Society, which was then considered a half-baked gang of visionaries. Although it was Chaplin who lured me into my first business meeting of Docfilm (and, to be perfectly candid, the mistaken belief that a girl named Marjorie was a member) I soon discovered what my rural and filmless childhood had given me no chance to know —that films were a marvelous and mixed medium, combining chance and patterns, passion and precision, life and craft, in mystifying and sometimes overwhelming ways. At Docfilm we had a scholarly bent; we went systematically through the arcane catalogues of the Museum of Modern Art Film Library, Brandon, Cinema 16. We showed *everything,* as a good film society should, trying to be stringently catholic, even to the point of booking films that only one member really fought for. And we had a profound sense of being on the unknown, growing edge of something: the new understanding of a beleaguered art, precious, endangered on every hand by commercialism, censorship, and the manifold sins that sound had made film heir to. We were disciples, and we spread the word as we could, with the devotion of disciples. We read and studied, we schemed to stay alive financially, we prepared long program notes, we worked many unpaid hours to carry out the actual arduous labor of publicizing and showing our films. It was lonely work, but serious, and in a way exhilarating.

Twenty years later, active film societies exist on literally hundreds of campuses. The distribution of 16mm films is becoming big business: Contemporary Films has merged with McGraw-Hill, Audio Films with Macmillan; even Brandon is reported negotiating a merger. Progress, surely? Or will the major corporations which have snatched up the formerly independent distributors play it safe, releasing only conventional, acceptable pictures? If another McCarthyism arises out of the frustrations of a continuing Vietnam war, will these corporate giants keep on supplying "subversive" films, as Brandon did? Or will the standards that apply to television and textbooks—precooked controversy, conventional wisdom—also be applied to film?

The old-established film schools (USC, UCLA, NYU) have been joined by others with full film programs; many other universities are gingerly offering film courses of one kind or another; colleges and secondary schools are incorporating film study into their curricula from one end of the country to the other. Film books need no longer be hunted up in secondhand bookstores; Rudolf Arnheim's *Film as Art,* which our Docfilm library possessed in its rare British edition, may be found in any paperback store and sells thousands of copies every year. *Film Quarterly,* which uses many long words and makes no attempt to be popular, may be seen on newsstands next to *Popular Mechanics* or *Hot Rod.*

And where young people during my Docfilm years thought of film as outside the pale of the established arts (drama, poetry, fiction, painting, and music were still the *real* arts, with histories, duly certified basic works, and accepted canons of taste) nowadays professors of literature bemoan their students' faint interest in literary art, and find them willing to talk seriously only about movies. Hairy young men who would have once said they were poets now declare themselves filmmakers, and invite girls over to see a few reels of their latest 8mm footage.

Is this satisfying spread of film enlightenment and activity perhaps only another manifestation of Callenbach's Second Law, *viz.,* "Success Is Failure"—though the principle itself was derived from a study of Hollywood career lines? Is the real frontier now elsewhere, in computer art, or portrait painting, or the home fabrication of Molotov cocktails? I have no answer, except to propose a lightning tour of the film scene as it seems to me to have evolved during the ten years *Film Quarterly* has existed; and that will lead us to still more questions.

THE STATE OF THE ART

Are the movies "falling apart," as Pauline Kael has charged, because the plot structures of many current (and popular) films are not the neatly built structures of earlier American movies? This is not merely a trivial debate over changing tastes; it raises the larger cultural question of what is happening to form in contemporary art generally. "Perhaps," writes Miss Kael, "people prefer incoherent, meaningless movies because they are not required to remember or connect," and she goes on to discuss the misfortune that is "the acceptance of art as technique." After some experience with teaching them, I do not share her worry that young audiences will be bulldozed into reacting to movies in the safe, anxious ways they have been taught to react to Shakespeare; but it seems to me that narrative form *has* certainly been taking a beating, and we critics have not been actively enough exploring the implications of this. I do not find the fracturing of old narrative standards a menace in itself. Jiggling a time sequence to no purpose seems to me exactly as tiresome as keeping a time sequence chronological to no purpose—no more and no less. An episodic structure, like that of Godard's *La Chinoise,* may seem intriguing to some viewers and irritating to others; but this phenomenon is at least partly explainable by differing expectations about the "allowable" forms of film. People who are reasonably willing to let poets write lyrics which are non-narrative do not always extend the privilege to film makers, whose control of the viewer's time is absolute and literal (unless he closes his eyes). Yet of course our reactions even to a strictly orthodox narrative film, like *The Thomas Crown Affair* or *The Graduate,* depend on many substantial non-narrative questions: whether we find the characters credible and interesting, whether the atmosphere created by the film seems in good faith, whether the imagery is rich or dull, whether the ideas conveyed in the style and in the dialogue have any relevance to our concerns, and so on. *Une Femme est Une Femme* and *Pierrot le Fou,* two Godard films I do not greatly prize, could have been made with conventional plot structures; but that would not have made them any more interesting. It is doubtful whether *La Chinoise,* or *8½,* or

This Sporting Life could be given any other treatment than they have. The real question, then, is whether contemporary structural innovations have not been essential for artistic reasons—whether, that is, the sacrifice of the kind of action "suspense" associated with the old narrative structures has not been obligatory for certain kinds of films. Films like *Persona* or *L'Avventura* do not goad us to keep wondering "What's going to happen next?" The implicit motto of most modern films is rather "What the hell is going on here?"

Miss Kael is very impatient with the idea that time is important as a "theme" in films. She hates *Marienbad;* and indeed *Marienbad* is a crucial case. For it is at least arguable that a film about obsession could literally not be made convincingly with the old linear casual structure —which is precisely what obsessions negate. Hence Robbe-Grillet and Resnais had to construct a style where the regular flow of time and causation did not obtain, or only haltingly. The result may be, as I think, a lasting work, or it may be, as some believe, an empty bore; but it is a singular achievement, a peculiarly French display of rigor and precision. Nobody is required to like it, or to like Descartes, or Citroën cars. But there is surely room for it in the canon of what cinema can do —unless we wish to close off certain areas of human experience as out of bounds to film makers.

Percy Lubbock's *Craft of Fiction* is a book for which we badly need a cinematic counterpart, because most major stylistic developments of the past decade have been matters of what we might call point-of-view. The narrative structure of the old Hollywood film in the thirties through fifties was that of the omniscient narrator, who could know everything and see everything at all times. The camera, like God, had "the whole world in his hands." Films were structured by universally accepted rules: unless a dissolve or a fade intervened, geographical and temporal continuity was assumed, reinforced by the aural continuity of the sound track. A film made on these stolid assumptions seems cloddish to us now. Even *Petulia,* with its arbitrary contrivances of structure, seems nearer to an honest artistic stance than the regular Hollywood article: we can take it seriously because its camerawork and editing *are not literal.* It is not made in the routine artistic bad faith that underlies the ordinary narrative film, say *The Heart Is a Lonely Hunter,* or *The Fox,* where no difficult questions of point of view have been allowed to arise out of the bland camera's presence.

Why do we now think it immoral of film makers to pretend to omniscience, when earlier viewers were perfectly willing to accord that as the artist's privilege or indeed his duty? One thing that has happened is that the visual image has lost its magic quality because of TV and *cinéma-vérité.* It has been borne in upon us by the casual sloppiness of TV camerawork that the existence of a visual image requires the presence of a taking lens, which some poor slob is operating. Traditional documentaries never lost the luster of artfulness; Flaherty's skies were filtered, and Grierson's workers were posed. But we now know, from the direct cinema films, what life looks like when it is captured with very little interference. We know instinctively, by the feel and movement of the image, that the theatrical film is built upon interference, control, preparation. We accept the presence of the camera there too, but we demand that the artist acknowledge its presence. In return we accord the artist certain new freedoms. His performers may now look at the lens—formerly a sacred taboo. His film may bear visible marks of having been worked upon: obtrusive editing, special titles. Most precious of all, he is no longer obliged to pretend that his film came into existence automatically or magically. The modern film is visibly constructed by the hand of man, and not by the eye of God. It has become, for sensitive viewers, slightly embarrassing to watch a film built on other assumptions—like watching a man who doesn't realize that he has a hole in his pants. The modern artist whom we find comfortable has sewed on a bright-colored patch, or is busy exploring the hole with his finger. With him, we know where we are.

THE STATE OF FILM CULTURE

Every television viewer—which means just about everybody—has some grasp of the changes outlined above. But understanding of film developments in the sense of following the appearance of new artists, making an effort to grasp the significance of new trends, has been spreading to a larger group of informed and curious students, film-society people, film makers, and so on. Clearly, the chosen people have multiplied. More Americans now know far more about films than they did in 1958. They have seen more films, and more varied kinds of films. They read more film books and magazines. They support film festivals in San Francisco and New York. It is no longer necessary for us to lecture on why film is an art; *Life* magazine takes care of that. We may not have a Cinémathèque such as they boast in Paris, but we have admirable repertory theaters in several major metropolitan areas. Censorship restraints on film have been chiseled away through the decade, thanks to legal actions by exhibitors and distributors, until only a few local ordinances remain; the screen has been accorded the same constitutional protections as other forms of expression. The feared Hollywood Code, by which a narrow Catholic moralism was forced upon a compliant industry, resulting in the hypocrisy and perverted puritanism of earlier decades, has been revised and reinterpreted, like some awkward early encyclical, to accommodate the big companies' need to compete in sexual candor as well as sadism and violence.

Before World War II, it would not have been far wrong to say that the only people who knew anything substantial about movies were the people in the studios. The situation has now changed so drastically that cynics ask whether anybody *in* the industry knows anything about movies—and that this is not an idle jest may be learned from those who have, for instance, gone through the experience of having their film publicized by a big movie company, or talked to a Hollywood movie-maker about his reactions to "foreign films." Perhaps it would be more accurate to say that people in the business care about the business; people outside care about films. There are now literally thousands of Americans outside the industry who have watched films carefully enough, or made enough films of their own, that they can tell when camerawork is incompetent or editing is sloppy; they can spot phony lighting; they laugh at idiotic dialogue; they can tell when a film maker is making it, and when he is just wasting their time. It is often startling for Hollywood film makers to come into contact with young people, even those outside film circles; one gathers that they had not expected to be found out, or subjected to such embarrassing questions. Intelligent film columns appear in most mass-circulation magazines, and in many smaller periodicals; they are read by millions of people.

Surveys of the general mass audience, nationwide, urban and rural, tells us it is younger and better educated than before. Even old-timers in the industry do not seem to talk any more about "the twelve-year-old mind." Theaters are not being called Bijou or Embassy any more, but Cinema II or New Metro. Mass audiences have no difficulty in following *Tom Jones* or *Help!,* perhaps because the visual acuity they presuppose is no greater than that of the better television commercials. Camp films—the would-be-serious middlebrow films of the thirties and forties—are popular not only in homosexual circles but because self-consciousness has come to seem inescapable anyway; so why not enjoy it in Bogey or Bette? The audiences are growing hippier, warier, less easy to fool. Yet they keep coming into the theaters; and money is going into the construction of new walk-in theaters, while drive-ins become more and more the exclusive preserve of the family trade and the young who need a place to make out.

THE STATE OF THE INDUSTRY

Hollywood, like Italy, may be "only a geographical expression"; its sound stages are filled nowadays with TV quickies, while many movies are shot elsewhere. Yet even after the dissolution of the old studio system and the rise of the "independent" method of film financing, the industry has hardly become the welter of small competing firms a naive economist might have expected. Some power has indeed been diffused, from the former studios toward their former employees: the high-priced stars, a diminishing band who have now incorporated themselves and operate on percentages not salaries. And the initiative has moved from studio executive offices to the offices of packagers—independent producers and agencies—who juggle tested properties from fiction and the stage with tested performers, and come up with satisfactory combinations. But there is still somebody the packages must be satisfactory to; and as it happens these are the major distributing firms—the remnants of the old film trust—which, like the body of a beheaded chicken, go on running around and flapping their wings.

The name of their game is desperation, for the old rules have failed, and the risks are rising. There is no such thing as a safe picture any more; audiences have grown unaccountably fickle and unpredictable. Things are obviously changing when *The Graduate* challenges *The Sound of Music* at the box office. But what are they changing to? Nobody knows, and everybody knows that nobody knows.

A healthy situation, ripe for important organizational innovations, one might imagine; yet the one thing that seems certain is that the industrial process of manufacturing films will *not* change. An occasional picture like *The Graduate* may succeed because vast numbers of young people think it is expressing their attitudes (with a terrible irony, they may be right). Such flukes can keep the game going for a long time. Over the next decade the budgets and crews of Hollywood (read "Hollywood-financed and -distributed") pictures will certainly grow still more extravagant. A business is measured by the dollar volume thereof; and the personal interests of its participants are served by monetary expansion, so long as the risks do not get out of hand, because there are bigger pies for everybody to get a slice of.

Going by most lists I know of, not one of the ten or twenty best films since the invention of the art has cost more than one million dollars to produce. Yet a picture with that small a budget is almost impossible to finance in the American film industry today. Americans think big. It is only the results whose size is questionable. And this is not merely an aberration of one small industry. The American method of making films is like the American method of waging war in Vietnam: it involves immense expenditures but it is indiscriminate in its objectives; it provides many lucrative jobs, utilizes ingenious technology, yet the operation is conducted out of touch with significant human reality. Both the war game and the film game have their own reality, of course: they are conducted with real guns, real cameras, and real people, some of whom mean well, at least when they begin to play. But the rules forbid taking into account certain discomfiting facts: that art is produced by artists, that people love their countries and defend them bitterly. Film makers who work like artists (who insist on doing their own work and controlling its finished form) are like Vietnamese who insist on running their own country. They refuse to play the game. They are a threat. Hence Godard's slogan: Create many Vietnams in the film industries of the world.

It is little realized that the American method of film manufacture has been spreading rapidly, in the past several years, on a wave of American finance that has at last penetrated European production to a significant extent. American control of the patterns of film distribution in Europe (and the rest of the capitalist world) was established by the twenties. American companies now control much production not only in England, where this is abetted by government subsidies intended to protect the home industry, but also in France and Italy. Budgets have been rising in Europe too; only the Swedes, with the thrifty example of Bergman always before them, seem to have escaped so far.

Moreover, through communication-satellite agreements and related developments, we must anticipate that in the next decade American interests will come to have an important degree of control over communication media throughout the capitalist world, and the international homogenization of films and television will make a Mustang commercial like *A Man and a Woman* look like virgin Gallic culture.

I do not argue that the emergence of individual talents, of the kind *Film Quarterly* has always watched for, has become impossible in the American film industry; but only a fatuous optimist would think it has been getting easier. We are currently witnessing a small boom in the stock of writers, largely on the strength of the unexpected success of *Bonnie and Clyde;* and greater influence for the writers or original scripts could hardly hurt an industry so parasitic on ideas formed and tested in other media. But the proving of new talents is rigorously commercial; if *Bonnie and Clyde* had failed like *Mickey One,* it would be cited as another case of insufficient caution in trusting untried materials. There are no modest successes in today's Hollywood, and the writer-producers or writer-directors will, like everybody else, have to make it big or not make it at all.

Once upon a time, we are told, the giant studios with their picture-a-week schedules year in and year out maintained a relatively rational apprenticeship system, with promising young men on low salaries making shorts, to show what they could do and learn their profession. Moreover, an astounding percentage of the men in their sixties and seventies who have until very recently been the workhorses of Hollywood (men like Ford, Hawks, Wellman, Vidor, Stevens, Cukor) got into the industry in its early days, before the studios had entered their full-blown factory phase. It was possible, in those days, for a young man with some talent and moderate gifts as a con man to persuade a small producer to let him try something with a couple of thousand dollars. No neophyte can be trusted with a couple of million. The result is that there is practically only one route of entry into film directing at present, and that is from television directing. Yet, since the early-fifties advent of Frankenheimer, Ritt, Lumet, and Mann, this route has not been traveled by any significant talents; evidently the experience of TV direction does something to people. They come through like Elliott Silverstein or Stuart Rosenberg: competent craftsmen in a small way, but with no original vision. Mike Nichols, with a string of Broadway staging successes as credentials, directed an excellent version of *Virginia Woolf;* but after *The Graduate* we realize that much of *Virginia Woolf's* stylistic vitality depended on Haskell Wexler's camerawork, and we look forward uncertainly to *Catch-22.* Francis Ford Coppola parlayed stage connections into a fashionable bit of kookery in *You're a Big Boy Now;* after *Finian's Rainbow* he is attempting a very personal project in *The Rain People,* which he is shooting with a workable-sized crew although with industry money.

Coppola's method of work—which is the method used by the great American pioneers, of course, as well as contemporary European directors—was only possible after lengthy and difficult union negotiations, and it is important to understand this aspect of industrial film-making. The industry has got the unions it deserves. The union position is simple: if movies are multimillion-dollar operations where stars, producers, and directors are paid fantastic sums, then the wealth should be spread around to the working men who push and haul, string the cables, run the machines. Heretofore, the unions have not been willing to recognize that other kinds of movies also exist, with modest budgets and where the film makers and actors are paid modest salaries, and which cannot sustain the costs of huge studio-type crews. Some movies are being made in the world, and even in the United States, by crews of a dozen men. Serious movies not only *can* be made by small crews, they *need* to be made by small crews. Sooner or later, union regulations must take account of the basic quantum-jump in film budgeting; rules that are fitting and proper for monster-budget pictures need to be complemented by rules that are sensible for small-budget pictures. In the long run, a film industry that has no place for small-budget films will find itself without new talents. Indeed it is the panicky realization that its old hands are retiring, and few youngsters are around to take their place, that has led the industry to support the American Film Institute and the film schools, with their schemes for the training of new directors.

It has not been lost upon industry figures that notions of cinematic style and interest have greatly widened since World War II; the commercial successes of *La Dolce Vita, The 400 Blows, Tom Jones, A Hard Day's Night* each pushed back a little the previously accepted ideas of what theatrical films should be. Not only the commercial confidence of the industry but its moral confidence seem to have suffered; the malaise of intelligent and talented Hollywood film-makers confronted by the free and original achievements of *8½* or *The Silence* or *Blow-Up* has been considerable. Nobody likes to feel he is being left behind, and one senses the bitterness when American directors defensively quote their box-office take as opposed to the Europeans'. They cry all the way to the bank, no doubt, but that's better than not crying at all.

OUTSIDE THE INDUSTRY

In any enterprise, distribution is the key. Faced with the massive caution of the established industry, film people in the past decade have pushed in other directions. Interest in foreign and short films has been fostered and served by the 16mm distributing firms and the 35mm importing firms; the result has been a kind of shadow industry, bypassing the regular theatrical system. Persistently, although against great obstacles, independent producers have made feature films for this market; and countless short-film makers have made films, sometimes for no market at all. Even the experimental film makers, who are not very interested in the business side of things, have organized cooperative distribution centers to book their films. The Film-Makers Co-op in New York led the way; now there is also the Canyon Cinema Co-op in San Francisco. Though undercapitalized and understaffed, they serve a growing number of people, and send back a high proportion of revenue to the film makers. (Thus, like co-ops in the grocery business, they give a competitive check against the profit-making firms.)

The volume of work being done in 16mm has become very large in recent years—that is, films made by experimentalists, students, documentary people, outside the special world of the 16mm sponsored film. Much of this work is not very good, but then neither is much industry work. What counts is that, compared to the days when Maya Deren and a few others championed the cause of the personal, "avant-garde" film, dozens of people with talent are busy, and their films are being seen. The center of creative gravity, that mysterious theoretical point, has moved in the United States to a point hovering over the boundaries between the industry and outside film-makers. When historians get around to adding up influences, the names of Bruce Conner, Ron Rice, and Jordan Belson are likely to loom larger than those of Richard Lester and Stanley Kubrick; for they are the men who invented the new forms that *Help!* and *The Trip* and *2001* later cannibalized.

In a curious way, film history is beginning to repeat itself. For new developments in 16mm technology (the light, portable camera, and the portable synchronized tape-recorder) have restored film to something like the simplicity it had in the earliest days of 35mm. We are approaching, in fact, a curious and critical point in our definition of what "a film" is. During the era of Hollywood's dominance, culminating in the elephantine budgets of today, a film has been something requiring the services of several hundred employees to manufacture, the investment of several million dollars, and the commitment of a giant organizational mechanism to distribute. But what if a film is, as it was once thought, only a band of images which can be made by anybody with talent and a couple of thousand dollars? What if both synchronous sound and image can be recorded by two men, operating without wires, cables, lights, reflectors, motor-generators, portable dressing rooms, refreshment trucks? What if it can be distributed through film societies, colleges, museums, 16mm-equipped art theaters? Above all, what happens if ambitious beginning film makers with the most talent begin to make films for this audience rather than to beat at the iron gates of Hollywood?

We face still other puzzling prospects in 8mm. A British device will shortly be available in this country which synchronizes any 8mm battery-driven camera to any tape recorder, at a cost of less than $100. Inexpensive editing and mixing devices will presumably follow. When this happens, any talented person will be able to make films with the flexibility of 35mm, though naturally without the photographic definition. And videotape recorders are now becoming cheap enough to be widely available. Does this matter? Judging from what has been happening with student films, if you give several hundred aspiring film-makers the equipment and stock to work with, at least a couple of them will turn out to be highly talented; one in five hundred may be a really interesting and original artist. Such ratios are not pejorative; they apply also to people who get the chance to make studio film. But what happens to this statistical game if ten thousand or a hundred thousand people begin to put themselves forward as film-makers?

Such a remarkable development, which is more than a gleam in the eye of Eastman Kodak, does not mean that we are about to enter a period when film art takes some kind of qualitative leap to higher levels. But it *does* mean that film at last can operate on the same basis as writing or painting: the means of production are within the grasp of any dedicated person, and the testing of talents can proceed in a more natural fashion. Jean Renoir, whose family had gained a modest fortune from his father's paintings, once remarked that it was a big help to a beginning film-maker if he was rich. What we can expect of the new technology is to diminish the extra obstacle to artistic achievement that the heavy costs of film-making have posed since film became heavy industry. This is not to say that it was easy to become Méliès or Porter or Griffith, any more than it has been easy to become

Bruce Baillie or Yoji Kuri or Chris Marker. Not is it to say that it will be easy, even given work of the highest caliber, to secure public circulation and recognition for it—just as it is not easy to get novels or poetry published. Great notoriety and financial success may now be coming more readily to certain artists, including film-makers, who touch a nerve of the mass society and have a talent for publicity, such as Andy Warhol. But for most serious film-makers, the practicalities of their situation will not be easy. Serious film-makers, however, know that only a fool expects the artist's situation or his work to be easy. Like science and politics, art is worth doing because it is *not* easy.

THE STATE OF OUR AUXILIARY INSTITUTIONS

The Museum of Modern Art in New York, together with the Cinémathèque in Paris, first led the way; today archives exist in many countries, industriously conserving both films and early machinery, film literature, and so on. General museums have begun to regard film as one of their proper concerns. The San Francisco Museum of Art struck out boldly with the Art in Cinema series in the fifties, followed by the early mixed-media shows called Vortex. Today museums across the country are sponsoring miniature "film festivals." Recently a novel and promising archive for experimental, personal films has been set up in the new Art Museum at the University of California, Berkeley; it will conserve the 16mm work of artists whose films have heretofore often been at the mercy of household fires and other hazards. The national collection of films in the Library of Congress has been reviewed and rationalized under a new film-trained curator; and recently, through grants from the American Film Institute, the remaining problem of transferring decomposing early films onto more lasting acetate stock has at last been solved. The history of the art, with certain painful exceptions in the form of apparently lost films (among them Stroheim's complete *Greed*), has been secured. And works of film history, though still rare, are being written; slowly but surely, historical scholarship in film is developing a tradition.

When Colin Young described a plan for an American Film Institute in these pages in 1961, it seemed a lovely idea but unlikely to happen. Today, a nongovernmental, part-industry, part-foundation organization exists, and is going ahead with ambitious plans to bolster our archives, provide grants for young independent film makers, perform scholarly and reference services, and improve American film education at all levels. Plans also exist—though fraught with various uncertainties—for feature films to be produced by new film makers under joint Institute-industry auspices, on "moderate" budgets (about twice Godard's or Bergman's).

Publishers, whose products were after all the first mass medium, no longer routinely reject manuscripts on film. Indeed books about film are sold in numbers that would have been unbelievable a decade ago: books that appeal to dedicated movie goers and also books of a specialized research nature. Many university libraries are building up respectable film collections that would have been hooted off the shelves by academicians earlier.

And the foundations? Their record is not a bright one, if we take seriously their press releases about providing "risk capital for culture." Ford's admirable $120,000 grant program to a dozen experimental film makers in 1964 reaped astonishing fruit: Belson's *Re-Entry,* Conner's *Report,* Emschwiller's *Relativity*—three films that will last. Yet a muddled and ignorant attack in *Time* led Ford timidly to draw back from a projected second round. (Nobody bothers to attack the ballet and music projects which consume enormously greater sums.) Recently the Rockefeller foundation began a modest and intelligent set of small grants to experimental film makers; and even the Guggenheim foundation, whose grants chiefly go to established academicians who don't need them, has given a couple of grants to film makers. A few ingenious souls have been able to pry money out of local or smaller foundations. But in general foundations wish to back respectable, already successful people; as one foundation mogul wrote to me, "We leave poverty programs to the federal government." In plain English, this means that they do not care about artists as much as about their own prestige, and that in particular they do not care about new artists, who are not yet widely known and do not yet have powerful friends and clients. It is well to keep in mind that, press releases aside, a foundation is basically an entity set up for tax and public-relations purposes. Foundation grants are erratic tidbits, useful but irrelevant to the long-range problem, which is how beginning artists can manage to eat while they are discovering if their talent is significant. That problem will only be solved when we have some kind of guaranteed minimum income, so that those strange and gifted individuals who wish to pursue unremunerative activities like writing or painting or film making can at least be sure they won't starve while they try it. Work, in the old sense of labor performed for another man's profit, in return for wages, is indeed going out of style. Millions of members of the expense-account middle class have learned this since the war, and it is at last getting through to ordinary working people and labor organizations. "Work" in the advanced technological society is becoming a formal and partly fictional phenomenon; one watches the dials and buttons, but it isn't necessary to actually *do* much. And so increasing numbers of people are able to contemplate what it would be like to work for something, or on something, that genuinely interests them. (As we students, members of a leisured class, used to do in Docfilm.)

A great race is on, in American society, between the massive forces of conflict and disintegration set in motion in Vietnam and the decay of the cities, and forces for new and freer ways of living which are being generated. Film is a weapon in that struggle, for only film can literally show it like it is. But film is also a prize: to the winners will go the images of the future.

Renata Adler

ON REVIEWING, I: TURNSTILES

How does a critic go about reviewing a film? How should he? Renata Adler, author of A Year in the Dark, *a collection of her film criticism for the* New York Times, *discusses these and other questions about the still imperfect art of film reviewing.*

THERE is probably no more unedifying and, in many ways, valueless kind of communication than everyone's always expressing opinions about everything. Not ideas, or feelings, or information—but opinions, which amount to little more than a long, unsubstantiated yes or no on every issue. People begin to identify themselves by opinion-clusters: on the basis of a few simple questions (Do you believe the Warren Report? Did you like *Bonnie and Clyde?*), you can project whole personalities and—better than on the basis of class or education—social groups. Since nothing more than endorsement or rejection is involved, arguments are reduced to a kind of *de facto* sarcasm, insult controversy, the unbacked scornful remark: "He *admires* McNamara," or "She *sobbed* during *Guess Who's Coming to Dinner*" might constitute a full description of you in some circles. Plain opinions are much overrated.

The problem is that reviews are read almost completely for opinions, and with movies this can be especially inadequate. Most movies are not very good. Most people know it and like to see them anyway. Without too much fuss or rave or polemic. One only wants a critical inventory of what to expect. I happen to think, for example, that *China Is Near, Poor Cow, Windflowers* and *The Power* are all pretty bad movies, at various levels of aspiration. *China Is Near* is an ambitious but dreary Italian provincial satire. *Poor Cow* is a false, colorful and sentimental movie of English working-class life of the genre of *Alfie.*

Windflowers is a frail, sincere underground lyric to draft evasion. And *The Power* is a straight, awful science-fiction picture that uses George Hamilton.

The important thing in each case, however, is not an opinion of how these movies rate on a scale of eternal values, but that a mixed review should serve as a turnstile which brings each reader to the kind of movie he would want to see. In each of them the tip-off is different; in reviewing the Italian film, the point is the director; in the British, the genre; in the underground, the aura; in the neighborhood movie, the fact that it stars George Hamilton. Since most people know in broad terms what kind of movies they like, it only takes describing the thing to suggest, regardless of whether the reviewer endorses the movie or not, whether the reader is going to want to go.

There is, however, the matter of the review in movie advertising. The practice of critical burbling seems to stem from a time when reviewers were considered part of the film industry, stringing superlatives together for the investor's sake. Now, I think, blurb excerpting and the kind of writing it leads to ("stunning," "engrossing," "an overwhelming experience") simply compromises everyone. It creates expectations which most movies—less part of the art than of the industry—simply are not meant to satisfy, and it makes it impossible to distinguish movies that are really . . . well, there you are.

Few things are more infuriating than standing in line in the cold for hours, subject to the extreme rudeness of the managements of nearly all New York theaters where successful movies are playing, and then seeing a disappointing film, which one would have liked well enough if only it had not been so extravagantly, unanimously praised. Readers either become distrustful or they are continually let down; copy sifters persist in using even honest reviews in misleading ways. As though audiences didn't really like to see so-so films. (Perhaps a solution would be to have reviewers write a few separate honest lines for inclusion in ads for a month or so, and see if audiences would go to anything that was not mis-labeled a masterpiece.) As it stands, the language of movie reviewing is simply debased.

That adjectives should remain apt and alive is important for the only function of a critic that really matters much: to recognize a distinguished work when it comes along, and keep it alive. That is the essence of his job. A corollary to that job is that, on a daily basis, in preparation for just such a work, he should try to keep audiences from being vulgarized. Or insulted. Or made uncertain.

There are so many things that ruin or disperse audiences: the scarceness of art; the badness of criticism; more than that, the recent tendency of films themselves to doublecross. One has to be always armed, these days, for the put-on. There are nervous audiences almost everywhere—laughing uneasily, for example, at jokes within movies which are only meant as characterization, not as comedy. Dick Hickock's pun on death and relieving oneself, in *In Cold Blood,* for example, "When you gotta go, you gotta go," always gets a laugh. No matter what one may think of the movie, it earns its responses at a higher level than that. What has thrown audiences out of balance is movies that try to have it both ways. An audience that is afraid to be caught dead serious at a put-on is a ruined audience.

I suppose that is why I prefer *The Power* to *Planet of the Apes. The Power* is willing to stay serious; the *Apes* wants to have a message and pretend it's fooling. I suppose, too, that is why I resent most of the movies in which the main character is posed briefly, unmistakably, in a Christ posture—only to have the film makers deny later on that they intended religious symbolism of any kind. It is the doublecross again. It leaves audiences feeling cheated and foolish, and sooner or later, jaded. It creates smart-alecks, an audience spoiled.

These, I would say, are the test of what reviewing is: not whether opinions agree with one's own from day to day, but whether they convey some inkling, by means of an inventory, of what one's own opinions will be. Whether they vulgarize. And more important, on the rare occasions when a beautifully made movie comes along, whether they call attention to it. *Charlie Bubbles,* I think, was such a film. Other reviewers thought *China Is Near* was. Both movies, naturally enough, are director's films, dominated by a single sensibility as most movies are not. It is a question of which sensibility one responds to. The question is important, a kind of critical watershed; it is the only place where critical opinion really matters. A reviewer's case rests on the things he deeply likes.

One of the interesting things about reviewing movies is finding a vocabulary for saying why. The question has been raised: What would happen if critics reviewed books as cinema buffs review films. X writes superb chapters, they might say; his use of the colon and comma is much imitated. Part of this is frivolous, of course; the main reason why book critics don't spend too much time on grammar is that everyone knows what writing style and grammar are.

In Truffaut's book of interviews with Hitchcock, the conversation dwells happily on the use of a champagne glass—bubbly in one shot, dead in the next—to denote the passage of time. It is a neat touch, but no one would make quite so much of a single well-turned phrase in a novel. There is so much more to say. In movies a lot remains to be worked out. In the meantime, a lot of the mystique of the "visual" seems to me silly and obscurantist. A movie works or it doesn't. Most people agree most of the time with the people they normally agree with about most other things about which movies work. It is only the vocabulary that is undeveloped still. I suspect one of the most productive areas for study is the television commercial. It is brief. It is often beautiful and extremely well made. It is an art that still has an evangelical message—as religious objects have. A perfect commercial is nearly an icon. A movie is still a mass project, on an architectural scale. The problem is how—beyond a simple yes or no or a complete *explication de texte*—the thing can be best discussed. Checking in with opinions is not really saying much.

Parker Tyler
IS FILM CRITICISM ONLY PROPAGANDA?

Parker Tyler, influential film critic and author of the Three Faces of the Film *and* Magic and Myth of the Movies, *examines the efforts of contemporary independent film-makers and the film critics responsible to them. Tyler's remarks were delivered at the Fourth New York Film Festival at Lincoln Center (1966).*

PERHAPS I am the most unpopular film critic in the world and maybe, despite my long record, I'm so unpopular because I'm not a very good propagandist for modern doctrines *in* film and *of* film. Let's look at the term propaganda. It means the systematic propagation of a special doctrine, religious, political, social, economic . . . artistic. . . . But what does the verb propagate signify? It merely means to multiply one's own kind, to reproduce, as do animals and, for that matter, vegetables. Is it that simple in regard to film? Perhaps, following the dictionary, it should be. But experience teaches us to suspect and examine the implications of dictionary definitions.

According to the dictionary, we might think that the duty of film criticism is to breed more film criticism of the same sort, the duty of films to breed more films of the same sort. From big Garbos, somehow, there should come little Garbos, who will grow up; from the avant-garde (apparently Garbo is still avant-garde) there should come more avant-garde, which will grow up. Surely it is clear that I'm being a little ironic, and that the whole point of film criticism viewed as propaganda is that it has a special doctrine, a viewpoint; that it is limited and exclusive, being for certain defined values and against other values, equally definable . . . that it can point, can divide the sheep from the goats, even within its own ranks; can develop theories of value, definition, analysis. Otherwise, it is no more than self-promotion, a variety of commercial advertising rigged up with gags, more or less refined and sophisticated. To cite an anology: It is not the function of film criticism to choose between grapefruit and nectarines as commodities for the discriminating palate, but rather to help create the best nectarines and the best grapefruit.

I'm sure that we who are serious desire that *better film criticism* stand for values, that it should be able to point and distinguish, speak a coherent language, and espouse, at its best, a vigorous, high-level doctrine. In this same hall, last year, I solemnly questioned that better film criticism *as it exists* stand for this; I assumed that critics are very much behind-hand in their natural work of propaganda. For my pains, I was applauded and I was also contradicted and looked at askance. I was told in print—by an authority who shall be nameless—that all the books that I saw as lacking and needful *had* been written. Now this was a childish admonition, based only on superstition and hearsay. If we really inspected such books, we might see attempts at the real thing, even near-successes, but widely recognized theories, anything like a lucid and comprehensive body of doctrine? No. Nothing like that save in the most limited sense. At least, if such exists, it hasn't been announced in the English language; nor, from what appears in *Cahiers du Cinema,* in the French language.

I'm devoting the rest of this talk to a series of propositions that won't take too long. The remainder of our time I suggest be taken up with discussing and confirming or denying my propositions, and with *evidence* rather than *rhetoric* and *prejudices.* For simplicity's sake, I'll call the film criticism that to me seems desirable Responsible Film Criticism.

First Proposition: *We cannot have responsible film criticism so long as there exists the sentimental fetish of the Good Old Days, both in Hollywood and European film capitals.*

Remarks: This attitude does not even represent "criticism" but should be called smart antiquarianism. It cites master directors and classic films by gauges and allusions whose values are completely obscure, to me, and so far as I know, untranslatable into any artistic or intellectual idiom known to any of the other arts. Note that the habit of antiquarianism does not rest chiefly on uniquely *filmic* values, on technical quantities, but on total historic results, on so-called film classics, whatever technical theories and assumptions the said classics may have had.

Second Proposition: *We cannot have responsible film criticism so long as nominally serious critics (here I can mention James Agee who was among the most talented) imitate the habits of journalistic reviewers.*

Remarks: What are the habits of journalistic reviewers and why are they so bad? Because of the journalistic reviewer's job, he must, even at his best, and most sincere and independent, assume that Hollywood (for example) has a standard of The Best, and that this is authoritative at any given time, by any given measure. But this rule of The Best, alas, is vitiated by having been industrially determined. Thus nothing could be more foolish than recognizing it. If producers created artistic standards, the very occupation of film critics would be superfluous and the discrimination of the audience rendered quite meaningless. I have often been asked: "Why aren't you writing criticism for one of the New York dailies or weeklies?" The answer is simple: Because I like far too little that happens in film. To hold their jobs, reviewers have to approve a minimum of the local products and the imported products. Of course, a few journalistic reviewers pretend not to accept Hollywood standards and interests—these are the ones who lambaste one day and laud the next—and perhaps they don't accept them, consciously, but unconsciously they are occupational victims of the same standards and interests. Moreover, most of even the better journalistic reviewers are habitual fakers; they vaunt having the know-how of a thing when actually their gift of the gab has simply succeeded in dominating the professional competition of critics in their own class. True know-how has very little to do with professional critical competence as it is.

THIRD PROPOSITION: *Responsible film criticism has been dealt a serious blow by the recent upsurge of the avant-garde in the direction of Pop Art, which has substituted mere qualities of smart novelty and unsmart impudence for creative meaning in film and represents a revolt of the amateurs against the professionals.*

Remarks: Here we are in focus with the theme of the present forums. The state of the Independent Cinema touches intimately the issue of film criticism as propaganda. We may reserve argument as to just how good the current avant-garde, or independent cinema, is. The avant-garde in theory, I maintain, must be serious and positive, not simply active and negative. It cannot be, with any growing profit, what it now overwhelmingly tends to be: a sort of anti-commercial demonstration protesting the segregation of small films from large: by "small" and "large" I refer roughly to their professional scale, not their length. . . . The fact is that the whole theory of the avant-garde has gradually, subtly, altered within the framework of modern social and political protest, and now proclaims itself as propaganda for a very loose and inferior doctrine. Today, we have exponents of the nominal Independent Cinema who welcome any creative-type manifestation, no matter what its artistic or nonartistic aims, no matter what its technical or professional qualifications. Why is the wildest, willfullest daydream (which may be quite banal) no less than the most naive and flabby documentary welcomed, sometimes, with equal fervor?

Let me extend the remarks on this proposition because actually it leads to the summary proposition that will be the whole point of my argument. The source of all radical intelligence in the arts, accounting for all past revolutions of style and taste, has been the desire to see, to hear, to write with greater keenness or greater scope, with more depth, grace, or comprehensiveness. To "change the mode"—even as late as the first two decades of this century—did not mean to lower the standard of quality, to level off the average, to be more democratically inclusive.

Now, however, the avant-garde is making a popular front among the underprivileged element in the arts. That would be all right, it would be fine, if their number was only underprivileged in *opportunity,* but too often independent filmmakers are also underprivileged in *talent.* It is a classic radical quality, in art or politics, to be aggressive and also to be "different." But to be both is not enough for the avant-garde with a high standard. The avant-garde today is like the miniskirt. It's new and it shows things. But some knees are beautiful and some are not.

Unfortunately, being a "useful" critic of the Independent Cinema is to be one who obeys blindly, a propagandist rule of order. But this rule is as elementary and as dated as the old campaign for free speech. Take the element of censorship. Nowadays, sex in the films—all kinds of sex—is being stripped nude inch by inch. Freedom of visual speech, I grant, is a vital issue, and opens up fresh opportunities. But a film, as an artistic entity, is not necessarily improved by being bold or candid in its sex scenes—quite the contrary, it may get worse. . . . It should be tacit that freedom of expression is no guarantee of merit. But, apparently, it needs to be said.

Now, speaking of the critics who devote themselves mostly to the Independent Cinema, I grant that some of the appreciative little monographs that appear, for instance, in *Film Culture,* are intelligent and display insight into artistic and filmic values. But, more frequently, one finds in the little film magazines the abandoned outpourings of some young or middle-aged enthusiast who wants to attract attention to himself or to a friend. If there is little discrimination about the artistic quality of independent filmmakers, there is almost as little about their critics. It strikes me very forcibly that good film criticism, *responsible* film criticism, is impossible, when so high a degree of tolerance is exercised toward manifestations of what roughly may still be termed the avant-garde. The social and political cause of Integration is one thing, the "Integration" of all grades of noncommercial film talent is . . . another.

I would say that today the reigning standard of the avant-garde is a deliberately cultivated amateurism. And amateurism, as systematically, "critically" encouraged, can be just as bad as its converse, professionalism. Certain kinds of "avant-garde" amateurism are mere parodies of professionalism. It is just as bad, this cult of amateurism, as the cult of professionalism propagated by the aforesaid journalistic reviewers. The avant-garde, in trying to displace its two declared enemies, the commercial film and the artistic academy, is morally beginning to equate itself with them. Here the business angle comes in. Economic survival has always been a major problem among ambitious artists who wished to change or improve standards. Famous writers and artists, notoriously, have starved during their lifetimes of neglect or uneven success. This, however, is a purely economic issue and its only solution, of course, is patronage.

Patronage, admittedly, is a limited solution. But its dogmatic converse is universal subsidy. As to this, one can remark that capitalism is a competitive system and that aspirants in the film have to compete even for foundation grants. We find, today, the avant-garde or Independent Cinema competing in the open market. The Cinematheque, here in New York, exists as a repertory theatre for the more radical filmmaking activities in this country. One strongly doubts that, however long it has been operating, the Cinematheque makes enough for itself or its filmmakers to be self-supporting. Unhappily most of their programs are very unfledged filmmaking and a good many have the same "charm" as the commercial "nudie" films a block away on 42nd Street. What does this mean? It means that if what I call responsible critical standards were applied to films shown at the Cinematheque, there would not be enough films for a repertory house.

As I imply, the regular commercial houses are guilty of exactly this indiscriminateness, with ordinary financial profit as the only motive. There, it is true, lies a difference. . . . It is often repeated that serious young filmmakers want to make only enough money to make more films and keep a roof over their heads, etc. It is natural for the young, ambitious, and inexperienced to think like that—but suppose, miraculously, the degree of their public success were to soar? They might well sing another tune. Look what happened to the really talented John Cassavetes! Hollywood swallowed him whole, as the whale did Jonah, and after making a film or two of rather striped merit, he issues forth now as—a Hollywood *actor.* We remember that the same thing happened to that greatly promising but now long-ruined film talent Orson Welles.

What strikes me in this respect is that if commercialism doesn't suck gifted young filmmakers into its art-annihilating system, it creates what medical scientists call an "antibody," which, to be effective, it seems, has to be as all-encompassing, as uncritical, overtolerant, and fashion-mongering in its own way as Hollywood is in its way. This is the danger for the Independent Cinema.

Thus my FOURTH PROPOSITION: *The independent film as an outgrowth of the avant-garde film is basically the social and economic antibody of the commercial film and directly tends to substitute for the vices of its opponent its own peculiar vices.*

Remarks: I argue that the context of this situation is the modern milieu of social-political-economic protest rather than any drive made by purely artistic protest; the implied logic: artists, too, ought to have jobs—it's too much the unionizing spirit of the old WPA on the rampage. . . . The fact is that a jaunty, more or less comic or campy, sort of nihilism has been spreading through the reels of a great number of 16mm film cameras. This has rightly been associated with certain radical movements in the arts, such as Dada, during the first quarter of this century. Very lately it has taken place in other arts—why not also in film? Why not, indeed? Yet what does it have to give? Very little that I can put a finger on. It often has mockery and spontaneity along with any number of faults. Mockery is feeble and infantile without real wit, and the current avant-garde, unlike the best Dadaists, has very little wit, and what it has is repetitious. In fact, underground and independent cinema is so structured and mooded that it seldom knows when it's being witty and pointed and when it's being stupid and futile. The moral of my proposition: Just contradicting a value or a form by giving it energy without intelligence is not in itself interesting, however much it rigs itself out with a new vogue. As we see by glancing at the current programs of New York's commercial houses, the cinema wholly dependent on financial profits is far from reluctant to take up the newest vogues in comedy and nudity. A few, but a very few, independent filmmakers, I would add, are offering substantial values above the level of current commercial values.

And I come to my FIFTH PROPOSITION: *Film criticism can be only propaganda for a naïve and gelatinous antibody of the film so long as mere technical antics involving sensation are deemed an adequate substitute for artistic, specifically filmic merit—for cinematic form, for emotional and intellectual values engendered through filmic means.*

Remarks: I think it a poor general tactic, that before the film itself has created a major body of superlative works of its own, it begin contracting formal liaisons with other arts. Mixed media may be amusing and modish; they certainly offer "expanded" opportunities. But the expansion and complication consequent on mixed media may be only distracting factors that cloud the results even if the results are "different" and more "amusing." I am sure there are great artistic possibilities in merging theatre with film, and involving the audience too. Though this is having an intensive revival just now, it isn't quite new. Historically, the stage itself has already leaked into the audience, assumed the audience as part of the theatrical dimension. Obviously it is harder—in a sense, impossible—for the film alone to do this; hence, the relevance of its joining with the stage.

In many senses, one can say, film is acting up: the Independent Cinema, it seems, is not so independent as not to want allies from other art media. I wonder, frankly, if the drive behind this multimoded manifestation of energy is even so artistic in character as to be called anti-art, as Dada used to call itself. We are already familiar with what is known as assemblage and collage in the plastic arts. The time has come when it is hard to tell a "found object," or *objet trouvé,* from an invented object because the invention tends so strongly toward the found. An undercurrent of recent creations in such styles has been that it doesn't matter what is happening, just so "something" is happening or has happened; its degree of resemblance to art or just mere intelligibility is irrelevant. It doesn't even have to amuse. It doesn't even have to be a sick joke. It can be a dead joke. A dead joke, one might say, in which live people participate. Perhaps, the jokers seem to be hinting, that is just what civilization has come to be: a dead joke with live character—actors.

Of course, I speak of the extreme. Many imagine, I guess, that there's much live honest fun of a "different" kind in the Independent Cinema and its mixed media. If so, I gather that it's so spontaneous, different, and independent that it forms an antibody to everything but its own propaganda. Sometimes it is argued that criticism has always been too destructive and thus inhibiting, whereas the ideal of critical commentary is interpretive: it should explain virtues and leave faults alone. But this, I say, is proper only to *program notes* and explicit statements made by filmmakers themselves about their aims.

For sixteen years, the New York film society, Cinema 16, under the guidance of Amos Vogel, now director of these Festivals,* provided a showcase for radical and extraordinary films (sometimes feature length but usually short) and I myself often contributed—I hope helpfully—to the program notes. Certainly one can not be against the exhibition of the rare film that otherwise, because of various taboos, would not be available to interested audiences.

But the mere "cause" of the underdog element in some field of creative endeavor should not be glamorized and fetishized to the point where no critical discrimination, no knowledgeable analysis, can be applied to the said underdog. Right within the independent film move-

* New York Film Festivals.

ment has appeared a term that well describes a pivotal part of its activity: *fetish footage.* Well, "fetish" footage may have various subjects, may mean to be tentative or final, may even be poetically inspired, but often it is embarrassingly close to being Home Movies, and little more. I see no good reason why this neo-professional sort of home-movie making should be celebrated as a cause and its viewers expected to be blind to comparative values or why really criticizing them should be regarded as—well—dastardly. If, in the presence of fetish footage or related activities, one mentions some "principle" of art, one is apt to be rebutted by a partisan of the current independent modes saying that one simply isn't in step with what's happening. If one refers to last year's sensations, these are no longer, perhaps, *au courant*—they may have been replaced by newer ones. This seems to me the avant-garde attitude overasserted to the point of lunacy.

Now, for my final and SIXTH PROPOSITION: *In escaping from the Establishment in the arts, in the largest sense, the avant-garde as it exists is concentrating most of its energy on being radical and revolutionary for the sake of being radical and revolutionary alone and NOT in behalf of any known art form, however "mixed." By a kind of implosion and explosion it is homogenizing all protest elements to this end by using a language of signs that possesses no scale of values, no intelligible aims, and therefore is beyond criticism.*

Remarks: It seems to me that this is not propaganda for anything at all like an art medium (say, the *film!*) but a propaganda of absolute parody. Nothing, I hasten to say, is to be excluded from parody. The old-fashioned silent film is parodied. Photographic skill is parodied. All human emotions and human dilemmas are subject to parody, presumably, and are parodied to the best ability of the parodist. It is not enough that old Hollywood films were naive and stereotyped and went in for the crudest human sentiment. This has to be expressed by the avant-garde over again to show that, as stupid and crude as it was, aesthetically and humanly speaking, one could really get some fun out of it. Oh, yes, I discovered that around 1940, and thereafter was called a surrealist film critic. But my purpose was to objectify and isolate the fun, which was ironic and satiric, not naive and credulous.

As for surrealism in film, we see what happened to a major filmmaker, Fellini, who made *8½* as a sort of parody of successful filmmaking; that is, the story of his failure is presumably more interesting and relevant than if he had succeeded in making the film he was supposedly trying to make. But Fellini already had a great deal of genuine know-how; I mean technical knowledge of all sorts. Nowadays, what is called the Independent Cinema wishes to be independent of mere know-how: one parodies know-how itself by showing one doesn't know how!

Of course there are some exceptions, some small filmmakers who do concentrate on know-how and somehow have escaped the domination of the parody-mania. One of them Ed Emshwiller, is to have a program in these special events. Several others have undeveloped poetic gifts and are floundering because of lack of means. Still others, because they have respect for form and the older avant-garde tradition are on the fringe of the Independent Cinema because they are considered too arty. Too straightforwardly arty, that is. But even the tongue-in-cheek arty, such as *Last Year at Marienbad,* is too straightforward for the latest movement in the avant-garde.

Here at the New York Film Festival, we can see just how far the colloquial designation of parody, which is "camp," has made an inroad on presumably serious big time filmmaking. We all know how James Bond has come to be rated. I just heard that his films are regarded by Willem de Kooning as superior to the small Independent Cinema. I wonder what De Kooning thinks of Morgan. But if we don't know, unless told by De Kooning, what he thinks of Morgan, we do know what Morgan thinks of King Kong. Morgan imagining himself as King Kong is a perfect realization of modern camp, however really entertaining the spectacle is.

I want to conclude with these remarks: Propaganda for the avant-garde, the underground, the independent cinema (mainly, I speak for America, of course) has been more effective than probably it is imagined by anyone, and actually has gotten quite out of the hands of those who wish to influence and determine the direction of the small cinema. When the avant-garde betrays its art, it betrays it into the hands of those to whom the dignity and the future of man, his glory and consciousness of godhead, the destiny of the great emotions and the great trials are all very incidental things. Nowadays we hear much talk of the power of communication systems, how all forms of human interchange, in their speed and multiplicity, affect the taste and the consciousness, and even the goals of human society. Some speak for mass—and massive—communication, others against it. The reason I lament the state of propaganda in film criticism is that film critics have developed no means of dealing authoritatively and competently with this very complex, fluid, and all too universal situation. One potent factor in it is the modern shibboleth to which I already referred: that of democratic tolerance of everything—one might call it everything, for everybody, everywhere. But this, I argue, is a universal issue for human society and not the immediate or proper concern for the avant-garde as such. In short, even if art be considered a weapon of propaganda, it should succeed in being art, should insist on being art, otherwise it cannot make its own particular role effective. Propaganda for a social principle, a social truth, if it be cast in an art medium, must also be propaganda for art, and it cannot be propaganda for art if it is propaganda for anti-art. There are those who would insist that film is not primarily an art medium, or even an entertainment medium, but an informational medium. Obviously then it is an ideal vehicle for political information as well as other kinds. I should hate to think, personally, that the chief destiny of the Independent Cinema—if it is not just to be an absolute parody of absolutely everything—is, on the contrary, to be a bureau of general information. So I too wish to raise a slogan: THE INDEPENDENT CINEMA INDEPENDENT OF ITS INDEPENDENCE OF *CRITICISM.*

THE GRADUATE
Four Reviews

Mike Nichols' The Graduate *was in many ways a watershed in American cinematic history. The first financially successful of the "personal" films—films in which the director seeks to express a personal viewpoint of a given aspect of our society—*The Graduate *marked the advent of the New American film. Because of its significance and influence, the film is deserving of critical study. Preceding Joseph Gelmis' article, "Mike Nichols Talks About 'The Graduate'" are four reviews of the movie: Hollis Alpert from* Saturday Review, *Bosley Crowther from the* New York Times, *Joseph Morgenstern from* Newsweek, *and Stephen Farber and Estelle Changas from* Film Quarterly.

Hollis Alpert
THE GRADUATE MAKES OUT

FROM a window of my apartment I have a view of a movie house on Manhattan's East Side, where, ever since last December, *The Graduate* has attracted long lines of patrons. During some of the coldest winter weekends, the lines extended around the corner all the way down the block, much like those at the Radio City Music Hall during holiday periods—except that the people waiting for the next showing were not family groups but mostly young people in their teens and early twenties. One night when it was eight degrees outside I passed the line and noticed how little they seemed to be bothered by the weather; they stomped their feet, they made cheerful chatter; it was as though they all knew they were going to see something good, something made for *them.* There were other cinemas nearby, but no one waited outside in the cold. *The Graduate* was the film to see.

It still is, although now, with the warm weather, I notice that older people have begun to intermix with the young crowd. Either *The Graduate* has begun to reach deep into that amorphous audience that makes the large hits or the elders have become curious about the movie their offspring have been going to see again and again. For that is what has been happening. *The Graduate* is not merely a success; it has become a phenomenon of multiple attendance by young people.

Letters from youthful admirers of the movie have been pouring in on Dustin Hoffman, the talented thirty-year-old actor who plays the unprepossessing twenty-one-year-old Benjamin Braddock. A strong theme of identification with Benjamin's particular parental and societal hang-ups runs through these letters, as it also does in the letters to Mike Nichols, the director with an uncanny knack for forging hits. They've been writing to Joseph E. Levine, who backed and has been presenting the film. One boy from Dallas wrote Levine, bragging that he had seen *The Graduate* more than any of his friends, no less than fifteen times.

I have seen *The Graduate* three times—once at a preview, twice with audiences—thus satisfying, I hope, the Columbia graduate student who questioned my qualifications to assess the film after only one viewing. "But you must see it at *least* three times," she told me at a brunch given by her literature professor. "You see, it has meanings and nuances you don't get on just one viewing." She, and many others in her age group, cultishly attach all sorts of significance to the most minor of details. In the film's opening moments, for example, Benjamin is seen in the cabin of a huge jet, blank-faced among rows of blank faces. "Ladies and gentlemen," the captain's voice announces, "we are about to begin our descent into Los Angeles." My graduate student interpreted this as symbolic of Benjamin's arrival in purgatory. Close to the end of the film, Benjamin is seen in an antiseptic church, outlined against a glass partition, his arms spread out. Many have interpreted this as suggesting a crucifixion theme, an interpretation, I have it on good authority, that was far from the minds of Mr. Nichols and Mr. Hoffman.

Viewers have made much of the symbolic use of glass and water in the film, signifying Benjamin's inability to get through, to communicate with the generation that has produced him. He peers through the glass of a tank at captive fish. At poolside, and in the pool, he looks out at his parents and their friends through the glass mask of a diving suit. At other times it is through sunglasses that he sees a home environment grown somewhat strange. Surely, Benjamin is alienated, but what is so odd here is that the generation-gappers who love the film regard this sense of estrangement as natural and normal, given the times and the middle-class values espoused by Benjamin's family and friends.

Hollywood has made strenuous attempts to appeal to the young film audience in the past, from Andy Hardy to Elvis Presley. There have been bikini beach parties, rock-'n'-roll orgies, Annette Funicello, and Peter Fonda on LSD, but the coin taken in from these usually cheap and sleazy quickies has been but a pittance compared to the returns from *The Graduate.* I need cite only the fact that *The Graduate* has already taken in more than $35,000,000 at the box office, after playing in only 350 of this country's theaters. Marlon Brando, the revered James Dean, and Presley never came near doing that. But this film, without the so-called stars for security, has now done better, financially speaking, than all but a dozen films of the past, and it still has thousands of drive-ins to play throughout the summer; it has yet to open anywhere abroad; and there are still those lines in front of the theater I see through my window. It is quite possible that *The Graduate* will become one of the three or four most profitable pictures *ever* made, perhaps as profitable as *The Sound of Music,* which has done so sensationally well that some critics renamed it *The Sound of Money.*

But how can these two industry landmarks be equated? *The Graduate* would appear to be squarely attacking all that *The Sound of Music* affirms so prettily: sugary sentiment, the sanctity of vows, whether religious or marital, the righteous rearing of children, melody over the mountains. The one has the well-scrubbed Julie Andrews and a dozen or so cute kids, all of them singing the Rodgers and Hammerstein lush gush as though it were the equal of Handel's *Messiah.* The other has the appealing but unhandsome Dustin Hoffman, Anne Bancroft playing a dissatisfied, alcholic bitch of a wife, and a musical score by Paul Simon (performed by Simon and Garfunkel) that, contrasted with *The Sound of Music*'s sentimental reverence, chants, "And the people bowed and prayed/To the neon god they made . . . " Yet a somewhat similar pattern of attendance has been noted about both films. The young audiences go to see *The Graduate* again and again. Housewives, matrons, women's clubbers went to see *The Sound of Music* again and again. We must hypothesize, then, that in this period of selective filmgoing there are at least two huge American audiences there for the right picture, one made up of the seventeens to the twenty-fives, the other of the over-thirty-fives. The Motion Picture Association now advertises its more adult fare as "suggested for mature audiences," but one wonders which is the more mature.

I have encountered some members of my generation—let us loosely call it the over-forties—who haven't liked *The Graduate.* More than that, it made them angry. It was almost as though they felt themselves personally attacked, and it has occurred to me that their reaction is less objective and critical than emotional and, possibly, subliminal. These friends do worry about their children, they have brought them up well, given them opportunities of education and aesthetic development, and they are quite certain they have managed to establish communication with their young. Their wives don't drink or seduce the neighbor's son. What's all this business about honesty and truth in *The Graduate?* The cards have been stacked against the middle-class parent and in favor of the rebellious "now" generation. They darkly hint at the commercial motives of Levine, Nichols, and company, who, it's true, hoped to come through at the box office, but had not the faintest notion they would come through so handsomely.

But *The Graduate* was not meant as an attack on a generation; it merely tells a *story,* as effectively as the makers knew how to do it. To understand the story it is necessary, however, to understand that Benjamin Braddock belongs to a milieu that has been termed the affluent society. He has never known financial insecurity—he has grown up among gadgets, among cars and swimming pools—and this he has taken so much for granted that it literally has no meaning for him. His parents, on the other hand, have presumably known hard times; they know the value, for them, of money, of material success, of things. When Benjamin comes of age, literally and symbolically, he finds himself vaguely rejecting all that his parents hold so dear. He finds himself a kind of object, the proud result of proper rearing, a reward of his parents' struggle in his behalf. Somehow, he feels, this is wrong, but he doesn't yet know what is right. What guides and counselors does he have? "Ben, I want to say one word to you, just one word," a friend of the family breathes in his ear at a welcome-home party. Benjamin awaits the word, among clinking glasses holding machine-made ice and good bourbon and Scotch. "Plastics" the fellow says, imparting the great secret to success in our time. "There is a great future in plastics." The young audiences howl, at least they did when I was there, and they're on the side of Benjamin and the movie, which pokes fun at the plastic society and those who believe in it.

It is also interesting that while Benjamin tunes out for a while, he doesn't turn on. He neither joins nor identifies with the hippies, the yippies, or the weirdies; he is still thoroughly middle-class, affluent variety. As he lazes purposelessly in the California sun his thoughts turn heavily to those of sex with Mrs. Robinson, whose frustrating marriage has borne her only one good result, her lovely daughter, Elaine. Elaine will soon have the benefits of her young womanhood, while the mother will sink into her bitter middle age. Unconscious envy on Mrs. Robinson's part turns into willful determination, and she reveals herself in her nudity to Benjamin's unwilling gaze. He first runs from her as from the very devil; after all, there are the proprieties, not to mention the taboos.

But then he backs into the affair with Mrs. Robinson, who uses him for the sex she doesn't get from Mr. Robinson. In only one moment does she allow Benjamin to reach her; their intimacy is, literally, skin deep.

When Benjamin stupidly assumes that affection is necessary in a furtive affair, the surprised Mrs. Robinson expels cigarette smoke into his mouth. She too is aware of and insistent on the taboos; Benjamin is never, ever to take Elaine out, for she assumes that by her actions she has cheapened both Benjamin and herself.

And, of course, he does, forced into it by his unaware parents. Some critics have felt that the film breaks in two around this point, that the first half is a "seriocomedy" and the second a kind of campus romance with a chase finale. But this criticism seems to overlook the unifying fact of its all being viewed and experienced through Benjamin, who is in a process of muddle, change, and development. He is a truth-seeker, trying to cut through to some acceptable level of meaning. He even tells the truth to the outraged Mr. Robinson about the affair with Mrs. Robinson: "We got into bed with each other. But it was nothing. It was nothing at all. We might—we might just as well have been shaking hands."

One of the great appeals of film to the young, and to the young in heart of all ages, is Benjamin's honesty. The most important thing in common between Elaine and Benjamin is that they share the urge to see honestly and clearly. But Elaine's emotions are still unstable. She allows herself to be rushed into a hasty, secret marriage with an available suitor, appropriately enough a medical student, a candidate for surgeondom.

It is the ending of the film that has annoyed some, and delighted many others. If it were not for the ending, I doubt that *The Graduate* would have aroused as much enthusiastic favor as it has among the somewhat inchoately rebellious young. The distraught Benjamin, madly seeking his lost Elaine—the pure, the good, the holy—manages to reach the church, but not (as is invariably the case in a Doris Day movie) in time, upon which his hoarse, despairing appeal causes Elaine to leave her newly wedded groom and the assembled relatives, and to take a bus to nowhere in particular with Benjamin. To hold off the outraged parents, the attendants, and the minister, Benjamin grabs a large golden cross and swings it menacingly, then uses it as a makeshift padlock on the church doors.

Curiously enough, the writer of the novel on which the film is based, Charles Webb, who was not much more than Benjamin's age at the time of writing, had fashioned a different ending—not *very* different, but crucial nevertheless. Benjamin, in the book, did arrive at the church in time, and there was no further "moral transgression" on his part involved, except, perhaps, for that bit of crosswielding. It turns out that Mr. Webb was disturbed by the changed ending. He wrote a letter to *The New Republic,* complaining about critic Stanley Kauffmann's laudatory interpretation of the film, and particularly by what

Kauffmann had approvingly termed the "film's moral stance." "As a moral person," Webb wrote, "he [Benjamin] does not disrespect the institution of marriage. In the book the strength of the climax is that his moral attitudes make it necessary for him to reach the girl before she becomes the wife of somebody else, which he does. In the film version it makes no difference whether he gets there in time or not. As such, there is little difference between his relationship to Mrs. Robinson and his relationship to Elaine, both of them being essentially immoral."

However, it does make a great deal of difference that in the film he does not get there in time, and the audiences have taken delight in just that fact. This film-bred, film-loving generation has seen that the ending is aimed, in a double-barreled kind of way, at what might be called general moral complacency in America, and also at Hollywood morality, which, from time immemorial, has felt it necessary to approve only the sexual love that occurs during the state of marriage, and that, up until only a decade ago, took place in twin beds, with at least one foot of the man on the floor.

Not only does Mr. Webb, in his letter, equate morality with marriage licenses, he overlooks the fact that even in his novel Elaine would already have taken out a marriage license by the time Benjamin reached her. And there is a thing called consummation. The Nichols ending (relatively little story tampering was done otherwise) is a bold stroke that not only is effective but gives the story more meaning. We now see clearly Mrs. Robinson's tragedy, that she was unable to break out of the hollow formality, the prosperous smothering surface of her own marriage. "It's too late," she screams at her daughter, who is about to head for Benjamin. Upon which Elaine, seeing it all clearly for the first time, screams triumphantly back, "Not for *me*."

But if that old Production Code has been forsaken, if Doris Day has at last been soundly spanked for her virginal sins, hasn't morality triumphed after all? Of course it has. Mike Nichols, perhaps without fully realizing it, has lined up old Hollywood with avant-garde Hollywood. He has contrived a truly moral ending, and a most positive one at that. Honesty wins the day. Sex without love has been put in its place. Ancient taboos have been struck down. Material values have been shown to be hollow. As uninhibited and refreshing as *The Graduate* is, we are still left in fantasy land. "Most of us," a friend of mine ruefully commented, "still miss the bus."

On the other hand, perhaps the reason this newly mature generation has taken so to *The Graduate* is that it thinks, assumes, imagines it can make the bus. Mike Nichols told of meeting, recently, one of the leaders of the Columbia University rebellion. The student had loved *The Graduate,* as had his associates in rebellion. "In a way," he told

Nichols, "it was what the strike was all about. Those kids had the nerve, they felt the necessity, to break the rules."

The Graduate represents a breakthrough of sorts in the Hollywood scheme of things, aside from its fine acting, its technical accomplishment, its vastly entertaining qualities. For it has taken aim, satirically, at the very establishment that produces most of our movies, mocked the morals and values it has long lived by. It is a final irony that it has thereby gained the large young audience it has been seeking and has been rewarded by a shower of gold.

Bosley Crowther
TALES OUT OF SCHOOL

SUDDENLY, here toward the year's end, when the new films are plunging toward the wire and the prospects of an Oscar-worthy long shot coming through get progressively more dim, there sweeps ahead a film that is not only one of the best of the year, but also one of the best seriocomic social satires we've had from Hollywood since Preston Sturges was making them.

It is Mike Nichols's and Lawrence Turman's devastating and uproarious "The Graduate," which came yesterday to the Lincoln Art and the Coronet.

Mark it right down in your datebook as a picture you'll have to see—and maybe see twice to savor all its sharp satiric wit and cinematic treats. For in telling a pungent story of the sudden confusions and dismays of a bland young man fresh out of college who is plunged headlong into the intellectual vacuum of his affluent parents' circle of friends, it fashions a scarifying picture of the raw vulgarity of the swimming-pool rich, and it does so with a lively and exciting expressiveness through vivid cinema.

Further, it offers an image of silver-spoonfed, bewildered youth, standing expectantly but with misgiving where the brook and the swimming-pool meet, that is developed so wistfully and winningly by Dustin Hoffman, an amazing new star, that it makes you feel a little tearful and choked-up while it is making you laugh yourself raw.

In outline, it may sound skimpy and perhaps a little crude—possibly even salacious in a manner now common in films. For all it is, in essence, is the story of this bright but reticent young man who returns from an Eastern college to his parents' swanky home in Beverly Hills, gets seduced rather quickly by the restless wife of his father's law partner, then falls in love with the lady's daughter and finds himself helplessly trapped in a rather sticky dilemma until he is able to dislodge himself through a familiar romantic ploy.

That's all. And yet in pursuing this simple story line, which has been adorned with delicious incidents and crackling dialogue in the screenplay by Calder Willingham and Buck Henry, based on a novel by Charles Webb, the still exploring Mr. Nichols has done such sly and surprising things with his actors and with his camera—or, rather, Robert Surtees's camera—that the over-all picture has the quality of a very extensive and revealing social scan.

With Mr. Hoffman's stolid, deadpanned performance, he gets a wonderfully compassionate sense of the ironic and pathetic immaturity of a mere baccalaureate scholar turned loose in an immature society. He is a character very much reminiscent of Holden Caulfield in J. D. Salinger's "Catcher in the Rye."

And with Anne Bancroft's sullenly contemptuous and voracious performance as the older woman who yearns for youth, Mr. Nichols has twined in the netting the casual crudeness and yet the pathos of this type.

Katharine Ross, another comparative newcomer, is beautifully fluid and true as the typical college-senior daughter whose sensitivities are helplessly exposed for brutal abrasion by her parents and by the permissive society in which she lives. Murray Hamilton is piercing as her father—a seemingly self-indulgent type who is sharply revealed as bewildered and wounded in one fine, funny scene. And William Daniels and Elizabeth Wilson fairly set your teeth on edge as the ha-cha, insensitive parents of the lonely young man.

Enhancing the veracity of the picture is first-rate staging in true locations and on well-dressed sets, all looking right in excellent color. And a rich, poignant musical score that features dandy modern folk music, sung (off-screen, of course) by the team of Simon and Garfunkel, has the sound of today's moody youngsters—"The Sound of Silence," as one lyric says.

Funny, outrageous and touching, "The Graduate" is a sophisticated film that puts Mr. Nichols and his associates on a level with any of the best satirists working abroad today.

Joseph Morgenstern
SUMMA CUM LAUDE

FOR his second film Mike Nichols has directed a faithful and devastatingly funny adaptation of *The Graduate,* Charles Webb's novel about a young man who loses his virginity to a family friend and his heart to her daughter. It has its faults, which largely proceed from its fidelity to the book, but the film provides an unforgettable portrait of a boy caught in the full panic of self-discovery and dragged screaming into manhood.

Like many another new college graduate, Benjamin Braddock is alienated. His only distinction is how much he has to be alienated from—a string of scholarly distinctions, a pair of rich parents, a Beverly Hills home done in California Ghastly with materials that God never dreamed of during that heavy week's work, a new Alfa-Romeo convertible, a scuba-diving suit, and all of it blighted by a bleak suspicion that his only mission in life is to mope.

Webb wrote the character beautifully to begin with, but it is Dustin Hoffman, in his first motion picture performance, who turns Benjamin into an endearing, enduring hero. He never seems sure of what his voice, eyes or hands are doing, or whose orders they are following. He nods his head whenever he doesn't quite know what he means, which is often. He is wrenchingly simple and vividly intelligent, even with his self-doubts, and his bumbling seduction scenes with the wife of his father's law partner, elegantly played by Anne Bancroft, are as funny as anything ever committed to film.

Nichols occasionally clutters his style with trick cuts and fashionable sound overlaps, but he moves easily from lacerating social satire to brittle neurotic comedy to surreal lyricism, and his work is greatly enhanced by Robert Surtees' photography and a superb score by Simon and Garfunkel. The director handles his excellent cast, which includes William Daniels, Murray Hamilton, Elizabeth Wilson and Katharine Ross, with serene skill and justified confidence. What he cannot handle is the book's fundamental flaw, the fact that Benjamin's subsequent romance is not merely with a girl his own age but with his mistress's daughter.

As a plot device this unifies the action and sharpens the contrast between generations—a predatory, hypocritical mother and a vulnerable, innocent daughter. It is only a device, though, and creates far more problems than it solves. Benjamin's affair with the older woman is wildly funny, revealing, and free. When he switches to the daughter, the comedy is suddenly forced to take itself desperately seriously, with grotesque and intricate complications of a mother-daughter relationship that must be accepted literally if they can be accepted at all.

The flaw is hardly catastrophic. Nichols negotiates the turn by stepping up his speed and closing with a chase just as wild and funny as Benjamin's first fling. He is a remarkably talented man, and in *The Graduate,* as in *Who's Afraid of Virginia Woolf?,* he has directed a piece of work from another medium with great skill and an underlying respect that compels him to operate within the bounds of its defects as well as its strengths. This is admirable, but it will be equally admirable and even more exciting when he takes his gifts beyond adaptations and allows himself the luxury of developing a film from an idea for a film, when he lays on the celebrated Nichols touch from scratch.

Stephen Farber and Estelle Changas
THE GRADUATE

MIKE NICHOLS'S name is so magical today that even if *The Graduate* had been the worst movie of the year, people would be buzzing reverently about it. As it is, *The Graduate* is only the most cleverly fashionable and confused movie of the year—and the responses, from critics and customers alike, have been ecstatic. We expected a lot—we're young, and so is Nichols; in addition to youth, he has money, talent, intelligence, irreverence. And after lots of quickie exploitation films about teenyboppers and acid-heads, *The Graduate* might have been the first movie about today's youth to tell it like it is. But Nichols has too much at stake to risk involving us. He's adored because he's hip and safe at the same time; his audiences know that he won't go too far.

The Graduate opens promisingly enough. Ben, a successful young Eastern college graduate, is returning home to Los Angeles, and Nichols immediately and effectively conveys his isolation by focusing exclusively on Dustin Hoffman's apprehensive face moving through the crowded LA airport. Nichols has said that he chose the thirty-year-old Hoffman (a talented comedian—to get that out of the way) to play his callow young hero because he had a face that suggested suffering. Hoffman himself thought there was something strange about the choice; he felt he wasn't suited to the part, which he described as "a young, conventional, squarejawed *Time* Magazine Man of the Year type." Hoffman was right of course. We soon learn that Ben, for all of his credentials and in spite of his vulnerable face, is clean-cut and stupid. He's supposed to be a champion college debater, but he can hardly form a sentence. In the first scenes he's thrown into his rich parents' cocktail and poolside parties; it's easy enough to caricature suburban phoniness, and we see quickly—Nichols provides a slick, superficial summary of anti-bourgeois satire of the last decade—everything that's wrong with LA society. But what does Ben see? He gapes a lot, but he never looks more than bewildered by what's going on. He certainly can't articulate any sort of protest. All he knows is that he wants his future to be "well . . . different. . . ." He really sweats to get that word out, but he doesn't seem capable of going further. When he's troubled, he stares into his bedroom aquarium.

Of course we're supposed to like Ben because he's victimized by all of those nasty, aging country clubbers. In the face of their boozing and their twaddle, he has a chunky innocence that is to endear him to us. Nothing is going on in his head, but because he's "mixed up," as he says at one point, and abused by his parents, audiences cluck over him and rush to give him credit for understanding anxieties that are actually beyond his grasp.

Nichols does use a few fine Simon and Garfunkel songs (written long before the film was conceived) to pump poetic and intellectual content into *The Graduate.* Because the songs, especially "The Sounds of Silence," are so concise, lyrical, eloquent, we're tempted to believe that the film contains their insights and that Ben understands them. We're supposed to assume that Ben shares Paul Simon's perceptions of "people talking without speaking, people hearing without listening" in a world whose "words of the prophet are written on the subway walls," but in truth Ben couldn't *begin* putting the world in that kind of order. He's only a beer-drinking *Time* magazine type, as Hoffman recognized, rather harmlessly stupid and awkward, but tricked up with a suffering face and an *Angst*-ridden song intent on persuading us that he's an alienated generational hero. And audiences eager to believe that all young people are sensitive and alienated and that all old people are sell-outs or monsters gratefully permit Hoffman's mannerisms and Paul Simon's poetry to convince them of a depth in Ben that the part, as written, simply does not contain.

The film's best scenes are the early ones in which Ben is seduced by the wife of his father's partner (superbly played by Anne Bancroft—her performance is reason enough to see the film). Bancroft, a young man's deliciously provocative sexual fantasy come to life, makes us aware that there *is* something to be said for women over thirty. When she's on, Ben might just as well roll over and play dead. Bancroft is engagingly wicked as Mrs. Robinson; she is at once supremely confident of her sexual power and mercilessly casual in the face of Ben's adolescent fear of her. Alone with him in her house, she takes calm delight in exposing her legs, while he ejaculates moral misgivings. Her sophistication enables her to see through his repeated protests: "You *want* me to seduce you, is that what you're trying to tell me, Benjamin?" she chants in poker-faced style. And finally, having trapped him in her daughter's bedroom, she remains utterly cool, while her daring flirtatious assault, comically caught by rapid cuts from bare bosom to Ben's anguished face, leaves him helplessly gasping, "Jesus Christ, Mrs. Robinson!"

Unfortunately, this is about the only scene which allows us to see that Ben is sexually attracted to Mrs. Robinson. Most of the time Nichols insists that Mrs. Robinson is repulsive because she is sexual and Benjamin lovable because he is not. Sheer boredom, Ben confesses, is the only thing which brings him to her time after time. And later he explains that bedding down with Mrs. Robinson meant nothing; it was "just another thing that happened to me . . . just like shaking hands." Apparently we are to believe, as Stanley Kauffmann has written, that Ben "sees the older woman's advances as a syndrome of a suspect society," and that he deserves congratulations for his indifference; what seems an astonishing blindness to Mrs. Robinson's very real sexiness is to be taken as a moral victory.

Ben's voice of morality, though, is rather unpleasantly self-righteous: "Do you think I'm proud that I spend my time with a broken-down alcoholic?" The scene in which he tries to liven up their evenings by getting Mrs. Robinson to *talk* to him has been much praised, and it *is* an interesting scene, though not for the reasons given, but because it presents Mrs. Robinson with more complexity than usual. When, in the middle of their abortive conversation, she orders Ben not to take out her daughter, the only reason he can guess for the command is that she thinks he isn't good enough for Elaine, and he announces angrily that he considers this liaison "sick and perverted." Bancroft's face, marvelously expressive of deeply rooted social and personal discontents, makes clear to us that this is *not* Mrs. Robinson's reason, that her reasons are much more intense and tortured than Ben suspects—mostly, presumably, an envy of youth and a fear of being cast off for her daughter—and deserve his sympathy, not his moralistic outrage. Ben is too insensitive to see that when she seems to acknowledge that she thinks her daughter too good for him, it's only out of desperation and confusion; she has feelings more intricate and disturbed than she knows how to explain to him. His rejection of her at this moment may look moral, but given the depth and the anguish of her emotional experience, it's a pretty ugly, unfeeling response. Mrs. Robinson's answer to Ben's plea that she talk to him—"I don't think we have much to say to each other"—proves to be quite accurate, but it doesn't expose her shallowness, as Nichols seems to have intended, it exposes *Ben's*. She has so much more self-awareness than he, and so many more real problems, why *should* she talk to him? Ann Bancroft is really too interesting for Nichols's sentimentalities about the generational gap, so he treats her characterization with no respect; after this scene, he turns her into a hideous witch, an evil Furie maniacally insistent on keeping Ben and her daughter apart. This goes along with the current urge to see the generational conflict as a coloring-book morality play—the young in white, the old in black—but it's a cheap dramatic trick.

What really wins the young audience to Ben is his compulsive pursuit of Mrs. Robinson's daughter Elaine in the second half of the film. His single-minded dedication to securing the girl he pines after may be the oldest staple of movie romance, but it is also manna to today's Love Generation. Elaine, though, is a problem. She's gorgeous, all right, she's earnest, and she smiles nicely, but what Ben sees in her beyond her lovely face is kept a secret from us. She does seem to be as clean-cut and stupid as he is. But since she wears her hair long and uncombed and goes to Berkeley (another put-on, much like Hoffman's suffering face), we're to assume that she's an extraordinary catch. Doesn't the fact that she dates and almost marries a smooth, starched medical student confirm the opposite? Ben, incidentally, doesn't even admit her physical attractiveness; his excuse for wanting her so desperately is that at last he has found someone he can talk to. What two such uninteresting people could talk about is a real stumper; and Nichols must have thought so too, for he bars us from one of their few conversations, placing them behind the windshield of Ben's convertible. Perhaps if Nichols were a more experienced film director, he could have convinced us of the vitality of Ben's and Elaine's love with some pungent, seductive visuals; but he relies only on modish out-of-focus shots of flowers and foliage (shots that looked a lot prettier in *Two for the Road* anyway).

All that does express their love is an old-fashioned Hollywood Kiss. On the first date, after treating her quite wretchedly, Ben tries to get her to stop crying and kisses her. And that does it. She forgets her humiliation and smiles. It's love at first sight, just like in the movies, but because the actors look casual and sensitive and alienated, audiences think their instant jello of a romance is "real." A little later Elaine learns of Ben's affair with her mother and flees back to Berkeley; he follows her there, and she comes to his room at night to ask why. But first she asks him to kiss her once more, and when he does, she's satisfied; her doubts are erased, and she's ready to marry him. It's all very reminiscent of Betty Grable cheerleader movies. And it's interesting that there seems to be no real sexual attraction between Ben and Elaine. Even their two or three kisses are awfully restrained. After receiving her second kiss, which looks about as exciting as a late-night cup of hot chocolate, Elaine darts quickly out of Ben's door. The movie is rather offensively prudish in splitting sex and love, implying that sexual relationships are sick and perverted, but that in a healthful Young Love relationship—why, sex is the furthest thing from the kids' minds. In this respect the film fits nicely with the flower talk about love, which for all of the bubbles and incense and the boast of promiscuity, is equally insipid, passionless, ultimately quite as sexless.

How bizarre it is that the vacuous Elaine who has been so easily conned into marrying the fraternity's ace make-out king, can cause such a cataclysmic change in Ben. He throws off his lethargy, chases after her and breaks up her wedding at the last minute, bellowing an anguished "Elaine" as he beats against the glass that separates him from the congregation. A minute later, when Ben punches Elaine's father in the stomach, when he beats off the suburbanites with a giant cross and locks the door with it, the audience cheers vigorously—and to give Nichols his due, it's a pleasing, outrageous image. But it's much too glib to turn Ben suddenly into a rebel hero—this same Ben who's spent most of the film staring blankly into his aquarium and lounging by his pool, transformed by a kiss from a sweet little coed into a fighter for his generation. The motivation may be phony, but we can all laugh at how the old folks get theirs in the end.

The Graduate, like Nichols's film of *Virginia Woolf,* has been applauded for its boldness—never before in an American movie, it is said, could a hero have slept with a woman and married her daughter. The premise *is* arresting, but it's interesting how Nichols blunts it, makes it as easy as possible for his audiences to accept the outrageous. By minimizing Ben's participation in the affair with Mrs. Robinson, by suggesting that it's boring and unpleasant to him, and then by leaving sex out of the relationship with Elaine altogether, the film scampers away from a situation that would be truly challenging and compelling—a young man with strong sexual desire for mother and daughter. Ben doesn't have any sexual desires, apparently, and his unwilling involvement in the affair with Mrs. Robinson lets us off too comfortably. And at a time of much irrelevant nudity and bedroom talk in the movies, this is one film that's entirely too fastidious; the absence of sex in *The Graduate* is a real failure (as it was in *The Family Way*) because the film is, to a large extent, *about* sexuality. But the urgency of Ben's triangular predicament is lost because we don't know much about what goes on in the bedroom, or even in Ben's fantasies. The incestuous longings that lie beneath the surface of the relationships are too uneasily sketched to carry much force. Any development of the oedipal rivalry between mother and daughter is also skimped. This hostility must be behind Mrs. Robinson's command that Ben not see Elaine, and if Elaine is human, she would have certain feelings of jealousy toward her mother. By making her outrage at Ben's affair *purely moral,* by ignoring its psychological content, the film misses an opportunity to explore its potentially explosive situation with depth and humanity—just as it cheated earlier by defining Ben's response to Mrs. Robinson in purely moral terms. Nichols titillates us with an intrigue that we haven't seen before in a movie, but he never gets close to feelings that would upset us. He knows how to startle, but he also knows how to please.

The movie as a whole is a Youth-grooving movie for old people. Nichols's young people have senile virtues—they're clean, innocent, upright, and cute too. Tired rich audiences can relax and say, "So *that's* what this youthful rebellion is all about; the kids want just what you and I want, Daddy—a happy marriage, a nice home, and they're really so well-behaved." Nichols doesn't risk showing young people who are doing truly daring, irreverent things, or even young people intelligent enough to seriously challenge the way old people live. All that ennobles Ben, after four years of college, is his virginity. He and Elaine are very bland, and that suits the old folks just fine; bankers and dowagers know that it's "in" to celebrate the young, and in *The Graduate* they can join the celebration with a minimum of fret or identification. The film is actually an insult to the young who aren't so goody-goody—young people who have complicated conflicts of loyalty and affection and who aren't able to make such a decisive moral rejection before they marry the most beautiful sweetheart of Sigma Chi.

Yet young people are falling for the film along with the old people, because it satisfies their most infantile fantasies of alienation and purity in a hostile world, their most simplistic notions of the generational gap, and their mushiest daydreams about the saving power of love. The movie swings on their side, though from a safe, rather patronizing position, and bleats that even when the middle-aged degenerates are cruelest, all you need is a closed-mouth kiss.

As for Nichols's film sense, he does seem to be learning. He still holds shots much too long or dresses them up much too self-consciously—as in the scuba-diving episode, a good idea ruined by clumsy direction. His images are mostly clichéd—not just blurs of flowers and sun-rippled water and car headlights reflecting on his lens, but even monkeys in the San Francisco zoo. He's good when you feel he's enjoying an unpretentiously silly, charming comic touch for its own sake, and he shows a nice eye for good-natured satiric detail (he's hardly a caustic talent)—Mrs. Robinson watching *The Newlywed Game* on TV, a daffy, myopic lady organist at Elaine's wedding. And perhaps it's not fair to give the impression that the film fails because of expediency and calculated compromise; it may be that Nichols actually did not know what he was doing. He has stated recently, in an interview, that Ben and Elaine are not to be envied at film's conclusion, and that Ben will end up exactly like his parents—which suggests attempts at a more harshly sardonic point of view than the film manages to convey. Why do people cheer so exuberantly and walk out so happily if the film means to criticize Ben? Have they all missed the point? Whatever Nichols's intentions, *The Graduate* never really seems to be attacking the young people; all that can be said is that it celebrates them with a strange lack of conviction, which may once have been meant as savage irony, but comes across only as particularly hollow and ineffective film-making. Along with his handling of actors, Nichols's only real success in the movie is with the same sort of lighthearted, inconsequential farce routines he's provided for Neil Simon's comedies on Broadway; there's no point in encouraging him to believe that he's the seriocomic prophet of the plastic generation. Maybe Nichols does have the talent to do something more important—so far he has the energy and the ambition—but we're not going to find out as long as an evasive gimmicky hoax like *The Graduate* is trumpeted as a milestone in American film history.

Joseph Gelmis
MIKE NICHOLS TALKS ABOUT *THE GRADUATE*

G: What story, if any, were you trying to tell with *The Graduate?*

N: I think it was the story of a not particularly bright, not particularly remarkable, but worthy kid drowning among objects and things, committing moral suicide by allowing himself to be used finally like an object or a thing by Mrs. Robinson, because he doesn't have the moral or intellectual resources to do what a large percentage of other kids like him do—to rebel, to march, to demonstrate, to turn on. Just drowning.

Then finding himself to some extent, finding a part of himself that he hadn't found, through connection with a girl. Finding passion, because of impossibility. Impossibility always leads to passion, and vice versa. Going from passion to a kind of insanity. Saving himself temporarily from being an object, through the passion and insanity. Getting what he thinks he wanted and beginning to subside back into the same world in which he has to live, with not enough changed. I think that's the story.

G: William Hanley and Calder Willingham had each written scripts for *The Graduate* which you didn't like. How did you happen to get together with Buck Henry?

N: I knew that Buck was extraordinary and funny and incredibly intelligent underneath all that kidding around. So we hired him. He never read anything but the novel. He never read the earlier scripts. He wrote an excellent, very long first draft. And then he and I spent literally six months working five, six hours a day. Now, three of those hours were spent goofing off and screwing around and making up horrifying stage directions for what Benjamin might be doing while he was driving along, playing with himself.

I took advantage of Buck to really figure out ways of shooting things. Like that whole montage—out of the pool, into Mrs. Robinson's bed, back and forth, ending up leaping out of the water, landing on Mrs. Robinson—Buck and I pieced together over days and days and days. Discovering Benjamin in the diving suit was entirely Buck's. That was in his first draft.

G: What inspired him to see Benjy in a diving suit? Is that from the book?

N: Yes. In the book, there's a whole scene where he's given a present and told to go ahead and open it. But Buck figured how to use it in the picture—to announce the thing and to have him suddenly discovered in the suit moving out toward the pool.

G: How much of the book of *The Graduate* did you use?

N: A great deal of the dialogue is straight from the book. Another portion of the dialogue—the "plastics" and such scenes—is entirely Buck's. The change of emphasis and the environment, Charles Webb, the author, didn't concern himself with at all. Reading the book, you think, "What's the matter with Benjamin?" We knew from the beginning that one of the problems was to make visible what was bugging him. But I get credit for a great many decisions and contributions that were Buck's.

G: One of the things that *The Graduate* has been said to have is those Christ symbols which frequently get read into films. You've insisted in public that you never intended any such symbolism. Could you explain the lyric reference in the song "Mrs. Robinson" to Jesus—"Jesus loves you more than you will know"—coming out of nowhere? And at the end of the film, it's been noted that Benjy raises his arms in church and moans like a man being crucified. Later he uses a crucifix to beat the congregation and then to lock them in their church. And whenever he's upset, he says, "Jesus" or "Christ."

N: So do we all.

G: Was there a second level of some sort that you were trying to play off the Christ thing?

N: *Good Christ, no!* . . . The line was there (in the song), one, because Paul (Simon) wrote it; two, because what it meant to me was a very specific attitude toward Mrs. Robinson. Do you remember when Salinger was talking about Seymour's mother-in-law? Do you remember that passage? He says, "She was born without a sense of the poetry that runs through life, all life, and yet she manages to go to matinees and have lunch with her friends and play cards. I find her unimaginably brave." And whatever "Jesus loves you more than you will know" meant to Paul, that's what it meant to me. And that's why I bought it for the picture.

Secondly, Benjamin's arms are not *outstretched.* They are *up.* He is pounding on the glass. There was an image that Buck and I had discussed. It came from endless talks between Dick Sylbert and me about the essence of Beverly Hills and California and all the glass and all the water and all the artificial grass. There's all this nature, but you're completely separated from it by glass. We had in our minds certain images having to do with glass, with water, with being separated, with being cut off. And our thought about Benjamin up there in the church was like a moth fluttering at a window. That's all.

G: And what about the crucifix?

N: Right. The crucifix is in the book. And I think it's very reasonably in the book because what the hell are you going to grab in a church if you're going to beat people off? You can't grab a priest. You can't grab a rock. The nearest thing was a giant metal crucifix. We had a technical problem. How's he going to keep all those hundreds of people from stopping him? Well, he's got to jam something in the door. What has he got in his hands? He's got the crucifix. Well, why doesn't he use it?

In the book, he just runs away. It's like "once out of the burning room." But I thought, "He's got to jam that door, or they're all going to follow him." Now, here's the point that should be made about all this. I suppose I must take the responsibility for all this Christ nonsense. Because if it's capable of being interpreted that way, I've got to take it. But it came about through a series of practical decisions, and it crossed none of our minds.

G: There are no set speeches in a complex film like *The Graduate* to tell the audience what the author's point, or message, or intent, or stance is. Instead, you offer a juxtaposition of images which you put together partly in the script and partly, as you said earlier, created from nothing in a cutting room. Well, some images are more supercharged or symbol-laden than others, as in the case of a crucifix. So that people understandably get more visceral stimulation and inferences than the director consciously intended. Do you feel we lose or gain when the ambiguity of supercharged images or objects causes an audience to see meanings you never consciously put in the film?

N: We gain. And I think it's part of what gets us all about movies. It's that movies are more than they were, just by virtue of being on film. I think a film can easily be more than the people who made it. I agree with you.

G: If ambiguity is a natural outcome of these images which are put together, at what point does an audience ever know what the director, the writer, or the "guiding consciousness" had in mind?

N: Never. You don't know in a novel. You certainly don't know in a play. Possibly a novel is a bad example, because it's explicit, whereas a play or movie is implicit by its nature. We will never know what a playwright had in his mind. And no one will ever know what a film director or a screenwriter had in his mind. It either hangs together and joins your life and becomes part of you and you trust it, or it doesn't.

It's very much like a person. You either trust a person, or you don't. You don't know why. It has nothing to do with what they say. It has nothing to do with how they look. Nobody knows what it has to do with. You buy them or you don't. I think it's the same with films. And we'll never know about each other. You'll never know really what I mean. I'll never know exactly what you mean. It's a kind of electricity that can sometimes be set up where we both get the illusion that we're saying the same thing or that we mean the same things.

G: Some critics felt *The Graduate* was brilliant in many ways but that it was structurally flawed, that the carefully constructed beginning was one kind of film, while the romance with the girl was another, bearing no relevance to it. Do you see any structural slippage?

N: It doesn't bother me, because it was deliberate on our parts. The picture changes in every way. The whole section with Mrs. Robinson is hard and glossy and Beverly Hills and cold and sexy in that way that things can be sexy when you get laid without a great deal of feeling. And with Elaine and his fantasy of Elaine, everything changes into a kind of fantasy prettiness.

My feelings about, for instance, the ending, what it means, who Elaine really is, what happens between her and Benjamin, are, at this point, just my feelings, and my opinion really doesn't have much more validity than anybody else's. Who's to say I'm right and somebody else is wrong? I have certain very specific thoughts about it. I've expressed them to kids, and they've been stunned and enraged. In my mind, it's always been that in five miles she's going to say, "My God, I haven't got any clothes."

G: You'd said elsewhere that in five or ten years Benjy will be just like his parents.

N: It would be my guess. If the picture's any good, then it means that you guess about the characters as you do about people you know. I don't know what's going to happen to me. Who's going to leave whom? Who's going to marry whom? Who's going to commit suicide? Who's going to be ruined? We don't know those things. You make guesses about the people you care for, just as you make guesses about characters.

A lot of us have the fantasy of breaking out, of dropping everything, of disappearing with that one girl, and extending a certain feeling forever, of taking the moment—let's say those three hours of your sitting with a girl and she's holding your foot and you think: "I would like her to go on holding my foot for the rest of my life. I don't want to go out and work. I don't want to go to dinner with those people I'm supposed to meet. I don't want to do anything. I want my life to be *this* and nothing else."

It's something everybody knows. And the fantasy of breaking through everything and living for that is a very powerful one. I think it can't be done. I think a lot of people, myself included, wish to God it could be done. And that's what the end means to me. That I'm moved by somebody who wants to try to do it, and I'm pulling for them. But I don't know if they can make it.

G: That final scene, according to Dustin Hoffman, was shot in a strained atmosphere, and both he and Katharine Ross were feeling exhausted and defeated so they didn't know whether to smile or to cry.

N: The end originally planned for the film was that they would get on the bus, turn, laugh, she would say, "Benjamin." He would say, "What?" which is all he ever said. She would kiss him, and the bus would go off. I never questioned it. But something very odd happened to me the day we were shooting that scene. I was rotten to the two of them, really rotten. And I told them—and I don't usually do this—I said, "Now, listen, it's a big deal and we've stopped traffic for miles and we've got a police car. You get on that bus and you better laugh. You hear me?"

They had tears in their eyes, they were so terrified. They got on the bus and they tried to laugh, and we kept rolling, and they tried to laugh some more. And then they finally gave up, and they thought, "I don't know what the hell he wants me to do."

And we rolled and we rolled and we rolled and we drove for miles. Then when I saw those rushes, I thought, "That's the end of the picture. They don't know what the hell to do, or to think, or to say to each other."

Members of the National Society of Film Critics
THE FUTURE OF FILM

Members of the National Society of Film Critics were asked to respond, at any length and in any manner they chose, to a list of questions designed to shed light on a few of the most important issues currently confronting both film-makers and critics. It was also hoped that in so doing, they might reveal a few of the general assumptions that underlie their day-to-day task of evaluating the new pictures.

These are the questions:

1. Do you regard film as the most relevant art of our time and do you think it will continue to maintain its hold on the modern sensibility in the years to come? If so, why? If not, why not?

2. Are we standing on the brink of a radically different film age? What influence on future film form and content do you expect from: cinéma vérité? the Underground film? mixed-media? technical developments such as those emphasized at Expo 67? the psychedelic subculture? what-have-you?

3. What of the American commercial movie? Can it go on as it is? If not, how much restructuring—and of what sort specifically—will be required artistically and economically if it is to remain a significant force on the world film scene?

4. Some critics, viewing current trends in movies, foreign and domestic, have expressed fear for the survival of plot, characterization and meaning as those terms have traditionally been understood. Do you share these fears? Please explain.

5. How much farther can the film go with sex and violence? Or do you think it has already gone too far?

Answers to them are arranged alphabetically by author.

HOLLIS ALPERT

1. All arts are relevant to our time, but film probably does hold the major place, due to its ability to transcend limitations of language,

geography and duration. Because film usually shares methods, techniques, and characteristics of other forms involving the use of words, plasticity, images, and motion, it is by no means a pure art, and this factor still makes it somewhat suspect in my eyes. The *pure* film-maker, if he exists at all, is bound to be a dull artist, for a sequence of images, without sound, words, story, etc,. is merely motion photography, and a diet of such, no matter how brilliantly edited, is something less than satisfying. Film's power comes from its ability to employ the other arts and communicative mediums, and this integrative quality is what seems to give it much of its fascination for so many. Through its developing technology and the exploration of cinematic technique, film is able to affect the feelings and emotions of the viewer more directly than the other arts, and a visual generation, made even more visual through habituation to the television screen, has thus taken it to its heart. Film involves, it convinces, because it seems *real*—it happens before one's very eyes—and it has the means, too, to render states of consciousness. Nevertheless, as most often used, film doesn't explore these states with the sensitivity of other and purer forms. Film as a form in its own right is still relatively crude, even fearful, the expense of production and the size of the audience making it so. Because there are forces at work expanding its current limitations the chances are excellent that it will engage a huge audience, made up of several levels of intellect and sensibility, for years to come.

2. I do not see a radically different film age moving upon us, but current directions do show promise of development and change. *Cinéma vérité* seems to appeal basically to the voyeuristic element in all of us, but the method is so presently riddled with self-consciousness (on the part of both film-maker and subject) that it takes on an almost inherent falseness. As a theatrical experience—that is, film shown publicly, to an audience—it is relatively primitive, in that it doesn't make more than the simplest use of the film techniques that are presently available. There is something also basically mean and degrading about much of *cinéma vérité;* we see, or think we see, self-exposure of the subjects, and audience instincts are being appealed to rather than emotions. The use of editing introduces, of course, another element of falseness. The Underground cinema hasn't much accomplishment to show for all the noise it has been making, and its value seems to lie in its exploration of some of the fringe areas of subject matter, as well as in erotic experimentation. Unfortunately, no large talents have as yet been attracted to the Underground mystique and, if they were, they would immediately be snapped up by the film establishment. If film stock were cheaper, cameras made miniaturized and inexpensive, we might eventually get better artistic results, but since films at their best call upon a variety of equipment and talent, the Underground movement seems likely to remain pretentious and propagandistic for some time to come. Mixed-media seems to me little more than tricks, noise,

and eyewash. As for the psychedelic subculture, it seems by its very nature to be antimeaning, antiart, essentially escapist, and inhibitory of artistic creation. Film may make some use of the visionary aspects of the psychedelic experience, just as it makes use of almost every form of experience to some degree. A radically different film culture is possible if film-makers grow courageous about using techniques that are available, but they must possess conceptualizing ability, for without an informing vision any innovative results are bound to be shallow.

3. The American commercial movie (which is to say the films that are made with a strong profit motive in addition to any others that may be present) is likely to go on as it is for quite a while, since behind it is an enormous concentration of financial power. This power is what dictates the nature of the commercial cinema to a large degree—audience tastes operate as checks and balances only. The power of the film financial Establishment has been recently enhanced through a kind of amalgamation with the television Establishment. Television residuals, in the form of lease to networks and syndication, now tend to amortize a large part of the production cost of a film, thus removing a considerable portion of the risk that has accompanied the making of films for the past fifteen years. With financial solidity generally comes conservatism, though undoubtedly there will be some seemingly benign sponsorship of films by the major talents—Antonioni and Kubrick, for instance, as well as by those who strike them as being potentially major talents, such as Lelouch, Furie and Schlesinger. Any cheerful prognosis must be based on the currently healthy state of the art house market in the United States, but it has been perceived by the financial powers that the art house audience reacts most strongly to films made by non-Americans. Thus, Universal is presently encouraging innovative production abroad—to take advantage of the art house market—while doing little to sponsor the younger American talents. Should the art house audience begin to support American commercial innovators (there is already disappointment and disillusion about foreigners such as Godard and Truffaut), we may see more liveliness in the American film which, at this time is, because of the financial stakes involved, mainly a producer's medium, even though some of these producers may also be directors. Because television is now a color medium (made so by the fact that advertisers prefer to show their messages in color), the commercial film will also become almost totally a color medium. Nor is this necessarily bad, for color is being used more inventively, with more pleasing aesthetic results, than ever before.

4. I share none of the fears of such critics mentioned. Story, character, and the emotions generated by these (which is what is usually meant by meaning, I guess) are what have kept audiences lovingly attached to movies for so long. This attachment will continue, I would imagine, so

long as movies involve them in this familiar and yet ever-new way. The fact that certain film-makers of minuscule talent have attempted to make themselves seem more important through the negation of narrative and characterization has caused a certain current confusion, particularly in young people enthusiastic about and attracted to film. Original story creation is difficult to achieve, and because some people are in a hurry to make films they delude themselves into thinking that they can dispense with subject, frame, characters, and a trajectory of action made meaningful and moving. If what they are rejecting are the cliché aspects of these obligations, they are undoubtedly correct, but when they also reject all creative responsibility for engaging and involving an audience, they are being at best pretentious and at worst phony. What makes Antonioni interesting is his unusual ability to tell stories through film, and he has been called, as a result, "a novelistic film-maker." But, then, so is Fellini a novelistic film-maker; Bergman, too, and such excellent craftsmen as Lean, Kubrick, Schlesinger and Clayton either depend on novels for their stories or go to the lengths of having one created, as Lean did, in a sense, for *Lawrence of Arabia.* Stanley Kubrick, for his new film, *2001,* A *Space Odyssey,* actually wrote a novel with Arthur Clarke in order to have a firm story structure for his undertaking. All this is indicative, it seems to me, and we can expect the emphasis on story only to increase.

5. Actual sex and violence, or sex and violence as subject matter? The only actual sex in films is the pornographic sex of the stag films, and the only actual violence is to be found in TV news film, shot during action in Vietnam or riots at home. Films use the illusion of sex and the illusion of violence as a means of convincing the audience of the "reality" of what they are seeing. When used to an excessive degree (as musical background sometimes is, too) it is to mask weaknesses in story structure and development by concentrating the audience attention on these details. We generally term such use "sensationalism." But if a story involves characters in a tale of intimate love, it is not necessarily excessive if sexual relations are also indicated, and each film has the right to be judged on its intentions. Quite obviously many films that use war as background or as crucial to the actions of characters are seldom as violent as the material—in actuality—would call for. Thus, when we question the use of sex or violence in a particular film we are questioning the taste of the film-maker, his degree of stress of these aspects, rather than their use per se. In semicomic fantasies, such as the James Bond series, we tend to accept a greater degree of violence, mainly because we willingly suspend our disbelief. We know it's going to be exaggerated; we know it's not real. But violence occurring in a seemingly real situation is often distasteful, if not downright painful, and our instinct is to protest. The cushion of illusion has been removed, so to speak. What a good many quite conscientious people are concerned about is the raising of the level of tolerance in the au-

dience toward portrayals of sex and violence, as shown by the commercial success of many films that feature these aspects, and our worry about the films is really a disguised worry about the audience. If we make the films go away, maybe we'll make that sensation-loving audience go away, too. Few critics who worried about the violence in *Bonnie and Clyde,* for example, were worried about its effect on themselves; it was always the other person. On the other hand, we do tend to demand of the film artist, as of the novelist, that he indicate to us his intention, his reason for showing us or telling us something, and when this is missing, or is unclear—when, in other words, the violence or sex seems purposeless—we automatically begin to suspect him. In sum, I rather doubt that the critic needs to be or should be a guardian of public morality or a shaper of public attitudes. As to the "effects" of the increased violence and sex in current films, that is best left to the social scientist to report on and analyze.

BRENDAN GILL

1. I regard all the arts as equally relevant in our time, and in all times. I think movies may become the most popular of the arts because TV threatens to become the chief means of communication and will make increasing demands on movie-makers of all sorts to help keep the glop flowing. (The need will be so great that some of the glop will turn out, largely by accident, to be pretty good, and a little of it will turn out not to be glop at all. This is what happened, and goes on happening, with the novel.)

2. No. When I was a boy, everybody talked about the fantastic advances that were to be made in my lifetime, but most of the technical resources we currently employ were employed by my grandparents. Moreover, children still get cavities in their teeth and still have the cavities filled with a nasty material that soon falls out. Advances on every front are pitifully slow.

3. The American commercial movie is going to be whatever TV chooses to make it be. The Paleys and Sarnoffs of this world care about nothing except making the greatest possible amount of money out of air that doesn't belong to them, and I assume that they will be glad to make movies much worse than the ones that Louis B. Mayer used to make. If they will not be glad, they will not be sorry. The only thing they know how to create from scratch are Jungle Jims.

4. The more plot vanishes, the more likely it is to reappear. It is like the body in painting—the beginning and the end, irrepressible. Besides, the emotion I feel in respect to trends in any field is never fear but exhilaration. All change is a manifestation of energy and ought to make us feel good, like drinking whiskey neat outdoors on a cold day.

5. A long way. I have yet to see a good movie life of John Greenleaf Whittier.

PHILIP T. HARTUNG

It is likely that film, right from its beginning, was a relevant art. Although people at the turn of the century considered the nickelodeon a plaything, they might have realized, if they had taken a closer look and given a thought to this amusing toy's possibilities, that the "Irwin-Rice Kiss," the Méliès films and the Porter films were the beginning of a new art. By the time Griffith swung into stride with two masterpieces, *The Birth of a Nation* and *Intolerance,* discriminating audiences were impressed that motion pictures *could be* more than a passing entertainment. Their impressions were strengthened during the following years by the appearance of such German pictures as *The Cabinet of Dr. Caligari* and *The Last Laugh,* such Russian semidocumentaries as *Potemkin* and *Ten Days That Shook the World,* and such American films as Erich von Stroheim's realistic *Greed* and the European-flavored *The Wedding March.*

As time and more films passed by, it dawned on the movie-going public, pushed a bit by the critics, that film was not only an art, but a relevant art that reflected the temper of the times. Perhaps even bad movies that have no connection with art, like *It* and *Our Dancing Daughters,* had enough truth in them to say something about the Jazz Age. And by the time directors were learning to use sound effectively in the thirties audiences were learning the difference between the arty and true cinematic art. Sometimes they even knew why they preferred *Little Caesar* and *Public Enemy* to *A Midsummer Night's Dream.* They appreciated along with the mad humor of the Marx Brothers the truth of the brilliant Marx satire on our mores. They saw the development and growth of Charlie Chaplin (and his wonderful portrait of Everyman who became known as the Little Tramp) from the days of the hilarious short comedies to the equally hilarious but more thoughtful longer pictures like *The Gold Rush, City Lights,* and *Modern Times,* and they began to recognize his genius—even in scathing satires like *The Great Dictator* and *Monsieur Verdoux* (which was ahead of its times and, alas, not well attended). And during the thirties, audiences, further impressed with the status given film by the Museum of Modern Art, began to see once-lowly movies as folk art. Perhaps even the Andy Hardy and Doctor Kildare pictures were art of a sort; and certainly Westerns, with their stunning photography and lively settling-of-the-west themes, stood as a kind of folk art.

During the forties and fifties, moviegoers began to know and select their film fare by the names of the directors. Stars were still attractions at the box office, but names like John Ford, Alfred Hitchcock and Orson Welles pulled in customers, too. And by the sixties audiences would go to films made by Fellini, Bergman, and Antonioni without asking who the actors were. The large number of books about cinema and the many film festivals that stressed motion pictures as art with minor concern for them as commercial entertainments also had much to do with the establishment of film as the most relevant art of our time. The very fact that so many schools now have courses and lectures in cinema is also indicative of the interest and influence of this art.

Cinema's appeal to young people and students would also indicate the survival of film as an art. No doubt some of the new technical developments, such as those displayed by Expo 67, and some of the new styles shown in the American Underground films and in the now international *cinéma vérité* have a lively and stimulating quality that is good for any art. But most of these movies, especially those using psychedelic effects, succeed in conveying something only for the moment. Their plotless themes and loosely-woven dialogue are so flash-in-the-pan that they are soon forgotten—and perhaps their techniques will soon be as forgotten as the once-much-touted 3-D and "smellie" films. The trouble with so many of the current movies, both Underground and aboveground, is that they put so much emphasis on nudity, sex, and violence-for-violence's-sake that they become a banal bore and defeat themselves.

Now that Hollywood is no longer the cinema capital of the world (in fact the world has no cinema center) and so many films are international with director, writer, technicians, actors, and perhaps even the producer and bankroll coming from different countries for a single picture, it is often impossible to put a nationality label on a movie. Whether this is good or bad, one cannot say. But as long as good movies turn up—films with vital plots and themes related in cinematic terms—then this most relevant art of our time will continue long, long beyond our time.

STANLEY KAUFFMANN

1. I think that film *is* the most relevant art today, in terms of audience appetite, but there are two paradoxes:

Timing. Film audiences have become more demanding as the impulse for and confidence in artistic creation seem to be declining. Possibly it is no accident that the rise of science, which made film possible, is connected with the quandaries in spirit and mind that have made the creation of films and of all art more difficult. The Lord giveth. . . .

Expense. This most universally desired art-form is also the most cumbersome and expensive. The most easily powerful of media is also the most difficult to use easily. Orson Welles once wryly said, "That is always the central fact about the film-maker as opposed to any other artist; he can never afford to own his own tools. The minimum kit is incredibly expensive, and one's opportunities to work with it are rather less numerous than might be supposed."

2, 4, 5. In violence, how can films go further than they have gone? We already have torture and killing on the home screens (TV news-reel clips of war). As for sex, I expect it to become ultimately frank—in foreign films, at least. Sex will be overused in fact by some film-makers as it has always been overused in masquerade by some; for others it will simply become one of the materials of art (as in modern literature). Censorship action will be taken from time to time, I suppose, with some temporary effect, but I doubt that the level of frankness will ever be pushed back permanently to, say, the 1950 level. The restrictive goal of secondary television sales will have some influence on American films, but even TV-audiences acceptability has broadened somewhat.

The Underground film—as distinct from the historical avant garde—seems to me pretty much an American reaction to an American condition. (There seems to be much less Underground activity abroad.) It is the result of a growing impulse to serious film-making in a country that has no tradition of the serious film—which is not to say that the United States has made no serious films. (Let's define a serious film as one which is made primarily because the maker himself wants to make it.) In France, for example, the New Wave did not have to go underground because there was a tradition of serious film-making toward which it could grow and which it could then reasonably hope to influence. The American Underground has had to try to develop a tradition as it went, which is why so many Underground films seem to be rebelling—in film terms—against "nothing." It is one thing to rebel against Duvivier and Delannoy, like the New Wave; it is another—it is in fact impossible—for a serious American film-maker to rebel against the Hollywood factory. This may be one reason why the best that can be said of so many Underground films is that they are promising.

The most striking development in the last few years has been the rise of *cinéma vérité,* which is of course linked to mechanical improvements in the hand-held camera and the portable tape-recorder. (I hear that they may soon be combined.) Inevitably this will mean, as has happened in writing and still photography, the aggrandizement of journalism as art. Socially, it will mean further and drastic changes in concepts of privacy.

I see little point in moaning about this. It will happen because we are all, to some extent, keyhole peepers. And now we can give our intrusions the spurious gloss of an insatiable hunger for truth. (Note the "vérité.") All I wish about it is that we could keep our attitudes honest and our statements rational. "Candid Camera" is "Candid Camera," on or off TV, and all the mystical pontifications about "direct cinema" will not change clever cinema journalism into the Second Coming. Let's just have the peep-shows. (*Once,* on each subject. After *Portrait of Jason,* who would want to see another two-hour film about a Negro male prostitute?)

Not much *cinéma vérité* is likely in any genuine sense to be art. But as photography had an effect on portrait painting by relieving it of certain obligations, so "direct cinema" may free the fiction film of naturalistic protocol and help it to concentrate on essences.

Mixed-media? My trouble with mixed-media so far is that they don't mix. Whenever film is a component, the occasion becomes for me a film show—*accompanied* by music and strobe lights and frugging. Film is far and away the most effective psychedelicacy.

3. The best American commercial films seem to be "growing up"—that is, keeping right on the dead-level of the moment in middle-class taste. Thus films like *Bonnie and Clyde* and *Cool Hand Luke* are very impressive, if one doesn't look too closely.

What I miss most at the moment in American films are musicals in the Donen-Minnelli vein. All we seem to get now are film versions of Broadway hit musicals. The Hollywood musical, at its best, was the most poetic and free-flying of American commercial films.

However, any arraignment of American films ought to note that this is the only country besides Japan with no regular system of subsidy or aid for its film-makers. The planned occasional awards by the American Film Institute are not equivalents. Subsidy would not guarantee fine results in the United States any more than it does abroad, but—as it does abroad—it would provide more of a fighting chance for personal, serious film-making.

ARTHUR KNIGHT

It is a sobering thought, as one begins to speak about the future of the film, that twenty years ago the pictures we are seeing today were the future. How much of it was predictable? To be sure, we could have anticipated a *Camelot* or a *Dr. Dolittle;* the musical spectaculars have been with us since the addition of a sound track, and will undoubtedly remain. But could we have predicted the wide screens, the stereophonic sound, the subtle color, and the flawless process work? Even after the 1964-65 New York World's Fair, which popularized the notion of multiscreen projection, who could have anticipated the fantastic multiples presented at Montreal's Expo 67? Somewhere today there are probably technicians at work who may so revolutionize the mechanisms of the medium as to make today's technical perfection seem as primitive as *The Jazz Singer.*

We have all learned enough film history, however, to realize that these changes in the medium do not come about automatically—or even because an inventor has a good, workable idea. Sound was introduced because Warner Brothers was about to go down the drain. The Vitaphone was, for them, a last, desperate grasping at a straw that might save the firm from bankruptcy. And the straw turned out to be the foundation block for a new, revitalized industry because the public responded in an overwhelming affirmative to the novelty. Similarly, wide screens, 3-D, even the idea for multiple screens had already been around for years before the movie companies took them up—and then solely because the small screens of television posed a threat that could only be answered by dramatic changes in the mode of theatrical presentation. Once the world is saturated with color TV, the film-makers unquestionably will be forced to respond with yet another technical innovation—possibly, this time, an extended use of the multiple screens.

But technology is only one aspect of film-making, and only in times of crisis does it become the dominant one. More important, and particularly today, is the intensified interaction between film-makers and film forms. In the studios, with their new emphasis upon the producer-director, corresponding a bit more closely to European precedents than in the days of the vast film factories, individuality is becoming not only accepted but prized. Not only are the Richard Brookses, the Stanley Kramers, and the David Leans handed virtual blank checks to do with as they wish, but such relative newcomers as John Frankenheimer and Norman Jewison are accorded the same deferential treatment. Meanwhile, Antonioni makes pictures for MGM, Vadim makes them for Columbia, and de Sica grinds them out for Joe Levine.

The fact is, though, that thanks to this trend, the Hollywood studio film has changed enormously—and will no doubt change more. Whereas once pictures came through stamped indelibly with the look of Fox or Metro or Paramount now they bear the unmistakable mark of the director, be he Robert Aldrich, Stanley Donen or Otto Preminger. For good or ill, they reflect his personality. But this reflection, it should be noted, is still within the context of the large-scale studio production, with script and star approval rigorously controlled by the executives who hold the purse-strings, and with films beamed for the broadest possible mass distribution. Under such conditions, a *Bonnie and Clyde* or *In the Heat of the Night* are quite remarkable—and a *Dutchman* or *Portrait of Jason* completely impossible.

It is against this background that one must place the phenomenal upsurge of the so-called Underground film-makers in recent years. These are people who, while attracted to the medium, know full well they aren't going to make it in Hollywood. Many of them have gone so far as to say quite specifically that they have no desire whatsoever to make it in Hollywood. The themes that interest them, the techniques that they prefer—such as *cinéma vérité*—they realize have no place in big studio production, nor would they be acceptable in mass distribution theaters. Instead, they address themselves to another audience altogether, the relatively new, relatively limited audience that gathers in on-campus film societies or for special "Movies Around Midnight" screenings in a scattering of art houses across the country.

What all of this points to, it seems to me, is a growing polarization of both films and audiences. We have already seen the construction (or alteration) of dozens of large theaters to accommodate such widescreen spectaculars as *The Greatest Story Ever Told, Grand Prix,* and *Camelot,* pictures that are held in a single house for as much as a year —and are, in fact, seen to their best advantage in those houses. Since spectacle has been an integral part of show business since Roman times, it is not unreasonable to assume that such multimillion-dollar efforts will continue, nor that, should the multiple screens ever come into vogue, they will be utilized for just such presentations.

At the same time, the most astonishing rise in theater construction in this country has been in the art house field. Twenty years ago, just after World War II, there were exactly a dozen art houses in the entire United States, most of them centered in New York. At that time, "art house" meant specifically those theaters that played foreign films exclusively; today, with more than two thousand such theaters in the field, the more popular—and accurate—term is "specialized cinemas," theaters that pick and choose adult fare regardless of its country of origin. In recent years, these have become the showcases for Hollywood's more "difficult" films—products of the new individuality that are a bit too unconventional for conventional releasing patterns; these play cheek-by-jowl with the best of the imports, appealing to the same type of audience, and for the same basic reasons.

Such theaters are, by and large, replacing the old neighborhood houses, the theaters where Hollywood's "B" product, now shunted to television, formerly received its major play-off. In many instances, the new "specialized cinemas" actually *were* the old neighborhood houses; they have merely been refurbished and a coffee urn set in the lounge. They may play to smaller audiences than once crowded in for the Saturday afternoon serials, but they are also more selective audiences and quite willing to scan a spectrum of films from *Alfie* to *Don't Look Back* to *Warrendale,* or from Jewison to Godard to Rickie Leacock. It is an audience—and a constantly growing one—that can supply a substantial economic base for the small film, the personal film, the individual film.

But there is also a third audience in the process of formation, an audience that wants no part of the spectaculars and can be lured only occasionally to see a Hollywood film that has gained a reputation or a European import that sounds interesting. That audience is to be found today in film societies, on university campuses, and in the art museums, and it is notably eager for the off-beat (as Janus Films profitably discovered when recently it went specifically into this market with its programs of outstanding shorts). For cinema, it represents the new growing edge.

If I have omitted television from this discussion—commercial, educational, or pay-TV—it is because I still think of it primarily as a means of transmission, not as an art. But should television ever take a more creative turn, we may well find that it will also importantly affect the future of the film, and in ways that we can not even begin to foresee. Mercifully, the clouded crystal ball is here impenetrable—but from the way TV looks today it seems all too likely that, twenty years from now, we will be finding *Hurry Sundown* listed for The Late Late Show.

JOSEPH MORGENSTERN

The second most relevant art of the foreseeable future will surely be film, preceded only by the mother art of weaponry. I have no idea if future generations will swear off books, but they will certainly continue to watch movies, tapes, trained fireflies or whatever else it may take to fill their eyes with dancing lights.

Predicting the immediate future is easy in the movie business—more love, sex, comedy, sex, perversion, sex, pubic hair, sex, passion, sex, violence, and possibly even sex. I have it on unimpeachable authority that one of the world's most eminent directors is investing his personal fortune in research and development of subminiature cameras and lights for the production of a Cinerama voyage up the vaginal canal. Whether the American commercial movie can endure depends largely on whether American commercialization can endure, and I fear that it can, for some time to come. What is more, or worse, American commercial movies will continue to exert vast influence throughout the world for some time to come. They base their appeal on the same materialism that motivates, like it or not, most of the underdeveloped world's revolutions of rising expectations. Hollywood knows what it is doing. The kitchen of a modern American ranch house was not designed to be loved, only to be desired.

Yet commerce and simple diversion will never be all. The serious film survives, flourishes fitfully and is changing before our slightly glazed eyes. Disorder is beginning to have its day—again. If the prospect is disturbing for those who prefer their regimes *anciens,* it is exhilarating and ventilating for artists who prefer their truths unvarnished. Disorder might well mean chaos in the end, but it might also mean a new way of looking at the strangely disordered things that people and societies do in the name of logic. Today's more astute and determined film-makers already have begun to show large audiences—so much larger than Joyce could reach in the twenties—that narrative conventions are needlessly restrictive at best and filthy frauds at worst, that a complex story can be evoked or a delicate mood spun by smashing time to smithereens, tossing possibilities and eventualities into the same pot with causes and effects and splitting beams as freely as scholars split hairs to yield several pictures on several screens of a supposedly simple event that is, on close inspection, just as simple as an atom.

Many film-makers will continue to reject a story as something more appropriately told to infants. An Underground will continue to exist as a means to its own artistic ends and as a valuable protest against order, coherence, typicality, normality, professionalism, and moderation. While some of its acolytes will suffer from and succumb to their own furtive yearnings for approbation, others will persist in showing up pieces of film or flashes of light that will frighten us, dazzle us, unsettle or outrage us but somehow command our attention and respect, and they will persist in doing this even if the rest of the country should take to the fallout shelters and drive them aboveground.

Yet there are stories and stories, and no reason to assume that film is locked on a course that will take it inexorably closer to pure abstraction and further from specific references to some recognizable reality. An artist can hardly be accused of turning his back on the world because he sees it in increasingly complex ways; a fly's compound eye is perhaps a far more useful instrument than a gopher's. Film-makers have only begun to explore the world outside the studio, hardly begun to study the world of science and nature, to educate the young, to find visual analogies to the nonfiction novel. What will they choose for subjects? Who knows? Who could have guessed in 1966 that the most compelling film heroes of 1967 would be a pair of scruffy bank robbers from the thirties? If the Apollo program succeeds, the most viable film form of the seventies may be the FitzPatrick travelogue in which we reluctantly take leave of our crater as the earth sinks slowly into a dusty sea.

Technology has played an incalculable role in the evolution of film and will continue to do so in the future. Just as the Leica made *Life* magazine possible, Morris Engel's portable cameras and sound equipment were vital for the beginning of the New Wave and were later refined for the *cinéma vérité* movement, which devised a whole esthetic theory about capturing objective truth without disturbing it, just to dignify the fun and excitement of using new hardware under conditions that people had never been able to shoot in before. Today's thoughtful young documentarians are more concerned, and properly so, with learning subjective truths about themselves and the way they look at their world. The truth shall set them free, but so shall even lighter and smaller equipment, faster lenses and emulsions and the inevitable acceptance of relatively economical 16-mm. as an acceptable format for all but the most vengefully spectacular productions.

Technology is also conspiring to change the way in which films are financed and to change the environment in which they are seen. This ought to be of paramount interest to anyone concerned with film as an art as well as a business. Present rivalries and lawsuits between Hollywood and the television industry notwithstanding, the future of film exhibition unquestionably lies in the home, thanks to recently developed playback devices that use a small tape cartridge in conjunction with a television set. It take a very slight effort of imagination to see the day when we will buy our movies as freely and easily as we now buy long-playing records, and watch them at our leisure in living, dancing holographic color. The prospect is enthralling until you realize that farsighted businessmen—far more farsighted than most of the artists they will hire and consume—are already at work on this future, laying it out, carving it up. What new Jack Warner sits in what new corner office of what new network subsidiary making plans and provisions for what whole new motion picture industry? It is a question that the film-maker ought to be answering as soon as possible, unless he wants to doom himself to continued subservience to bankers and front-office goons. It is a question that the consumer ought to be asking too, unless he wants to buy his first new cartridge at the A & P, take it home, switch it on, settle into the ankle-deep carpet and waist-deep cushions of his family room and watch his wall-sized screen as the camera moves in for a first, epoch-making peek into the eyepiece of a softly whirring nickelodeon.

ANDREW SARRIS

1. Film is relevant to some aspects of our time and irrelevant to others. For example, the pot scene is reflected more in pop music than in pop movies. There can never be a cinematic equivalent of Vladimir Nabokov's *Pale Fire.* Television has taken over many of the sociological tasks of the motion picture medium. I happen to derive more pleasure from film than from any other art, but that is *my* sensibility speaking, not necessarily modern sensibility. I enjoyed movies before they were intellectually fashionable, and I shall enjoy them long after they have gone out of fashion. I can no more renounce movies than literary men can renounce books. I have never felt it necessary, however, to re-

nounce any other art form in order to defend film. To choose one's own area of specialization is not to repudiate any other area. Movies are only a part of modern culture, and it is too early to tell how important they will seem in the next century.

2. *Cinéma vérité* has already exercised a profound influence on film form. *(J'entends la vérité mais je ne vois pas le cinéma.)* Underground film is merely journalistic jargon. Mixed-media have little to do with film as such. The psychedelic subculture goes back to the twenties.

3. The premise of this question seems dubious. With Fellini unemployed, Bergman only intermittently successful with the public, Rosi wasted on Cinderella stories with Sophia Loren, Antonioni in America, Kurosawa in limbo, and Godard boycotted by American distributors, it would seem that foreign art films are in much deeper trouble than American commercial movies. We must remember that Hollywood is no longer in Hollywood but has spread its imperial boundaries to the Thames, the Seine, the Tiber, and Danube, and even the Volga.

4. The survival of plot, characterization, and meaning will depend on the ability of artists to replenish the supply of plot, characterization, and meaning. The old motivational plot structure is probably dead, but that is all to the good. I think film will profit by the relaxation of taboos to the extent that new subject matter is made available to the medium.

5. The film will go only as far as artists can take it. I don't believe film has gone too far. In sex, it has not yet caught up with literature. In violence, it still lags behind politics.

RICHARD SCHICKEL

Film is the pack rat of the arts. It constantly raids not only its own past history but the entire range of our culture for bright baubles of material and techniques; it is this something-from-everybody, something-for-everybody mode of operation that gives movies their centrality in the modern sensibility. In this day of intensive specialization by individuals it is not uncommon—indeed, it is the norm—to find intellectuals who cheerfully admit that they know nothing about music or dance or drama or even the modern novel, but I have yet to meet anyone, intellectual or not, who can bring himself to admit that he knows nothing about the movies. If he is under fifty years old, they are, quite simply, part of his formative experience, like mother or grade school. To accuse him of ignorance on the subject of film is to accuse him of ignorance about modern life—an unbearable affront and, undoubtedly an error as well. Everybody *does* know something about movies, whatever the limits of intelligence or insight he brings to bear on that knowledge. This knowledgeability has grown astonishingly in the postwar decades, what with the TV late shows serving as an easily available—if imperfect—archive, the art theater increasing everyone's cosmopolitanism and the college film society or course creating an art spirit—one might even say fervor—among a group that, in another day, might have placed their developing creative energies in the service of one of the more traditional arts—the theater, for instance. I really can't imagine, in the light of all this, the position of the movies declining within the foreseeable future; indeed, I think their hold on us will only increase.

I think past history gives us a clue as to how film-makers will use new styles and techniques as they are developed. We are already beginning to see *cinéma vérité* camera work in blatantly commercial films just as we are beginning to see, far too often in my opinion, editing techniques and camera set-ups borrowed from such diverse sources as the TV commercials, the New Wave, even the Underground in American studio productions. Right now we are in a stage, familiar to us from history, where innovations are being used simply out of a desire to use them, regardless of their appropriateness to the scene or the story or the controlling mood the director may be trying to establish (Richard Lester's *How I Won the War* is the most flagrant recent example of this disjunction between technique and didactic intention). What will happen, I am sure, is that what is useful in all this stuff will be incorporated in what amounts to a new standard film style with which the routinizers of the industry can live comfortably and which will eventually seem as familiar to us as, say, the old Warner studio style. The same thing will happen with the next wave of innovation—and the next and the next—world without end.

As to some of the technological innovations that are, in effect, entirely new weapons systems, related to the presently dominant film technology in about the same way that an ICBM is related to the old Springfield rifle, the incorporative mode will work less easily on them. Enormous outlays for special theatrical installations would have to be made and even then it is doubtful if the sorts of things that so excited people at Expo 67 could be made available in more than a few metropolitan areas. There they might run for years as tourist attractions and eventually pay off their backers handsomely. But such exhibitions would not encourage much experiment with the basic problems of content these systems pose or even much fresh production since a few whatchamacallits will serve the producers as well as many. Thus they may well endure as sideshows, but I doubt that they will prevail as the main line of future film production.

It is often argued that giantism of this sort is less of a threat to the future of the film as we know it than the miniaturizing effect of television. Its madcap purchase of theatrical film presently guarantees producers against serious loss of money on any film that can conceivably be shown on the home screen and this, of course, will have the tendency to dehumidify the much-discussed trend toward more frank portrayals of sex-and-violence. (Ah, the delicious agony of the typical producer—should he steam up his product in the hope of making a killing in the theaters or tone it down in order to insure a TV sale? Poor wretch, he'll probably try to do both and end up a schizophrenic failure.) One is aware, too, that we are but a half-step away from this gizmo you can clip on your television set in order to project through it films of one's choosing. And cable TV is already here. Thus, it seems to me that films made directly for use at home and distributed by some means other than networking are a distinct possibility. Inevitably, they will be different, to some degree, from the movies we presently see. One's psychological set as he peers into a small screen in his living room is entirely different from what it is looking at a large screen in a large room filled mostly with strangers. Please note that I said the films would be different, not better. No substantial improvement of an art form has ever resulted from mere technological change; everything depends on the use to which individuals put their new tools.

As to plot, characterization, and meaning in this revolutionary age, I expect them all to endure, if not to prevail. The methods by which film-makers convey these essentials have, generally speaking, grown more elliptical and telegraphic, which is mostly a good thing, although some of them, caught up in the excitement of the new visual techniques, have tended to forget that they are not an end in themselves. I expect the balance to be redressed as time goes on. In regard to that strange Siamese twin sex-and-violence, it seems to me more a social than a filmic problem. Our world has, with astonishing rapidity, set aside its long-cherished taboos about discussion of sex and, I fear, its inhibitions against violence. The movies reflect this, but then, so does the front page of *The New York Times.* I sometimes think it unfortunate that the end of the long fight for freedom of the screen should coincide with these large-scale changes in social values, for a good many film-makers have been irresponsible in exploitation of our present try-anything, do-anything mood. What I have yet to see from Hollywood are mature explorations of mature sexuality—the kind of thing visible in such foreign films as *Dear John* and *La Guerre Est Finie.* Partly, this is the result of the crassest kind of commercialism, Partly, it is a reflection, again, of the galloping adolescentism of a society which more and more resembles the teen-ager rolling dirty words around on his tongue merely because previously forbidden fruit is so terribly tasty. Will we grow up? I can't be sure, but I do have, at bottom, a faith in the ability of this nation to grow and to change. I know that is not a very fashionable belief at the moment *(pace, The New York Review of Books),* but until there is definitive proof to the contrary, I am going to cling to it. Therefore, I believe that even the most corrupt of our institutions—and the movie industry is surely one of them—will somehow manage to catch up with the rest of the world in this matter as well as in many others. I hope so, for my sensibility was nurtured on the American film and I would like to see it come through.

WILFRID SHEED

Having been subjected to a mess of novels in the last few years, not to mention a thrombosis of theater, I would suggest that the whole art of fiction is in crisis, as to both matter and form, and that movies partake of this crisis along with all their other little crises. This subject is too big to deal with here, but let me give one obvious example. On Broadway, we all used to moan in chorus over the commercial theater, but off-Broadway never turned out that much better. The plays tended to be either sterilely private or caricatures of pop cultures—parasites on the main commercial body.

The situation seems to be not dissimilar as between Hollywood and the off-Hollywood Underground. American fiction-workers are soaked to the marrow in pop culture and trivial self-analysis; there is, at the moment, no vigorous alternative to either. However sensitive and intelligent the writer, he is trapped by his education and his stereotyped hang-ups. Hollywood continues, by definition, to bring up the rear of sensibility. That is what it's for. Possibly (to bow briefly in the direction of the questionnaire) it will become, like the bestselling novel, the sole repository of the old furniture, plot, character and such, and this would be too bad, because it has no ideas of its own about any of these. And without serious models to copy from, it will sink beneath the level of Kathleen Winsor.

The most relevant contemporary art, I would rather hysterically contend, is still written fiction, because it can use all the tricks of the other arts. Not only can the novelist use movie-script techniques, he can also use the movie experience of his readers to make them see the scene the movie way. Or he can make it a theater scene. Above all, he can use touch and smell in a manner that only a few movie-masters (Buñuel comes to mind) have approached.

The future of the Expo hijinks is hard to graph at this point. Some of these new techniques will require such outlandishly designed theaters that one doesn't foresee very many of them; possibly some master complex might be concocted—a cross between Lincoln Center and a planetarium—to take the children to. I found I got used to the trick effects at Expo very quickly and became impatient with the vaporing substance. Whether it is worth making full-length serious movies at this expense is hard to say—the history of Cinerama suggests otherwise. In any event, normal screens and ultra-small screens, will certainly survive.

JOHN SIMON

1. Film is clearly the most relevant art of our time; only television may be more relevant, but it isn't an art. The relevance of film lies in its being more international and available than fiction (more easily translatable and ready for export); in its ability to convey the entire spectrum of human experience and imagination most convincingly to people who have neither; in its having the means to make points with greater rapidity than any art except poetry—which, however, has fallen into disfavor, even in coffee houses. It is the art form patronized by the young, who have inherited the world, and who love movies because of the ease with which they go down—like rock-'n'-roll or pills. None of this means of course, that film is *ipso facto* an art; on the contrary, it means that film must fight all the harder for becoming or, as the case may be, remaining one. About its future, I cannot be sure; though considering the rate at which film is progressing, both artistically and technically, its supremacy is not likely to be challenged easily or soon.

2. All "film ages" are different, just as all ages of drama, fiction, painting, or music are. And if one interprets an age as being more than just a moment in history, the differences between ages are bound to be radical. *Cinéma vérité* seems to me suited only to documentaries and television, and then only in limited doses; the truth of art is very different from the truthfulness of reportage. Underground films strike me as distinguished from the other kind mostly by being considerably worse. Working by himself on a low budget (or none), the film-maker can only masturbate; for his love of film to bear offspring, the collaboration of others and some money is needed—you cannot raise a family on nothing. Mixed-media and new techniques may prove useful when a way can be found to integrate them into patterns of meaningful communication. For the time being, they are too insecure and (consequently) overbearing to adapt themselves to normal emotional, intellectual, and artistic needs. As for psychedelics, they have nothing to do with art. But they may be fun.

3. Seeing that the American commercial movie has gone on more or less unchanged for—is it decades? centuries?—there is no reason to assume it will have to mend its ways in the foreseeable future. To make matters worse, inane Europeans of the *Cahiers du Cinéma* and *Sight and Sound* variety (not to mention the hordes of unsightly and unsound movie buffs) have an unholy craving for the wretched refuse of our teeming shores, which they love to enshrine in their cultist pantheons. But good criticism and the increasing interest in film among cultivated people may make a difference eventually. The change I hope for is an American film of which the individual film-maker remains in full control, rather than one made to front- or box-office specifications. This, of course, will require a taste for small- or medium-

sized films made on sensible budgets, as well as more subsidy for young, independent film-makers. Here film criticism can exercise a beneficial function by attacking the Hollywood (or other) hokum with uncompromising rigor. Misguided enthusiasts who must find something good in late Hitchcock or Hawks or Ford are merely retarding the cause of film as art.

4. Plot, characterization, and meaning are indeed beleaguered in the new coterie cinema, whether it be the Godard-, Mekas-, or Warhol-oriented one. This is no different from the current predicament of the other arts; let us hope that it is a transitory manifestation. If not, we shall have a life without culture or a culture without life in it. What we need is an end to slavish permissiveness, the new philistinism, in the name of being "with it"—to all the junk peddled by the Imperial Suppliers of New Clothes, Here, again, better education and criticism—fostering, if nothing else, enlightened skepticism—might eventually sweep away the garbage.

5. I do not think there is a specifiable limit for either sex or violence. Whatever serves a given artist's purpose best—provided he is a true artist—is right; whatever conveys the point to be made most artistically and efficaciously is good and proper. I realize that this is too vague to be of any use to potential censors, but, then, I am against all censorship of any kind. Considered criticism can and must be the only form of restraint. In the area of sex, at any rate, I consider puritanism a far worse thing than overindulgence; all that need and can be hoped for is the development of the public's taste. Those who want to seek their damnation in inferior movies will find it—there or elsewhere.

SELECTED BIBLIOGRAPHY

Adler, Renata. *A Year in the Dark.* New York: Random House, 1969.

Agee, James. *Agee on Film: Five Film Scripts.* Boston: Beacon Press, 1964.

———. *Agee on Film: Reviews and Comments.* Boston: Beacon Press, 1958.

Alpert, Hollis, and **Andrew Sarris.** *Film 68/69.* New York: Simon & Schuster, 1969.

Antonioni, Michelangelo. *Screenplays.* New York: Orion Press, 1963.

Arnheim, Rudolph. *Film.* London: Faber & Faber, 1933.

———. *Film As Art.* Berkeley: University of California Press, 1957.

———. *Toward a Psychology of Art.* Berkeley: University of California Press, 1967.

Baddeley, W. High. *The Technique of Documentary Film Production.* New York: Hastings House, 1963.

Balázs, Bela. *Theory of the Film.* New York: Roy, 1953.

Barry, Iris. *D. W. Griffith: Film Master.* New York: Museum of Modern Art, 1940.

Battcock, Gregory, ed. *The New American Cinema.* New York: E. P. Dutton, 1967.

Bazin, Andre. *What Is the Cinema?* Berkeley: University of California Press, 1967.

Bergman, Ingmar. *Four Screenplays of Ingmar Bergman.* New York: Simon & Schuster, 1965.

Bluestone, George. *Novels into Film.* Berkeley: University of California Press, 1966.

Bogdanovich, Peter. *The Cinema of Alfred Hitchcock.* New York: Museum of Modern Art, 1963.

Callenbach, Ernest. *Our Modern Art, the Movies.* Chicago: Center for Study of Liberal Education for Adults, 1955.

Casty, Alan, ed. *Mass Media and Mass Man.* New York: Holt, Rinehart & Winston, 1968.

Chaplin, Charles. *My Autobiography.* New York: Simon & Schuster, 1964.

Cowie, Peter, ed. *International Film Guide.* New York: A. S. Barnes & Co., (annual).

Crist, Judith. *The Private Eye, the Cowboy and the Very Naked Girl.* New York: Holt, Rinehart & Winston, 1967.

Crowther, Bosley. *The Lion's Share.* New York: E. P. Dutton, 1957.

Davy, Charles. *Footnotes to the Film.* London: Lovat, Dickson & Thompson, 1937.

Didion, Joan. *Slouching Toward Bethlehem.* New York: Farrar, Straus & Giroux, 1968.

Donner, Jorn. *The Personal Vision of Ingmar Bergman.* Bloomington: Indiana University Press, 1964.

Eisenstein, Sergei M. *Film Sense.* New York: Harcourt, Brace & World, 1942.

———. *The Film Form.* New York: Harcourt, Brace & World, 1949.

Fielding, Raymond, ed. *A Technological History of Motion Pictures and Television.* Berkeley: University of California Press, 1967.

Gassner, John, and **Dudley Nichols.** *Great Film Plays.* New York: Crown, 1959.

———. *Twenty Best Film Plays.* New York: Crown, 1943.

Geduld, Harry M., ed. *Film Makers on Film Making.* Bloomington: Indiana University Press, 1967.

Gelmis, Joseph. *The Film Director as Superstar.* New York: Doubleday & Co., 1970.

Gish, Lillian, and **Ann Pinchot.** *Lillian Gish: The Movies, Mr. Griffith and Me.* Englewood Cliffs, New Jersey: Prentice-Hall, 1969.

Graham, Peter. *A Dictionary of the Cinema.* New York: A. S. Barnes & Co., 1968.

Griffith, Mrs. D. W. *When the Movies Were Young.* New York: E. P. Dutton, 1925.

Hardy, Forsyth. *Grierson on Documentary.* London: W. H. Allen, 1945.

Houston, Penelope. *The Contemporary Cinema.* Baltimore: Penguin, 1963.

Hughes, Robert, ed. *Film: Book 2—Films of Peace and War.* New York: Grove Press, 1962.

Jacobs, Lewis. *Introduction to the Art of the Movies.* New York: Noonday Press, 1960.

———. *The Rise of the American Film.* New York: Harcourt, Brace & World, 1939.

Kael, Pauline. *I Lost It At the Movies.* Boston: Little, Brown & Co., 1965.

———. *Kiss, Kiss, Bang, Bang.* Boston: Little, Brown & Co., 1968.

Kauffmann, Stanley. *A World on Film.* New York: Harper & Row, 1966.

Knight, Arthur. *The Liveliest Art.* New York: Crowell Collier & Macmillan, 1957.

Kracauer, Siegfried. *Caligari to Hitler.* Princeton, New Jersey: Princeton University Press, 1947.

———. *Theory of Film.* New York: Oxford University Press, 1960.

Kuhns, William. *Environmental Man.* New York: Harper & Row, 1969.

Lahue, Kalton C. *World of Laughter.* Norman, Oklahoma: University of Oklahoma Press, 1966.

Larsen, Otto N., ed. *Violence and the Mass Media.* New York: Harper & Row, 1968.

Lawson, John Howard. *Film in the Battle of Ideas.* New York: Mainstream, 1953.

———. *Film: The Creative Process.* New York: Hill & Wang, 1964.

Leprohon, Pierre. *Michelangelo Antonioni.* New York: Simon & Schuster, 1963.

LeRoy, Mervyn. *It Takes More than Talent.* New York: Alfred A. Knopf, 1953.

Lindgreen, Ernest. *The Art of the Film.* London: Allen & Unwin, 1963.

MacCann, Richard Dyer, ed. *Film: A Montage of Theories.* New York: E. P. Dutton, 1966.

———. *Film and Society.* New York: Charles Scribner's Sons, 1964.

Macdonald, Dwight. *On Movies.* Englewood Cliffs, New Jersey: Prentice-Hall, 1969.

McBride, James. *The Contemporary American Avant-Garde Program Notes.* New York: Gallery of Modern Art, 1964.

McLuhan, Marshall. *Understanding Media.* New York: McGraw-Hill, 1964.
———. and **Edmund Carpenter.** *Explorations in Communications.* Boston: Beacon Press, 1960.
Manvell, Roger. *The Film and the Public.* Baltimore: Penguin, 1955.
Michael, Paul, ed. *The American Movies Reference Book.* Englewood Cliffs, New Jersey: Prentice-Hall, 1969.
Montagu, Ivor. *Film World: A Guide to Cinema.* Baltimore: Penguin, 1965.
Morris, Lloyd. *Not So Long Ago.* New York: Random House, 1949.
Nicoll, Allardyce. *Film and Theater.* New York: Thomas Y. Crowell, 1936.
Nizhny, Vladimir. *Lessons with Eisenstein.* New York: Hill & Wang, 1962.
O'Leary, Liam. *The Silent Cinema.* New York: E. P. Dutton, 1965.
Pudovkin, V. I. *Film Technique and Film Acting.* New York: Grove Press, 1960.
Ramsaye, Terry. *A Million and One Nights.* New York: Simon & Schuster, 1926.
Reed, Rex. *Conversations in the Raw.* New York: Harcourt, Brace & World, 1969.
———. *Do You Sleep in the Nude?* New York: New American Library, 1968.
Renan, Sheldon. *An Introduction to the American Underground Film.* New York: E. P. Dutton, 1967.
Robinson, W. R., *ed. Man and the Movies.* Baton Rouge: Louisiana State University Press, 1967.
Ross, Lillian. *Picture.* New York: Holt, Rinehart & Winston, 1952.
Rotha, Paul, and **Richard Griffith.** *The Film till Now.* New York: Funk & Wagnalls, 1949.
Rotha, Paul; Sinclair Road; and **Richard Griffith.** *Documentary Film.* London: Faber & Faber, 1963.
Sarris, Andrew. *Interviews with Film Directors.* New York: Bobbs-Merrill, 1967.
Schickel, Richard. *Movies.* New York: Basic Books, 1964.
———, and **John Simon,** eds. *Film 67/68.* New York: Simon & Schuster, 1968.
Schillaci, Anthony. *Movies and Morals.* Notre Dame: Fides Press, 1968.
Schramm, Wilbur, ed. *Mass Communications.* Urbana: University of Illinois Press, 1960.
Seldes, Gilbert. *The Great Audience.* New York: Viking Press, 1951.
———. *The Public Arts.* New York: Simon & Schuster, 1956.
Sennett, Mack. *King of Comedy.* New York: Doubleday & Co., 1954.
Sontag, Susan. *Against Interpretation.* New York: Farrar, Straus & Giroux, 1966.
Spottiswoode, Raymond. *A Grammar of the Film.* Berkeley: University of California Press, 1950.
Stephenson, Ralph, and **J. R. Debrix.** *The Cinema as Art.* Baltimore: Penguin, 1965.
Talbot, Daniel, ed. *Film: An Anthology.* New York: Simon & Schuster, 1960.
Taylor, John Russell. *Cinema Eye, Cinema Ear.* New York: Hill & Wang, 1964.
Tyler, Parker. *Three Faces of the Film.* New York: A. S. Barnes & Co., 1960.
———. *Magic and Myth of the Movies.* New York: Holt, Rinehart & Winston, 1947.
Walker, Alexander. *Sex in the Movies.* Baltimore: Penguin, 1966.
White, David Manning, and **Richard Averson.** *Sight, Sound and Society.* Boston: Beacon Press, 1968.
Wolfe, Tom. *The Kandy-Kolored Tangerine-Flake Streamline Baby.* New York: Farrar, Straus & Giroux, 1965.